HEALTH
PSYCHOLOGY

Psychology: Revisiting the Classic Studies

Series Editors:
S. Alexander Haslam[1] and Joanne R. Smith[2]
[1]School of Psychology, University of Queensland, Brisbane, Australia
[2]School of Psychology, University of Exeter, Exeter, UK

Psychology: Revisiting the Classic Studies is a new series of texts aimed at students and general readers who are interested in understanding issues raised by key studies in psychology. Volumes centre on 12–15 studies, with each chapter providing a detailed account of a particular classic study and its empirical and theoretical impact. Chapters also discuss the important ways in which thinking and research have advanced in the years since the study was conducted. They are written by researchers at the cutting edge of these developments and, as a result, these texts serve as an excellent resource for instructors and students looking to explore different perspectives on core material that defines the field of psychology as we know it today.

Also available:

Health Psychology
Mark Tarrant and Martin S. Hagger

Clinical Psychology
Graham Davey

Cognitive Psychology, second edition
Michael W. Eysenck, David Groome

Personality and Individual Differences
Philip Corr

Organisational Psychology
Niklas K. Steffens, Floor Rink, Michelle
K. Ryan

Social Psychology, second edition
Joanne R. Smith and S. Alexander
Haslam

Developmental Psychology, second edition
Alan M. Slater and Paul C. Quinn

Brain and Behaviour
Bryan Kolb and Ian Wishaw

HEALTH PSYCHOLOGY
REVISITING THE CLASSIC STUDIES

EDITED BY:
MARK TARRANT
MARTIN S. HAGGER

S Sage

1 Oliver's Yard
55 City Road
London EC1Y 1SP

2455 Teller Road
Thousand Oaks, California 91320

Unit No 323-333, Third Floor, F-Block
International Trade Tower Nehru Place
New Delhi - 110 019

8 Marina View Suite 43-053
Asia Square Tower 1
Singapore 018960

Editor: Martin Perchard
Assistant Editor: Emma Yuan
Production Editor: Neelu Sahu
Copyeditor: Sarah Bury
Proofreader: Brian McDowell
Indexer: KnowledgeWorks Global Ltd
Marketing Manager: Fauzia Eastwood
Cover Design: Wendy Scott
Typeset by KnowledgeWorks Global Ltd
Printed and bound by CPI Group (UK) Ltd,
Croydon, CR0 4YY

Library of Congress Control Number: 2022951333

British Library Cataloguing in Publication data

A catalogue record for this book is available from the
British Library

ISBN 978-1-5297-7188-6
ISBN 978-1-5297-7187-9 (pbk)

At Sage we take sustainability seriously. Most of our products are printed in the UK using responsibly
sourced papers and boards. When we print overseas we ensure sustainable papers are used as
measured by the Paper Chain Project grading system. We undertake an annual audit to monitor our
sustainability.

Contents

About the Editors

Mark Tarrant is Professor of Psychology at the University of Plymouth, UK. His work focuses on the development and evaluation of group-based behaviour change interventions for supporting health. He has published more than 70 articles and book chapters, including in leading international journals (e.g., *Psychological Science*, *Health Psychology Review*), and has been funded by major research councils (e.g., NIHR, MRC, ESRC) and charities (e.g., Stroke Association).

Martin S. Hagger is Distinguished Professor of Health Psychology at the University of California, Merced, Professor (Behaviour Change) in the Faculty of Sport and Health Sciences, University of Jyväskylä, Finland, and Adjunct Professor and Research Consultant in the School of Applied Psychology, Griffith University. His research applies social cognition and motivational theory to predict, understand, and change health behaviours. He has published over 400 articles, chapters, and books, and served as editor of major scholarly peer-reviewed journals.

About the Contributors

Sarah V. Bentley is a Research Fellow at the University of Queensland. Sarah's research targets three domains: the psychometric articulation and measurement of social identity and social connectedness; assessing the impact of social identity processes on psychological function and well-being; and working collaboratively with stakeholders in organisational, educational, and clinical domains to design, deliver, and validate social identity informed psychological interventions. The emphasis of Sarah's work lies in understanding – and harnessing – the power of positive social connection, as well as understanding – and managing – the pitfalls of social disconnection.

Felicity L. Bishop is a Professor of Health Psychology at the University of Southampton where she leads a programme of mixed methods research around complementary therapies and placebo effects in health care. Her interdisciplinary research has attracted funding from NIHR, Versus Arthritis, and others, and has been published in leading medical, health psychology, and social science journals. With an extensive network of national and international collaborations, Felicity has held visiting positions at Harvard and at the Australian Centre for Integrative and Complementary Medicine at The University of Technology Sydney (UTS). Her current focus is on developing and testing novel and engaging ways to harness placebo effects in medical practice.

Roger Booth is Associate Professor of Immunology and Health Psychology in the Faculty of Medical and Health Sciences at the University of Auckland. As well as teaching immunology, psychoneuroimmunology and mind–body health at the university, Roger's research centres on the effects of emotions and emotional expression on inflammation and immunity, particularly in relation to wound healing and immune responses to vaccines.

Elizabeth Broadbent is a Professor of Health Psychology at the University of Auckland. She teaches postgraduate research methods and psychoneuroimmunology.

Her research interests include psychological stress, the development of interventions to empower patients and reduce distress, and social robotics in healthcare. She is a Fellow of the Royal Society of New Zealand, and the Academy of Behavioral Medicine Research, USA.

Roderick D. Buchanan is an Honorary Fellow in the History and Philosophy of Science Program at the University of Melbourne. He is the author of *Playing with Fire: The Controversial Career of Hans J. Eysenck* (2010). He has published on the history of psychology and psychiatry, for example: 'Psychotherapy (The History of Psychotherapy in the Modern Era)' (2019) with Nick Haslam, and 'The Enduring Appeal of Psychosocial Explanations of Physical Illness' (2018) with Nick Haslam and Wade Pickren.

Linda D. Cameron is Professor of Psychology at the University of California, Merced. Her research focuses on developing health communications and interventions for individuals who have or are at risk for cancer, heart disease, and other illnesses. Her research takes a self-regulation perspective by evaluating cognitive and emotional processes influencing health behaviours and illness experiences. She focuses on both theoretical and applied aspects of issues with the parallel goals of developing theoretically-based interventions and refining psychological theory. Research lines include the development and evaluation of emotion regulation interventions for women with breast cancer and adults with histories of adverse childhood experiences, the influence of imagery in health communications, and the effects of graphic warnings on tobacco products in deterring use. Within the university's Health Sciences Research Institute, she is Director of the Translational Research Center and Co-Director of the Rapid Response Core of the Nicotine and Cannabis Policy Center.

Mark Conner is a Professor of Applied Social Psychology at the University of Leeds, UK. His research focuses on predicting and changing health behaviours. His more recent work has focused on affective predictors of health behaviour and simple interventions such as implementation intentions, goal planning, and the question-behaviour effect. He has co-edited one of the key books in this area, *Predicting and Changing Health Behaviour* (with Paul Norman, 2015), and has over 300 publications in peer-reviewed journals. His research has attracted funding from NIHR, MRC, ESRC, and various charities. He has been co-Editor-in-Chief (2011–2019) of the journal *Psychology and Health*.

Rik Crutzen is Professor of Behaviour Change & Technology at the Department of Health Promotion, Care and Public Health Research Institute, Maastricht University, in the Netherlands, and is an Honorary Professorial Fellow within the Melbourne School of Psychological Sciences, University of Melbourne, Australia.

Ryan J. Goffredi is a Graduate Student Instructor at University of Missouri – Columbia. His research areas include self-determination theory, the agentic self, narrative identity, positive psychology, and applied psychological interventions aimed at increasing well-being. His ongoing work focuses on the power of core values and self-concordant goal striving for health and well-being across the lifespan. He also has an interest in game-based learning and exploring the efficacy of incorporating gaming into higher education courses to facilitate student engagement and learning.

Nick Haslam is Professor of Psychology at the University of Melbourne. He received his PhD in clinical psychology at the University of Pennsylvania and then taught at the New School for Social Research before returning to Australia. Nick's research interests include personality, group perception, and psychiatric classification, and he has published extensively on these topics, among others.

Jolanda Jetten is Professor of Social Psychology and an Australian Research Council Laureate Fellow at the University of Queensland. Her research is concerned with group processes, social identity and intergroup relations, and she explores how these processes play a role in mental health and well-being. Her Laureate research is concerned with responding to collective level change, including adjustment and resilience in the aftermath of disasters.

Marie Johnston, BSc, PhD, is Emeritus Professor of Health Psychology at the University of Aberdeen in Scotland and a registered Health and Clinical Psychologist. Her research focuses on behaviour and health, especially on behaviour change interventions. Most recently, her work has been on building ontologies of behaviour change interventions with Susan Michie at University College London (www.human behaviourchange.org/) and investigating adherence to COVID-19 transmission-reducing behaviours as part of the Covid Health and Adherence Research In Scotland (CHARIS) project led by Diane Dixon at the University of Aberdeen. She works with multiple disciplines to ensure that behavioural science theory and methods are integrated into studies of evidence-based practice. Her work has been supported by national, international, and charitable funders and she has over 400 publications.

Anke Karl is a Neuroscientist and Clinical Psychologist conducting translational clinical research specialising in biopsychological mechanisms of recovery from trauma, posttraumatic stress disorder (PTSD), and protective factors and their role for trauma-focused psychological therapies. She is director of the biobehavioural lab at the Mood Disorders Centre (MDC) at the University of Exeter, UK, and an associate psychological psychotherapist at the MDC's AccEPT clinic.

Laura A. King received her AB in English Literature and Psychology from Kenyon College and her PhD in Personality Psychology from the University of California, Davis. She was on the faculty of Southern Methodist University for 10 years prior to moving to the University of Missouri, Columbia, where she is a Curators' Distinguished Professor of Psychological Sciences. A personality/social psychologist, Laura's research concerns well-being, especially meaning in life and folk theories of The Good Life. Whatever the topic, her work reflects an enduring interest in what is healthy and functioning about people and recognising psychological functioning in everyday people and their everyday lives. She has published over 100 articles and chapters. Laura has served as editor or associate editor for a number of journals and was the first woman to edit the *Journal of Personality and Social Psychology: Personality Processes and Individual Differences*.

Gerjo Kok is Professor Emeritus of Applied Psychology at Maastricht University, the Netherlands. In his research and teaching, he focuses on behaviour change, especially in the area of health promotion. He is also one of the authors of the Intervention Mapping protocol.

Evelyne de Leeuw is Professor of Urban Health and Policy at the University of New South Wales, Sydney (Australia). She is Editor-in-Chief of the OUP journals *Health Promotion International* and *Infrastructure and Health*, and of the Palgrave book series 'Studies in Public Health Policy Research'. Her own research plays out at the interface of urban planning, public health, and political science.

Warren Mansell is currently Professor of Mental Health at the School of Population Health, Curtin University, Perth, Australia. He received his DPhil at the University of Oxford, and his clinical psychology doctorate at the Institute of Psychiatry, University of London. He developed his academic career at the University of Manchester, UK, where he utilised perceptual control theory in mental health interventions, and tested the theory in experimental studies of behaviour, computational models, and robotics. His current focus is on the applications of the theory to consciousness, and towards developing scalable solutions for universal mental health and well-being.

Paul Norman is a Professor of Health Psychology at the University of Sheffield. His research focuses on the application of social cognition models (e.g., theory of planned behaviour, health belief model, protection motivation theory) to the prediction of health behaviour. His more recent work has focused on developing and testing interventions to change health behaviour, including the use of online interventions. He has co-edited one of the key books in this area, *Predicting and Changing Health Behaviour* (with Mark Conner, 2015), and has over 150 publications in peer-reviewed journals. His research has attracted funding from NIHR, MRC, ESRC, and various charities. He has been Secretary (2000–2006) and President (2010–2012) of the European Health Psychology Society and Editor-in-Chief (2001–2006) of the journal *Psychology and Health*.

Robert A.C. Ruiter is Professor of Health and Social Psychology at Maastricht University, the Netherlands. His research and teaching focus on identifying determinants of behaviour change and the design and testing of behaviour change programmes. He is co-author of *Intervention Mapping* (2019). He applies this protocol to topics in the domains of health, traffic safety, and environmental health in both the Netherlands and the Global South.

Christopher (Chris) A. Sanders earned his BA from California State University, Bakersfield, and his MA from San Francisco State University. He is currently an ABD doctoral candidate at the University of Missouri and his work primarily concerns well-being and social factors, combining interests in both positive psychology and social psychology. His main ongoing research programme explores how demographics, social class, criminal status, and physical appearance influence well-being within our current social climate, but he has also published more broadly on the topic of positive psychology and the interventions discussed in that field.

Fabio Sani is a Professor of Social and Health Psychology at the University of Dundee. His general research interest concerns the impact of social relationships and group life on both physical and mental health, from either an epidemiological or a phenomenological perspective. His major research projects have been funded by the Economic and Social Research Council (ESRC) of the UK, the British Academy, and the Scottish Government. He has published over 70 scientific papers and four books, and has been an associate editor of the *European Journal of Social Psychology*.

Kennon M. Sheldon is a Curators' Professor of Psychology at the University of Missouri. He is known for his work in self-determination theory, positive psychology, happiness, self-concordance, and goal setting. He is the author of more than 300 articles or books, including *Freely Determined: What the New Psychology of the Self Tells Us about How to Live* (2022).

Benjamin Schüz is professor of public health at the University of Bremen. His research focuses on social inequalities in health and how health behaviours and determinants of health behaviours contribute to these.

John Weinman is Professor of Psychology applied to Medicines, and Director of the Centre for Adherence Research & Education at King's College London. His research focuses on factors influencing recovery from illness and treatment, including surgery, patient self-management, and adherence. He was founding editor of *Psychology & Health: An International Journal*. He has visiting professorships in UCL, Denmark, and Ireland, and was awarded a lifetime achievement award and Honorary Fellowship by the British Psychological Society. He is Fellow of the European Health Psychology Society, American Academy of Behavioral Medicine Research, King's College London, the Academy of Social Sciences, and a Distinguished International Affiliate of the APA Division of Health Psychology.

Tarli Young is a Postdoctoral Research Fellow at the University of Queensland. Tarli's research focuses on understanding and improving well-being and mental health in adult populations. Her current work centres on the development and testing of interventions that harness a Social Identity Approach to Health. She also researches meaning in work, social well-being, mindfulness, and ethics.

1

Introduction: Health Psychology Revisiting the Classics

Martin S. Hagger and
Mark Tarrant

WHAT IS HEALTH PSYCHOLOGY?

Many of the most prominent and pressing problems facing society relate to human health. For example, communicable (e.g., upper-respiratory tract infections, HIV/AIDS, tuberculosis) and non-communicable diseases and conditions (e.g., cardiovascular disease, diabetes, depression and mental health conditions) account for a majority of premature deaths, disability, and hospitalisations and emergency care worldwide (WHO, 2014, 2020, 2021). This has been brought into sharp focus in the impact of relatively recent regional epidemics and global pandemics of communicable diseases such as Ebola, Avian influenza, Zika, and COVID-19. Analogously, the past 40 years have seen a widespread rise in the prevalence of non-communicable diseases and associated health-compromising conditions, such as obesity, to the extent that they have reached pandemic proportions. Global health and medical organisations and governmental departments highlight healthcare policies and interventions, particularly the development of effective treatments, management strategies, and prevention methods and campaigns, as a priority for the promotion of population good health and the eradication of ill-health (Ferraro et al., 2020; WHO, 2004). Given that many of these health illnesses and conditions have their roots, at least in part, in human behaviour, researchers have advocated for a prominent role of the behavioural and social sciences, particularly psychology, to provide evidence-based solutions that may promote prevention and management of these conditions (e.g., Bonell et al., 2020; Glanz & Bishop, 2010).

Psychology is a relatively 'young' scientific discipline compared to other sciences and, as it has matured, it has diversified into multiple applied disciplines focused on developing theory and evidence to explain mental phenomena and behaviour in key areas relevant to society. *Health psychology* is one of these comparatively 'new' sub-disciplines that has come to be accepted as a core division of the study in psychology. This sub-discipline now sports a critical mass of theorists, researchers, and practitioners who apply the science and practices of health psychology to the pressing health issues, and has established national and global organisational structures that represent their interests and foster advancements in scientific discovery in the sub-discipline and its translation into health practice.

As an applied sub-discipline, health psychology draws its influences from other pre-existing core (e.g., cognitive and social psychology) and applied (e.g., clinical psychology) sub-disciplines within the parent discipline. It is from these sub-disciplines that health psychologists derive the scope, assumptions, theoretical approaches, and methods of study and practice in this field of study (Gurung, 2018; Murray, 2014a). In fact, the researchers and practitioners who were at the forefront of this developing sub-discipline had academic roots in one or more of these other, contributing, applied sub-disciplines. For example, many of the leading theoretical approaches applied to investigate and inform health phenomena, including health behaviour, responses to, and management of, illness and disease, and stress and coping, are derived from social psychological theory (see Carver & Scheier, 1982; Conner & Norman, 2015; Fishbein et al., 2001; Hagger et al., 2020). Importantly, early health psychologists drew upon a generalised set of common principles regarding knowledge generation, research, and practice that were shared with many other psychology sub-disciplines, with a strong focus on the application of scientific principles and evidence bases, and these principles have endured as the discipline has matured and grown in its recognition, utilisation, and application (Friedman, 2014; Smith, 2003; Straub, 2022; Taylor & Stanton, 2020).

Formally, health psychology is the scientific study of the psychological and behavioural factors and processes that relate to health and illness (Leventhal et al., 2008; Smith, 2003; Taylor & Stanton, 2020). It is, therefore, an interdisciplinary sub-discipline of psychology, and, as suggested earlier, draws its perspectives, methods, and practices from multiple sub-disciplines within psychology, as well as allied behavioural, social, and health sciences. Health psychologists seek to generate evidence of the factors that impact health-related outcomes and behaviour, and the mechanisms and processes involved. Examples of the key areas and topics of focus for health psychologists include: studying the interface between individuals' mental representations (e.g., beliefs, perceptions, traits, judgements, social roles, and identity) and health and illness processes and outcomes (Leventhal et al., 2008); the psychological, biological, socio-demographic, and socio-environmental determinants of adoption and maintenance of, or desistence from, health behaviours, and the processes and mechanisms involved (Baum & Posluszny, 1999; Mann & Kato, 1996; Miller et al., 2009; Rodin & Salovey, 1989; Schneiderman et al., 2001; Taylor et al., 1997; Williams et al., 2002); the role of emotional responses (e.g., anxiety, stress) and capacities (e.g., coping, resilience) and their reciprocal relations with illness incidence and progression (Rodin & Salovey, 1989; Taylor et al., 1997); and the development of therapies, methods, and interventions aimed at the management and prevention of ill-health, health behaviour change, and the promotion of good health and well-being (Adler & Matthews, 1994; Boll et al., 2002; Hagger et al., 2020; Stanton et al., 2006).

As an interdisciplinary sub-discipline, health psychology also shares many common elements with the sub-disciplines that informed its development. For example, health psychology owes a great deal to advancements in the sub-discipline of clinical psychology, and, broadly speaking, many of the theories, approaches, and issues in which health psychologists engage are also those that concern clinical psychologists (Baum & Posluszny, 1999; Boll et al., 2002; Smith, 2003). For example, both clinical and health psychologists have interests in promoting positive mental health and psychological well-being, and, as a consequence, aim to develop efficacious means to detect and manage conditions that threaten good mental health, such as anxiety, depression, and chronic stress. Many of the approaches and methods used by clinical and health psychologists to promote and manage health, therefore, converge, in the application of broad therapies such as cognitive behavioural therapy to manage mental health conditions (Rachman, 2009; Whittington, 2019). Many researchers and practitioners in both domains would acknowledge this overlap and recognise the commonalities in approaches and focus areas of study (Boll et al., 2002). However, there are also divergences. For example, most clinical and health psychologists would agree that clinically-diagnosed conditions, such as bipolar disorders or post-traumatic stress disorders, tend to be the focus and domain of clinical psychologists, while the management and prevention of physical illness in health populations tends to be the domain of health psychologists.

The key point here is that health psychology has boundaries that are somewhat 'fuzzy', and has substantive overlaps with other sub-disciplines. Those trained in health psychology, and are actively engaged in its application, are acutely aware of these commonalities. While there is very broad consensus on the core or central topics of focus and study in disciplines such as clinical and health psychology, there is also recognition that there are topics of study where the interests and approaches of these sub-disciplines align. Alongside this, therefore, there is recognition that advances in the sub-disciplines that share commonalities with health psychology have extensively informed its development, and there is tacit acknowledgement that the ground-breaking studies that made important contributions to the development of these other psychology sub-disciplines also made concomitant advances in health psychology.

A common theme in definitions of health psychology is the focus on a *biopsychosocial* approach to generating knowledge and informing practice in health contexts (Barkway & O'Kane, 2019; Schneiderman et al., 2001; Straub, 2022; Vögele, 2015). Although this term is somewhat vague, its adoption seeks to emphasise the necessity of moving beyond unidimensional approaches to the study of health-related phenomena towards multi-factorial, interdisciplinary approaches. For example, a sole focus, or heavy emphasis on, biological or medical models of health and illness has been criticised as both reductive and insufficient as a means to provide a comprehensive understanding of health processes. An overarching guiding perspective for health psychologists, therefore, is to draw from multiple perspectives, including the medical and biological approaches, but also incorporating perspectives from multiple sub-disciplines of psychology and the other social and behavioural sciences, to arrive at optimally comprehensive, fit-for-purpose models and means to explain phenomena in health and illness. Coupled with the adoption of scientific methods, health psychology is, therefore, well placed to take a systematic, evidence-based approach to developing means to explain health and illness phenomena, and inform practices and interventions that may assist in resolving some of the most prescient health challenges facing society in the 21st century (Murray, 2014b).

As with many other sub-disciplines in psychology, key 'milestone' scientific discoveries in the domain of health psychology can be identified that have made indelible, 'step-change' contributions to its development. These include developments in the theory and conceptual bases of the scientific study of health psychology, developments in key sub-fields within health psychology that laid the foundations of particular areas of research and practice, advances in methods and measurement that have provided health psychologists with the tools to investigate phenomena in health psychology, and key methods, strategies, and intervention approaches that have advanced the application, practice, and translation of health psychology knowledge to promote health (Smith, 2003; Taylor & Stanton, 2020). This book, in keeping with others in this series, aims to provide those with an interest in health psychology with an overview of some of the 'classic' studies that have shaped health psychology. These are studies that exemplify the scientific innovation and ingenuity that health psychologists have applied to advance the scientific understanding of health and behaviour, over the years, and have served to lay the foundation for subsequent innovation in knowledge generation and practice.

In the next section we outline the process we adopted to identifying the 'classic' studies included in this book. To be sure, this is no 'accidental' list – we applied a rigorous, systematic approach which involved consultation with multiple expert sources to inform our decision and we provide a full, unabridged, and transparent account of our process so that the reader is fully informed of how we arrived at our selection. Importantly, we welcome the inevitable disputes and debates over our selections and the process used, recognise the inherent subjectivity entailed in the development of a list of this kind, and acknowledge that such debates themselves are important to advance perspectives on how knowledge and discovery in health psychology have developed and inform the development of the sub-discipline going forward.

WHAT DEFINES A CLASSIC STUDY IN HEALTH PSYCHOLOGY?

Foremost in our minds when assembling a text on 'classic' studies in an inherently interdisciplinary psychological sub-discipline such as health psychology is what, exactly, constitutes a 'classic' study – what does a 'classic' study in health psychology 'look like'? Inevitably, as alluded to in the previous section, identifying 'classic' studies in any discipline is a challenging endeavour – in many ways, what defines a 'classic' is not always readily quantifiable by any metric, or through basis in evidence, that is likely to satisfy the 'scientist' in many of those who seek to do so. While tracking quantifiable metrics such as numbers of citations and other usage statistics may provide some information that may inform thinking on what constitutes as 'classic', that is really only superficial 'surface' evidence detached from the content of the study. And reliance on such metrics would be an inherently flawed approach – although classic studies are often highly cited, studies that are generally considered weak research, with substantive limitations or deficiencies, can be also highly cited, and are often highly cited *because* they are examples of weak research!

So we recognised the imperative of adopting other, less tangible, methods to identify our 'classic' health psychology studies for this book. One way of doing so is to collate broad expert opinion on the studies highly revered in the field, particularly among those who have substantive experience in conducting research and advancing theory in health psychology themselves, or those who have written authoritatively on the subject of health psychology, or been highly active in applying health psychology methods and practices (e.g., Jorm, 2015; Miche et al., 2013; Teixeira et al., 2020). This is the approach we took in the current text, leveraging the pooled knowledge of experts in order to inform our decisions on the 'classic' studies that ultimately made the 'cut' to be included in the current text. We note that it is also an approach that has also been taken by other editors in this series (see Davey, 2019).

An important endeavour in this regard is the identification of the experts themselves, which presented us with an initial challenge insofar as we recognised the imperative of ensuring broad representation and coverage of topics as well as discipline and national representation. For example, we were aware that psychologists working in different academic systems or global regions may differ in their perspectives on what constitutes a 'classic'. Similarly, there may be a degree of within-area bias among the consulted experts – they are more likely to favour studies conducted in their specific areas. Identification of a broad-based expert 'panel', therefore, was an issue to which we dedicated considerable thought, and we found we had not only to draw on our own expertise and knowledge of networks of researchers within health psychology, but also rely on the broader knowledge of colleagues to identify appropriate expert panel members.

A principal consideration in the process of identifying 'classics' in health psychology is arriving at a set of essential criteria on which to judge candidate 'classic' studies that would be broadly acceptable to, and be considered valid by, health psychologists. Fortunately, a number of readily-available sources, authored by those who have sought to evaluate the contribution of research studies in various fields, exist which could inform our thinking (e.g., APA Task Force on Health Research, 1976; Davis et al., 2015; Glanz & Maddock, 2000). These criteria include studies that make a substantive general innovation or advancement of theory, practice, or generalised approaches to key topics in health psychology, as well as studies that made specific advances in theory or methods that made an indelible mark on health psychology research or practice, and are still in use or inform current thinking. So, innovation and contribution that has an enduring effect on health psychology as a sub-discipline and represents a 'step change' in ideas, methods, or practice is important to the identification of a 'classic'.

Alongside this, it is also important that a 'classic' study: clearly identifies the research gap or issue it is attempting to address and summarises contemporary thinking of the time and how the research advances that thinking; is methodologically sound, including study design, data collection or collation, and appropriate analysis – although we acknowledge that methods move on quickly and some of the methods of 'classic' studies may have dated somewhat relative to the current 'zeitgeist'; and is communicated clearly and effectively. A final essential criterion of a 'classic' study is its capacity to inform and shape the direction of research and practice going forward. Accordingly, authors of the chapters on each 'classic' study presented in this book have dedicated considerable time to explore how the identified 'classic' has impacted the field and served as an impetus for advancing knowledge going forward. For example, Johnston (Chapter 12) explains how Michie and co-workers' taxonomy of behaviour change techniques paved the way for common, standardised descriptions of interventions in health psychology and also the development of elaborated means to describe how such interventions 'work' in changing behaviour. Similarly, Cameron (Chapter 10) describes the role that research on fear appeals has had on the development of campaigns that use emotionally-aversive messages (e.g., graphic warning labels on tobacco products) and their effectiveness.

It is also important to acknowledge that 'classics' in a given sub-discipline likely take on a multitude of different formats and designs. For example, advancements in some psychology sub-disciplines can often be traced to individual empirical studies, such as Stanley Milgram's (1963) experiments on obedience in social psychology (see Reicher & Haslam, 2017), or David Clark's (1986) study on panic disorders in clinical psychology (see Waddington, 2019). The same can be applied in health psychology – although as an applied field that draws from multiple sub-disciplines, many studies that have advanced the field take the form of non-empirical conceptual and theoretical research contributions that draw from a wider body of research and highlight their innovation and contribution to this relatively new and emerging sub-discipline. As a consequence, we maintained an open mind when it came to the types of studies that were identified as classics in this book. A brief perusal of the final selection of health psychology 'classics', will reveal that some report the results and implications of ground-breaking empirical studies in the traditional sense, which adopt scientific methods and seek to directly test a set of hypotheses (e.g., Cohen et al.'s (1991) experiments on stress and the common cold, see Chapter 5; or Leventhal et al.'s (1965) experimental test of the effects of fear arousal on attitudes towards vaccination, see Chapter 10). However, the 'classics' targeted in other chapters are not traditional reports of empirical research but, instead, are seminal conceptual or theoretical reviews that not only summarise the contemporary state of the research on the area at the time, but also advance thinking by proposing new ideas and hypotheses that influence the progression of the field and set the agenda for future research (e.g., Ajzen's (1998) conceptual analysis of theories and models of health behaviour, see Chapter 2; or Sallis et al.'s (2006) conceptual overview of multilevel ecological approaches to behavioural interventions, see Chapter 4).

In some disciplines in psychology, such as social psychology, what constitutes a 'classic' study is often clear. As Joanne Smith and Alex Haslam (2017) point out in their introduction to *Classic Studies in Social Psychology*, a defining feature of many social psychology classics is that they are well known beyond the field of social psychology, including some that are widely known among the general public. But in health psychology, the answer to the question of what constitutes a 'classic' study is perhaps more nuanced and, in many cases, quite subjective, and, as we intimated previously, there may be considerable variability in studies labelled as 'classics' among health psychologists. And, of course, the answer to the question is also framed by the metric used to define the status of a nominated study: while article citation counts may give an indication of academic, scientific impact, citation counts have obvious limitations, as we outlined above, and the wider *societal value* of a given study is inherently harder to assess (Aksnes et al., 2019). Yet, in an applied discipline such as health psychology, this latter form of research quality may be at least as important as other indicators of impact – this emphasis is also explicit in the stated priorities of the funding bodies that support our research (e.g., National Institute for Health and Care Research in the UK).

Finally, we recognised that a 'list' of 'classic' studies will, inevitably, need to encompass the breadth of key sub-fields in health psychology. This has two important implications: first, we needed to clearly identify the sub-fields that are broadly considered essential or 'core' to those who conduct research or work in health psychology; and, second, there was the imperative of identifying a candidate 'classic' study that not only fulfilled our aforementioned criteria of what constitutes a 'classic', but also had 'best fit' as representative of its respective sub-field. As a consequence, one of our key strategies in nominating 'classic studies' for inclusion this book was to identify a panel of experts with broad, representative expertise in multiple subfields of health psychology. This strategy also contributed to developing convergence on which of the candidate studies made the 'final cut'. This meant that we had to settle on potential classics that were worthy of the 'classic' moniker, but were also the most suitable representative of innovation and advancement in their sub-field – in many ways the 'uber-classic'. The upshot of this approach was that quite a few studies that fulfilled the 'classic' criteria necessarily fell by the wayside in the selection process. Inevitably, this is a further side effect of a highly selective and subjective approach to identifying 'classics' in a given sub-discipline: some of the identified health psychology sub-fields would be home to multiple 'classic' studies, but only one could be the nominee. Again, we stress the subjectivity of our selection procedure, and we fully expect there are those that would not agree with our decision in particular sub-fields and would, instead, have nominated another study as the representative 'classic' in its area. As before, we recognise, acknowledge, and embrace this diversity in opinion, and, in many respects, hope that this book catalyses their continuation as they, in themselves, serve to promote engagement in the sub-discipline and foster healthy, informative knowledge exchange on how health psychology has developed and what contributions have shaped the field and determine its future direction.

IDENTIFYING THE CLASSIC STUDIES

We started with a number of questions that framed our approach to identifying the 'classic' studies for inclusion in this book: To what extent do we focus on work that sought to impact health directly, such as clinical intervention studies, versus studies that contributed to the understanding of the psychological mechanisms underpinning health problems, or works that fundamentally sought to advance theorising around a particular topic? Should we target studies that propose or review specific, highly influential theories that have widespread application in the psychological study of health, even if these theories were not originally developed in the health psychology field (e.g., the theories of reasoned action and planned behaviour, self-determination theory)? What should the balance be between a focus on specific health conditions (e.g., stress), phenomena (e.g., placebo effects), or approaches (e.g., the health beliefs model)?

CONSENSUS EXERCISE

To identify our 'panel' of experts, we capitalised on our network of colleagues working in different sub-areas of health psychology. We initially contacted a small group of immediate colleagues, and canvassed their opinion on influential studies in health psychology that they considered to be classics. This entirely non-representative exercise served to 'pilot' our ultimate approach and develop an initial 'long list' of candidate 'classic' studies for consideration for inclusion in the book. This initial exercise immediately served to reinforce the scale of the challenge we faced, aptly captured by a comment from one colleague during the process:

> I don't know where to start – sorry. I think this would be different for different people ... It's a big field – are you interested in theories/theory-building studies, interventions, mechanisms-evaluation, methodological papers, systematic reviews, or all of the above?

Several of the studies nominated by our colleagues ultimately made it onto the 'short list' of candidate 'classics', and subsequently into the book itself, perhaps illustrating some degree of consensus among our peers from the start. However, we knew that we were still some way from delivering a final list of agreed 'classics' that satisfactorily and broadly represented scholarship in the sub-discipline. Our next step, therefore, was to assemble and consult a broader panel of experts from the wider community of researchers and practitioners working in health psychology. We distributed a short online survey across the community via learned society list servers (e.g., *the Society for Behavioural Medicine; the Society for Personality and Social Psychology; the British Psychological Society, Division of Health Psychology*), and requested members to list up to three representative studies in health psychology they considered 'classics'. Members were also offered the option to nominate classic *topics* they considered should be included, in lieu of nominating specific *studies*.

Ultimately, 48 studies were nominated by our broader expert 'panel' – we also had several other colleagues reach out directly to us to suggest 'classic' studies and topics. The set of nominees was impressive, and consistent with our goal of gaining broad coverage of sub-areas within health psychology. Nominees covered areas such as behaviour change, social networks and health, models of health behaviour, psychoneuroimmunology, stress responses and appraisals, placebo effects, health inequalities, personality, and psychotherapeutic interventions. It was also encouraging to note a degree of convergence among the nominated studies and topics. The onus was then on us, as editors, to refine the list that comprised the final list of nominated 'classics'. In doing so, we gave close consideration to ensuring representativeness and balance in the studies in terms of their impact and contribution, design and approach, attention to theory and mechanisms, and lasting impact and longevity. As before, we freely acknowledge the level of subjectivity inherent in this exercise, and we hope that readers will recognise these studies as fitting the criteria of a 'classic' study, while simultaneously recognising its limitations and using this to spur further debate.

A CHRONOLOGY OF HEALTH PSYCHOLOGY CLASSICS

The 13 'classic' studies presented in this book span the period from the 1950s to the 2010s. Some interesting observations emerge when surveying the 'timeline' of the emergence and development of health psychology that this collection of studies represents. Prior to the late 1970s, the psychological study of health and illness was shaped by the broad interests and methodological approaches, and the studies here reflect this *uni*disciplinary perspective. For example, in the 1950s and 1960s, there was a scientific drive to identify explanatory factors contributing to major public health challenges of the time, notably coronary heart disease. The pervading influence of research in personality psychology at the time, and the subsequent emergence of the social cognition approach in psychology, are captured in two of the early 'classic' studies: Friedman and Rosenman's (1959) study on Type A personality (see Chapter 7), and Leventhal et al.'s (1965) paper on fear appeals, with particular focus on the impact of arousal and action plans on attitudes and behaviour (see Chapter 10).

The 1970s saw the emergence of an interest in how social factors impacted health. Research on this topic coincided with the emergence of health psychology as a sub-discipline and, reflecting this, drew on multiple perspectives in its approach. The two classic papers from this decade, on inequality (Marmot et al., 1978; see Chapter 8) and social networks (Berkman & Syme, 1979; see Chapter 9), capture this emergence, coinciding, for example, with significant developments in the field of social psychology (e.g., research on group and intergroup relations; Tajfel, 1978), and reflecting a wider societal debate about the reliance on broad social categories, such as race, sex, and nationality, in health policy making.

By the end of the 1970s, several major sub-disciplines in psychology, including personality, cognitive, and social psychology, had developed and come to be recognised as foundational or core to the discipline. At this time, several applied areas of the discipline were formalised, including health psychology itself. For example, the 1970s also saw the proposal and popularisation of the biopsychosocial model (see Schneiderman et al., 2001; Straub, 2022) and establishment of the Division of Health Psychology (Division 38) of the American Psychological Association in 1978. Defining health psychology as an interdisciplinary sub-discipline and field of professional practice formally established the application of psychological approaches and methods in health contexts, and helped to advance the evidence-based approach to research and the application of psychological theory and methods in health contexts that is the established approach today.

The six studies published in the 1980s and 1990s capture the diversity of application of new approaches in this emerging sub-discipline, and cover topics such as stress (Cohen et al., 1991; Chapter 5), response expectancy (Kirsch, 1985; Chapter 11), psychoneuroimmunology (Kiecolt-Glaser et al., 1995; Chapter 6), and emergent integrative theory (Carver & Scheier, 1982; Chapter 3). One of the 'classic' studies from this era (Pennebaker et al., 1988; Chapter 13) represents an early example of the translational application of health psychology research, in keeping with the dual focus emphasised by Division 38 of conducting health psychology research and also *practising* it. The translational relevance of health psychology is further emphasised in the 'classic' study by Ajzen (1998; Chapter 2) on models of health behaviour, which acknowledged the contribution of many of the seminal theories developed in the 1970s to the identification of health behaviour determinants, but also signalled a shift in focus from health behaviour prediction to seeking to *impact* health on a larger scale, with an emphasis on identifying potentially modifiable factors that contribute to the behaviours related to health and ill-health, and the psychological mechanisms involved.

Finally, the three chapters covering the period since 2000 focus more on how individuals can be supported to improve their health, and draw on some of the preceding theories in doing so (Seligman et al., 2005, Chapter 14; Sallis et al., 2006, Chapter 4; Michie et al., 2013, Chapter 12).

ORGANISATION OF THE CHAPTERS

While locating the 'classic' studies in this book in the context of a chronological timeline permits an appreciation of their contribution to the wider progression of the sub-discipline of health psychology, we chose to organise the studies along four themes: (i) Theory (Chapters 2, 3, and 4), (ii) Biological processes (Chapters 5, 6, and 7), (iii) Social processes (Chapters 8, 9, and 10), and (iv) Interventions (Chapters 12, 13, and 14). The purpose of this structure is to reflect on the *collective* contribution of research inquiry that defines key sub-areas of health psychology. We chose this approach over a chronological presentation so as not to imply that 'older' contributions are in some way dated, or have waned in influence.

The Berkman and Syme study is an excellent example: Jetten et al. (Chapter 9) point out that this study was important because it illustrated the marked effect of social connectedness on health, and it is only relatively recently that the prescient impact of this work has been recognised, in part due to the emergence of new theoretical frameworks since this classic was published (e.g., Jetten et al., 2012).

Chapter structure

Largely in keeping with other texts in the series, a substantive proportion of each chapter focuses on the description and critical appraisal of the 'classic' studies themselves, including consideration of the health context in which the study is located. This focus serves a principal objective of this text: to introduce readers to the 'classic' studies in health psychology. Moreover, a key goal of the book is that each 'classic' study be used as a catalyst for a discussion on how research inquiry and practice in the representative sub-area of health psychology have developed subsequently, or inspired the inception of an entire new field of research or inquiry in health psychology. For example, Michie et al.'s (2013) behaviour change technique taxonomy is seen as an influential stepping stone in the development of a new 'science' of behaviour change (see Chapter 12). Consequently, each chapter also focuses on the broader implications for the subject area, including how the classic study inspired subsequent research, and in some cases also highlighting how thinking, theory, and methods have moved on or changed since the publication of the 'classic'. For example, Karl (Chapter 13) highlights the methodological innovations that were prompted by Pennebaker et al.'s (1988) research on psychotherapeutic interventions. It is through illuminating these broader implications that the 'classic' nature of the studies in this book can be truly appreciated.

In addition to providing a review of the 'classic' study, authors were encouraged to provide 'sidebars' that detail specific topics of interest relating to the 'classic' study or in the sub-area of their chapter. In some cases, the sidebars have been used to distinguish key terms or provide definitions (e.g., distinguishing between placebo effects and placebo responses: Chapter 11), or to present additional study findings (e.g., gender differences in the relationship between social connectedness and health: Chapter 9), or controversial issues or methods that are topics of current debate (e.g., discussion of the self-selection bias in health psychology research: Chapter 14). Some authors have also drawn attention to other seminal or 'neo-classic' studies that follow from the focal study. For example, Sani (Chapter 5) reviews Cohen et al.'s (1991) 'classic' study, but this study was actually one of five reported by Cohen and his colleagues that investigated the link between stress and susceptibility to the common cold. The studies together became known as the 'Common Cold Project', and brief summaries of these are provided in a side bar in that chapter. Finally, each chapter provides links and references to further reading and resources that readers can use to gain greater insight into practices, methods, and implications of the findings of the topics covered by the 'classic' study and the developments in the discipline since.

HONOURABLE MENTIONS

As outlined previously, our expert consensus approach to nominating the 'classic' studies that are the subject of each chapter of this book was simultaneously rigorous and subjective, such that we welcome the inevitable debate we expect our final list of 'classics' to generate. We also freely admit we were somewhat uncomfortable with identifying just one 'classic' in each sub-field of health psychology given that there are a multitude of other studies that are worthy 'classic' designates but did not make the final cut. In order to provide a consolatory, but, again inevitably unsatisfactory, redress to these omissions, we provide here an honorable mention of some of the candidate studies identified in our nomination procedures that fulfil the criteria of a 'classic' for each of the sub-fields addressed in the 13 chapters of the book.

Chapter 2: Models of Health Behaviour

We considered other conceptual studies that proposed some of the most influential and well-used theories and models of health behaviour. Prominent among these were by Albert Bandura (e.g., Bandura, 1986), whose Social Cognitive Theory and self-efficacy construct has been a pre-eminent perspective and construct, respectively, in research aimed at understanding and changing health behaviour, and studies. Other candidates were articles that proposed or summarised additional classic studies, such as Ronald W. Rogers' (1975) proposal of Protection Motivation Theory and Rosenstock's (1974) overview of the Health Belief Model, both of which have been instrumental in informing thinking on the determinants and processes related to health behaviour. However, Ajzen's seminal review was identified as the 'classic' in this area principally because it eminently collated the collective impact of this 'social cognition' class of theories, and specified how they had informed behavioural research and intervention in the health domain explicitly, and his agenda-setting precis of how this research continues to inform thinking and practice on health behaviour going forward.

Chapter 3: Control Theory

As Mansell clearly outlines, the conceptual origins of Control Theory owe much to the work of William T. Powers (e.g., Powers, 1973) in translating concepts from systems approaches in engineering to the study of behaviour. As such, candidate nominees for the application of the influential Control Theory were Powers' key writings in which he proposed the general feedback theory of human behaviour (e.g., Powers et al., 1960a, 1960b). However, Carver and Scheier's (1982) article was the nominated 'classic' as it not only introduced researchers in the health domain to a hitherto relatively unknown approach, but provided the clear theoretical basis and practical implications of its application in health behaviour domains.

CHAPTER 4: THE ECOLOGICAL APPROACH

As Ruiter and colleagues note, Sallis et al.'s (2006) message, as expressed in the 'classic' study that is the focus of Chapter 4, was not necessarily considered 'new' at the time of its publication: the authors dedicate considerable space to discussing the historical underpinnings of the ecological approach – including the works of Urie Bronfenbrenner. In fact, several studies by Bronfebrenner and co-authors' were early contenders for inclusion as 'classic' studies for this text (e.g., Bronfenbrenner, 1977). What Sallis et al.'s work served to achieve, however, was to give prominence to the ecological approach within the sub-discipline of health psychology and, for this reason, it was the 'classic' study designated to represent this approach.

CHAPTER 5: STRESS AND HEALTH

This was identified as a high priority area of focus within the sub-discipline of health psychology by our panel, with several candidate studies nominated, including: Lazarus and Folkman's (1984) seminal work distinguishing between primary and secondary stress appraisals Carver, Scheier, and Weintraub's (1989) work, which focused on the measurement of coping strategies; and Shelley Taylor's writings on illusions of control and optimism and their importance for mental health (e.g., Taylor & Brown, 1988), and later empirical tests of these ideas (e.g., Taylor et al., 1992). With their primarily psychological focus, such studies have made valuable contributions to the sub-discipline of health psychology. But Cohen et al.'s (1991) report of the 'common cold studies' stood out as the pioneering contribution in this field because it provided a new, integrative approach that linked biological, environmental, and psychological perspectives to the study of stress. And, as Sani points out in Chapter 5, these studies were a decisive stimulus for the broad development of research into the stress–health link, and also stimulated key questions that remain as relevant today as they did 30 years ago when the 'classic' study was published.

CHAPTER 6: PSYCHONEUROIMMUNOLOGY

With its unarguable impact on health psychology, as well as the indelible mark it made in other allied disciplines, inclusion of the work of Kiecolt-Glaser and colleagues as the 'classic' contribution in the area of psychoneuroimmunology was the leading choice. However, the most substantive challenge was deciding on *which* study to include, as numerous potential 'classics' from these authors were suggested to us by our panel. However, as noted by Weinman and co-authors in Chapter 6, Solomon and Moos' (1964) early cross-disciplinary collaboration provided a vision for future theory and research in this area, and forms a prominent backdrop for Kiecolt-Glaser et al.'s (1995) own investigations, and therefore fully deserves an honourable mention here. Segerstrom and Miller's (2004) large meta-analysis is also worth noting, not because we considered it as a 'classic' study *per se*, but because it so powerfully illustrates the scale of interest in, and impact of, research on this topic.

CHAPTER 7: PERSONALITY AND HEALTH

It is interesting to note that the target 'classic' article in this context reports an empirical study that applied intuitively appealing and clearly defined theoretical predictions in an empirical study, that, ultimately, under more extensive research and scrutiny, led to its debunking. Nevertheless, the study had far-reaching implications and lessons that informed research on personality in health domains, particularly theoretical perspectives and research designs and methods. On this basis, the 'classic' selection is a sound one, even if its 'classic' status is for somewhat different reasons from other 'classics' in this book. Nevertheless, this meant we had to overlook other studies that also made substantive contributions to the development of personality research in health, such as seminal empirical research and reviews of research examining how personality traits relate to longevity and mortality (e.g., Bogg & Roberts, 2004; Friedman et al., 1993).

CHAPTER 8: HEALTH INEQUALITIES

Although it is not as directly situated in the sub-discipline of health psychology in the same way as many of the other 'classic' studies in this book, Marmot et al.'s (1978) study was selected as the 'classic' on health inequalities because its findings have had a marked impact on the development of and progress in this area in the four decades since its publication. And as Schüz notes in Chapter 8, this study has materially contributed to greater recognition of social inequality in research in psychology more generally. The broad scope and impact of some of the studies that have followed the works of Marmot and colleagues are testament to this contribution, some of which resonate with other topics considered in this text, including contemporary work that has considered psychological and moderators of the effects of inequality (e.g., Godin et al., 2010; Schüz et al., 2017).

CHAPTER 9: SOCIAL NETWORKS AND HEALTH

While earlier studies had proposed theory or provided data suggesting that social connectedness is important to health (e.g., Maddison & Viola, 1968), Jetten and colleagues note that Berkman and Syme's (1979) study was the first to demonstrate this *directly*. Critically, the study stimulated several further studies on the topic, including some that made important methodological advances along the way to convincingly replicating the original effects (e.g., House et al., 1982). But Berkman and Syme's original enjoys 'legacy classic' status because its findings can be seen as underpinning a large programme of research that has burgeoned only relatively recently. And it is this latter body of work, and associated developments in social identity theory and research, that guided Jetten and colleagues to further isolate the impact on health of social connectedness in their re-analysis of the original Berkman and Syme data.

CHAPTER 10: FEAR APPEALS AND ILLNESS PERCEPTIONS

In the context of effects of fear appeals and threat on health decisions and behaviour, Howard Leventhal and co-workers' contribution was an obvious choice and featured prominently in the nominees across our expert panel survey. Leventhal et al.'s (1965) work is also often elevated to 'classic' status. In fact, other contributions by Leventhal, such as the Common-Sense Model of Illness Self-regulation, which provided a more elaborated model of coping and behaviour in the health domain, and notion of illness perceptions or representations could also have been the focal 'classic' article, and feature prominently in Cameron's chapter (Chapter 10). However, it would be remiss not to acknowledge other potential 'classic' contributions in the domain of threat and appraisal in health psychology, such as Janis and colleagues' (Janis & Feshbach, 1953; Janis & Terwilliger 1962) experimental tests of responses and resistance to fear arousing communications, or seminal reviews of the application of these approaches in health domains, such as pictorial warning labels (Brewer et al., 2018).

CHAPTER 11: PLACEBO EFFECTS

Several candidate 'classic' studies on this topic were proposed by our expert panel. One candidate was Crum and Langer's (2007) study in which they demonstrated that experimentally increasing people's perceptions of their own physical activity levels had a marked impact on health, including weight (loss) and (reduced) blood pressure, despite no apparent change in physical activity behaviour. Similarly, Stewart-Williams and Podd's (2004) comprehensive and integrative discussion of response expectancy and classical conditioning accounts for the placebo effect was also nominated. In addition, although Kirsch's (1985) 'classic' theoretical contribution to placebo effects was the nominated 'classic' on this topic, several other studies by Kirsch and colleagues were suggested, including two meta-analyses of anti-depressant efficacy data submitted to the US Food and Drug Administration that demonstrated an even more pronounced placebo effect than the 'classic' study (Kirsch, Deacon et al., 2008; Kirsch, Moore et al., 2002). While some research in this area clearly represents a challenge to the response expectancy account, Kirsch's (1985) formulation stimulated a debate that continues to shape the science of placebo effects.

CHAPTER 12: BEHAVIOUR CHANGE

Michie and co-workers' seminal expert consensus study and comprehensive and systematic approach to the development of the Behaviour Change Technique Taxonomy is a fitting target article for this chapter on behaviour change, and is fast becoming a modern 'classic' in both its content and method. Nevertheless, it was not the first taxonomy developed, and Abraham and Michie's (2008) initial taxonomy of behaviour change techniques was pioneering of this approach, and served as the platform for the development of subsequent taxonomies of behaviour change techniques. Other important contributions in the behaviour change field that are worthy of mention when identifying 'classics' are contributions by researchers who developed psychologically-based motivational methods of behaviour change, such as Carl Rogers' (1951) client-centered therapy and William R. Miller's (1983) motivational interviewing approaches.

CHAPTER 13: PSYCHOTHERAPEUTIC INTERVENTIONS

As Anke Karl points out in Chapter 13, Pennebaker and colleagues' work on expressive writing as a health intervention was informed by a long history of work that has explored psychosomatic explanations for health and illness. Other contributions by Pennebaker were considered (e.g., Pennebaker & Beall, 1986), along with work on other therapeutic approaches, such as the transtheoretical approach (Prochaska & DiClimente, 1982). Ultimately, we chose Pennebaker et al. (1988) as the 'classic' study because of its broad impact on health psychology, both in terms of its understanding of health processes and its applied contribution to the field of psychotherapy.

CHAPTER 14: POSITIVE PSYCHOLOGY

Contributions by Martin Seligman and colleagues were at the forefront of our panel's consideration when nominating the focal 'classic' study in positive psychology, and although a number of candidates from the same author were considered, we settled on the broad overview and summary of research as the focal seminal contribution (Seligman et al., 2005). However, primary research articles that served to be foundational in the inception and development of this sub-area should not be overlooked, such as prior work on pessimism as a risk factor for physical illness (Peterson et al., 1988). Contributions by other luminaries in the field were also considered and deserve a mention, such as those by Ed Diener and Sonja Lyubomirsky on subjective well-being and happiness (e.g., Diener, 2000; Lyubomirsky et al., 2005).

CONCLUDING REMARKS

As we have outlined in the current chapter, identifying 'classic' studies in health psychology was a challenging, controversial, and highly subjective endeavour. And while we adopted a rigorous and systematic process, we recognise that inevitably such an attempt may fall short of its goal in the eyes of some, both in terms of what is labelled and included as a 'classic' health psychology study, and what is omitted! We do not, therefore, make any grandiose claim that the classic studies presented herein represent a definitive or exhaustive list of classic studies. Rather, we prefer to view it as a starting point that will inspire readers to review the nominated 'classic' studies in each chapter, as well as other studies, stimulate further discussion on the important discoveries in this discipline, and, perhaps, inspire them to develop their own list of 'classic' studies. Ultimately, and despite the inherent subjectivity of the process, we hope that readers will agree with us that the chapters that comprise this text present a representative collection of 'classic' studies that together capture the diversity of topics in health psychology while also highlighting its substantial and lasting impact.

REFERENCES

Abraham, C., & Michie, S. (2008). A taxonomy of behavior change techniques used in interventions. *Health Psychology*, *27*(3), 379–387. https://doi.org/10.1037/0279-6133.27.3.379

Adler, N., & Matthews, K. (1994). Health psychology: Why do some people get sick and some stay well? *Annual Review of Psychology*, *45*(1), 229–259. https://doi.org/10.1146/annurev.ps.45.020194.001305

Ajzen, I. (1998). Models of human social behavior and their application to health. *Psychology and Health*, *13*, 735–739.

Aksnes, D. W., Langfeldt, L., & Wouters, P. (2019). Citations, citation indicators, and research quality: An overview of basic concepts and theories. *SAGE Open*. https://doi.org/10.1177/2158244019829575

APA Task Force on Health Research. (1976). Contributions of psychology to health research: Patterns, problems, and potentials. *American Psychologist*, *31*, 263–274. https://doi.org/10.1037/0003-066X.31.4.263

Bandura, A. (1986). *Social foundations of thought and action: A social-cognitive theory*. Englewood Cliffs, NJ: Prentice-Hall.

Barkway, P., & O'Kane, D. (2019). *Psychology: An introduction for health professionals*. Oxford: Elsevier.

Baum, A., & Posluszny, D. M. (1999). Health psychology: Mapping biobehavioral contributions to health and illness. *Annual Review of Psychology*, *50*(1), 137–163. https://doi.org/10.1146/annurev.psych.50.1.137

Berkman, L. F., & Syme, S. L. (1979). Social networks, host resistance, and mortality: A nine-year follow-up study of Alameda County residents. *American Journal of Epidemiology*, *109*, 186–204. https://doi.org/10.1093/oxfordjournals.aje.a112674

Bogg, T., & Roberts, B. W. (2004). Conscientiousness and health-related behaviors: A meta-analysis of the leading behavioral contributors to mortality. *Psychological Bulletin*, *130*(6), 887–919. https://doi.org/10.1037/0033-2909.130.6.887

Boll, T. J., Perry, N. W., Rozensky, R. H., & Johnson, S. B. (2002). *Handbook of clinical health psychology: Medical disorders and behavioral applications*. Washington, DC: American Psychological Association.

Bonell, C., Michie, S., Reicher, S., West, R., Bear, L., Yardley, L., Curtis, V., Amlôt, R., & Rubin, G. J. (2020). Harnessing behavioural science in public health campaigns to maintain 'social distancing' in response to the COVID-19 pandemic: Key principles. *Journal of Epidemiology and Community Health*, *74*, 617–619. https://doi.org/10.1136/jech-2020-214290

Brewer, N. T., Hall, M. G., & Noar, S. M. (2018). Pictorial cigarette pack warnings increase quitting. *Health Psychology Review*, *12*, 129–132. https://doi.org/10.1080/17437199.2018.1445544

Bronfenbrenner, U. (1977). Toward an experimental ecology of human development. *American Psychologist*, *32*(7), 513–531. https://doi.org/10.1037/0003-066X.32.7.513

Carver, C. S., & Scheier, M. F. (1982). Control-theory: A useful conceptual framework for personality-social, clinical, and health psychology. *Psychological Bulletin*, *92*, 111–135.

Carver, C. S., Scheier, M. F., & Weintraub, J. K. (1989). Assessing coping strategies: A theoretically based approach. *Journal of Personality and Social Psychology, 56*(2), 267–283.

Clark, D. M. (1986). A cognitive approach to panic. *Behaviour Research and Therapy, 24*(4), 461–470. https://doi.org/10.1016/0005-7967(86)90011-2

Cohen, S., Tyrrell, D. A. J., & Smith, A. P. (1991). Psychological stress and susceptibility to the common cold. *New England Journal of Medicine, 325*(9), 606–612. https://doi.org/10.1056/nejm199108293250903

Conner, M. T., & Norman, P. (2015). *Predicting and changing health behaviour: Research and practice with social cognition models* (3rd ed.). Maidenhead: Open University Press.

Crum, A. J., & Langer, E. J. (2007). Mind-set matters: Exercise and the placebo effect. *Psychological Science, 18*(2), 165–171. https://doi.org.10.1111/j.1467-9280.2007.01867.x.

Davey, G. C. L. (2019). Introduction. In G. C. L. Davey (Ed.), *Clinical psychology: Revisiting the classic studies* (pp. 1–8). London: Sage.

Davis, R., Campbell, R., Hildon, Z., Hobbs, L., & Michie, S. (2015). Theories of behaviour and behaviour change across the social and behavioural sciences: A scoping review. *Health Psychology Review, 9*(3), 323–344. https://doi.org/10.1080/17437199.2014.941722

Diener, E. (2000). Subjective well-being: The science of happiness and a proposal for a national index. *American Psychologist, 55*, 34–43. https://doi.org/10.1037/0003-066X.55.1.34

Ferraro, R. A., Davis, D. M., Blumenthal, R. S., & Martin, S. S. (2020). *Comparison of dietary and exercise recommendations on both sides of the Atlantic*. Washington, DC: American College of Cardiology.

Fishbein, M., Triandis, H. C., Kanfer, F. H., Becker, M., Middlestadt, S. E., & Eichler, A. (2001). Factors influencing behavior and behavior change. In A. Baum, T. A. Revenson, & J. E. Singer (Eds.), *Handbook of health psychology* (pp. 3–17). Mahwah, NJ: Lawrence Erlbaum.

Friedman, H. S. (2014). Revolutionary health psychology versus scientific health psychology – commentary on Murray (2012). *Health Psychology Review, 8*(2), 238–241. https://doi.org/10.1080/17437199.2013.770048

Friedman, H. S., Tucker, J. S., Tomlinson-Keasey, C., Schwartz, J. E., Wingard, D. L., & Criqui, M. H. (1993). Does childhood personality predict longevity? *Journal of Personality and Social Psychology, 65*, 176–185. https://doi.org/10.1037/0022-3514.65.1.176

Friedman, M., & Rosenman, R. H. (1959). Association of specific overt behavior pattern with blood and cardiovascular findings. *JAMA, 169*(12), 1286–1296. https://doi.org/10.1001/jama.1959.03000290012005

Glanz, K., & Bishop, D. B. (2010). The role of behavioral science theory in development and implementation of public health interventions. *Annual Review of Public Health, 31*, 399–418. https://doi.org/10.1146/annurev.publhealth.012809.103604

Glanz, K., & Maddock, J. (2000). On judging models and theories: Research and practice, psychology and public health. *Journal of Health Psychology, 5*(2), 151–154. https://doi.org/10.1177/135910530000500203

Godin, G., Sheeran, P., Conner, M., Belanger-Gravel, A., Cecilia, M., Gallani, B. J., & Nolin, B. (2010). Social structure, social cognition, and physical activity: A test of four models. *British Journal of Health Psychology, 15*(1), 79–95. https://doi.org/10.1348/135910709x429901

Gurung, R. A. R. (2018). Health psychology. In Kenneth D. Keith (Ed.), *Culture across the curriculum: A psychology teacher's handbook.* (pp. 449–463). Cambridge: Cambridge University Press. https://doi.org/10.1017/9781316996706.024

Hagger, M. S., Cameron, L. D., Hamilton, K., Hankonen, N., & Lintunen, T. (Eds.). (2020). *The handbook of behavior change.* Cambridge: Cambridge University Press. https://doi.org/10.1017/9781108677318

House, J. S., Robbins, C., & Metzner, H. L. (1982). The association of social relationships and activities with mortality: Prospective evidence from the Tecumseh community health study. *American Journal of Epidemiology, 116,* 123–140. https://doi.org/10.1093/oxfordjournals.aje.a113387

Janis, I., L., & Feshbach, S. (1953). Effects of fear-arousing communications. *Journal of Abnormal and Social Psychology, 48,* 78–92. https://doi.org/10.1037/h0060732

Janis, I. L., & Terwilliger, R. F. (1962). An experimental study of psychological resistances to fear arousing communications. *Journal of Abnormal and Social Psychology, 65,* 403-410. https://doi.org/10.1037/h0047601

Jetten, J., Haslam, C., & Haslam, S. A. (Eds.). (2012). *The social cure: Identity, health and well-being.* London: Psychology Press. https://doi.org/10.4324/9780203813195

Jorm, A. F. (2015). Using the Delphi expert consensus method in mental health research. *Australian & New Zealand Journal of Psychiatry, 49*(10), 887–897. https://doi.org/10.1177/0004867415600891

Kiecolt-Glaser, J. K., Marucha, P. T., Malarkey, W. B., Mercado, A. M., & Glaser, R. (1995). Slowing of wound healing by psychological stress. *The Lancet, 346,* 1194–1196.

Kirsch, I. (1985). Response expectancy as a determinant of experience and behavior. *American Psychologist, 40,* 1189–1202. https://doi.org/10.1037/0003-066X.40.11.1189

Kirsch, I., Deacon, B. J., Huedo-Medina, T. B., Scoboria, A., Moore, T. J., & Johnson, B. T. (2008). Initial severity and antidepressant benefits: A meta-analysis of data submitted to the Food and Drug Administration. *PLoS Medicine, 5*(2), e45. https://doi.org/10.1371/journal.pmed.0050045

Kirsch, I., Moore, T. J., Scoboria, A., & Nicholls, S. S. (2002). The emperor's new drugs: An analysis of antidepressant medication data submitted to the U.S. Food and Drug Administration. *Prevention & Treatment, 5*(1), Article 23. https://psycnet.apa.org/doi/10.1037/1522-3736.5.1.523a

Lazarus, R. S., & Folkman, S. (1984). *Stress, appraisal, and coping.* New York: Springer.

Leventhal, H., Singer, R., & Jones, S. (1965). Effects of fear and specificity of recommendation upon attitudes and behavior. *Journal of Personality and Social Psychology, 2*(1), 20–29. https://doi.org/10.1037/h0022089

Leventhal, H., Weinman, J., Leventhal, E. A., & Phillips, L. A. (2008). Health psychology: The search for pathways between behavior and health. *Annual Review of Psychology, 59,* 477–505. https://doi.org/10.1146/annurev.psych.59.103006.093643

Lyubomirsky, S., Sheldon, K. M., & Schkade, D. (2005). Pursuing happiness: The architecture of sustainable change. *Review of General Psychology, 9*(2), 111–131. https://doi.org/10.1037/1089-2680.9.2.111

Maddison, D., & Viola, A. (1968). The health of widows in the year following bereavement. *Journal of Psychosomatic Research, 12,* 297–306. https://doi.org/10.1016/0022-3999(68)90084-6

Mann, T., & Kato, P. M. (1996). Diversity issues in health psychology. In T. Mann & P. M. Kato (Eds.), *Handbook of diversity issues in health psychology* (pp. 3–18). New York: Springer.

Marmot, M. G., Rose, G., Shipley, M., & Hamilton, P. J. (1978). Employment grade and coronary heart disease in British civil servants. *Journal of Epidemiology and Community Health*, *32*(4), 244. https://doi.org/10.1136/jech.32.4.244

Michie, S., Richardson, M., Johnston, M., Abraham, C., Francis, J., Hardeman, W., Eccles, M. P., Cane, J., & Wood, C. E. (2013). The Behavior Change Technique Taxonomy (v1) of 93 hierarchically clustered techniques: Building an international consensus for the reporting of behavior change interventions. *Annals of Behavioral Medicine*, *46*, 81–95.

Milgram, S. (1963). Behavioral study of obedience. *Journal of Abnormal and Social Psychology*, *67*, 371–378. https://doi.org/10.1037/h0040525

Miller, W. R. (1983). Motivational interviewing with problem drinkers. *Behavioural Psychotherapy*, *11*(2), 147–172. https://doi.org/10.1017/S0141347300006583

Miller, G., Chen, E., & Cole, S. W. (2009). Health psychology: Developing biologically plausible models linking the social world and physical health. *Annual Review of Psychology*, *60*(1), 501–524. https://doi.org/10.1146/annurev.psych.60.110707. 163551

Murray, M. (2014a). Social history of health psychology: Context and textbooks. *Health Psychology Review*, *8*(2), 215–237. https://doi.org/10.1080/17437199.2012. 701058

Murray, M. (2014b). The time has come to talk of many things: Some comments on Ogden and Friedman. *Health Psychology Review*, *8*(2), 246–250. https://doi.org/ 10.1080/17437199.2013.798830

Pennebaker, J. W., & Beall, S. K. (1986). Confronting a traumatic event: Toward an understanding of inhibition and disease. *Journal of Abnormal Psychology*, *95*(3), 274–281. https://doi.org/10.1037//0021-843x.95.3.274

Pennebaker, J. W., Kiecolt-Glaser, J. K., & Glaser, R. (1988). Disclosure of traumas and immune function: Health implications for psychotherapy. *Journal of Consulting and Clinical Psychology*, *56*, 239–245.

Peterson, C., Seligman, M. E., & Vaillant, G. E. (1988). Pessimistic explanatory style is a risk factor for physical illness: A thirty-five-year longitudinal study. *Journal of Personality and Social Psychology*, *55*, 23–27. https://doi.org/10.1037/0022-3514. 55.1.23

Powers, W. T. (1973). *Behavior: The control of perception*. Chicago, IL: Aldine.

Powers, W. T., Clark, R. K., & McFarland, R. L. (1960a). A general feedback theory of human behavior: Part I. *Perceptual and Motor Skills*, *11*(1), 71–88. https://doi. org/10.2466/pms.1960.11.1.71

Powers, W. T., Clark, R. K., & McFarland, R. L. (1960b). A general feedback theory of human behavior: Part II. *Perceptual and Motor Skills*, *11*(3), 309–323. https://doi. org/10.2466/pms.1960.11.3.309

Prochaska, J. O., & DiClemente, C. C. (1982). Transtheoretical therapy: Toward a more integrative model of change. *Psychotherapy: Theory, Research & Practice*, *19*(3), 276–288.

Rachman, S. (2009). Psychological treatment of anxiety: The evolution of behavior therapy and cognitive behavior therapy. *Annual Review of Clinical Psychology*, *5*(1), 97–119. https://doi.org/10.1146/annurev.clinpsy.032408.153635

Reicher, S., & Haslam, S. A. (2017). Obedience: Revisiting Milgram's shock experiments. In S. A. Haslam & J. R. Smith (Eds.), *Social psychology: Revisiting the classics* (2nd ed., pp. 108–129). London: Sage.

Rodin, J., & Salovey, P. (1989). Health psychology. *Annual Review of Psychology*, *40*, 533–579. https://doi.org/10.1146/annurev.ps.40.020189.002533

Rogers, C. (1951). *Client-centred therapy*. Boston, MA: Houghton-Mifflin.

Rogers, R. W. (1975). A protection motivation theory of fear appeals and attitude change. *Journal of Psychology*, *91*(1), 93–114. https://doi.org/10.1080/00223980.1975.9915803

Rosenstock, I. M. (1974). Historical origins of the health belief model. *Health Education Monographs*, *2*, 328–335. https://doi.org/10.1177/109019817400200403

Sallis, J. F., Cervero, R. B., Ascher, W., Henderson, K. A., Kraft, M. K., & Kerr, J. (2006). An ecological approach to creating active living communities. *Annual Review of Public Health*, *27*(1), 297–322. https://doi.org/10.1146/annurev.publhealth.27.021405.102100

Schneiderman, N., Antoni, M. H., Saab, P. G., & Ironson, G. (2001). Health psychology: Psychosocial and biobehavioral aspects of chronic disease management. *Annual Review of Psychology*, *52*(1), 555–580. https://doi.org/10.1146/annurev.psych.52.1.555

Schüz, B., Li, A. S.-W., Hardinge, A., McEachan, R. R. C., & Conner, M. (2017). Socioeconomic status as a moderator between social cognitions and physical activity: Systematic review and meta-analysis based on the Theory of Planned Behavior. *Psychology of Sport and Exercise*, *30*, 186–195. https://doi.org/10.1016/j.psychsport.2017.03.004

Segerstrom, S. C., & Miller, G. E. (2004). Psychological stress and the human immune system: A meta-analytic study of 30 years of inquiry. *Psychological Bulletin*, *130*(4), 601–630. https://doi.org.10.1037/0033-2909.130.4.601

Seligman, M. E. P., Steen, T. A., Park, N., & Peterson, C. (2005). Positive psychology progress: Empirical validation of interventions. *American Psychologist*, *60*, 410–421. https://doi.org.https://doi.org/10.1037/0003-066X.60.5.410

Smith, J. A., & Haslam, S. A. (2017). An introduction to classic studies in social psychology. In S. A. Haslam & J. A. Smith (Eds.), *Social psychology: Revisiting the classic studies* (2nd ed., pp. 1–10). London: Sage.

Smith, T. W. (2003). Health psychology. In J. A. Schinka & W. F. Velicer (Eds.), *Handbook of psychology: Research methods in psychology* (Vol. 2, pp. 241–270). New York: John Wiley & Sons Inc.

Solomon, G. F., & Moos, R. H. (1964). Emotions, immunity and disease. *Archives of General Psychiatry*, *11*, 657–674.

Stanton, A. L., Revenson, T. A., & Tennen, H. (2006). Health psychology: Psychological adjustment to chronic disease. *Annual Review of Psychology*, *58*(1), 565–592. https://doi.org/10.1146/annurev.psych.58.110405.085615

Stewart-Williams, S., & Podd, J. (2004). The placebo effect: Dissolving the expectancy versus conditioning debate. *Psychological Bulletin*, *130*(2), 324–340.

Straub, R. O. (2022). *Health psychology: A biopsychosocial approach* (7th ed.). New York: Worth Publishers.

Tajfel, H. (1978). *Differentiation between social groups: Studies in the social psychology of intergroup relations*. London: Academic Press.

Taylor, S. E., & Brown, J. D. (1988). Illusion and well-being: A social psychological perspective on mental health. *Psychological Bulletin*, *103*(2), 193–210.

Taylor, S. E., Kemeny, M. E., Aspinwall, L. G., Schneider, S. G., Rodriguez, R., & Herbert, M. (1992). Optimism, coping, psychological distress, and high-risk sexual behavior among men at risk for acquired immunodeficiency syndrome (AIDS). *Journal* of Personality and Social Psychology, 63(3), 460–473. https://doi.org.10.1037// 0022-3514.63.3.460.

Taylor, S. E., Repetti, R. L., & Seeman, T. (1997). Health psychology: What is an unhealthy environment and how does it get under the skin? Annual Review of Psychology, 48, 411–447. https://doi.org/10.1146/annurev.psych.48.1.411

Taylor, S. E., & Stanton, A. L. (2020). Health psychology (11th ed.). New York: McGraw-Hill.

Teixeira, P. J., Marques, M. M., Silva, M. N., Brunet, J., … Hagger, M. S. (2020). Classification of techniques used in self-determination theory-based interventions in health contexts: An expert consensus study. Motivation Science, 6(4), 438–455. https://doi.org/10.1037/mot0000172

Vögele, C. (2015). Behavioral medicine. In J. D. Wright (Ed.), International encyclopedia of the social & behavioral sciences (2nd ed.). Oxford: Elsevier.

Waddington, L. (2019). Panic disorder as a psychological problem: Building on Clark (1986). In G. C. L. Davey (Ed.), Clinical psychology: Revisiting the classic studies (pp. 135–156). London: Sage.

Whittington, A. (2019). The origins of cognitive therapy: Building on Beck (1964). In G. C. L. Davey (Ed.), Clinical psychology: Revisiting the classic studies (pp. 41–60). London: Sage.

WHO. (2004). WHO global strategy on diet, physical activity & health. Geneva: World Health Organization.

WHO. (2014). Global status report on noncommunicable diseases 2014. Geneva: World Health Organization.

WHO. (2020). WHO guidelines on physical activity and sedentary behaviour. Geneva: World Health Organization.

WHO. (2021). WHO Discussion Paper on the development of an implementation roadmap 2023–2030 for the WHO Global Action Plan for the Prevention and Control of NCDs 2023–2030. Geneva: World Health Organization.

Williams, P. G., Holmbeck, G. N., & Greenley, R. N. (2002). Adolescent health psychology. Journal of Consulting and Clinical Psychology, 70, 828–842. https://doi.org/10.1037/ 0022-006X.70.3.828

2 | Models of Health Behaviour: Revisiting Ajzen (1998)

Ajzen, I. (1998). Models of human social behavior and their application to health. *Psychology and Health, 13*, 735–739.

Mark Conner and Paul Norman

BACKGROUND

Many people engage in certain behaviours (e.g., physical activity) and avoid others (e.g., eating a high fat diet) because of their impact on health outcomes (e.g., to get fitter, to lose weight). Interest in such health behaviours is based on the proposition that they tend to be related to reduced risk of morbidity and mortality (Belloc, 1973). It is also assumed that by changing these behaviours individuals can improve their health. Much of the research supporting these propositions comes from epidemiological studies looking at differences in health outcomes between individuals who do or do not engage in these behaviours. For example, a study conducted in Alameda County, California, identified seven features of lifestyle that together were associated with lower morbidity and mortality: not smoking, drinking alcohol only in moderation, sleeping 7–8 hours per night, exercising regularly, maintaining a desirable body weight, avoiding snacks, and eating breakfast regularly (Belloc, 1973).

Health psychologists have made an important contribution to work on this topic by developing 'models' that outline the proximal determinants of health behaviour, and summarise or represent *how* these determinants relate to health behaviour. These models focus on social cognition factors or 'constructs' that inform people's decisions to participate in a given 'target' behaviour, including perceptions of health risk, the effectiveness of the behaviour to reduce these risks, social pressures to perform the behaviour, and control over performance of the behaviour. The relative importance of these factors in determining who performs various health behaviours constitutes the basis of different models (Conner & Norman, 2015). These models seek to specify the key constructs that determine health behaviour and, in doing so, they identify key constructs that might be targeted when attempting to change such behaviours.

Ajzen's (1998) article, which is the focus of this chapter, considered the content of these models and their application to explaining people's health behaviours. In this chapter we provide some background to Ajzen's article, identify three important aspects or contributions of the article, and examine two important developments of health behaviour models that have occurred subsequent to the article. In doing so, we provide descriptions of the key models of health behaviour, provide an overview of research on the use of these models to both predict and change health behaviour, and summarise their contribution and relevance to the field.

DETAILED OVERVIEW

Icek Ajzen, an American social psychologist, has played a key role over the last 40 years in helping to refine behavioural scientists' modelling of the social cognition determinants of behaviour (see Sidebar 2.1). Alone, and in conjunction with colleague Martin Fishbein, he has, over this period, developed a parsimonious model of social behaviour that has been widely employed to explain health behaviours, *the Theory of Planned Behaviour* (Fishbein & Ajzen, 2010). Ajzen's (1998) article appeared in one of two special issues of the journal *Psychology and Health* that focused on self-regulation and health, and followed a widely-cited 1995 book on the use of various models for predicting and changing health behaviours, with updated editions in 2005 and 2015 (Conner & Norman, 2015). Ajzen's (1998) article was an important commentary on the key health behaviour models at the time and was also influential in relation to subsequent developments in this area. In the article, Ajzen made an important distinction between content-specific and content-free models of human behaviour, and then identified two major insights that can be made with these models; namely, to provide a better prediction of health behaviour and to help the design of more effective interventions.

Sidebar 2.1. Social Cognition

Social cognition is an approach to predicting behaviour originating in social psychology that focuses on cognitions (or thoughts and feelings) as processes which intervene between observable stimuli and responses in real-world situations (Fiske & Taylor, 2013). A major focus of social cognition is on how individuals direct their thoughts and behaviour to be consistent with their self-perceptions and to help achieve their goals (i.e., self-regulation). Self-regulation involves the setting of goals, cognitive preparations, and the ongoing monitoring and evaluating of goal-directed activities. Social cognition models describe the key cognitions and their interrelationships in this process of self-regulation and have been widely applied to predict health behaviours. The Theory of Planned Behaviour (Ajzen, 1991) is one example of a social cognition model.

CONTENT-SPECIFIC VERSUS CONTENT-FREE MODELS OF HUMAN BEHAVIOUR

Ajzen's (1998) article made a key distinction between content-specific and content-free models of human behaviour that have been applied to health behaviours. Content-specific models are formulated specifically to focus on the domain of interest, such as health. In contrast, content-free models are specified at a higher level of generality and, as such, should apply to a broad range of domains (e.g., health, environment, educational, occupational). Key content-specific models in the health domain include the Health Belief Model (Janz & Becker, 1984) and Protection Motivation Theory (Rogers, 1983), whereas the key content-free models that have been applied to the health domain include Social Cognitive Theory (Bandura, 1986) and the Theory of Planned Behaviour (Ajzen, 1991). Next, we provide brief overviews of these models.

The *Health Belief Model* (HBM) is one of the oldest and most widely used content-specific models of health behaviour (see Conner & Norman, 2015, for a review; Figure 2.1). Developed in the 1960s, the model specifies a set of 'common sense' constructs associated with the adoption of health behaviours that are amenable to change. Key model constructs are the *perceived susceptibility* to experiencing a health problem, the *perceived severity* of the consequences of the health problem, and the *perceived benefits* of, and *perceived barriers* to, the health behaviour taken to respond to the health threat. *Cues to action* and *health motivation* are two other variables commonly included in the model. Cues to action include a diverse range of 'triggers' to the individual taking action and are commonly divided into factors which are internal (e.g., physical symptoms) or external (e.g., mass media campaigns) to the individual (Janz & Becker, 1984). Health motivation represents an individual's general readiness to be concerned about health matters, i.e., certain individuals may be predisposed to respond to cues to action due to the value they place on their health (Becker, 1974). In the HBM, as well as other models, other

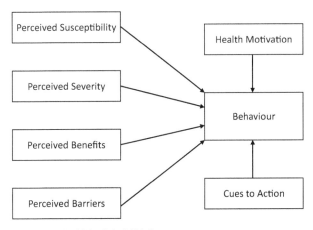

Figure 2.1 Health Belief Model (HBM)

influences on health behaviour, such as demographic factors or psychological characteristics (e.g., personality, peer pressure), are assumed to exert any effect through the key constructs in the model.

Protection Motivation Theory (PMT) is another popular content-specific model, originally developed as a framework for investigating the effectiveness of fear appeals. It has been widely used to predict health protective behaviour (see Conner & Norman, 2015, for a review; Figure 2.2). Rogers (1983) argued that when faced with a health threat, individuals engage in two appraisal processes: threat appraisal, which focuses on the source of the health threat, and coping appraisal, which focuses on the evaluation of a recommended protective behaviour. These two appraisal processes form the basis of PMT as a model of health behaviour. Within PMT, an individual's *perceived vulnerability* to, and the *perceived severity* of, the health threat increase the likelihood of a protective behaviour, whereas *rewards associated with a maladaptive response* decrease the likelihood of a protective behaviour. In addition, *response efficacy* and *self-efficacy* increase the likelihood of a protective behaviour, whereas *response costs* decrease the likelihood of a protective behaviour. *Protection motivation* (i.e., intention) results from these two appraisal processes and is the sole proximal determinant of protective behaviour.

Social Cognitive Theory (SCT; Bandura, 1986) is, in contrast, a content-free model of human behavior, a key construct of which has come to be regarded as one of the most powerful predictors of health behaviour – *self-efficacy*. Self-efficacy

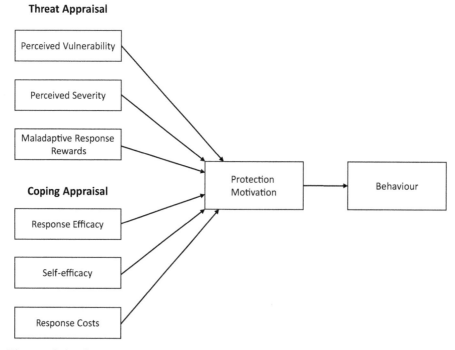

Figure 2.2 Protection Motivation Theory (PMT)

expectancies refer to beliefs about one's ability to perform a specific action to attain a desired outcome. Self-efficacy beliefs can be seen as *self-regulatory* insofar as they determine whether actions will be initiated, how much effort will be expended, and how long action will be sustained in the face of obstacles and failures. According to SCT, self-efficacy beliefs are a key predictor of *goals* (i.e., intention) and are also directly predictive of behaviour (see Conner & Norman, 2015, for a review; Figure 2.3). In addition to self-efficacy expectancies, SCT proposes that *outcome expectancies* – i.e., beliefs about the possible consequences of performing a behaviour – are predictive of goals. Goal setting is also influenced by perceived *socio-structural factors* – i.e., the impediments (barriers) or facilitators (opportunities) that reside in living conditions and health, political, economic or environmental systems (Bandura, 1986). Goals, in turn, are used to guide behaviour.

The *Theory of Planned Behavior* (TPB; Ajzen, 1991), is another content-free model of human behavior that has been widely applied to predict a variety of behaviors including health behaviors (see Conner & Norman, 2015, for a review; Figure 2.4). This theory is an extension of its precursor, Theory of Reasoned Action (Ajzen & Fishbein, 1980), and has been further developed into the Reasoned Action Approach (Fishbein & Ajzen, 2010). The TPB proposes that the proximal determinant of behaviour is the individual's *behavioural intention* to engage in that behaviour, which represents an individual's motivation or decision to exert effort to perform the behaviour. Behavioural intention is determined by three constructs: (i) *attitude*, an individual's overall evaluation of the behaviour based on their beliefs about the likely consequences of the behaviour; (ii) *subjective norms*, an individual's beliefs about whether significant others

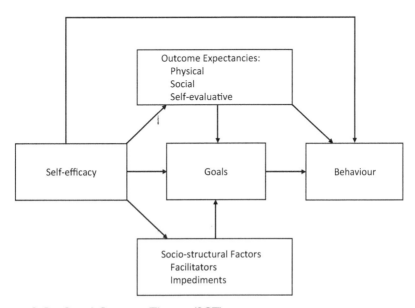

Figure 2.3   Social Cognitive Theory (SCT)

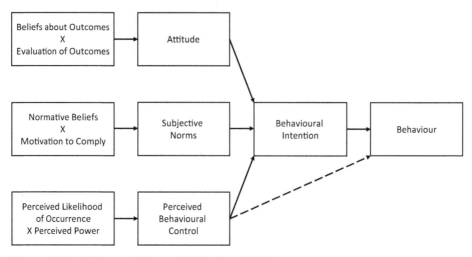

Figure 2.4 Theory of Planned Behaviour (TPB)

think they should engage in the behaviour based on their beliefs about what specific others (e.g., friends, family) think; and (iii) *perceived behavioral control*, an individual's perception of the extent to which performance of the behaviour is within their control based on beliefs about internal (e.g., personal skills, abilities) and external (e.g., opportunities, barriers) control factors. This construct is similar to self-efficacy from SCT. Perceived behavioural control can also influence behaviour directly, in addition to its effect through behavioural intentions.

Content-specific models, such as the HBM and PMT, might be expected to be more predictive of health behaviour than content-free models, such as SCT and the TPB, as they were specifically developed to predict health behaviour. By contrast, content-free models sacrifice generality and may potentially lead to the need to develop different models for different domains of human social behaviour (e.g., voting, consumer, or religious behaviour). However, although there have been a limited number of direct comparisons of models (e.g., Dzewaltowski et al., 1990), reviews generally have not supported the view that content-specific models explain more variance in people's health intentions and behaviour compared to content-free models (Conner & Norman, 2015). However, an interesting development in relation to content-specific models of health behaviours has been the idea that models may need to distinguish types of health behaviour (see Sidebar 2.2). In emphasising the importance of generally applicable models, Ajzen clearly saw an advantage to content-free compared to content-specific models. It is notable that neither content-specific nor content-free models have come to dominate work on models of health behaviour. One of the potential weaknesses of research on health behaviour has been the lack of direct comparisons of models.

Sidebar 2.2. Types of Health Behaviour

Ajzen's (1998) review of models of health behaviour noted the distinction between content-free models (e.g., SCT, TPB) and content-specific models (e.g., HBM, PMT). The latter have been specifically developed to predict health behaviour rather than other human social behaviours. Within the health behaviour domain there has been some consideration of even more specific models that might better predict specific types of health behaviours. For example, a common distinction among health behaviours is between protection (or approach) behaviours, where doing more of the behaviour benefits health (e.g., physical activity, eating low fat foods), and risk (or avoid) behaviours where doing less of the behaviour benefits health (e.g., being sedentary, eating fruit and vegetables). It is argued that the constructs key to predicting approach and avoid behaviours may be different.

Another distinction is between the initiation and maintenance of health behaviours. Many health behaviours, such as healthy eating and physical activity, provide little or no health benefit unless they are maintained over prolonged time periods. The models of health behaviour considered here primarily focus on the initiation of health behaviour. However, it is likely that the factors that determine the maintenance of health behaviour will be different from those that are important in the initiation of health behaviour. A number of models that focus on the key constructs important in the maintenance of health behaviour have been developed (see Conner & Norman, 2015, for a review). For example, self-determination theory (Deci & Ryan, 1985) focuses on the idea that motivation or intention to act needs to be internalised in order for a health behaviour to be maintained. So while the initiation of a health behaviour may be possible even when the motivation is external (e.g., following a health professional's recommendation), such motivation is unlikely to be sufficient to maintain the behaviour. Instead, the motivation needs to be internalised – i.e., the individual needs to fully accept the regulation of the behaviour as internally determined. For example, in a systematic review of applications of self-determination theory to physical activity and exercise, Teixeira et al. (2012) reported that identified regulation (i.e., performing the behaviour to pursue personally valued outcomes rather than for the behaviour itself) was more predictive of initial and short-term exercise adherence, whereas intrinsic motivation (i.e., performing the behaviour for the intrinsic satisfaction of the behaviour itself) was more predictive of long-term exercise adherence.

PREDICTING HEALTH BEHAVIOUR

Ajzen (1998) argued that in identifying the key constructs that determine health behaviour, these models provide a useful knowledge-summarising function. They also provide an account of how these different constructs drive behaviour.

For example, the TPB describes how intention mediates or 'explains' effects of attitudes, subjective norms, and perceived behavioural control on behaviour. Each of the main models of health behaviour considered in this chapter has been widely applied to the prediction of health behaviour. In this section, we consider the efficacy of each model as a means to explain health behaviour.

Quantitative reviews of research with the HBM indicate that the model's constructs are typically weakly correlated with behaviour, although correlations for perceived benefits and barriers are usually stronger than those for perceived susceptibility and severity. For example, Carpenter (2010) reported that the barriers component had a medium-sized effect on health behaviour, while benefits and severity had small–medium-sized effects, and susceptibility a very small-sized effect.

Research testing PMT indicates that coping appraisal variables (i.e., response efficacy, self-efficacy, response costs) tend to have stronger associations with protection motivation and health behaviour than do threat appraisal variables (i.e., perceived vulnerability, perceived severity). For example, Milne et al. (2000) reported that response costs, self-efficacy, and perceived vulnerability had medium-sized effects on protection motivation, but perceived vulnerability and perceived severity only had small-sized effects. In turn, protection motivation had a medium–large-sized effect on future behaviour, consistent with the proposed structure of the PMT.

Research that has used SCT to predict health behaviours has focused almost exclusively on self-efficacy and outcome expectancies, although some applications of SCT have also assessed goals and socio-structural factors. For example, Young et al. (2014) reported a systematic review and meta-analysis of 44 studies that had applied SCT to the prediction of physical activity. On average, SCT explained 31% of the variance in physical activity. Self-efficacy and goals were consistently associated with physical activity, whereas outcome expectancies and socio-structural factors were not.

Considering the TPB, McEachan et al. (2011) reported significant medium–large-sized correlations between attitudes, subjective norms, perceived behavioural control and intention, and between intention, perceived behavioural control and behaviour. Overall, the TPB explained 44% and 19% of the variance in health-related intentions and behaviour, respectively. Taken together, these reviews suggest that, overall, intention/protection motivation and perceived behavioural control/self-efficacy are the strongest predictors of health behaviour.

INTERVENTIONS TO CHANGE HEALTH BEHAVIOUR

Ajzen (1998) also highlighted that, to the extent to which these models are able to predict health behaviour, they should also provide a basis for designing interventions to change health behaviour, by identifying potential targets for change (e.g., perceived risk, self-efficacy). Over the past 25 years, a growing number of studies have sought to develop and test interventions to change health behaviour based on these models.

For example, the HBM has been used to inform the design of interventions to change various health behaviours, including interventions focusing on smoking cessation, healthy eating, condom use, screening and breast self-examination (see Conner & Norman, 2015; Hagger et al., 2020, for reviews). For example, Jones et al. (2013) reviewed 18 HBM-based interventions to increase adherence to medical regimes, finding that 14 had significant effects on adherence behaviour, although intervention effectiveness was unrelated to which contsructs were targeted. However, Sheeran et al. (2013) reported that interventions that successfully heightened perceptions of susceptibility or severity produced small but significant changes in behaviour.

One of the strengths of PMT is that it has been subjected to many experimental tests in which specific variables are manipulated and effects on PMT cognitions, protection motivation and behaviour are assessed. Milne et al. (2000) reviewed experimental tests of PMT through a meta-analysis of cognition changes following manipulations of specific PMT variables, finding larger effects on perceived vulnerability and severity than on response efficacy, self-efficacy, and response costs. However, when the effects of manipulating specific PMT variables on protection motivation are considered, manipulations of self-efficacy are typically found to be more effective than manipulations of other PMT constructs. Unfortunately, analyses of the longer-term impact of such manipulations on behaviour are rarely conducted. In contrast, PMT-based interventions have been found to have significant effects on behaviour in relation to fruit and vegetable intake, saturated fat intake, condom use, and skin cancer preventive behaviours, often over extended follow-up periods. However, non-significant PMT interventions have been reported in relation to exercise, adherence to physiotherapy, and eating guidelines after bariatric surgery (see Conner & Norman, 2015; Hagger et al., 2020, for reviews).

Reviews have reported positive effects for interventions based on SCT for physical activity (Stacey et al., 2015) and other behaviours (see Hagger et al., 2020). However, as with the use of SCT to predict health behaviour, most studies have focused on the self-efficacy construct. For example, in their review of interventions to increase physical activity in community-dwelling older adults, French et al. (2014) reported that interventions that successfully increased self-efficacy had a medium-sized effect on physical activity. More generally, Sheeran et al. (2016) reported that experimentally-induced increases in self-efficacy produce medium-sized changes in both intention and behaviour.

The TPB has been used in intervention studies for a range of health behaviours (see Conner & Norman, 2015; Hagger et al., 2020, for reviews). For example, Tyson et al. (2014) reported a small but significant effect size from a meta-analysis of 34 TPB intervention studies focusing on reducing heterosexual risk behaviours. In addition, experimental evidence indicates that manipulating TPB constructs leads to changes in intentions and behaviour. For example, meta-analyses of experimental and intervention studies indicate that studies that produce significant changes in attitudes, norms, and perceived behavioural control or self-efficacy produced medium-sized changes in intentions and small-to-medium-sized changes in behaviour (Sheeran et al., 2016; Steinmetz et al., 2016).

Despite some encouraging findings, a key criticism of models of health behaviour is that they are not models of behaviour *change* (Ajzen, 2015; Sniehotta et al., 2014). As noted above, while these models may help identify the key constructs that predict engagement in a specific behaviour and might be targeted in an intervention, they provide limited insight into how to change these key constructs in order to change behaviour. Moreover, reviews focusing on health behaviour change interventions that are explicitly based on theoretical models have only found limited support for their greater effectiveness compared to interventions not based on such models (Prestwich et al., 2014). One of the reasons that such work has tended not to find robust effects is because interventions are often only very loosely based on models of health behaviour, not always targeting all constructs included in a model (Jones et al., 2013), thereby leading to 'theory-inspired' rather than 'theory-based' interventions (Michie et al., 2017).

EVALUATING THE CONTRIBUTION OF AJZEN (1998)

An important point made by Ajzen (1998) was the value of theory as a way to systematise knowledge in a particular area. He noted that models of human social behaviour provide a useful way to summarise such knowledge and that these models may usefully serve this function in the health behaviour domain. Different models present both potentially different key constructs influencing behaviour and different structures within which these constructs are arranged. In comparing the key constructs in different models, there is the concern over whether the same construct is given different labels in different models or whether the same label is used for two different constructs. These are longstanding concerns in psychology and the behavioural sciences in general that apply well beyond models of human behaviour (see descriptions of 'jangle' and 'jingle' fallacies by Block, 1995). These considerations are important in the development of new models of human behaviour, in revising and updating such models, and in comparing different models. However, the dearth of research focusing on comparing different models of health behaviour and on making theoretical rather than empirical comparisons is notable.

Ajzen (1998) also drew attention to the opposing forces of *sufficiency* versus *parsimony* in evaluating and further developing health behaviour models. This is an issue that to this day remains a contentious one in relation to models of health behaviours. Those who focus on sufficiency considerations point particularly to the fact that models of health behaviour only explain a modest proportion of the variance in health behaviour (e.g., Sniehotta et al., 2014). The suggestion is that the inclusion of additional constructs might provide more complete models of health behaviour that explain more variance in health behaviour. Others have also emphasised the need to identify *all* the constructs that predict a health behaviour when the focus is on identifying targets for interventions designed to change behaviour (Head & Noar, 2014). There is some merit in this view when the focus is on changing behaviour because there is a desire to identify all the key determinants of behaviour in order to target them in an intervention. Adding further constructs to a model will generally better explain behaviour (i.e., more variance in behaviour accounted for; empirical justification), although this may be trivial or limited to one particular behavioural domain. Others (e.g., Ajzen, 1998) focus on parsimony and favour simpler models that only include key constructs shown to be influential across a range of domains. Although strongly in favour of parsimony, Ajzen (1998) also emphasises that models of human behaviour should be open to the inclusion of additional constructs where there are strong empirical and theoretical arguments for their inclusion. In this regard, Ajzen comments on the additional constructs of moral norms and affective factors as constructs where there might be evidence for adding them to the TPB, but notes that this may only apply to specific behaviours.

DEVELOPMENTS IN HEALTH BEHAVIOUR MODELS

In this section we draw attention to two developments in relation to health behaviour models that have occurred subsequent to Ajzen's (1998) article, and that can be partly traced back to it. The first comprises work on past behaviour and habit, and the development of dual process models; the second comprises work addressing the intention–behaviour gap and the development of 'stage' models of behaviour.

ROLE OF PAST BEHAVIOUR AND HABIT AND DEVELOPMENT OF DUAL PROCESS MODELS

The role of past behaviour in models of health behaviour has attracted much attention. Past behaviour is typically found to be the strongest predictor of future behaviour, explaining variance over and above that explained by variables included in models of health behaviour (e.g., McEachan et al., 2011). Ouellette and Wood (1998) have argued that past behaviour can determine future behaviour through one of two routes, depending on the frequency of past behaviour and the stability of the context (i.e., time and place) in which the behaviour is performed.

For behaviours that are performed relatively infrequently in unstable contexts, past behaviour provides individuals with information that shapes their beliefs about the behaviour which, in turn, determine intention and future behaviour (i.e., a conscious response). Such an account is consistent with the structure of the models of health behaviour covered in this chapter. When past behaviour is found to have a direct effect on future behaviour, it is because key social cognition variables have not been assessed (Ajzen, 1991) – i.e., the model is not sufficient. One approach to this issue is therefore to include additional variables in the models so that they account for more of the variance in health behaviour. However, this has to be balanced against the drive for parsimony, as highlighted in Ajzen's (1998) article.

In contrast, for behaviours that are performed relatively frequently in stable contexts, the impact of past behaviour on future behaviour may reflect the operation of habitual responses that do not require the mediation of intention. Thus, the repeated execution of the same behaviour (i.e., response) in the same context (i.e., cue) is likely to lead to formation of a habitual response. The behaviour is then performed automatically and efficiently with little effort or conscious awareness in response to the relevant stimulus cue. Moreover, as behaviour becomes more habitual, intentions (and other social cognition variables) may lose their predictive validity. Gardner et al. (2011) reported a strong effect of habit strength on nutrition behaviour and physical activity. In addition, some studies included in their review found that intention became a weaker predictor of behaviour as habit strength increased. These findings are consistent with the idea that there are two important influences on people's behaviour – reflective (i.e., determined by people's intentions) and non-reflective (i.e., determined by habitual processes) – and have led to the development of dual process models that can be used to explain health behaviour.

The Reflective-Impulsive Model (RIM) developed by Strack and Deutsch (2004) represents one such important dual process model. In the RIM, two separate but interacting systems are distinguished that together guide behaviour: reflective and impulsive. The reflective system is seen as reasoned, conscious, and intentional, and many of the models outlined in this chapter attempt to describe the key constructs influencing behaviour in this system. In contrast, the impulsive system consists of associative clusters that have been created by temporal or spatial coactivation of external stimuli, affective reactions, and associated behavioural tendencies. Once an association or link is established in the impulsive system, then a simple perceptual input can automatically trigger an affective evaluation and associated behaviour.

Reviews have summarised evidence for the impact of impulsive processes on health behaviour (Hagger et al., 2020; Sheeran et al., 2013). For example, studies have found that high consumers of alcohol exhibit increased attentional bias towards alcohol-related cues and that training to reduce attentional bias can reduce alcohol consumption and delay short-term relapse among those with alcohol dependence. Similarly, research has shown that activating, or priming, goals outside conscious awareness can influence behaviour. For example, Papies and Hamstra (2010) showed that priming the goal of dieting via a subtle exposure to a poster led to a reduced number of snacks being consumed by restrained eaters. While such findings highlight the importance of non-conscious processes on health behaviour, there is evidence to suggest that the effect of unconscious primes can be overridden by other active, conscious, goals (Sheeran et al., 2013). Research is needed to assess: (i) the relative predictive power of reflective and impulsive influences on health behaviours; (ii) when reflective and impulsive influences may act independently or interact to produce health behaviour; and (iii) whether 'implicit' interventions influence behaviour though conscious as well as non-conscious processes.

INTENTION–BEHAVIOUR GAP AND DEVELOPMENT OF STAGE MODELS

Behavioural intention is the key predictor of behaviour in many models of health behaviour (e.g., PMT, TPB). Although intention is typically the strongest correlate of future behaviour in models of health behaviour, intention does not perfectly predict behaviour (which is often referred to as the 'intention–behaviour gap'; Sheeran, 2002). For example, Orbell and Sheeran (1998) examined the discrepancy between people's intentions and their subsequent behaviour by classifying people as intenders versus non-intenders and then examining whether or not they enacted the target behaviour. Their findings were striking. Only 53% of intenders success-fully performed the behaviour in question, whereas 93% of non-intenders did not. These findings therefore indicate that the intention–behaviour gap is primarily due to people not acting on their intentions. (see also Rhodes & de Bruijn, 2013)

The intention–behaviour gap has attracted a lot of research attention over the past 25 years, with research focusing on variables that may moderate the strength of the intention–behaviour relationship (see Sidebar 2.3) and techniques, such as implementation intentions, that help individuals to bridge the intention–behaviour gap (see Sidebar 2.4). Another approach has been the development of stage models of health behaviour in which different social cognition variables are proposed to be important in different stages. For example, one of the most prominent stage models of health behaviour, the Health Action Process Approach (HAPA; Schwarzer, 1992), makes a distinction between a pre-intentional (i.e., motivational) phase, which outlines the processes that lead to an individual forming an intention to engage in a behaviour, and a post-intentional (i.e., volitional) phase, which outlines the processes through which people act on their intentions. Different social cognition variables are proposed to be important in each phase (Figure 2.5).

Sidebar 2.3. Moderators of the Intention– Behaviour Relationship

In recent years, there has been a focus on the factors that much reduce (i.e., moderate) the strength of the intention–behaviour relationship. For example, higher levels of perceived behavioural control are assumed to lead to intentions being better predictors of behaviour (see McEachan et al., 2011, for a review). A key moderator of intention–behaviour relationships in the health domain appears to be the temporal stability of intentions. Intentions that are stable over time appear to be more likely to predict behaviour over considerable periods of time. For example, Conner et al. (2002) showed that stable inten-tions predicted healthy eating behaviour over a period of six years. Similarly, Sheeran and Abraham (2003) showed intention stability to moderate the inten-tion–behaviour relationship for exercising and to explain the impacts of other moderators of the intention–behaviour relationship (i.e., intention certainty, past behaviour, self-schema, anticipated regret, attitudinal control). Factors that lead to more stable intentions (that are more predictive of behaviour) are a focus of ongoing research.

Sidebar 2.4. Implementation Intentions

Gollwitzer (1993) makes the distinction between goal (or behavioural) intentions and implementation intentions. Goal intentions are concerned with intention to perform a behaviour or achieve a goal (i.e., 'I intend to achieve x') whereas implementation intentions are concerned with plans as to when, where, and how the goal intention is to be translated into behaviour (i.e., 'I intend to initiate the goal-directed behaviour x when situation y is encountered'). Implementation intentions commit an individual to a specific course of action when certain environmental conditions are met, and help translate a goal intention into action. For example, an individual may have a behavioural intention to go running, but may not translate this into action if they do not form an implementation intention that specifies when, where, and how they will go running. It is argued that by making implementation intentions individuals pass control over to the environment and then the environment acts as a cue to action. Forming an implementation intention can therefore be seen as a volitional process that complements motivation processes.

Implementation intentions have been widely studied as a means to change health protection behaviours (see Conner & Norman, 2015, for a review). For example, Orbell et al. (1997), at the end of a questionnaire about breast self-examination, asked half the women to indicate when and where in the next month they intended to perform breast self-examination. At one-month follow-up they found that 64% of these women had performed breast self-examination in the intervening month compared with only 16% of women who had not made an implementation intention, despite no difference in goal intentions for the two groups. Fewer studies have examined implementation intentions in relation to health risk behaviours.

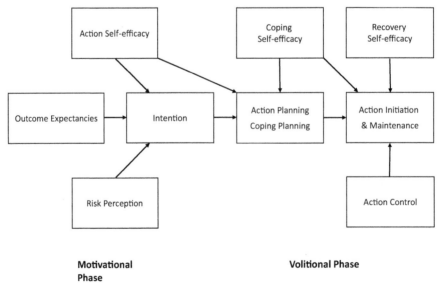

Figure 2.5 Health Action Process Approach (HAPA)

The HAPA outlines three determinants of intention in the motivational phase. First, risk perception refers to the individual's perceived susceptibility to the health threat. Second, outcome expectancies refer to the perceived consequences of a behaviour. Third, action (or task) self-efficacy refers to the individual's confidence in their ability to perform the behaviour, and is also proposed to have a direct effect on initial health behaviour, independent of intention. Intention is regarded as a 'watershed' between this initial goal-setting (i.e., motivational) phase and a subsequent goal pursuit (i.e., volitional) phase.

The HAPA outlines a different set of social cognition variables that are important in the volitional phase of health behaviour. Specifically, action planning and coping planning are important for translating intentions into behaviour. Action planning refers to the making of specific plans (e.g., implementation intentions) that help people enact their intentions. In contrast, coping planning refers to the making of specific plans to overcome anticipated barriers that may hinder individuals from enacting their intentions. The theory also identified 'phase specific' forms of self-efficacy. Maintenance or coping self-efficacy – i.e., beliefs about one's capability to cope with such barriers – is important in this phase. Having initiated behaviour, it is often necessary to maintain it. The HAPA outlines three aspects of action control that are important in this context: namely, self-monitoring (i.e., monitoring ongoing levels of performance of the behaviour), awareness of standards (i.e., being aware of the desired level of performance), and self-regulatory effort (i.e., making an effort to perform the behaviour as much as intended). Finally, recovery self-efficacy – i.e., beliefs about one's capability to get back on track after a setback – is important in ensuring the maintenance of behaviour following setbacks.

The HAPA has been used to predict a range of health-related behaviours, including physical activity, healthy eating, condom use, smoking cessation, sunscreen use, and detection behaviours (see Conner & Norman, 2015, for a review). In the most comprehensive review of the HAPA to date, Zhang et al. (2019) reported that outcome expectancies and action self-efficacy had medium–large-sized effects and risk perceptions had small-sized effects on intention; intention had medium–large-sized effects on action planning, coping planning, and behaviour; and action self-efficacy, maintenance self-efficacy, recovery self-efficacy, action planning, and coping planning all had medium–large-sized effects on behaviour. These findings are consistent with the theoretical structure of the HAPA.

The HAPA has also been used as a basis for interventions to change health behaviour, with a particular focus on forming action and coping plans to aid the translation of strong intentions into behaviour. HAPA-based interventions have been reported in relation to physical activity, dietary behaviour, vaccination uptake, sunscreen use, breast self-examination, dental flossing, and hand hygiene behaviours (see Conner & Norman, 2015; Hagger at al., 2020, for reviews). For example, Vayisoglu and Zincir (2019) reported that a HAPA-based health education intervention increased influenza vaccination rates in patients with chronic obstructive pulmonary disease. The intervention also increased risk perceptions, outcome expectancies, action self-efficacy, coping self-efficacy, intention, and planning.

A key strength of the HAPA is that it explicitly outlines different phases/stages of health behaviour and, in particular, focuses on the post-intentional variables that are important for translating intentions into behaviour and for maintaining behaviour. Other models of health behaviour covered in this chapter tend to focus exclusively on the motivation phase. The HAPA also has received strong support both as a model to predict health behaviour, but also as a model to inform the design of effective interventions, although few HAPA studies have examined the role of action control in conjunction with action and/or coping planning in the volitional phase.

CONCLUSIONS

Health behaviours have been demonstrated to have important consequences for both the quality and length of life through their influence on various health outcomes. Thus, individuals need to increase their participation in health protection behaviours and decrease participation in health 'risk' behaviours for positive health outcomes to accrue. Considerable research has focused on models of health behaviours as a basis for attempting to change their occurrence, as outlined in Ajzen's (1998) article. These models describe the key constructs underlying these behaviours and their interrelationship, and represent an important approach to predicting health behaviours. The key constructs in these models can help explain how behaviour change interventions work (i.e., mechanisms of action) and represent important targets for such interventions. However, more research is required on the specific behaviour change techniques that may be employed to effectively change these constructs or 'mechanisms of action' (see Johnston, Chapter 12, this volume).

FURTHER READING

Conner, M., & Norman, P. (2015). (Eds.). *Predicting and changing health behaviour: Research and practice with social cognition models* (3rd ed.). Maidenhead: Open University Press.

An edited collection of chapters on the key social cognition models applied to health behaviours.

Ajzen, I. (2015). The theory of planned behaviour is alive and well, and not ready to retire: A commentary on Sniehotta, Presseau, and Araujo-Soares. *Health Psychology Review, 9,* 131–137. https://doi.org/10.1080/17437199.2014.883474

Sniehotta, F. F., Presseau, J., & Araujo-Soares, V. (2014). Time to retire the theory of planned behaviour. *Health Psychology Review, 8,* 1–7. https://doi.org/10.1080/17437 199.2013.869710

A critique of the TPB and response from the theory author.

Sheeran, P., Gollwitzer, P. M., & Bargh, J. A. (2013). Nonconscious processes and health. *Health Psychology, 32,* 460–473. https://doi.org/10.1037/a0029203

An editorial to a special issue of a journal devoted to impulsive influences on health behaviours.

REFERENCES

Ajzen, I. (1991). The theory of planned behavior. *Organizational Behavior and Human Decision Processes*, *50*, 179–211. https://doi.org/10.1016/0749-5978(91)90020-T

Ajzen, I. (1998). Models of human social behavior and their application to health. *Psychology and Health, 13*, 735–739.

Ajzen, I. (2015). The theory of planned behaviour is alive and well, and not ready to retire: A commentary on Sniehotta, Presseau, and Araujo-Soares. *Health Psychology Review*, *9*, 131–137. https://doi.org/10.1080/17437199.2014.883474

Ajzen, I. & Fishbein, M. (1980) *Understanding Attitudes and Predicting Social Behavior*. Englewood-Cliff, NJ: Prentice-Hall.

Bandura, A. (1986). *Social foundations of thought and action: A cognitive social theory*. Englewood Cliffs, NJ: Prentice-Hall.

Becker, M. H. (1974). The health belief model and sick role behavior. *Health Education Monographs*, *2*, 409–419. https://doi.org/10.1177/109019817400200407

Belloc, N. B. (1973). Relationship of health practices to mortality. *Preventive Medicine*, *2*, 67–81. https://doi.org/10.1016/0091-7435(73)90009-1

Block, J. (1995). A contrarian view of the five-factor approach to personality description. *Psychological Bulletin*, *117*, 187–215. https://doi.org/10.1037/0033-2909.117.2.187

Carpenter, C. J. (2010). A meta-analysis of the effectiveness of health belief model variables in predicting behavior. *Health Communication*, *25*, 661–669. https://doi.org/10.1080/10410236.2010.521906

Conner, M., & Norman, P. (Eds.). (2015). *Predicting and changing health behaviour: Research and practice with social cognition models* (3rd ed.). Maidenhead: Open University Press.

Conner, M., Norman, P., & Bell, R. (2002). The theory of planned behavior and healthy eating. *Health Psychology*, *21*, 194–201. https://doi.org/10.1037/0278-6133.21.2.194

Deci, E. L., & Ryan, R. M. (1985). *Intrinsic motivation and self-determination in human behavior*. New York: Plenum.

Dzewaltowski, D. A., Noble, J. M., & Shaw, J. M. (1990). Physical Activity Participation: Social Cognitive Theory versus the Theories of Reasoned Action and Planned Behavior, *Journal of Sport and Exercise Psychology*, *12*(4), 388–405. https://doi.org/10.1123/jsep.12.4.388

Fishbein, M., & Ajzen, I. (2010). *Predicting and changing behavior: The reasoned action approach*. London: Psychology Press.

Fiske, S. T., & Taylor, S. E. (2013). *Social cognition: From brains to culture* (2nd ed.). London: Sage.

French, D. P., Olander, E., Ahisholm, A., & McSharry, J. (2014). Which behavior change techniques are most effective at increasing older adults' self-efficacy and physical activity behavior? A systematic review. *Annals of Behavioral Medicine*, *48*, 225–234. https://doi.org/10.1007/s12160-014-9593-z

Gardner, B., de Bruijn, G.-J., & Lally, P. (2011). A systematic review and meta-analysis of applications of the self-report habit index to nutrition and physical activity behaviours.

Annals of Behavioral Medicine, *42*, 174–187. https://doi.org/10.1007/s12160-011-9282-0

Gollwitzer, P. M. (1993). Goal achievement: The role of intentions. In W. Stroebe & M. Hewstone (Eds.), *European Review of Social Psychology* (Vol. 4, pp. 141–185). New York: Wiley.

Hagger, M. S., Cameron, L. D., Hamilton, K., Hankonen, N., & Lintunen, T. (Eds.). (2020). *The handbook of behavior change*. Cambridge: Cambridge University Press.

Head, K. J., & Noar, S. M. (2014). Facilitating progress in health behaviour theory development and modification: The reasoned action approach as a case study. *Health Psychology Review*, *8*, 34–52. https://doi.org/10.1080/17437199.2013.778165

Janz, N. K., & Becker, M. H. (1984). The health belief model: A decade later. *Health Education Quarterly*, *11*, 1–47. https://doi.org/10.1177/109019818401100101

Jones, J. J., Smith, H., & Llewellyn C. (2013). Evaluating the effectiveness of health belief model interventions in improving adherence: A systematic review. *Health Psychology Review*, *8*, 253–269. https://doi.org/10.1080/17437199.2013.802623

McEachan, R. R. C., Conner, M., Taylor, N. J., & Lawton, R. J. (2011). Prospective prediction of health-related behaviors with the Theory of Planned Behavior: A meta-analysis. *Health Psychology Review*, *5*, 97–144. https://doi.org/10.1080/17437199.2010.521684

Michie, S., Carey, R. N., Johnston, M., Rothman, A. J., de Bruin, M., Kelly, M. P., & Connell, L. E. (2017). From theory-inspired to theory-based interventions: A protocol for developing and testing a methodology for linking behaviour change techniques to theoretical mechanisms of action. *Annals of Behavioral Medicine*, *52*, 501–512. https://doi.org/10.1007/s12160-016-9816-6

Milne, S., Sheeran, P., & Orbell, S. (2000). Prediction and intervention in health-related behavior: A meta-analytic review of protection motivation theory. *Journal of Applied Social Psychology*, *30*, 106–143. https://doi.org/10.1111/j.1559-1816.2000.tb02308.x

Orbell, S., Hodgkins, S., & Sheeran, P. (1997). Implementation intentions and the theory of planned behavior. *Personality and Social Psychology Bulletin*, *23*, 945–954. https://doi.org/10.1177/0146167297239004

Orbell, S., & Sheeran, P. (1998). 'Inclined abstainers': A problem for predicting health-related behaviour. *British Journal of Social Psychology*, *37*, 151–165. https://doi.org/10.1111/j.2044-8309.1998.tb01162.x

Ouellette, J., & Wood, W. (1998). Habit and intention in everyday life: The multiple processes by which past behavior predicts future behaviour. *Psychological Bulletin*, *124*, 54–74. https://doi.org/10.1037/0033-2909.124.1.54

Papies, E. K., & Hamstra, P. (2010). Goal priming and eating behavior: Enhancing self-regulation by environmental cues. *Health Psychology*, *29*, 384–388. https://doi.org/10.1037/a0019877

Prestwich, A., Sniehotta, F. F., Whittington, C., Dombrowski, S. U., Rogers, L., & Michie, S. (2014). Does theory influence the effectiveness of health behavior interventions? Meta-analysis. *Health Psychology*, *33*, 465–474. https://doi.org/10.1037/a0032853

Rhodes, R. E., & de Bruijn, G. J. (2013). How big is the physical activity intention-behaviour gap? A meta-analysis using the action control framework. *British Journal of Health Psychology*, *18*, 296–309. https://doi.org/10.1111/bjhp.12032

Rogers, R. W. (1983). Cognitive and physiological processes in fear appeals and attitude change: A revised theory of protection motivation. In J. T. Cacioppo & R. E. Petty (Eds.), *Social psychophysiology: A source book* (pp. 153–176). New York: Guilford Press.

Schwarzer, R. (1992). Self-efficacy in the adoption and maintenance of health behaviors: Theoretical approaches and a new model. In R. Schwarzer (Ed.), *Self-efficacy: Thought control of action* (pp. 217–243). London: Hemisphere.

Sheeran, P. (2002). Intention–behavior relations: a conceptual and empirical review. In W. Strobe & M. Hewstone (Eds.) *European Review of Social Psychology* (Vol. 12, pp. 1–30). New York: Wiley.

Sheeran, P., & Abraham, C. (2003). Mediator of moderators: Temporal stability of intention and the intention–behavior relationship. *Personality and Social Psychology Bulletin*, *29*, 205–215. https://doi.org/10.1177/0146167202239046

Sheeran, P., Gollwitzer, P. M., & Bargh, J. A. (2013). Nonconscious processes and health. *Health Psychology*, *32*(5), 460–473. https://doi.org/10.1037/a0029203

Sheeran, P., Maki, A., Montanaro, E., Bryan, A., Klein, W. M. P., Miles, E., & Rothman, A. J. (2016). The impact of changing attitudes, norms, and self-efficacy on health-related intentions and behavior: A meta-analysis. *Health Psychology*, *35*, 1178–1188. https://doi.org/10.1037/hea0000387

Sniehotta, F. F., Presseau, J., & Araujo-Soares, V. (2014). Time to retire the theory of planned behaviour. *Health Psychology Review*, *8*, 1–7. https://doi.org/10.1080/17437 199.2013.869710

Stacey, F. G., James, E. L., Chapman, K., Courneya, K. S., & Lubans, D. R. (2015). A systematic review and meta-analysis of social cognitive theory-based physical activity and/or nutrition behavior change interventions for cancer survivors. *Journal of Cancer Survivorship*, *9*, 305–338. https://doi.org/10.1007/s11764-014-0413-z

Steinmetz, H., Knappstein, M., Ajzen, I., Schmidt, P., & Kabst, R. (2016). How effective are behavior change interventions based on the Theory of Planned Behavior? A three-level meta-analysis. *Zeitschrift fur Psychologie/Journal of Psychology*, *224*(3), 216–233. https://doi.org/10.1027/2151-2604/a000255

Strack, F., & Deutsch, R. (2004). Reflective and impulsive determinants of social behaviour. *Personality and Social Psychology Review*, *8*, 220–247. https://doi.org/10.1207/s15327957pspr0803_1

Teixeira, P. J., Carraca, E., Markland, D. A., Silva, M. N., & Markland, D. A. (2012). Exercise, physical activity, and self-determination theory: A systematic review. *International Journal of Behavioral Nutrition and Physical Activity*, *9*, 78. https://doi.org/10.1186/1479-5868-9-78

Tyson, M., Covey, J., & Rosenthal, H. E. S. (2014). Theory of planned behavior interventions for reducing heterosexual risk behaviors: A meta-analysis. *Health Psychology*, *33*, 1454–1467. https://doi.org/10.1037/hea0000047

Vayisoglu, S. K., & Zincir, H. (2019). The health action process approach-based program's effects on influenza vaccination behaviour. *Journal for Nurse Practitioners*, *15*, 517–524. https://doi.org/10.1016/j.nurpra.2019.04.004

Young, M. D., Plotnikoff, R. C., Collins, C. E., Callister, R., & Morgan, P. J. (2014). Social cognitive theory and physical activity: A systematic review and meta-analysis. *Obesity Reviews*, *15*, 983–995. https://doi.org/10.1111/obr.12225

Zhang, C. Q., Zhang, R., Schwarzer, R., & Hagger, M. S. (2019). A meta-analysis of the health action process approach. *Health Psychology*, *38*, 623–637. https://doi.org/10.1037/hea0000728

3

Control Theory: Revisiting Carver and Scheier (1982)

Carver, C. S., & Scheier, M. F. (1982). Control-theory: A useful conceptual framework for personality-social, clinical, and health psychology. *Psychological Bulletin, 92*, 111–135.

Warren Mansell

BACKGROUND

In a seminal article for the field, Carver and Scheier (1982) introduced control theory, a new conceptualisation for understanding behaviour that was to have wide-reaching resonance for researchers and practitioners in health, clinical, and social psychology. The article provided an accessible explanation and application of control theory, based on Powers' (1973) earlier theory of human behaviour, and brought it to a much wider audience. In fact, Carver and Scheier's article was published in 1982, nearly a decade after Powers' theoretical treatise, which itself was a culmination of work that began in the 1950s, and was eventually published in 1960 (Powers et al., 1960a, 1960b). Yet it was in the early 1980s, soon after the publication of Carver and Scheier's article, that Powers' proposal – that the human mind operates as a hierarchy of negative feedback control sub-systems – truly entered the academic psychology lexicon and began to be applied in health psychology.

Psychological theories are faced with the considerable challenge of providing clear, testable explanations of human behaviour. In addition to theories in the dominant traditions of behaviourism and cognitivism, a third strand of theories in psychology are based on the way that *control* is explained and implemented within the fields of biology and engineering, theories that were based on Powers' pioneering work. The broad construct of control was central to the study of psychology in general, and stress and health specifically, long before publication of Carver and Scheier's classic article. The detrimental effects on stress and health on the uncontrollability of aversive experiences in animals was studied throughout the 1950s and 1960s (for a review, see Mineka & Henderson, 1985). This led to the conceptualisation of 'learned helplessness' as a key factor in chronic stress and depression (Seligman, 1972). Yet, since that time, psychologists have attempted to combine the concept of control with other 'human' factors, in order to try to explain the impacts on human health. There was, and remains, an assumption, that humans are not simply affected by their degree of control, because of their more complex internal, mental experiences. This is likely to be a misunderstanding for a number of reasons, but nonetheless it carved out the backdrop of the developments in social cognition models during the 1960s and 1970s (see also Norman and Conner, Chapter 2, this volume).

The social cognition theories included control-related constructs such as perceived control (Rothbaum et al., 1982), locus of control (Rotter, 1966), intrinsic and extrinsic motivation (Maddi & Kobasa, 1981), the focus of self-awareness as an object (Duval & Wicklund, 1972), and self-efficacy (Bandura, 1977. Each of these constructs, and the theories to which they pertain, were supported empirically, and each is still used to guide current theory and research. In general, important conclusions derived from these theoretical approaches are that people who reported less stress and better well-being were those who tended to attribute events to their own control, pursue activities that fit with their own standards and needs, focus attention on their surroundings, and report a high self-efficacy.

Yet, research on each of these approaches remained compromised by findings that the effects varied widely across contexts, between different measures, or between different groups of participants (for a review, see AbuSabha & Achterberg, 1997). For example, health and well-being are associated with an internal locus of control, but in some contexts, such as within-group interventions to change health behaviour, studies had found that it is more favourable to hold an external locus of control (Strudler, Wallston, & Wallston, 1978). While attention towards the environment, and away from the self, is often associated with less anxiety and depression, increased self-awareness can enhance self-control for certain tasks, such as tolerating pain when squeezing a handgrip (Alberts et al., 2011). While people reporting high self-efficacy generally have better well-being, when studying an individual over time, improvements in performance at various tasks are often preceded by a *drop* in self-efficacy, as the individual learns from their mistakes (Vancouver et al., 2001). The general picture is that social cognition theories are supported, on average, but the frequent exceptions or reverse effects indicate that a finer-grained model that accounts for individual differences and varying contexts may be needed. It also highlighted the need to clearly specify conditions and contexts or auxiliary assumptions which bounded their predictions (see Trafimow, 2012).

Social cognition theories also share another feature; they are *system* theories rather than *functional, sub-system* theories (Barnard, 2004; Vancouver, 2005). System theories describe psychological constructs in order to explain observations of behaviour, but they do not provide the mathematical specifications of the sub-systems that, together, allow this mechanism to be simulated. Some social cognition theories tend to be based on verbal descriptions or schematic 'box-and-arrow' models. This makes them hard to apply in a way that takes account of the idiosyncratic way that individuals develop and might act differently within different environmental contexts (Mansell & Huddy, 2018). On the other hand, sub-system theories provide sufficient detail to construct and test working models formed from specific components. For example, within control theory, multiple *control units* are connected together in branching hierarchies, and each control unit is an organised set of components (e.g., the comparator), each of which has a mathematical function. The dynamic changes in behaviour of an individual over time, and across contexts, can be modelled and predicted by sub-system models of this kind. While some proponents of social cognition theories have characterised such machine-like approaches to human psychology as 'austere materialistic reductionism' (Bandura & Locke, 2003, p. 92), many others have welcomed this more dynamic and functionalist approach (e.g., AbuSabha & Achterberg, 1997; Riley et al., 2016).

A sub-system framework for clinical, health, and social psychology could provide a means to address the issue that social cognition theories tend to attain some support, but are also subject to a variety of exceptions and inconsistent findings. Potentially, a broader framework that specifies the functioning of systems whose components vary according to the individual and context could accommodate the empirical findings. For example, how might a sub-systems framework model intrinsic and extrinsic motivation? How might the focus of attention be operationalised? The application of control theory has contributed to filling this evidence gap. In the following sections the principles of control theory, as introduced to the community of health, clinical, and social psychologists by Carver and Scheier (1982) will be explained, and how their application of this approach advanced the theoretical landscape at this time, and continues to do so.

DETAILED OVERVIEW

Carver and Scheier's (1982) classic article provided the first introduction of engineering control theory directly and explicitly to the field of health psychology. This is a significant reflection on the relatively slow pace of scientific dissemination and dialogue across disciplines. Engineering control theory was first applied in psychology in the 1940s to human performance (Craik, 1947, 1948; Wiener, 1948), and yet in contemporary health psychology, control theory is now regarded as a key theoretical perspective that informs many other theories in the field (Mansell, 2020; Webb et al., 2010). Carver and Scheier's article is undoubtedly responsible, in part, for that change in perspective, with numerous academic articles on this approach emerging over the subsequent decade. Yet, it is also the case that the implications of control theory for the research and practice of health psychology remain relatively unexplored, and the likely reasons for this will also be explained. Several features of Carver and Scheier's article may account for its impact, and these will be covered in turn, alongside evidence for the impact within contemporary health psychology, and the related fields of social and clinical psychology.

BEHAVIOUR AS CONTROL

Carver and Scheier (1982) provided a specific control theory account of human behaviour, consistent with Powers' proposal of control theory in the 1960s and 1970s. Powers was a medical physicist whose interdisciplinary training and insights allowed him to apply control engineering concepts within medical and health contexts that were highly amenable to health psychologists. For most health psychologists, Carver and Scheier's article was most likely to be their first introduction to control theory. Yet the impact of Powers' work now extends to fields allied to health psychology, including developmental psychology (Plooij, 2020), neuroscience (Yin, 2020), organisational psychology (Vancouver, 2020), and psychiatry and psychopathology (Mansell, 2021).

Classic control theory in engineering is based on feedback, which relies on there being a 'closed loop' between an agent (e.g., a person or patient) and the environment (e.g., the objects and features of a healthcare or medical environment, such as a clinic or hospital). This means that the actions of the agent on the environment are sensed by the agent itself, so that it can adjust its behaviour accordingly. Within classic control theory, the feedback is described as 'negative' because it cancels out the effects of disturbances from the environment that push the agent away from its reference point or *reference value*. For example, an air conditioning system is a simple negative feedback control system that blows out hot air if it senses the temperature of the room dropping below the target temperature, or cold air if it senses the temperature rise above the target value.

The concept of the negative feedback loop provided an antidote to the behavioural theories of the time, which had claimed behaviour must be understood by the external observer. In addition, the loop is explicitly based on homeostatic systems that are well understood within the wider fields of medicine and health. In their article, Carver and Scheier adopted the term 'self-regulation' to describe their control theory model and related approaches, and this term gained wide acceptance in the field.

It is vital to note, however, that the most unique insight within Powers' writings was not translated explicitly in the Carver and Scheier's (1982) article. This can be summarised in the title of Powers' primary text: *Behavior: The control of perception* (Powers, 1973). Powers realised that negative feedback systems responsively control their *perception* of the variable they are controlling, such as temperature. For example, a temperature sensor within an air conditioner unit can be tinkered with so that it will not control successfully. What this means, in turn, is that the target value for a sensed experience is set *within* the agent itself. Thus, the 'behaviour' of an agent is the process of it controlling its input to keep the input at a reference value.

The above account may sound obvious when applied to a machine like an air conditioning system. But what about when it is applied to people? The behaviours observed in other people, particularly those assumed to be learned as habits, are actually attempts to control perceptual experience according to Powers' control theory. If this is the case, should a health psychologist be researching how to use learning theory to reduce specific health behaviours, like smoking, or would it be more effective to generally help people find wider opportunities for managing and understanding their feelings of stress, the likely controlling source behind their smoking (Mansell, 2020)? Even an 'habitual' behaviour like smoking involves control of perception – how else can a smoker consistently hold a cigarette with the appropriate tension, orient it to the face, and locate its tip in the mouth? The controlled perception of 'tip of cigarette in mouth' is at a lower level in a hierarchy to the control of 'smoke inhaled'. To explain this further leads to the next feature of Carver and Scheier's article – how 'goals' and 'behaviours' can be better understood as a layered hierarchy of control systems.

THE CONTROL HIERARCHY

Arguably, it is the hierarchical organisation of goals within Powers' (1973) theory that has been the most influential aspect of Carver and Scheier's article on the wider field of psychology. Powers was clear that each level controls its own input by setting the desired inputs of the level below. Carver and Scheier echoed this as they described the basic working principle of the control hierarchy: 'At each level of hierarchy, the results of behavior are presumably assessed by monitoring perceptual input information at the appropriate level of abstract, and by comparing it with the reference values from the level above' (p. 113). In addition, Carver and Scheier specified each of the levels of the hierarchy proposed by Powers and illustrated them in a diagram (see Figure 3.1). In doing so, they elegantly spanned the gap from control of simple perceptual experiences, through sequences and plans, upwards to more traditionally 'cognitive' and humanistic constructs at the higher levels, such as *principles* (e.g., honesty, kindness) and *system concepts* of the self and others. Thus, a control hierarchy is a branching fractal network of many control sub-systems, rather like the roots of a tree. For example, there would be many different principles (e.g., honesty, commitment, safety) that would be maintained at the level below a system concept of the self (e.g., to be a responsible person), and, in turn, there would be many different programs of action (e.g., to return some notes, to lock the front door when leaving the house) that would be experienced for each principle through setting references for the perceptual results of actions at lower levels in the hierarchy. Figure 3.1 provides an illustration of one branch of such a hierarchy. The 'functional-blue-print' architecture of control theory stands in contrast to the schematic, 'box-and-arrow' diagrams of the majority of social cognition theories.

The importance of Carver and Scheier's introduction to the control hierarchy is hard to underestimate, even though it had earlier precedents. Early neuroscientists, such as Hughlings Jackson in the 19th century, had proposed a hierarchical organisation of the brain (Meares, 1999). Another influential control systems model, published at the same time as Powers' first publication, called Test-Operate-Test-Exit (TOTE) had a hierarchical organisation (Miller et al., 1960). Even within the decade that the classic article emerged, the hierarchical organisation of behaviour within the field of ethology had been proposed (Dawkins, 1976). Yet, in every

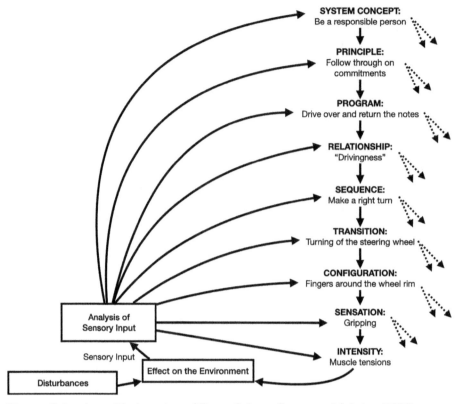

Figure 3.1 A modified version of Figure 3 from Carver and Scheier (1982) to provide a concrete illustration of Powers' control hierarchy

Note. The example is that of a young man making a turn while driving to a friend's house on an errand. The diagram illustrates the terminology for each level of Powers' (1973) hierarchy, and a concrete example at each level. At each level, an output signal sets the reference values for the next level down. The 'analysis of sensory input' actually represents a series of input functions at each level. The revised diagram includes the disturbances in the environment that are counteracted by actions, and the dotted arrows represent other branches of the hierarchy.

one of these theories, the hierarchy described units of *behaviour*. Take a moment to consider this idea: it may seem rather strange and unlikely. It is as though the agent's nervous system had an *observer's* perspective of its actions coded into its architecture. On the contrary, Powers (1973) proposed that all that is coded within a control hierarchy is specification of desired *input* – the neural specifications for perceptual variables that are controlled during action. For example, to drink a sip of tea, a branching hierarchy of controlled perceptual variables would be involved. Going from the top of the hierarchy, the tea would need to be perceived in the mouth, which in turn would require perceiving the cup to tilt towards the mouth. This perception, in turn, requires that the cup is perceived to be close to the mouth, which in turn requires the perceived distance of the cup to the mouth to be controlled as the cup is brought up from the table, and at the same time the vertical orientation of the cup and its perceived acceleration would need to be controlled, so that it does not spill.

It is notable that the concept of a control hierarchy introduced by Carver and Scheier to the psychological community has informed the development of many related models and theories, but little direct research. The theoretical articles have often used the hierarchy to integrate other social cognition theories. For example, terror management theory proposes that individuals' management of the fear or terror experienced when considering one's own mortality is a high-level goal that is implemented by a range of lower-level strategies (Pyszczynski et al., 1990). The control hierarchy has also informed the development of a model of purpose in life (McKnight & Kashdan, 2009), an integrative model of the effects of goal conflict on distress (Kelly et al., 2015), and a comprehensive review of the benefits of pursuing high-level goals (Höchli et al., 2018). Empirical studies are rare, maybe because direct assessments of the hierarchy of goals are methodologically laborious, and idiographic, making them harder, but not impossible, to subject to statistical analysis (see Sidebar 3.1).

Sidebar 3.1.   The Laddering Technique as a Method to Generate Goal Hierarchies

One method that has been used to assess goal hierarchies, and, in so doing, provides a means to test this aspect of control theory, is known as the 'laddering technique'. For example, the technique has been used to generate idiosyncratic goal hierarchies for weight-loss behaviour (Pieters et al., 1995). The experimenter begins by asking the participant to identify a focal goal, which is usually the behaviour that is at the focus of their awareness. Within health psychology, it is typically a habit they would like to break, or a new activity they would like to take up and maintain, such as 'losing weight'. The participant is then asked 'Why is this important to you?' in order to generate the goals at the next level up. These may be documented by the researcher or participant in boxes above the focal goal (Pieters et al. decided on four boxes). Then the participant is asked the same question again, about each of their goals in the four boxes to elicit goals at a higher level, and these are again noted down in boxes above. The technique can also be used to go down levels by asking 'How would you go about doing this?'. In recent years, the validity of the laddering technique in generating personalised goal hierarchies has been demonstrated for user-determined goals, as a potential aid to psychological formulation for therapy (Wilcoxon et al., 2016). Within this study, the method also helped to identify goals at the same level that may be in conflict with one another.

FOCUS OF ATTENTION

For Carver and Scheier (1982), the description of the control hierarchy introduced a purpose and mechanism for focal attention: 'the highest level of control operating at any given moment corresponds to the level to which the person is focally attentive at that moment' (p. 118). They echoed Powers (1973) by proposing that focal attention is often directed at the program level – the level at which plans are being implemented and decisions are being made to switch plans or correct them in real time. The fact that attention is typically focused at the planning level may explain why the Test-Operate-Test-Exit (TOTE) architecture took sequential planning as its basis for control (Miller et al., 1960). Yet, within Powers' control hierarchy, control is conceptualised as continuing automatically throughout the higher and lower levels of the hierarchy while attention itself is focused at a specific level. Carver and Scheier (1982) suggested that once a plan is made, attention can then focus on lower levels of the hierarchy to adjust the means of executing a plan if it is unsuccessful.

A substantial body of research leading up to the Carver and Scheier article involved testing the hypothesis that 'self-focused attention' leads to greater efforts at maintaining prescribed standards during a specific task (e.g., Scheier & Carver, 1977). This work, in turn, influenced psychological models of social anxiety and social phobia, which proposed that socially evaluative environments (e.g., speeches, interviews) heighten self-focus and therefore the use of internal information, such as feelings of anxiety, to compare against higher level internal standards (e.g., 'to not feel like a nervous wreck'). This exacerbates social anxiety and may impair social performance. On balance, the evidence supports this proposal (Bögels & Mansell, 2004). Carver and Scheier's explanation of self-focused attention within the context of a control hierarchy appears to have also influenced the development of a number of widely known, and empirically supported, models of self-focused attention. These include models of binge eating, suicide, and other harmful behaviours, as the escape from self-awareness (Heatherton & Baumeister, 1991), and transdiagnostic models are used to inform psychological treatment (e.g., Ingram, 1990; Wells & Matthews, 1994).

SPECIFYING THE CONTROLLED VARIABLE

Carver and Scheier's article made clear the direct relevance of control theory for maintaining health, which is typically about matching a variable – such as blood pressure, weight, and shape – with a reference standard. Moreover, the standard is situated within a hierarchy in which the means for maintaining the variable at a desired state (e.g., keeping a balanced diet to reduce blood pressure) are at lower levels, and the reasons why the variable is controlled are situated at higher levels (e.g., to live long enough to see my daughter grow up). Carver and Scheier point to the importance of specifying the correct controlled variable for effective health management. If the variable is not a reliable index of health – for example, if it is an uncorrelated 'feeling' – then attempting to control it can be ineffective and lead to disengagement with health management. Their article elaborates on a range of questions relevant to health that can be answered by relating to the hierarchical organisation of control systems.

There appears to be little research that has tested for the controlled variable within a health context to support this aspect of the classic article. Again, this may be because it requires a different kind of methodology and statistical analysis. The selection of a controlled variable is typically specific to the individual and the current context, and confirming the variable that is being controlled requires collecting behavioural data to show that the individual is counteracting disturbances in their environment to keep the variable at the desired standard. Multiple variables at different levels of a control hierarchy are controlled simultaneously, and so only a small sample of these is likely to be subject to research. The methodological tools for this research are only recently becoming synthesised and disseminated (Marken, 2021). They include methods such as experimental control tasks (Marken et al., 2013), hierarchical task analysis (Marken, 1999), and computational modelling of control systems (Mansell & Huddy, 2020). Within the health domain, research on the controlled variable includes research on errors in medical prescriptions (Marken, 2003), control of perceived distance in computerised exposure to spider fears (Healey et al., 2017), and control of blood glucose levels and goal achievement in Type 1 diabetes (Pitt & Mansell, 2021).

SCIENTIFIC BACKGROUND FOR LATER WORK

A final lasting impact of Carver and Scheier's classic article is that it set the stage for their later work, especially their application of control theory to the experience and functions of emotion. This is most clearly elaborated in their book, *On the self-regulation of behavior* (Carver & Scheier, 1998). Their exploration of the possibilities of control theory has allowed them to develop empirically-supported models of resilience (Carver, 1998), optimism (Carver et al., 2010), and the functions of positive and negative affect (Carver & Scheier, 1990). Their model of affect is based on the proposal that a meta-monitoring system senses the rate of progress towards or away from a reference value (goal), and that this rate and direction have reference standards themselves (Carver & Scheier, 1990). If the rate of progress is less than a standard, then negative affect is experienced, but if it is faster, positive affect is experienced. The positive affect signals that the individual can reduce effort at the current goal ('coasting') and shift their focus to other goals, and contemporary research supports such a proposal (Thürmer et al., 2020).

DEVELOPMENTS

RETURNING TO POWERS: PERCEPTUAL CONTROL THEORY IN THE 21ST CENTURY

In the last 20 years, research on control theory in psychology has returned to the original and later work of Powers (Mansell & Marken, 2015), which has had implications for methodology and practice beyond those proposed by Carver and Scheier (1982). In particular, Powers' writings make it clear that his version of control theory, now commonly referred to as perceptual control theory (PCT), proposes that perceptual input, rather than behavioural output, is controlled. It also proposes that chronic, unresolved conflict between goals undermines control and can be experienced as distress. Importantly, Carver and Scheier point out how conflict is salient to the experience of stress within their 'Directions for the Future' section, but their research programme did not explore its implications. Conflict is actually critical to the understanding of control. Within a complex control system such as the human mind, there will be a multitude of inputs that compete to be maintained at their reference values, and there will be some controlled variables that are controlled at opposing values; this results in conflict. One example within the health sphere is the intake of high carbohydrate foods, which for many people has both a high reference value (e.g., to provide a distraction from stress) and a low reference value (e.g., to stay a desirable weight). As a consequence, people who strongly endorse these opposing goals may experience more ups and downs in weight from week to week (Rosenhead & Mansell, 2015).

Another essential component of Powers' original description of PCT is reorganisation. This is the learning algorithm required to modify and optimise a control system. It works in tandem with what Powers (1973) called *intrinsic* systems. These are the homeostatic control systems in the brain and body that are biologically prepared, such as those governing body temperature, salt ions, and blood glucose levels. When errors in these systems are not automatically corrected, their increase in error drives random changes in the functions and parameters of the control hierarchy. For example, a control system may increase its sensitivity to error (gain) which in turn enhances its control. When there is conflict, however, the process of reorganisation needs to be directed at a specific control unit – the hierarchically-superordinate system responsible for setting incompatible reference standards. Within the health example described above, it might be focused on the goal of maintaining self-worth, which is at a higher level than either distraction from stress, or staying at a certain weight. Within PCT, it is the locus of reorganisation in the hierarchy that reflects the focus of attention, and so provides a point of convergence between Carver and Scheier's consideration of attentional focus. Carver and Scheier also pointed the way to a theory of consciousness in *On the self-regulation of behavior* (Carver & Scheier, 1998) (see Sidebar 3.2).

Sidebar 3.2. Consciousness in Control Theory

Early accounts of perceptual control theory proposed that consciousness is focused on a specific region of the hierarchy, where reorganisation occurs (Powers et al., 1960a, 1960b). In an elaboration of this view, Carver and Scheier (1998) suggested that the focus of consciousness is located at the level of sequences in the hierarchy, from where it can form new 'construals' of whatever lower level inputs are in its 'lens' at that moment; Powers would term these construals as *input functions* at high levels in the perceptual hierarchy. The idea that consciousness serves the role of generating new meanings of its input is becoming increasingly accepted within contemporary psychology and neuroscience (e.g., Seth & Bayne, 2022). However, contemporary models conceptualise meaning abstraction as a form of prediction, rather than as the specification of a controlled variable. Therefore, most recently, an integrative control theory perspective on consciousness has attempted to unify contemporary theories and evidence on consciousness through an architecture based on Powers' control theory (Mansell, 2023). This new model retains the focusing role of awareness within the hierarchy as utilised by Carver and Scheier (1982), but it requires the principles of control of input, conflict, and reorganisation to form the basis of a working model. Arguably, an accurate model of consciousness is necessary to fully understand how people can make lasting changes in their health-related behaviour.

Through studying PCT directly, contemporary psychologists have pursued research on identifying the perceptual inputs that are controlled by an individual, using a methodology known as the 'test for the controlled variable' (for a review, see Marken, 2021). In addition, PCT informs the development and evaluation of method of levels (MOL) therapy, a conversational intervention that helps clients to shift and focus their attention in order to restore control over their lives and reduce distress (Carey, 2006). Because MOL therapy is based on a universal theory of control (PCT) rather than based on a theory of a specific mental health diagnosis, it aims to address a wide range of mental health problems and presenting issues. MOL therapy has therefore been applied across a wide range of settings, including outpatient primary and secondary care, psychiatric inpatient wards, high schools, and prisons (for a review, see Grzegrzółka, & Mansell, 2021).

CONCLUSION

The control theory explanation of behaviour was derived from the original development of controlled systems in the fields of biology and engineering, and, prior to Carver and Scheier's (1982) classic article, had only limited application in the field of psychology via cybernetics and human factors. Carver and Scheier spearheaded a new awareness of control theory in clinical, health, and social psychology that spawned a variety of research programmes and related theoretical models. The focus of attention within a hierarchy provided the most fruitful area of research. Within contemporary work, there is now wide consensus that well-being and resilience involve the capacity for an individual to shift and sustain their focus of attention up and down the levels within a hierarchy of goals (Höchli et al., 2018; Mansell, 2020; Watkins, 2011; Wells & Matthews, 1994). Carver and Scheier's article made suggestions regarding research on the controlled variable in health behaviour that has not, to date, received much in-depth research attention, and it omitted key principles of Powers' theory regarding the control of input, conflict, and reorganisation. Yet, without Carver and Scheier's extensive descriptions of the theory and their own research programme stemming from their article, even the term 'control theory' would most likely be novel to clinical, health, and social psychologists. With the renewed research and applications derived from Powers' original theory throughout the previous decade, and the suitability of control theory for idiographic research and computational modelling, the future holds incredible promise for this fundamental, interdisciplinary theory.

FURTHER READING

Carver, C. S., & Scheier, M. F. (1990). Origins and functions of positive and negative affect: A control-process view. *Psychological Review, 97*(1), 19–35.

In this article, Carver and Scheier go beyond their original control theory model to hypothesise that various forms of affect reflect the rate of goal progress over time and therefore provide informational feedback for a 'metacontrol system' that governs goal engagement and disengagement. For example, positive affect is felt when goals are met at or beyond the expected rate, and can allow switching to alternative goals.

Powers, W. T. (1973). *Behavior: The control of perception*. Chicago, IL: Aldine.

This book is the main source of Carver and Scheier's (1982) control theory, and contains a range of detail, including neural specifications, mathematical models, descriptions of each perceptual level, modes of operation (controlled, automatic, imagination, and passive observation), memory, learning through reorganisation, the role of conflict, and methodological implications.

ACKNOWLEDGEMENT

This chapter is dedicated to the memory of William T. Powers, who passed away in 2013, and Charles Carver, who passed away in 2021.

REFERENCES

AbuSabha, R., & Achterberg, C. (1997). Review of self-efficacy and locus of control for nutrition-and health-related behavior. *Journal of the American Dietetic Association, 97*(10), 1122–1132.

Alberts, H. J., Martijn, C., & De Vries, N. K. (2011). Fighting self-control failure: Overcoming ego depletion by increasing self-awareness. *Journal of Experimental Social Psychology, 47*(1), 58–62.

Bandura, A. (1977). Self-efficacy: Toward a unifying theory of behavioral change. *Psychological Review, 84*(2), 191–215.

Bandura, A., & Locke, E. A. (2003). Negative self-efficacy and goal effects revisited. *Journal of Applied Psychology, 88(1)*, 87–99.

Barnard, P. J. (2004). Bridging between basic theory and clinical practice. *Behaviour Research and Therapy*, *42(9)*, 977–1000.

Bögels, S. M., & Mansell, W. (2004). Attention processes in the maintenance and treatment of social phobia: Hypervigilance, avoidance and self-focused attention. *Clinical Psychology Review*, *24*(7), 827–856.

Carey, T. A. (2006). *The method of levels: How to do psychotherapy without getting in the way*. Menlo Park, CA: Living Control Systems Publishing.

Carver, C. S. (1998). Resilience and thriving: Issues, models, and linkages. *Journal of Social Issues*, *54(2)*, 245–266.

Carver, C. S., & Scheier, M. F. (1982). Control-theory: A useful conceptual framework for personality-social, clinical, and health psychology. *Psychological Bulletin*, *92*, 111–135.

Carver, C. S., & Scheier, M. F. (1990). Origins and functions of positive and negative affect: A control-process view. *Psychological Review*, *97*(1), 19–35.

Carver, C. S., & Scheier, M. F. (1998). *On the self-regulation of behaviour*. Cambridge: Cambridge University Press.

Carver, C. S., Scheier, M. F., & Segerstrom, S. C. (2010). Optimism. *Clinical Psychology Review*, *30*(7), 879–889.

Craik, K. J. (1947). Theory of the human operator in control systems: The operator as an engineering system. *British Journal of Psychology. General Section*, *38*(2), 56–61.

Craik, K. J. (1948). Theory of the human operator in control systems. II. Man as an element in a control system. *British Journal of Psychology*, *38*(3), 142.

Dawkins, R. (1976). Hierarchical organisation: A candidate principle for ethology. In P. P. G. Bateson & R. A. Hinde (Eds.), *Growing points in ethology*. Cambridge: Cambridge University Press.

Duval, S., & Wicklund, R. A. (1972). *A theory of objective self awareness*. London: Academic Press.

Grzegrzółka, J., & Mansell, W. (2021). How do we help people regain control over their lives? An introduction to method of levels therapy. *Psychiatria i Psychologia Kliniczna*, *21*(1), 45–59.

Healey, A., Mansell, W., & Tai, S. (2017). An experimental test of the role of control in spider fear. *Journal of Anxiety Disorders*, *49*, 12–20.

Heatherton, T. F., & Baumeister, R. F. (1991). Binge eating as escape from self-awareness. *Psychological Bulletin*, *110*(1), 86–108.

Höchli, B., Brügger, A., & Messner, C. (2018). How focusing on superordinate goals motivates broad, long-term goal pursuit: A theoretical perspective. *Frontiers in Psychology*, *9*, 1879.

Ingram, R. E. (1990). Self-focused attention in clinical disorders: Review and a conceptual model. *Psychological Bulletin*, *107*(2), 156–176.

Kelly, R. E., Mansell, W., & Wood, A. M. (2015). Goal conflict and well-being: A review and hierarchical model of goal conflict, ambivalence, self-discrepancy and self-concordance. *Personality and Individual Differences*, *85*, 212–229.

Maddi, S. R., & Kobasa, S. C. (1981). Intrinsic motivation and health. In H. I. Day (Ed.), *Advances in intrinsic motivation and aesthetics* (pp. 299–321). Boston, MA: Springer.

Mansell, W. (2020). Changing behavior using control theory. In M. S. Hagger, L. D. Cameron, K. Hamilton, N. Hankonen, & T. Lintunen (Eds.), *The handbook of behavior change* (pp. 120–135). Cambridge: Cambridge University Press.

Mansell, W. (2021). The perceptual control model of psychopathology. *Current Opinion in Psychology*, *41*, 15–20.

Mansell, W. (2023). An integrative control theory perspective on consciousness. *Psychological Review*. https://doi.org/10.1037/rev0000384

Mansell, W., & Huddy, V. (2018). The assessment and modeling of perceptual control: A transformation in research methodology to address the replication crisis. *Review of General Psychology*, *22(3),* 305–320.

Mansell, W., & Huddy, V. (2020). Why do we need computational models of psychological change and recovery, and how should they be designed and tested? *Frontiers in Psychiatry*, *11*, 624.

Mansell, W., & Marken, R. S. (2015). The origins and future of control theory in psychology. *Review of General Psychology*, *19(4),* 425–430.

Marken, R. S. (1999). PERCOLATe: Perceptual control analysis of tasks. *International Journal of Human–Computer Studies*, *50*(6), 481–487.

Marken, R. S. (2003). Error in skilled performance: A control model of prescribing. *Ergonomics*, *46*(12), 1200–1204.

Marken, R. S. (2021). The study of living control systems: A guide to doing research on purpose. Cambridge: Cambridge University Press.

Marken, R. S., Mansell, W., & Khatib, Z. (2013). Motor control as the control of perception. *Perceptual and Motor Skills*, *117*(1), 236–247.

McKnight, P. E., & Kashdan, T. B. (2009). Purpose in life as a system that creates and sustains health and well-being: An integrative, testable theory. *Review of General Psychology*, *13*(3), 242–251.

Meares, R. (1999). The contribution of Hughlings Jackson to an understanding of dissociation. *American Journal of Psychiatry*, *156*(12), 1850–1855.

Miller, G. A., Eugene, G., & Pribram, K. H. (1960). *Plans and the structure of behaviour*. New York: Holt.

Mineka, S., & Hendersen, R. W. (1985). Controllability and predictability in acquired motivation. *Annual Review of Psychology*, *36*(1), 495–529.

Pieters, R., Baumgartner, H., & Allen, D. (1995). A means-end chain approach to consumer goal structures. *International Journal of Research in Marketing*, *12*(3), 227–244.

Pitt, M., & Mansell, W. (2021). What are the relationships between glycaemic control, psychological distress, and goal attainment in Type 1 diabetes? Assessing the acceptability and feasibility of a case series informed by PCT. Paper presented at the Annual Conference of the International Association of Perceptual Control Theory (IAPCT), Manchester, UK.

Plooij, F. X. (2020). The phylogeny, ontogeny, causation and function of regression periods explained by reorganizations of the hierarchy of perceptual control systems. In W. Mansell (Ed.), *The Interdisciplinary Handbook of Perceptual Control Theory (pp. 199-225)*. Academic Press.

Powers, W. T. (1973). *Behavior: The control of perception*. Chicago, IL: Aldine.

Powers, W. T., Clark, R. K., & Farland, R. M. (1960a). A general feedback theory of human behavior: Part I. *Perceptual and Motor Skills*, *11*(1), 71–88.

Powers, W. T., Clark, R. K., & McFarland, R. L. (1960b). A general feedback theory of human behavior: Part II. *Perceptual and Motor Skills, 11*(3), 309–323.

Pyszczynski, T., Greenberg, J., Solomon, S., & Hamilton, J. (1990). A terror management analysis of self-awareness and anxiety: The hierarchy of terror. *Anxiety Research, 2*(3), 177–195.

Riley, W. T., Martin, C. A., Rivera, D. E., Hekler, E. B., Adams, M. A., Buman, M. P., ... & King, A. C. (2016). Development of a dynamic computational model of social cognitive theory. *Translational Behavioral Medicine, 6(4),* 483-495.

Rosenhead, J., & Mansell, W. (2015). Conflict over reasons to eat tasty food predicts weight fluctuation over 6 weeks. *The Cognitive Behaviour Therapist, 8*, e4. https://doi.org/10.1017/S1754470X15000045.

Rothbaum, F., Weisz, J. R., & Snyder, S. S. (1982). Changing the world and changing the self: A two-process model of perceived control. *Journal of Personality and Social Psychology, 42*(1), 5–37. https://doi.org/10.1037/0022-3514.42.1.5

Rotter, J. B. (1966). Generalized expectancies for internal versus external control of reinforcement. *Psychological Monographs, 80*(1), Whole No. 609.

Scheier, M. F., & Carver, C. S. (1977). Self-focused attention and the experience of emotion: Attraction, repulsion, elation, and depression. *Journal of Personality and Social Psychology, 35*(9), 625–636.

Seligman, M. E. (1972). Learned helplessness. *Annual Review of Medicine, 23*(1), 407–412.

Seth, A. K., & Bayne, T. (2022). Theories of consciousness. *Nature Reviews Neuroscience, 23*, 439–452.

Strudler Wallston, B., & Wallston, K. A. (1978). Locus of control and health: A review of the literature. *Health Education Monographs, 6*(1), 107–117.

Thürmer, J. L., Scheier, M. F., & Carver, C. S. (2020). On the mechanics of goal striving: Experimental evidence of coasting and shifting. *Motivation Science, 6*(3), 266–274. https://doi.org/10.1037/mot0000157

Trafimow, D. (2012). The role of auxiliary assumptions for the validity of manipulations and measures. *Theory & Psychology, 22*(4), 486–498. doi.org/10.1177/0959354311429996

Vancouver, J. B. (2005). The depth of history and explanation as benefit and bane for psychological control theories. *The Journal of Applied Psychology, 90(1),* 38-52.

Vancouver, J. B. (2020). Perceptions of control theory in industrial-organizational psychology: disturbances and counter-disturbances. In W. Mansell (Ed.), *The Interdisciplinary Handbook of Perceptual Control Theory* (pp. 463-501). Academic Press.

Vancouver, J. B., Thompson, C. M., & Williams, A. A. (2001). The changing signs in the relationships among self-efficacy, personal goals, and performance. *The Journal of Applied Psychology, 86*(4), 605–620.

Watkins, E. (2011). Dysregulation in level of goal and action identification across psychological disorders. *Clinical Psychology Review, 31*(2), 260–278.

Webb, T. L., Sniehotta, F. F., & Michie, S. (2010). Using theories of behaviour change to inform interventions for addictive behaviours. *Addiction, 105*(11), 1879–1892.

Wells, A., & Matthews, G. (1994). *Attention and emotion: A clinical perspective.* Hove, UK: Erlbaum.

Wiener, N. (1948.) Cybernetics, or control and communication in the animal and the machine. New York: John Wiley & Sons, Inc.

Wilcoxon, L., Hulme, L., Hussain, H., Fowler, E., & Mansell, W. (2016). Assessment of personal goal hierarchies development and validation of a new measure. www.researchgate.net/publication/289522469_Assessment_of_Personal_Goal_Hierarchies_Development_and_Validation_of_a_New_Measure/link/568e4c8608aeaa1481b00c2d/download

Yin, H. (2020). The crisis in neuroscience. In W. Mansell (Ed.), *The Interdisciplinary Handbook of Perceptual Control Theory* (pp. 23-48). Academic Press.

4

The Ecological Approach: Revisiting Sallis, Cervero, Ascher, Henderson, Kraft, and Kerr (2006)

Sallis, J. F., Cervero, R. B., Ascher, W., Henderson, K. A., Kraft, M. K., & Kerr, J. (2006). An ecological approach to creating active living communities. *Annual Review of Public Health, 27*, 297–322.

Robert A. C. Ruiter, Evelyne de Leeuw, Rik Crutzen, and Gerjo Kok

BACKGROUND

Sallis and colleagues' (2006) paper is considered a classic because it stresses the importance of adopting a so-called 'ecological approach' to understanding the determinants of health and its promotion. Ecological approaches go beyond the individual level and include social environments, physical environments, and policies as important factors that influence people's health (Sallis et al., 2006, p. 298). Sallis and colleagues argued that health and well-being are not only determined by individual thoughts, feelings, and action, but should be seen in a broader perspective that takes account of the varied influences on people's daily lives, including, for example, their upbringing and schooling, work, and living environments. The authors advocated for an approach to health promotion that not only targets the intra-individual and interpersonal levels through educational interventions that aim to change psychological and social influences on behaviour, but that also accounts for the external influences that support (or hinder) people in pursuing personal health and well-being. Sallis et al.'s contribution to the health psychology literature can be summarised as a plea for multi-level interventions that target individuals, social environments, physical environments, *and* policies to promote population health. Concurrently, they argued that this multi-level approach to health promotion can only thrive if multiple disciplines in the social, geographical, and environmental sciences work together in building a transdisciplinary research field and it is supported by collaborative, long-term funding policies that allow for open-ended outcomes (Sallis et al., 2006).

At the time, Sallis et al.'s message was not necessarily considered 'new' but served to bring the ecological perspective into mainstream thinking about health behaviour and assisted in giving prominence to the ecological profile within the field of health psychology, evidenced not least by the substantial number of citations it has accumulated over the years. The current chapter revisits the key perspective from Sallis et al.'s research, how this has influenced thinking about the determinants of health, and its legacy in inspiring research that applies ecological approaches to health and behaviour. Following an overview of the paper and the historical context that informed its key messages, the chapter moves on to discuss how the paper informed new and novel perspectives on the ecological approach to health promotion, including the emergence of systems thinking. The final part of the chapter considers ways to incorporate complexity in health promotion programme development and research.

DETAILED OVERVIEW

Sallis et al. (2006) stressed the importance of multi-level interventions to promote physical activity for health benefits and illness prevention at the population level. Their thesis was that promoting physical activity in people's daily life (referred to as 'active living') can only be realised by 'multi-level interventions based on ecological models and targeting individuals, social environments, physical environments, and policies' (p. 298). Accordingly, their ecological model includes factors at the intrapersonal, interpersonal/cultural, organisational, physical environment, and policy levels across four domains of human activities: leisure-time, mobility, work, and home. Sallis and colleagues' key hypothesis was that interventions will be most effective when implemented at multiple levels and are the result of collaborations among multiple disciplines that combine their research methods to create new *transdisciplinary approaches*.

Sallis et al. suggested that an ecological approach to health promotion needs to combine ecological levels and environments. Ecological levels include intrapersonal, behavioural, built environment, and policy levels. Environments include the information environment (e.g., media), social cultural environment (e.g., social support), natural environment (e.g., air quality), and the policy environment (e.g., zoning codes). In turn, within each of these, different settings can be distinguished such as the healthcare setting, the home setting, the work setting, and the recreational setting. The distinctions among levels, environments, and settings were not necessarily clear, but, generally speaking, environments can be thought of as having different settings that function at different levels. For example, cycling promotion policies can be thought of as a product of the policy environment at the municipality or provincial policy level when situated within a recreational setting, or at the organisational (company) level when situated within the work setting. The realisation of safe cycle routes, in turn, is shared under the built environment level that will become part of the natural *environment* and serve different settings in which people live, attend school, and go to work.

To illustrate the complexity of the ecological approach in the promotion of population health, Sallis and colleagues made the point that multi-level interventions need to be informed by research from different fields, including public health and behavioural science, urban planning and transportation studies, leisure and recreation studies, public policy, economics, and political science research. Specifically, they called for a research agenda that not simply allows for the summative input of different disciplines, each adding their own unique concepts and theoretical models, but to organise scientific collaborations targeting research outcomes that are of collective interest to the collaborating partners. Examples were provided that demonstrate the complexity of environmental and policy issues that cannot be fully understood or solved by a mono-disciplinary approach, but need to be approached from multiple perspectives that eventually yield insights and outputs that expand the outcomes of interest in the individual fields. For example, within the Dutch context, health researchers would traditionally see the decision to realise a new long-distance cycle route from a recreational perspective, providing an opportunity to become more physically active. However, when working with transportation researchers, the promotion of *active* transport is seen as another option (e.g., cycling to work). Viewing the problem from a cross-disciplinary perspective brings to the fore other outcomes for prioritisation, in this case ensuring that using a bicycle compares favourably with (or better than) car use in terms of travel time and safety. Public policy researchers, in turn, might use that same initiative as a case study to demonstrate how commuting to work by bicycle can enhance people's physical and mental health, thus convincing employers and health insurance companies to provide incentives for car users to switch to cycle use. And political scientists may use the initiative to enrich their models of successful advocacy by demonstrating the need to have converging argumentation from different layers in the population and environmental levels.

Through interdisciplinary working, it was argued, research methods and statistics that are traditionally strong in one discipline can be introduced to other disciplines. However, Sallis et al. also warn that ecological approaches bring challenges in terms of organising, conducting, publishing, and financing the research. One such challenge is the inherent complexity of multi-level research, which involves different stakeholders at different ecological levels with different responsibilities and allegiances. Bringing researchers from different disciplines together might also easily instigate a debate about research methods and paradigms that are more acceptable in one domain than in the other. While such debates can be productive, funding bodies typically prioritise the generation of products that provide ready-made solutions to societal problems rather than on implementing new scientific approaches that leave room for outcomes that were not foreseen at a project's outset. Sallis et al. hypothesised that accumulating experiences with multi-level research will bring factors and hypotheses related to the ecological approach more to the foreground and increase efforts to put research findings into practice, which in turn may influence the funding landscape and allow for further cross-disciplinary, multi-level, research. Although notable exceptions can be found (see, for example, the Amsterdam Healthy Weight Approach introduced later in this chapter in Sidebar 4.2), long-term health programmes involving the collaboration of different research disciplines, such as the Active Living Research Programme that started in 2001 and formed the basis of the Sallis et al. paper, are scarce. The Active Living Research Programme is still active and now focuses on the implementation of new health practices and policies, beyond, but not limited to, the promotion of physical activity, that are supported by empirical and theoretical evidence (see https://activelivingresearch.org).

HISTORICAL CONTEXT OF THE ECOLOGICAL APPROACH TO HEALTH PROMOTION

When Sallis et al. published their article, it was against the backdrop of considerable earlier work that had elaborated on the ecological approach to health and behaviour. When considering the ecological approach, many researchers and authors in health contexts refer to the earlier ideas of American psychologist Urie Bronfenbrenner on the role of the environment in explaining human development. Bronfenbrenner (1977) criticised earlier 'unidirectional' theories that studied the influence of a single aspect of the environment on human development. Instead, he argued for research that accounts for the dynamic influences of the complex environments in which people live and the interactions within these environments that have an impact on individual development. Bronfenbrenner described those environments as a nested arrangement of social structures, each contained within the next: (i) a microsystem of interrelations among the developing individual and the environment in an immediate setting that contains them (e.g., home, school, workplace); (ii) a mesosystem that incorporates the interactions among the different micro-settings, the result of which may influence the individual's development (e.g., parents talking with school about their child's development); (iii) an exosystem that extends the mesosystems with both formal and informal social structures (e.g., social norms, information and transportation services, built environment) that do not directly impact on the individual, but indirectly influence them as they affect one of the microsystems (e.g., local policies to support parents financially to allow their children to join a sports club); and (iv) the macrosystem, referring to the already established society and culture within which the individual is developing, and how elements such as the socioeconomic status, ethnicity, geographic location and political ideologies, and cultural norms affect the individual's development through their influence on the structure and functioning of the micro-, meso-, and exosystems (e.g., national policies that promote sport participation in children).

McLeroy and colleagues (1988) were among early scholars who warned against simplifying health promotion as programmes that try to change individuals. They renamed Bronfenbrenner's 'systems' as factors at the intrapersonal, interpersonal, institutional, community, and public policy levels, and argued for intervening at all these levels of analysis. McLeroy et al. saw active involvement of the target population, programme users, and stakeholders at the different levels in the development process as the main vehicle to: (i) ensure environmental support for implementation and institutionalization of health promotion interventions; (ii) support individual behaviour change; (iii) evaluate health promotion outcomes at multiple levels; (iv) understand that stimulating individuals to change behaviour is not sufficient when the sources of ill-health are environmental; and (v) avoid victim blaming, because that may result in coercion and restriction of individual rights.

A 1996 special issue of the *American Journal of Health Promotion* (Stokols et al., 1996) gave further impetus to the developing approach advocated by Sallis et al. (2006). One article in the collection (Richard et al., 1996) presented a visualisation of the ecological approach by separating intervention settings from intervention targets. Intervention settings were defined as the 'living systems' that operate around the individual, identified as the organisation, community, society, and supranational settings. Within those settings, health promotion programmes are aimed at distinct types of intervention targets, for example: the individual members of an 'at-risk' population; the interpersonal environment of people and small groups those individual members are linked to the organisations to which they belong; the communities in which they live; and the political 'players' in the community and societal settings. Richard et al. argued that, following this structuring of intervention targets and intervention settings, it follows that the more a health promotion programme integrates individual and environmental targets across a variety of settings, the more it can be deemed to be *ecological*.

Another article in the special issue (Green et al., 1996) reflected on the strengths and limitations of the ecological perspective in health promotion settings. According to these authors, a principal advantage of the ecological approach is its emphasis on considering unforeseen effects, given that these might extend the boundaries of the system in which a health programme is located. Another claimed advantage was the view that an individual's health is mediated by behaviour–environment interactions. Specifically, the ecological approach argues that while the environment is a determinant of individual behaviour, the behaviour of individuals, groups and organisations also impacts the environment, with the implication that individuals can thus be given control over both internal and external determinants of their health. Finally, Green et al. emphasised the value of accounting for individual variability in responses across different environments, stressing that there is no 'one-size-fits-all' intervention in health promotion: the effectiveness of a change method therefore always depends on its fit with the people, the health issue at stake, and the environments in which it is to be applied (see Schaalma & Kok, 2009). In terms of limitations of the ecological approach, Green et al. (1996) highlight its inherent complexity, as evidenced in the difficulty in setting boundaries to enable a clear research focus and the emphasis on observable behaviour and environments, rather than studying underlying biological, psychological, and social processes that explain phenomena within controlled experimental designs.

The ecological approach garnered considerable interest among scholars in the fields of public health and health psychology, and the Sallis et al. (2006) paper can be seen as a classic example of that popularity. However, it was the first international conference on health promotion in Ottawa in 1986, under the auspices of the World Health Organization (WHO), that served as the platform for introducing the ecological approach to practitioners in the domain of health promotion. The resulting *Ottawa Charter for Health Promotion* (World Health Organization, 1986) acknowledged a programme of work that included multi-level perspectives and determinants of health (de Leeuw & Harris-Roxas, 2016) and called for the creation of supportive environments, reorienting healthcare towards health rather than disease, and investing in individual and community capability to promote population health. The Charter identified stakeholder (advocate) involvement, empowerment of individuals and groups (enable), and inter-sectoral collaboration (mediate) as the operational strategies within those action areas. It also built on Milio's (1986) assertion that policies for health are integral to health promotion because policies shape opportunities for health and drive health equity. The Ottawa Charter was therefore innovative in that it embraced a broader, systemic, and integrated agenda for the creation and maintenance of health. In short, it aimed to focus on a *health* system rather than a *care* system (Kelly & Charlton, 2003). Sidebar 4.1 provides an example of how the ecological approach has been brought into the practice of health promotion.

Sidebar 4.1. Planning for Health Promotion

The PRECEDE-PROCEED planning model for health promotion (Green & Kreuter, 2005) was the first planning framework for health promotion programmes that explicitly acknowledged environmental factors as important determinants of health and health behaviour. The model promoted the ecological approach by making an environmental assessment part of the problem diagnosis phase, and by identifying the social and physical factors that facilitate or hinder the behaviour (e.g., cultural norms, accessibility of healthcare services) or directly influence the health outcome (e.g., air pollution). This ecological assessment complements the behavioural and educational assessments, which identify the behaviours that positively contribute to health, and the person-related factors that should be in place to initiate and sustain the required behaviour change. These factors include enabling (e.g., skills), reinforcing (e.g., incentives), and cognitive or predisposing factors (e.g., beliefs, perceptions, attitude).

Notably, the authors of Intervention Mapping (IM) (Bartholomew Eldredge, Markham et al., 2016; Bartholomew Eldredge, Parcel et al., 2001) built on the PRECEDE-PROCEED model but more explicitly described the actions needed for the planning, development, implementation, and evaluation of health promotion programmes. The six-steps protocol is recognised for its comprehensiveness in developing solutions for complex behavioural problems (O'Cathain, Croot, Duncan et al., 2019; O'Cathain, Croot, Sworn et al., 2019). In thinking about the problem and solutions, IM stresses three main working principles:

(1) the use of theory and evidence, (2) community and stakeholder participation, and (3) adopting an ecological approach. Bartholomew Eldredge and colleagues adapted the ecological model of Richard et al. (1996), in which individuals exist within groups (interpersonal), which in turn are embedded in organisations and higher order systems (called ecological levels): community, society, and supranation. Following this, health is seen as mediated by both behaviour and environment, and health promotion programmes therefore need to impact on multiple levels, as well as prepare for programme adoption and implementation. Accordingly, the potential impact of an intervention depends on the quality of the programme in addressing change at the different ecological levels and the quality of programme use reflected in implementation completeness and fidelity. Finally, the identification of key people – referred to as environmental agents – that influence the existence or intensity of each environmental condition at the different ecological levels is considered essential to the use of the ecological approach in IM. Once the agents and their behaviours have been identified, the planner can select determinants and methods to change them using theory from the individual and higher ecological levels, including organisational change theories, community empowerment approaches, and theories of public policy (Bartholomew Eldredge et al., 2016; Kok et al., 2016).

LINEAR VS. DYNAMIC ECOLOGICAL INFLUENCES ON HEALTH

The above historical perspective on the introduction of the ecological approach to health promotion theory and practice touches on a possible inherent paradigmatic conflict between the approach introduced by Sallis et al. (2006) and the systems views advocated by other forms of health promotion (e.g., the Ottawa Charter; WHO, 1986). The latter challenged the linearity between ecological levels and suggested that agents and events in systems can operate simultaneously to influence, with synergy, broader change. An example of such multi-purpose and multi-layered engagement for change is the WHO Healthy Cities movement. A healthy city is one that puts health to the forefront in all its policies and continuously creates supportive environments for health (de Leeuw, 1999; de Leeuw et al., 2014). The call for the paradigm shift towards a social ecological approach to health promotion that provides a framework for 'understanding the dynamic interplay among persons, groups, and their sociophysical milieus', as formulated by Stokols et al. (1996, p. 283), is arguably still warranted. Or, rather, perhaps what is needed is paradigm *integration* whereby a systems model of health is adopted in which the introduction of a given health promotion programme is evaluated according to its impact on the ecosystem in which it is implemented, alongside development of an understanding of how that impact occurs (Green et al., 1996). The development and implementation of large-scale socio-ecological programmes that allow this kind of integration and analysis is faced with major challenges and no doubt less practised than preached. This is a topic to which this chapter now turns.

DEVELOPMENTS

FROM ECOLOGICAL LEVELS TO SYSTEMS THINKING TO COMPLEX INTERVENTIONS

Complex social phenomena have multiple ecological levels, which are characterised as environments (Bronfenbrenner, 1977) or settings (Richard et al., 1996). In recent years, the conceptualisation of the decision-making environment for promoting health as a complex adaptive system has gained strong foothold, as can be seen in ecological approaches to health promotion in urban areas such as the WHO Healthy Cities Network (Chughtai & Blanchet, 2017; Kim et al., 2022). The way these levels are believed to work together in influencing individual behaviour has evolved from Sallis et al.'s (2006) thinking in processes of linear effects, with agents at one level having influence on individuals in lower levels (and vice versa), towards seeing social phenomena as complex adaptive systems in which multiple factors at different ecological levels continuously interact (Hawe, 2015a, 2015b).

In the domain of public health, where the complexity of health problems is generally high and decision-making contexts continuously change, systems thinking implies that behaviour change can only be attained if there is simultaneous action that addresses the totality of personal and external factors that promote healthy behaviours. Such 'whole system' or 'complex adaptive system thinking' approaches require a coordinated and integrated effort that involves policy actors and stakeholders from inside and outside public health, including local governments, private partners, and public institutions, and stimulates multi-level action and cross-sectoral working. Furthermore, it should have the capacity to respond to changes in a continuously evolving structure of complex relationships among personal, social, physical, and policy factors (Hawe, 2015a, 2015b). Precisely this 'complex intervention' perspective has also been the driver of 'Whole-of-Government', 'Joined-up-Government', 'Integrated Governance', and other integrative approaches to policy making and governance – not just for health, but across large societal challenges, including climate change, food security, and mobility (de Leeuw, 2021).

Systematically described public health examples of complex interventions are still scarce and, according to Bagnall and colleagues (2019), mainly limited to the domain of obesity prevention. Their systematic review of 65 articles suggested that multi-component community interventions that include elements of adaptive complex systems thinking (e.g., broad engagement of stakeholders and community, meaningful relationships among key players, embedment of health programmes in local policies) can have positive effects on behavioural and physiological indices of health (e.g., nutrition, BMI) and strengthen community capacity to instal health-promoting environments (e.g., road safety, green areas). Several drivers of successful complex interventions were identified, including: strong involvement of key partners, sufficient time to build meaningful relationships, trust and community capacity, good governance and use of a common language, embedding initiatives within a broader political context, local evaluation of local-level interventions, and sufficient financial support and resources. However, they also concluded that a systematic approach towards development, implementation, and evaluation of complex interventions is still in its infancy (Bagnall et al., 2019). Sidebar 4.2 provides an illustrative example of a community-based health promotion programme that functions along the working principles of a complex adaptive system strategy.

Sidebar 4.2. The Amsterdam Healthy Weight Approach

The Amsterdam Healthy Weight Approach programme was initiated by the City of Amsterdam in 2012 to reduce overweight and obesity rates in children aged 0–18 years over a period of 20 years (Sawyer et al., 2021; UNICEF et al., 2020). The working principles of complex adaptive system thinking were applied by implementing 'multi-level actions aiming to modify the local political, physical, social, health education, and care environment in multiple settings (the home, neighborhood, school, health care, and city)', stimulating 'cross-sectoral working across municipal sectors (responsible for public health, spatial planning, sport, education, welfare, poverty reduction, economic affairs, youth, and neighborhood work) and public, private, and community partners to develop and implement actions', and further adopting 'a learning approach to enable program adaptation in response to change in the complex adaptive system comprising the local environment (i.e., Amsterdam)' (Sawyer et al., 2021, p. 592). For a detailed description of the logic model of change underlying the Amsterdam Health Weight Approach, see Sawyer et al. (2021).

Data used in the evaluation of the programme came from annual health monitoring of the municipal youth health services of Amsterdam and are representative of all Amsterdam children with similar gender, age, ethnicity, and social economic position (City of Amsterdam, 2017). BMI data from the programme's first five years (2012–2017) showed that, in contrast to global trends of increased obesity rates in urban settings, the estimated prevalence of overweight or obesity in 2–18 year-olds in Amsterdam declined from 21% to 18.7%. Questionnaire data showed that health behaviours, such as the breastfeeding of babies, consumption of non-sugary drinks, and physical activity, have improved over the same period in Amsterdam youth.

The Amsterdam Healthy Weight Approach has since been extended to the promotion of other health behaviours. For example, by following the first four steps of Intervention Mapping and adopting a 'Health-in-All Policies' framework, Belmon and colleagues (2022) created a blueprint for intervention development to promote children's sleep health across relevant policy sectors, again in the City of Amsterdam. A logic model describing the individual and external determinants of poor sleep hygiene was combined with an overview of the existing organisational structures and related policy sectors that could be leveraged to promote better sleep behaviours in children by working with multiple stakeholders across ecological levels (e.g., parents, teachers, community workers). A set of programme objectives and opportunities for promoting sleep health was then specified, after which policy advisers were provided with a blueprint for possible interventions to support this across multiple policy sectors of the city. These sectors included education, sports, youth healthcare, social services, and public health services.

Integration of Ecological Models in Health Promotion

The Sallis et al. (2006) paper described an ecological approach to societal problems that are related to health and well-being, in this case physical activity/active living. However, the approach has been shown to be generalizable to issues other than those specific to physical activity (see Sidebar 4.2). The multi-level approach has clearly become a source of inspiration for other researchers across the health promotion field and especially among researchers working on interventions related to 'health-for-all'. Indeed, over the past decade, health promotion practice has seen an increase in utilisation of multi-level programmes. Synthesising the literature on newly introduced ecological models in this area, Richard and colleagues (2011) concluded that the ecological approach had gained a strong foothold in health promotion, with both physical activity and dietary behaviour research having become more 'ecological' compared to other areas of research.

However, Kok et al.'s (2008) earlier research had already concluded that the evidence-base underpinning use of the ecological approach is relatively weak. These authors interviewed 43 coordinators of 47 multi-level ecological programmes. Most programmes were found to include two or three ecological levels, with organisational modification being the most common ecological approach, followed by policy and community changes. Kok et al. also reported that systematic descriptions of the methods used to change organisations and influence communities and public policy were scarce and, importantly, limited in scope. To build a stronger evidence base for the ecological approach in population health, the authors made a plea for better, systematic descriptions of the strategies (applied methods for change) of multi-level health promotion programmes, following up on similar pleas published in the wider health psychology literature (Michie & Abraham, 2008; Peters et al., 2015). Behaviour change taxonomies have since been introduced that can help in providing these more detailed descriptions of the active ingredients of an intervention (Kok et al., 2016; Michie et al., 2013), although these remain mostly limited to the individual level rather than providing definitions of change methods at higher ecological levels.

Sallis and Owen (2015) reflected on the conditions that may strengthen ecological programmes. They argued that behaviour change is maximised when environments and policies support healthful choices, when social norms and social support are strong, and when individuals are motivated and educated to make healthful choices. Four core principles were advanced: (1) multiple levels or factors influence health behaviours, (2) influences interact across levels, (3) multi-level interventions are most effective in changing behaviour, and (4) ecological models are more powerful when they are tailored to specific health behaviours. The authors presented data in two new health domains, physical activity and tobacco control, to support their argument. However, they also acknowledged key weaknesses of ecological models, including their lack of specificity about the most important hypothesised influences. Accordingly, a challenge of working with ecological models is to develop operational models that lead to testable hypotheses and also provide useful guidance for interventions. As Sallis and Owen (2015, p. 61) put it, the final goal is to 'create environments and policies that make it convenient, attractive and economical to make healthful choices, and to motivate and educate people about those choices'. Such a goal aligns with the Ottawa Charter perspective to 'make healthier choices the easier choice': if an infrastructure is developed that enables performance of desired behaviours (e.g., mixed density urban planning, bicycle paths, walkability), and is supported by appropriately informed policy, behaviour (change) becomes more easily developed and maintained (cf. Committee on Capitalizing on Social Science and Behavioral Research to Improve the Public's Health, Division of Health Promotion and Disease Prevention, Institute of Medicine, 2001).

Recent conceptualisations of the ecological approach stress the high complexity of health problems and argue for a complex adaptive system approach in order to devise effective solutions to these. A central element of a complex intervention approach is collaboration among different policy sectors, including beyond the health sector (see de Leeuw, 2017). De Leeuw argues for cross-sectoral engagement, grounded in a multi-level governance perspective that is dependent on deliberate and participatory engagement of communities. Examples of the impact community engagement has on health outcomes are often limited, methodologically, preventing firm conclusions, but research points to the idea that community engagement generally leads to better social outcomes (e.g., housing management, perceptions of crime, information flows between communities and service providers), which ultimately may contribute to better health (Milton et al., 2012). Nonetheless, as de Leeuw (2017, p. 343) concludes: 'full community participation and empowerment, particularly in influencing policy and systems change for health, remain the bedrock of health promotion'.

In line with Sallis et al.'s (2006) ecological model of active living that influences interact across levels, Mkhitaryan et al. (2020) described a hybrid approach to incorporate complexity in health promotion programme development. Their point of departure is that commonly used planning frameworks for health promotion programmes often oversimplify human behaviours despite acknowledging their inherent complexity. For instance, frameworks include chains of lists (in logic models) instead of richer structures considering loops and the dynamicity of relations between factors at various levels. While integrating many aspects of complexity in logic models may be possible, it also runs the risk of producing artefacts that become equally complex instead of equipping intervention planners and health researchers with decision-making tools to estimate intervention effects.

Key elements in a hybrid approach described by Mkhitaryan et al. (2020) are 'Fuzzy Cognitive Maps' (FCMs). Intuitively, a FCM can be conceptualised as comprising two parts: (1) a network, and (2) a computational, or 'simulation', engine that can estimate the effects of introducing an intervention along with how the intervention introduction interacts with factors at different levels. The network represents factors (at various levels) as 'nodes', which are interconnected by means of causal antecedents and consequents represented by directed edges. FCMs also reflect other key information, that nodes and edges have values which specify how to update the model when conducting a simulation (e.g., a test of introducing an intervention at a certain level). Mago et al. (2013) have developed a FCM to analyse

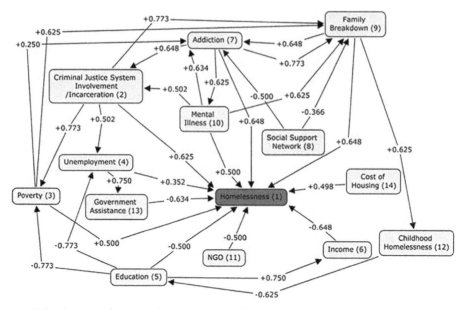

Figure 4.1 Impact of various factors on homelessness

Source: Mago, V. K. et al. (2013). Analyzing the impact of social factors on homelessness: A Fuzzy Cognitive Map approach. BMC Medical Informatics and Decision Making, 13, 94. https://doi.org/10.1186/1472-6947-13-94. Reprinted under the terms of the Creative Commons Attribution License (http://creativecommons.org/licenses/by/2.0)

a complex social problem: childhood homelessness (Figure 4.1). In line with de Leeuw (2017), this FCM example shows that engagement by sectors other than health is necessary.

CONCLUSIONS

Sallis et al.'s (2006) paper has been pivotal in our thinking about health, its causes, and how to improve it. It built on an earlier argument about the need for systems thinking, introduced by Bronfenbrenner, in the health field. The notions of interconnectedness and complex reciprocal dynamics in shifting systems were also seen in other disciplines and social arenas at the time, and this continued into the 21st century (e.g., see Doxiadis, 1970, for a theory on human settlement and well-being that was grounded in the ecological approach). As suggested recently by Brenner and Katsikis (2021), to understand and change our collective and individual health and well-being we must be able to grasp its complexity. As suggested above, the tools to do this effectively are now starting to emerge. Approaches and initiatives such as Health in All Policies, Whole of Governance structures, and tools such as Fuzzy Cognitive Maps are informing the specification and operationalisation of the total ecological system with its interlocking and reciprocating dynamics between levels and environments. Sallis and colleagues have opened a door that we can now walk through towards a better understanding of individual, collective, ecosystemic, and planetary health. As such, their much cited 2006 paper deserves its place among the classics in Health Psychology.

FURTHER READING

de Leeuw, E. (2017). Engagement of sectors other than health in integrated health governance, policy, and action. *Annual Review of Public Health, 38*, 329–349.

Provides an introductory overview of joined-up policy making and implementation for health (also known as 'Health in All Policies').

Hawe, P. (2015). Lessons from complex interventions to improve health. *Annual Review of Public Health*, *36*, 307–323. https://doi.org/10.1146/annurev-publhealth-031912-114421.

Demonstrates that complexity is not overwhelming but can be analytically approached and used for intervention development and implementation.

Sawyer, A., den Hertog, K., Verhoeff, A. P., Busch, V., & Stronks, K. (2021). Developing the logic framework underpinning a whole-systems approach to childhood overweight and obesity prevention: Amsterdam Healthy Weight Approach. *Obesity Science & Practice, 7*(5), 591–605. https://doi.org/10.1002/osp4.505.

Provides an example of applying the working principles of a complex systems approach in the development of a health promotion programme.

REFERENCES

Bagnall, A.-M., Radley, D., Jones, R., Gately, P., Nobles, J., van Dijk, M., Blackshaw, J., Montel, S., & Sahota, P. (2019). Whole systems approaches to obesity and other complex public health challenges: A systematic review. *BMC Public Health*, *19*(1). https://doi.org/10.1186/s12889-018-6274-z

Bartholomew Eldredge, L. K., Markham, C. M., Ruiter, R. A. C., Fernández, M. E., Kok, G., & Parcel, G. S. (2016). *Planning health promotion programs: An Intervention Mapping approach* (4th ed.). San Francisco, CA: Jossey-Bass.

Bartholomew Eldredge, L. K., Parcel, G. S., Kok, G., & Gottlieb, N. H. (2001). *Intervention mapping: Designing theory- and evidence-based health promotion programs*. Mountain View, CA: Mayfield.

Belmon, L. S., van Stralen, M. M., Harmsen, I. A., den Hartog, K., Ruiter, R. A. C., Chinapaw, M. J. M., & Busch, V. (2022). *Promoting children's sleep health: Intervention Mapping meets Health in All Policies*. Manuscript under review.

Brenner, N., & Katsikis, N. (2021). Hinterlands of the capitalocene. In O. Abingdon (Ed.), *Global urbanism* (p. 34). London: Routledge. https://doi.org/10.4324/9780429259593-6

Bronfenbrenner, U. (1977). Toward an experimental ecology of human development. *American Psychologist*, *32*(7), 513–531. https://doi.org/10.1037/0003-066X.32.7.513

Chughtai, S., & Blanchet, K. (2017). Systems thinking in public health: A bibliographic contribution to a meta-narrative review. *Health Policy and Planning*, *32*, 585–594. https://doi.org/10.1093/heapol/czw159

City of Amsterdam. (2017). *Amsterdam will become the healthiest city for children: Review 2012–2017, part 2.* https://assets.amsterdam.nl/publish/pages/967207/review_2011-2017_amsterdam_healthy_weigth_programme_wcag.pdf

Committee on Capitalizing on Social Science and Behavioral Research to Improve the Public's Health, Division of Health Promotion and Disease Prevention, Institute of Medicine (2001). Promoting health: Intervention strategies from social and behavioral research. American Journal of Health Promotion, 15(3), 149–166. https://doi.org/10.4278/0890-1171-15.3.149

de Leeuw, E. (1999). Healthy cities: Urban social entrepreneurship for health. *Health Promotion International*, *14*(3), 261–269. https://doi.org/10.1093/heapro/14.3.261

de Leeuw, E. (2017). Engagement of sectors other than health in integrated health governance, policy, and action. *Annual Review of Public Health*, *38*(1), 329–349. https://doi.org/10.1146/annurev-publhealth-031816-044309

de Leeuw, E. (2021). Intersectoral Action. Oxford Bibliographies, 25 August 2021. DOI:10.1093/OBO/9780199756797-0203. www.oxfordbibliographies.com/view/document/obo-9780199756797/obo-9780199756797-0203.xml

de Leeuw, E., & Harris-Roxas, B. (2016). Crafting health promotion: From Ottawa to beyond Shanghai. *Environnement, Risques & Santé, 15*, 461–464. https://doi.org/10.1684/ers.2016.0921

de Leeuw, E., Tsouros, A. D., Dyakova, M., & Green, G. (Eds.). (2014). *Healthy cities: promoting health and equity – evidence for local policy and practice: Summary evaluation of Phase V of the WHO European Healthy Cities Network.* Geneva: World Health Organization. Regional Office for Europe. https://apps.who.int/iris/handle/10665/137512

Doxiadis, C. A. (1970). Ekistics, the science of human settlements. *Science, 170*(3956), 393–404. https://doi.org/10.1126/science.170.3956.393

Green, L. W., & Kreuter, M. W. (2005). *Health promotion planning: An educational and ecological approach* (4th ed.). New York: McGraw-Hill Professional.

Green, L. W., Richard, L., & Potvin, L. (1996). Ecological foundations of health promotion. *American Journal of Health Promotion, 10*(4), 270–281. https://doi.org/10.4278/0890-1171-10.4.318

Hawe, P. (2015a). Lessons from Complex Interventions to Improve Health. *Annual Review of Public Health, 36*, 307–323. https://doi.org/10.1146/annurev-publhealth-031912-114421

Hawe, P. (2015b). Minimal, negligible and negligent interventions. *Social Science & Medicine, 138*, 265–268. https://doi.org/10.1016/j.socscimed.2015.05.025

Kelly, M. P., & Charlton, B. (2003). The modern and postmodern in health promotion. In R. Bunton, S. Nettleton, & R. Burrows (Eds.), *The sociology of health promotion: Critical analyses of consumption, lifestyle and risk* (pp. 77–90). London: Routledge.

Kim, J., de Leeuw, E., Harris-Roxas, B., & Sainsbury, P. (2022). Four urban health paradigms: The search for coherence. *Cities.* http://dx.doi.org/10.1016/j.cities.2022.103806

Kok, G., Gottlieb, N. H., Commers, M., & Smerecnik, C. (2008). The ecological approach in health promotion programs: A decade later. *American Journal of Health Promotion: AJHP, 22*(6), 437–442. https://doi.org/10.4278/ajhp.22.6.437

Kok, G., Gottlieb, N. H., Peters, G. J. Y., Mullen, P. D., Parcel, G. S., Ruiter, R. A. C., Fernández, M. E., Markham, C., & Bartholomew, L. K. (2016). A taxonomy of behaviour change methods: An Intervention Mapping approach. *Health Psychology Review, 10*(3), 297–312. https://doi.org/10.1080/17437199.2015.1077155

Mago, V. K., Morden, H. K., Fritz, C., Wu, T., Namazi, S., Geranmayeh, P., Chattopadhyay, R., & Dabbaghian, V. (2013). Analyzing the impact of social factors on homelessness: A Fuzzy Cognitive Map approach. *BMC Medical Informatics and Decision Making*, *13*, 94. https://doi.org/10.1186/1472-6947-13-94

McLeroy, K. R., Bibeau, D., Steckler, A., & Glanz, K. (1988). An ecological perspective on health promotion programs. *Health Education Quarterly*, *15*(4), 351–377. https://doi.org/10.1177/109019818801500401

Michie, S., & Abraham, C. (2008). Advancing the science of behaviour change: A plea for scientific reporting. *Addiction (Abingdon, England)*, *103*(9), 1409–1410. https://doi.org/10.1111/j.1360-0443.2008.02291.x

Michie, S., Richardson, M., Johnston, M., Abraham, C., Francis, J., Hardeman, W., Eccles, M. P., Cane, J., & Wood, C. E. (2013). The Behavior Change Technique Taxonomy (v1) of 93 hierarchically clustered techniques: Building an international consensus for the reporting of behavior change interventions. *Annals of Behavioral Medicine*, *46*(1), 81–95. https://doi.org/10.1007/s12160-013-9486-6

Milio, N. (1986). Multisectoral policy and health promotion: Where to begin. *Health Promotion*, *1*(2), 129–132.

Milton, B., Attree, P., French, B., Povall, S., Whitehead, M., & Popay, J. (2012). The impact of community engagement on health and social outcomes: A systematic review. *Community Development Journal*, *47*(3), 316–334. https://doi.org/10.1093/cdj/bsr043

Mkhitaryan, S., Giabbanelli, P. J., de Vries, N. K., & Crutzen, R. (2020). Dealing with complexity: How to use a hybrid approach to incorporate complexity in health behavior interventions. *Intelligence-Based Medicine*, *3-4*, 100008. https://doi.org/10.1016/j.ibmed.2020.100008

O'Cathain, A., Croot, L., Duncan, E., Rousseau, N., Sworn, K., Turner, K. M., Yardley, L., & Hoddinott, P. (2019). Guidance on how to develop complex interventions to improve health and healthcare. *BMJ Open*, *9*(8), 1–9. https://doi.org/10.1136/bmjopen-2019-029954

O'Cathain, A., Croot, L., Sworn, K., Duncan, E., Rousseau, N., Turner, K., Yardley, L., & Hoddinott, P. (2019). Taxonomy of approaches to developing interventions to improve health: A systematic methods overview. In *Pilot and Feasibility Studies* (Vol. 5, Issue 1, pp. 1–27). Pilot and Feasibility Studies. https://doi.org/10.1186/s40814-019-0425-6

Peters, G.-J. Y., de Bruin, M., & Crutzen, R. (2015). Everything should be as simple as possible, but no simpler: Towards a protocol for accumulating evidence regarding the active content of health behaviour change interventions. *Health Psychology Review*, *9*(1), 1–14. https://doi.org/10.1080/17437199.2013.848409

Richard, L., Gauvin, L., & Raine, K. (2011). Ecological models revisited: their uses and evolution in health promotion over two decades. *Annual Review of Public Health*, *32*, 307–326.

Richard, L., Potvin, L., Kishchuk, N., Prlic, H., & Green, L. W. (1996). Assessment of the integration of the ecological approach in health promotion programs. *American Journal of Health Promotion*, *10*(4), 318–328.

Sallis, J. F., Cervero, R. B., Ascher, W., Henderson, K. A., Kraft, M. K., & Kerr, J. (2006). An ecological approach to creating active living communities. *Annual Review of Public Health*, *27*(1), 297–322. https://doi.org/10.1146/annurev.publhealth.27.021405.102100

Sallis, J. F., & Owen, N. (2015). Ecological models of health behavior. In K. Glanz, B. K. Rimer, & K. Visnawath (Eds.), *Health behavior: Theory, research, and practice* (5th ed., pp. 43–64). San Francisco, CA: Jossey-Bass.

Sawyer, A., den Hertog, K., Verhoeff, A. P., Busch, V., & Stronks, K. (2021). Developing the logic framework underpinning a whole-systems approach to childhood overweight and obesity prevention: Amsterdam Healthy Weight Approach. *Obesity Science & Practice*, *7*(5), 591–605. https://doi.org/10.1002/osp4.505

Schaalma, H., & Kok, G. (2009). Decoding health education interventions: The times are a-changin'. *Psychology & Health*, *24*(1), 5–9. https://doi.org/10.1080/088704408 01995802

Stokols, D., Allen, J., & Bellingham, R. L. (1996). The social ecology of health promotion: Implications for research and practice. *American Journal of Health Promotion*, *10*(4), 247–251. https://doi.org/10.4278/0890-1171-10.4.247

UNICEF, City of Amsterdam, & EAT. (2020). *The Amsterdam Healthy Weight Approach: Investing in healthy urban childhoods: A case study on healthy diets for children.* London: UNICEF.

World Health Organization (1986). *The Ottawa Charter for Health Promotion*. Geneva: World Health Organization (WHO). www.who.int/publications/i/item/ottawa-charter-for-health-promotion (retrieved 30 August 2022).

5

Stress and Health: Revisiting Cohen, Tyrrell, and Smith (1991)

Cohen, S., Tyrrell, D. A. J., & Smith, A. P. (1991). Psychological stress and susceptibility to the common cold. *New England Journal of Medicine, 325*, 606–612.

Fabio Sani

BACKGROUND

From 1986 to 1989, a research team led by Sheldon Cohen embarked on a methodologically novel study on stress and illness (Cohen, Tyrrell, & Smith, 1991). In this study, a sample of healthy adults reported the extent to which they had experienced recent life events as stressful (i.e., as unpredictable, uncontrollable, and overloading). Then, the study participants were exposed to the common cold virus, with different groups of participants receiving different strains of the virus. Observations made after this exposure revealed that participants who had felt more stressed over recent weeks were more likely to catch a cold, no matter to which specific strain of the virus they had been exposed. These results compellingly demonstrated that the appraisal of life events as stressful may reduce resistance to infectious illness. The study, which was reported in a 1991 article titled 'Psychological stress and susceptibility to the common cold' published in the prestigious *New England Journal of Medicine*, had a marked impact on the research community, and it is now recognised as a classic in the field of health psychology.

The rationale and objectives of Cohen et al.'s (1991) study were inspired by literature from three broad perspectives on stress and health – namely, the biological, environmental, and psychological perspectives – that developed in a relatively independent fashion across the 20th century. These perspectives are briefly outlined below.

THE BIOLOGICAL PERSPECTIVE

The biological perspective on stress and health was pioneered by Walter Cannon, a physiology professor from Harvard Medical School (Cannon, 1939/1963). Cannon's main assertion was that changes in the outer world that threaten to change the body's internal environment activate self-regulated physiological adjustments aimed at either avoiding the threat or restoring the former state. He defined this general process as *homeostasis*. Cannon also postulated that different threats would lead to different emotional reactions, which in turn would prompt different types of physiological adjustments. He proposed, for instance, that threats triggering either anger or fear lead to deeper respiration or the shifting of the blood away from the stomach and intestines to the heart, the central nervous system, and the muscles. This particular response – which Cannon called *fight or flight* – was assumed to allow the individual to mobilise mental and physical abilities in order to face the task of either fighting or escaping effectively.

The endocrinologist Hans Selye developed Cannon's theory and produced a more nuanced expression of the biological perspective on research about stress and health. He argued that a living organism that is exposed to noxious agents and stressors for a prolonged period of time will react with a universal pattern of physiological responses aimed at maintaining homeostasis. Selye contended that this innate protective reaction, which he defined as *general adaptation syndrome* (Selye, 1956), is based on three stages. The first stage concerns the 'alarm reaction'. This initial response of the body to a perceived threat is characterised by a state of physiological arousal that prepares the organism for a fight-or-flight response. In the second stage, called 'resistance', arousal decreases and the body tries to adapt to the stressor. The various forms of tissue damage and vulnerability to illness associated with this attempt at resisting the stressor were defined as 'diseases of adaptation'. If the stressor does not subside and the resistance stage lasts too long, the organism will move to the third stage: 'exhaustion'. This is characterised by a depletion of bodily resources and 'adaptive energy', accompanied by a decline in the organism's ability to respond to stressors, and an increased likelihood of diseases such as cardiovascular problems, arthritis, and asthma, and ultimately death.

THE ENVIRONMENTAL PERSPECTIVE

Cannon and Selye's work demonstrating the effects of environmental factors on health had a strong impact on researchers, especially those with an interest in psychosomatic medicine and social psychiatry. These researchers conceptualised environmental factors in terms of particular 'life events', and created instruments aimed at discovering the normative level of stress associated with each particular event. This allowed the investigation of the effects of single events or classes of events, as well as the accumulated effects of a series of events, on the onset of disease.

This approach was pioneered by Holmes and Rahe (1967), who created the *Social Readjustment Rating Scale* (SRRS). This scale listed 43 events (e.g., revision of personal habits, death of spouse, fired at work) commonly linked to the inception of illness. Holmes and Rahe proposed that the level of stress associated with an event was proportional to the degree of change required to adapt to the event itself. Events entailing a greater 'change from the existing steady state' (1967, p. 217) required a greater adaptive effort and therefore caused a greater level of stress. A study conducted by Holmes and Masuda (1974) explored the magnitude of the change required by each of the 43 events, which was expressed in *life change units* (LCU). The event with the highest LCU was found to be *death of a spouse* (100 LCU). Other events with relatively high LCU were *divorce* (73 LCU) and *jail term* (63 LCU). At the lower end there were events such as *holidays* (13 LCU) and *minor violations of the law* (11 LCU).

Holmes and Rahe's (1967) approach was criticised for portraying life events as being 'objectively' stressful, thereby ignoring the subjective significance of the events (Horowitz et al., 1979). In an attempt to address these issues, Brown and Harris (1986) developed the *Life Events and Difficulties Schedule* (LEDS). This instrument was based on a semi-structured interview aimed at eliciting a detailed account of any reported event together with the meaning and importance attached to it by the respondent. However, the researchers also compared a respondent's appraisal of an event with what it was assumed to be the typically expected appraisal. Clearly, while acknowledging the importance of the subjective meaning attached to an event, the LEDS proved to be yet another instrument that assumed the existence of an 'objective' level of stress produced by specific events.

THE PSYCHOLOGICAL PERSPECTIVE

Researchers bringing a psychological perspective to the study of stress and health contended that a given life event does not generate an objective, universal level of stress. On the contrary, the stress produced by an event will depend on how that event is construed by the particular individual. The most prominent and influential proponents of this approach were Richard Lazarus and Susan Folkman (1984). These authors defined stress as: 'a relationship between the person and the environment that is appraised by the person as taxing or exceeding his or her resources and endangering his or her well-being' (p. 21). This definition conceptualises stress as a complex *transaction* where factors concerning the characteristics of the situation (novelty, predictability, ambiguity, time in relation to the life-cycle), as well as factors related to the individual (commitments, beliefs), will be responsible for the *subjective* appraisal of the transaction. Lazarus and Folkman considered cognitive appraisal as largely *evaluative*, and postulated the existence of two types of appraisal, which received the names of *primary* and *secondary* appraisal respectively.

Primary appraisal concerns the evaluation of the specific meaning of the individual/environment transaction and the significance of that transaction for the individual's well-being. This is like asking oneself: 'Am I in trouble or being benefited, now or in the future, and in what way?' A transaction may be appraised as stressful either because the individual has already sustained some damage, as in the case of illness or loss of a loved one, or because the individual is anticipating harm or loss, or because the person can see potential for gain or growth.

Secondary appraisal occurs when a transaction is perceived as stressful and one must evaluate how the situation can be managed. The fundamental question in this case is: 'what, if anything, can be done about it?' Importantly, asking what can be done about a stressful or challenging situation implies the evaluation of *coping* options. Lazarus and Folkman defined coping as 'constantly changing cognitive and behavioral efforts to manage specific external and/or internal demands that are appraised as taxing or exceeding the resources of the person' (1984, p. 141), and proposed that coping strategies can be either problem-focused or emotion-focused. *Problem-focused* coping strategies aim at managing or changing the problem causing the distress. Importantly, these strategies do not always imply acting upon the external environment. In fact, they may be directed at the self, such as when an individual decides to learn new skills and procedures that might help them cope with the perceived stressor. *Emotion-focused* coping strategies concern the regulation of the emotional response to the problem through, for instance, minimisation, avoidance, selective attention, or positive comparison.

DETAILED OVERVIEW

PSYCHOLOGICAL STRESS AND SUSCEPTIBILITY TO THE COMMON COLD: THE COHEN ET AL. (1991) STUDY

By the end of the 1980s, the three perspectives outlined above contributed to an integrated assumption that was widely endorsed by researchers. According to this assumption, the perceived inability to cope with environmental demands produces negative psychological states, which in turn lead to changes in the immune system that suppress host resistance to infection and increase risk of illness. This hypothesis was consistent with results stemming from prospective studies that found a link between family stressors and the occurrence of respiratory problems in family members. For instance, in a study involving 58 young children in North Carolina, Boyce et al. (1977) found life changes within family routines (e.g., morning rituals, meals, homecoming) to be strongly associated with both severity and duration of respiratory illnesses. Another study, this time involving 235 members of 94 Australian families assessed over a period of six months for stressful life events, found that perceived stress was associated with significantly more symptom days of respiratory illness (e.g., runny nose, sore throat, hoarse cough, fever: Graham et al., 1986).

However, in their paper on psychological stress and cold susceptibility, Cohen et al. (1991) pointed out two serious limitations of these earlier studies. First, they argued that people exposed to many stressful events may also be just more likely to come into contact with cold and influenza viruses. Second, they suggested that possible mechanisms explaining why stress might influence susceptibility were not considered. Cohen and his colleagues addressed these limitations by (i) using an innovative research paradigm based on the controlled exposure of research participants to rhinovirus and subsequently observing participants' health status under quarantine conditions, and (ii) exploring potential mediators of the link between psychological stress and illness susceptibility.

STUDY METHOD

Study participants were 420 (154 men and 266 women) healthy individuals aged 18–54 years. They were asked to stay for a few weeks at the Common Cold Unit in Salisbury, a southern English town. On arrival, participants took a blood test for immune assessment and completed a variety of measures.

The predictor variable, *psychological stress*, was assessed with three measures that were eventually combined into a single stress index. First, participants went through a list of 67 major stressful events, some of which could have happened to the participant themselves and some to others they were close to, and indicated the specific events during the previous 12 months that had exerted a negative impact on their own lives. Second, participants reported the intensity of each of 15 negative emotions (e.g., nervous, sad, angry) during the preceding week. The third measure of psychological stress was the 10-item *Perceived Stress Scale* (Cohen & Williamson, 1988). This was a shortened version of the 14-item scale originally designed by Cohen, Kamarck, and Mermelstein (1983). This scale had been created to overcome limitations of instruments that tried to assess stress objectively, and embraced a conception of stress as stemming from one's subjective perception of the stressfulness of events (Sidebar 5.1 presents details of the construction and nature of this important scale).

Sidebar 5.1. The Perceived Stress Scale

Cohen, Kamarck, and Mermelstein (1983) were concerned about the psychometric limitations of existing measures of objective and subjective stress. They noted that measures of objective stress assumed that events are, in and of themselves, the precipitating cause of illness. This was in contradiction with work demonstrating that pathology is caused by the way in which the event is subjectively appraised on the basis of personal and contextual factors (Lazarus & Folkman, 1984). Scales of subjective stress had two major problems. First, these scales assumed that an individual's global perceived stress broadly coincides with the number of stressful events reported. Second, these scales failed to take into account chronic stress from ongoing life circumstances, as well as stress produced by events not listed on the scale, expectations about future events, and events occurring to close friends and family.

Cohen and his colleagues took a different approach. They produced a *Perceived Stress Scale* (PSS) based on items asking participants how often, in the last month, they had felt unable to cope with events that appeared: unpredictable (e.g., 'In the

(Continued)

(Continued)

last month, how often have you been upset because of something that happened unexpectedly?'); uncontrollable ('In the last month, how often have you been angered because of things that were outside of your control?'); and overloading (e.g., 'In the last month, how often have you felt difficulties were piling up so high that you could not overcome them?'). This scale overcomes limitations of both objective measures of stress, by focusing entirely on the appraisal of events rather than the events in themselves, and subjective measures of stress, by allowing participants to think about any sort of event, including events concerning close others.

An important reason behind the creation of the PSS was to have an instrument that could provide valuable 'information about the relationship between stress and pathology' (Cohen et al., 1983, p. 385). To ensure that this was indeed the case, the researchers conducted two validation studies. These studies revealed that the link between PSS and physical symptoms was reduced but remained statistically significant after psychological symptoms were controlled for, thereby confirming that the PSS did not confound stress appraisal and pathology. Also, importantly, these studies demonstrated that PSS, while correlated with life events, predicted mental and physical health symptoms better than life-event scores.

The PSS scale has been extremely well received by the research community, at least if it is judged from the numerous translations of it, and from the citations received by the 1983 paper where the scale first appeared, which are currently more than 33,000.

Cohen and his colleagues also assessed a set of variables that could provide alternative explanations for the hypothesised relationship between psychological stress and cold. These included serological status (i.e., the amount of antibodies to the specific virus that participants would eventually be exposed to), some demographic variables, allergic status, weight, the season, the number of participants housed together, and whether any participants housed in the same apartment were infected.

Other measures concerned variables that could play a role in the link between psychological stress and susceptibility to cold. These were personality, health practices, white-cell counts, and immunoglobulin levels. Concerning *personality*, researchers focused on three aspects, namely self-esteem, personal control, and extroversion/introversion. The latter was deemed especially important as a control variable, because of evidence suggesting a greater vulnerability to cold among introverted people (Totman et al., 1980). Regarding *health practices*, researchers assessed nicotine intake (through cotinine levels), alcohol consumption, exercise, quality of sleep, and dietary practices. White-cell counts and immunoglobulin levels were assessed by performing blood assays.

Subsequently, 394/420 participants were given nasal drops containing a low dose of one of five respiratory viruses (rhinovirus Types 2, 9, and 14; respiratory syncytial virus; or coronavirus 229E), with the remaining 26 participants receiving saline drops. The viral doses were meant to resemble those that are common in person-to-person transmission. Participants were quarantined in large apartments, either alone or with one or two others, for two days before and seven days after receiving the nasal drops. During the whole quarantine period, participants were examined daily by a clinician for respiratory signs and symptoms (e.g., sneezing, watering of the eyes, nasal obstruction, sinus pain, cough). The number of facial tissues used by participants was also counted. Approximately 28 days after the challenge, participants went through a second immune assessment (blood was taken by participants' own physicians and sent to the Common Cold Unit).

STUDY FINDINGS

After the study, a physician judged whether participants had symptoms indicating the presence of a clinical cold. Of those exposed to a virus, 148 (38%) were found to have a clinical cold, with the highest incidence observed among those who had received coronavirus (61.1%) and the lowest among those who had been given rhinovirus Type 9 (23.3%). None of the 26 participants who were given saline drops developed a cold.

The focal analysis of the study was obviously concerned with the link between psychological stress and susceptibility. This analysis showed that the likelihood of developing a cold after the virus challenge was greater among those with higher scores on the stress index. Specifically, participants with a score in the highest quartile were 2.16 times more likely to develop a cold than those in the lowest quartile, after statistically partialling out the effects of all control variables. Importantly, these effects were the same across all five types of virus to which participants were exposed (see Figure 5.1).

The same effects were also found for participants with and without virus-specific antibodies at baseline. Specifically, among participants with a positive serological status (i.e., participants who had the virus-specific antibodies at baseline), a cold was developed by 18.7% of those with low stress (i.e., stress below the median value) and 25.5% of those with high stress (i.e., stress above the median value). Regarding participants with a negative serological status (i.e., participants who did not have the virus-specific antibodies at baseline), a cold was developed by 43.7% of those with low stress and by 55.2% of those with high stress. The analyses also showed similar effects for participants housed with someone who became infected and participants without any infected apartment mate. Specifically, among those not housed with an infected person, a cold was developed by 20.8% of participants with low stress and 32.6% of participants with high stress. For those who had an infected person in their house, a cold was developed by 37.2% and 44.6% of participants respectively with low stress and with high stress. All these results were obtained after adjusting for several control variables (e.g., age, sex, allergic status).

The researchers also examined factors that might mediate the link between psychological stress and cold. However, neither white-cell populations nor total immunoglobulin levels mediated this link. Also, and somewhat surprisingly, not

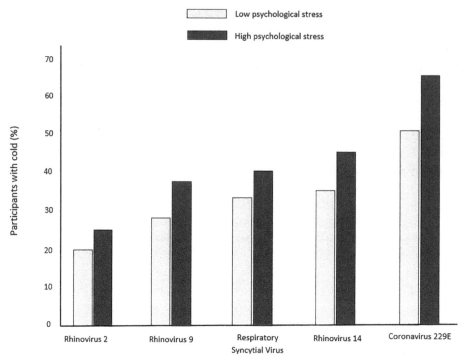

Figure 5.1 Participants with low psychological stress (index values below the median) and high psychological stress (index values above the median) who developed a cold in each challenge-virus group

Adapted from Figure 3 in Cohen, Tyrrell, and Smith (1991)

even unhealthy practices, such as smoking or drinking excessively, could explain the relationship between stress and cold. The researchers also considered the possibility that developing a cold might result not from different reactions to stressors, but from differences in some of the personality characteristics that were assessed. However, data analyses confirmed that this was not the case.

STUDY CONCLUSIONS

The study unambiguously demonstrated that greater psychological stress is associated with increased susceptibility to the common cold virus. However, contrary to expectations, there was no evidence that individuals who were more stressed were more likely to catch the cold because they were more inclined to adopt unhealthy behaviours. Even the immune measures assessed in the study did not mediate the link between psychological stress and susceptibility. The question of why stress is linked to susceptibility was therefore unanswered.

FOLLOW-UP STUDIES

Encouraged by the results produced by this study, Cohen and his colleagues conducted four additional studies, all based on the exposure of participants to rhinovirus. These studies further explored the role of immunity in the link between stress and susceptibility, and investigated the influence of psychosocial variables (i.e., interpersonal relations and child socioeconomic environment) on stress, coping, and health. The original study together with these additional studies are now known as the 'common cold studies' (see Sidebar 5.2).

Concerning immunity specifically, the studies broadly suggested that under chronic stress, immune cells become insensitive to cortisol, thereby making the body incapable of turning off the immune system's production of inflammatory chemicals (Cohen, 2021). However, the clearest results stemming from the studies concerned the implications of social relationships and child socioeconomic environment for stress, coping, and health (Cohen, 2005). It is to these specific results that this chapter now turns.

Sidebar 5.2. The Common Cold Studies

Cohen and his colleagues conducted five studies in which healthy participants were exposed to common cold viruses. The research paradigm constituted a novel and powerful methodological innovation, and has been praised for its precision in how stress and a variety of psychosocial factors related to stress were operationalised (O'Connor et al., 2021). Each study produced rich data that were published in multiple papers. Here are the main characteristics of these studies.

- *British Cold Study* – Conducted from 1986 to 1989. Involved 399 English participants aged 18–54 years. Primary focus was on psychological stress and its association with common cold susceptibility.

- *Pittsburgh Cold Study 1* – Conducted from 1993 to 1996. Involved 276 participants aged 18–55 from Pittsburgh, Pennsylvania. Extended the British Cold Study by assessing the effects of stressful life events and social integration on susceptibility to common cold.

- *Pittsburgh Cold Study 2* – Conducted from 1997 to 2001. Involved 334 participants aged 18–54 from Pittsburgh, Pennsylvania. Focus was on the role of childhood socioeconomic status (SES) and personality in common cold susceptibility.

- *Pittsburgh Mind-Body Center Study* – Conducted from 2000 to 2004. Involved 193 participants aged 21–55. Focus was on the role of social interactions, mood, and health behaviours in common cold susceptibility.

- *Pittsburgh Cold Study 3* – Conducted from 2007 to 2011. Involved 213 participants aged 18–55 from Pittsburgh, Pennsylvania. Extended work on the role of childhood environment in common

(Continued)

(Continued)

cold susceptibility by including additional retrospective measures of childhood and adolescent experience (e.g., parental social participation, family structure).

Collectively, these studies compellingly demonstrated that psychological stress is linked to an increased vulnerability to infectious diseases in individuals who are otherwise healthy. Data stemming from these studies strongly suggest that the inability of the body to turn off the immune system's production of inflammatory chemicals is at least partly responsible for this link. These studies have also confirmed that negative social relationships constitute a source of stress, increasing vulnerability to infectious disease, while positive relationships act as buffers against stress, thereby decreasing vulnerability. Finally, these studies have shown that low socioeconomic status in early childhood increases vulnerability.

IMPACT OF SOCIAL RELATIONSHIPS AND CHILD SOCIO-ECONOMIC ENVIRONMENT ON SUSCEPTIBILITY TO INFECTIOUS DISEASES

INTERPERSONAL DIFFICULTIES INCREASE SUSCEPTIBILITY

The Pittsburgh Cold Study 1 (Cohen et al., 1998) explored the effects of life stressors on common cold susceptibility, and found that participants with chronic stressors were at a greater risk of catching a cold when compared with participants without chronic stressors. However, the extent of risk varied on the basis of the type of chronic stressors reported by participants. For instance, when focusing on stressors lasting for six months or more, risk of catching a cold after the viral challenge was almost three times as large for those having interpersonal difficulties with family and friends, compared to those with either other types of stressors or no stressors at all. This is fully consistent with research demonstrating that relationships characterised by abuse, discrimination, exploitation, and bullying can have marked impacts on health (Boden et al., 2016; Cuevas et al., 2020).

A DIVERSITY OF RELATIONAL CONTEXTS DECREASES SUSCEPTIBILITY

In the Pittsburgh Cold Study 1, participants completed a social network index before undergoing the viral challenge (Cohen et al., 1997). The index counted the number of different relational contexts (parent, spouse, friend, workplace) in which a participant was involved. Results showed the risk of catching a cold for the least connected participants (i.e., those involved in three or fewer relational contexts) to be 4.2 times larger than the risk for the most connected ones (i.e., those involved in six or more relational contexts). Since a relational context may, in principle, be problematic, and therefore detrimental to health, it can be assumed that the overall beneficial effect of greater connectedness is due to the fact that most relational contexts tend to have a positive valence (see Jetten, Bentley, and Young, Chapter 9, this volume, for a detailed discussion of the impact of social connectedness on health).

SUPPORTIVE RELATIONSHIPS BUFFER THE NEGATIVE IMPACT OF INTERPERSONAL DIFFICULTIES ON SUSCEPTIBILITY

Analyses conducted by Cohen, Janicki-Deverts, Turner, and Doyle (2015) on data collected in the Pittsburgh Cold Study 3 explored the possibility that the negative impact of interpersonal conflict could be buffered by positive aspects of social relationships, such as perceived support and hugs. Results confirmed that perceived social support and received hugs acted as buffers against susceptibility to infectious disease induced by interpersonal conflict. Specifically, an increased frequency of conflict was found to predict a rise in infection risk, but perceived support attenuated the risk, with hugging explaining 32% of the attenuating effect of perceived support. In short, hugging effectively conveyed perceived social support.

LOW SOCIOECONOMIC STATUS IN EARLY CHILDHOOD IS LINKED TO GREATER SUSCEPTIBILITY

Pittsburgh Cold Study 2 focused specifically on the effects of childhood socioeconomic environment on susceptibility. Data analyses conducted by Cohen et al. (2004) revealed low income and wealth during early childhood to be associated with decreased resistance to colds in adulthood. Specifically, susceptibility to colds decreased with the number of childhood years during which a participant's parents owned their home. Furthermore, having had parents who did not own their home during a participant's early life but did during a participant's adolescent years, still put a participant at the same increased risk as those participants whose parents never owned their home. This points to low socioeconomic status in early childhood years as a particularly noxious factor in terms of building resistance to infectious disease.

INTEGRATING DIFFERENT RESEARCH PERSPECTIVES ON STRESS AND COPING

Taken together, the common cold studies have provided rich insights into the processes involved in the link between stress and health. These insights have contributed to a greater integration of the biological, environmental, and psychological perspectives on stress and health. Such an integrative perspective can be represented in terms of a stage model of the processes leading from life events to disease. Below, I outline the various stages in this model (see Figure 5.2 for a diagrammatic illustration), which is broadly based on the model proposed by Cohen, Gianaros, and Manuch, (2016).

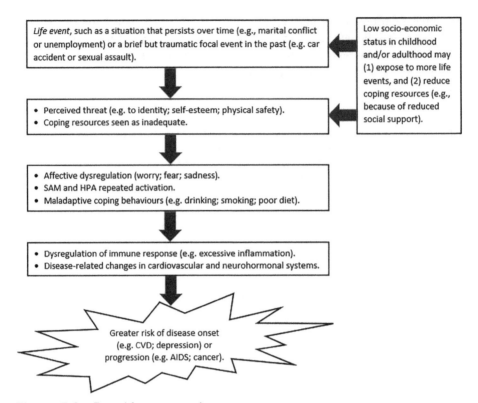

Figure 5.2 From life events to disease

Broadly based on Cohen et al.'s (2016) stage model of the stress process

The model poses life events as the origins of stress and disease, with events that involve other people having the potential to be especially noxious. This is what emerged from Pittsburgh Cold Study 1 (Cohen et al., 1998) discussed above, and more recent studies have largely confirmed these findings. For example, in a longitudinal study of adolescent girls, Slavich et al. (2020) found that problematic interpersonal events increased depression. This is consistent with research revealing the health-damaging implications of particularly aversive forms of interpersonal interactions, such as child maltreatment (Edwards et al., 2003), workplace bullying (Hansen et al., 2013), and discrimination based on either ethnicity (Harris et al., 2006) or sexual orientation (Denton et al., 2014). However, in line with the psychological perspective on stress and health, the model specifies that a particular event will trigger a stress response only if the event is simultaneously perceived as a threat to important aspects of the self, such as identity, self-esteem, aspirations, or physical safety, and as exceeding one's coping resources.

Importantly, the model emphasises that people with low socioeconomic status are typically exposed to a greater number of unfavourable life events, such as abuse, discrimination, accidents, and unemployment (e.g., Walsh et al., 2019). In addition, there is evidence that people with low socioeconomic status tend to have lower perceived availability of support (Weyers et al., 2008), and to engage more often in downward social comparisons, which create and reinforce feelings of inadequacy and deficiency (Layte & Whelan, 2014). The model assumes that lower perceived support and more frequent downward social comparisons will increase the likelihood of events being perceived as threatening and unmanageable, and therefore as increasing risk of illness. This is consistent with findings from Pittsburgh Cold Study 2 (Cohen et al., 2004), described above.

Perceiving life events as threatening may have three interrelated consequences. First, an individual's affective sphere may become dysregulated. One may engage in ruminative thinking about the event and its possible consequences, and feel preoccupied, hopeless, or sad. Second, perceiving a life event as threatening leads to repeated activation of the sympathetic adrenal medullary (SAM) axis and the hypothalamic pituitary adrenal (HPA) system. The activation of the SAM axis involves the adrenal medulla and the release of adrenaline/noradrenaline. This creates physiological arousal and produces the fight-or-flight response. The activation of the HPA system involves the adrenal cortex producing corticosteroids such as cortisol, which help the body to return to a steady state once the threat is over. While the activation of these two systems is a highly adaptive response to acute stress, when problematic life events persist and danger does not cease, the repeated activation of these systems can be hazardous to health (Sapolski, 2004). Third, life events that are perceived as a threat may lead one to engage in maladaptive behaviours, such as smoking tobacco and alcohol consumption (Ng & Jeffery, 2003), or eating foods that are high in sugar and fat (Torres & Nowson, 2007), which are meant to help one cope with the threat but will actually damage health.

At this point, the model postulates that emotion dysregulation, repeated activation of physiological systems, and maladaptive coping behaviours lead to disease-related changes in cardiovascular and neurohormonal systems, and to dysregulation of immune response. It is worth emphasising that research has given special attention to the effects that stress may have on inflammation, which is an important indicator of dysregulation of immune response (see Weinman, Broadbent, & Booth, Chapter 6, this volume). For instance, Kiecolt-Glaser et al. (2005) found couples' blister wounds to heal substantially more slowly following marital conflicts than after supportive interactions.

Finally, the model highlights that immune dysregulation and changes in cardiovascular and neurohormonal systems will increase the risk of either disease *onset*, as has been observed for cardiovascular disease and depression, or disease *progression*, as is likely to be case with, for instance, HIV and cancer (Cohen, Janicki-Deverts, & Miller, 2007).

It is worth noting that the proposed link between perceived stress and illness via health behaviours was not confirmed by the Cohen, Tyrrell, and Smith (1991) classic study. However, this study took into account only recent stressful events and focused specifically on infectious diseases. There are, however, good reasons to assume that chronic stress may lead to various types of illnesses via health behaviours. For instance, literature on stress and health in indigenous Australians suggests that chronic stress may lead to obesity, metabolic syndromes, and cardiovascular disorders via unhealthy diet and alcohol and drug abuse (Sarnyai et al., 2016).

To conclude, it is necessary to emphasise that, although the model includes an ordered series of stages, not all the stages are necessarily required (Cohen et al., 2016). For instance, one may feel capable of coping with a given environmental demand through constant monitoring, which may lead one to think that the demand does not pose a threat. However, a demand requiring prolonged monitoring may deplete cognitive capacities, which may in turn impact negatively on health-related decisions (Cohen et al., 1986). Also, although the model is unidirectional, various types of feedback loops may take place. For instance, certain coping behaviours, such as excessive alcohol consumption, could cause life events such as loss of a job or marital conflict, which in turn can present a psychological threat (Leonard & Eiden, 2007).

CONCLUSIONS

By the end of the 1980s, the combination of three major perspectives – biological, environmental, and psychological – contributed to a broadly consensual understanding of the processes involved in stress and health. Specifically, it was assumed that an individual's perceived inability to cope with environmental demands produces aversive psychological states, leading in turn to the suppression of host resistance to infection and increased risk of illness. The 1991 classic study discussed in this chapter compellingly demonstrated the plausibility of such an assumption, by showing that greater psychological stress makes people more susceptible to developing an infectious illness, through the use of a novel and powerful research paradigm. The results of this study stimulated a series of follow-up studies which shed further light on the processes – especially the psychosocial ones – linking stress to infectious disease. According to O'Connor, Thayer, and Vedhara (2021), the 1991 study together with the follow-up ones have revolutionised the field of stress and health, and the evidence they have produced 'has done much to quash the skeptical view that stress is a modern-day complaint with no lasting consequences for health' (p. 678). These studies not only hold a central position in the health psychology literature, but have been key in the development of psychoneuroimmunology (Cohen & Herbert, 1996), and have contributed to the credibility and establishment of the biopsychosocial approach to health and illness (Engel, 1977).

Undoubtedly, the current understanding of stress and health can be enriched in various ways. For instance, the common cold studies, and the literature on stress and health more generally, have typically focused on the role played by either interpersonal (micro-level) or socioeconomic (macro-level) processes. However, as contended by the social identity approach to health (Haslam et al., 2018), people's interactions and interpersonal relationships often take place within the context of the social groups of which they are a part (family, school, workplace, etc.). Importantly, the extent to which one subjectively identifies with these groups determines whether relationships and encounters within the context of these groups are stress-producing or stress-buffering, and are therefore beneficial or detrimental to health. So, for instance, greater identification with a group appears to be linked with both lower psychological stress (Sani et al., 2012) and lower depressive symptomatology (Sani et al., 2015). This points to the importance of paying greater attention to what we could consider as meso-level processes, in research and theory about stress and health.

To conclude, thanks to Cohen et al.'s classic study and the common cold studies that it stimulated, work on stress and health has made considerable progress across the last three decades. We now know for certain that stress and health are linked, and we understand much about the complex processes that account for this relationship. However, important questions remain unanswered in relation to each single stage in the process. To name just three issues concerning life events, we don't know whether past stressful events moderate responses to current ones, whether specific types of stressful events are linked to specific disease, and how different types of stressful events may impact health across different development stages (Cohen, Murphy, & Prather, 2019). A task of future research will be to address these challenging questions.

FURTHER READING

Cooper, C. L., & Dewe, P. (2004). *Stress: A brief history*. Oxford: Blackwell.

This is a relatively short, yet highly readable and informative text on the history of stress research.

Kabat-Zinn, J. (2013). Full catastrophe living: How to cope with stress, pain and illness using mindfulness meditation (revised ed.). London: Piaktus; New York: Bantam Books.

If you are interested in mindful meditation as an evidence-based technique for coping with stressful life circumstances, then there is nothing better than this one. This is the most recent and updated edition.

Lazarus, R. S., & Folkman, S. (1984). *Stress, appraisal, and coping*. New York: Springer.

It remains to date the most inspiring book about the psychology of stress and coping.

Sapolski, R. M. (2004). *Why zebras don't get ulcers* (3rd ed.). New York: Henry Holt.

This is an enjoyable and informative book on stress and health from a predominantly biological perspective. The first edition of this book appeared in 1994, but I suggest you read the third edition published in 2004.

The Common Cold Project

For plenty of details about the objectives, design and measures of all the cold studies conducted by Cohen and his colleagues, see the website 'The Common Cold Project': cmu.edu/common-cold-project/.

REFERENCES

Boden, J. M., van Stockum, S., Horwood, L. J., & Fergusson, D. M. (2016). Bullying victimization in adolescence and psychotic symptomatology in adulthood: Evidence from a 35-year study. *Psychological Medicine*, 46, 1311–1320. doi: 10.1017/ S0033291715002962.

Boyce, W. T., Jensen, E. W., Cassel, J. C., Collier, A. M., Smith, A. H., & Ramey, C. T. (1977). Influence of life events and family routines on childhood respiratory tract illness. *Pediatrics*, *60*, 609-615. doi: 10.1542/peds.60.4.609

Brown, G. W., & Harris, T. O. (1986). Establishing causal links: The Bedford College studies of depression. In H. Katsching (Ed.), *Life events and psychiatric disorders*. Cambridge: Cambridge University Press.

Cannon, W. B. (1939/1963). *The wisdom of the body*. New York: Norton.

Cohen, S. (2005). The Pittsburgh Common Cold Studies: Psychosocial predictors of susceptibility to respiratory infectious illness. *International Journal of Behavioral Medicine*, *12*, 123–131. http://repository.cmu.edu/psychology/274

Cohen, S. (2021). Psychosocial vulnerabilities to upper respiratory infectious illness: Implications for susceptibility to coronavirus disease 2019 (COVID-19). *Perspectives on Psychological Science*, *16*, 161–174. doi: 10.1177/1745691620942516

Cohen, S., Doyle, W. J., Skoner, D. P., Rabin, B. S., & Gwaltney, J. M. (1997). Social ties and susceptibility to the common cold. *JAMA*, *277*, 1940–1944. doi: 10.1001/jama.1997.03540480040036

Cohen, S., Doyle, W. J., Turner, R., Alper, C., & Skoner, D. P. (2004). Childhood socioeconomic status and host resistance to infectious illness in adulthood. *Psychosomatic Medicine*, *66*, 553–558. doi: 10.1097/01.psy.0000126200.05189.d3

Cohen, S., Evans, G. W., Krantz, D. S., & Stokols, D. (1986). *Behavior, health, and environmental stress*. New York: Plenum Press.

Cohen, S., Frank, E., Doyle, W. J., Skoner, D. P., Rabin, B. S., & Gwaltney, J. M. (1998). Types of stressors that increase susceptibility to the common cold in healthy adults. *Health Psychology*, *17*, 214–223. doi: 10.1037/0278-6133.17.3.214

Cohen, S., Gianaros, P. J., & Manuck, S. B. (2016). A stage model of stress and disease. *Perspectives on Psychological Science*, *11*, 456–463. doi: 10.1177/1745691616646305

Cohen, S., & Herbert, T. B. (1996). Psychological factors and physical disease from the perspective of human psychoneuroimmunology. *Annual Review of Psychology*, *47*, 113–142. doi: 10.1146/annurev.psych.47.1.113

Cohen, S., Janicki-Deverts, D., & Miller, G. E. (2007). Psychological stress and disease. *JAMA*, *298*, 1685–1687. doi: 10.1001/jama.298.14.1685

Cohen, S., Janicki-Deverts, D., Turner, R. B., & Doyle, W. J. (2015). Does hugging provide a stress-buffering social support? A study of susceptibility to upper respiratory infection and illness. *Psychological Science*, *26*, 135–147. doi: 10.1177/0956797614559284

Cohen, S., Kamarck, T., & Mermelstein, R. (1983). A global measure of perceived stress. *Journal of Health & Social Behavior*, *24*, 385–396. www.jstor.org/stable/2136404

Cohen, S., Murphy, M. L. M., & Prather, A. A. (2019). Ten surprising facts about stressful life events and disease risk. *Annual Review of Psychology*, *70*, 577–597. doi: 10.1146/annurev-psych-010418-102857

Cohen, S., Tyrrell, D. A. J., & Smith, A. P. (1991). Psychological stress and susceptibility to the common cold. *New England Journal of Medicine*, *325*, 606–612. doi: 10.1056/NEJM199108293250903

Cohen, S., & Williamson, G. (1988). Perceived stress in a probability sample of the United States. In S. Spacapan & S. Oskamp (Eds.), *The social psychology of health* (pp. 31–68). Newbury Park, CA: Sage.

Cuevas, A. G., Ong, A. D., Carvalho, K., Ho, T. et al. (2020). Discrimination and systemic inflammation: A critical review and synthesis. *Brain, Behavior, & Immunity*, *89*, 465–479. doi: 10.1016/j.bbi.2020.07.017

Denton, F. N., Rostosky, S. S., & Danner, F. (2014). Stigma-related stressors, coping self-efficacy, and physical health in lesbian, gay, and bisexual individuals. *Journal of Counseling Psychology*, *61*, 383–391. doi: 10.1037/a0036707

Edwards, V. J., Holden, G. W., Felitti, V. J., & Anda, R. F. (2003). Relationship between multiple forms of childhood maltreatment and adult mental health in community respondents: Results from the Adverse Childhood Experience study. *American Journal of Psychiatry*, *160*, 1453–1460. doi: 10.1176/appi.ajp.160.8.1453

Engel, G. L. (1977). The need for a new medical model: A challenge for biomedicine. *Science*, *196*, 129–136. doi: 10.1126/science.847460

Graham, N. M. H., Douglas, R. M., & Ryan, P. (1986). Stress and acute respiratory infection. *American Journal of Epidemiology*, *124*, 389–401. doi: 10.1093/oxford journals.aje.a114409

Hansen, Å. M., Hogh, A., Garde, A. H., & Persson, R. (2013). Workplace bullying and sleep difficulties: A 2-year follow-up study. *International Archives of Occupational & Environmental Health*, *3*, 1–10. doi: 10.1007/s00420-013-0860-2

Harris, R., Tobias, M., Jeffreys, M., Waldegrave, K., Karlsen, S., & Nazroo, J., (2006). Racism and health: The relationship between experience of racial discrimination and health in New Zealand. *Social Science & Medicine*, *63*, 1428–1441. doi: 10.1016/j.socscimed.2006.04.009

Haslam, C., Jetten, J., Cruwys, T., Dingle, G. A., & Haslam, S. A. (2018). *The new psychology of health: Unlocking the social cure*. London: Routledge. doi: 10.4324/9781315648569

Holmes, T. H., & Masuda, M. (1974). Life change and illness susceptibility. In B. S. Dohrenwend & B. P. Dohrenwend (Eds.), *Stressful life events: Their nature and effects* (pp. 45–72). New York: John Wiley and Sons.

Holmes, T. H., & Rahe, R. H. (1967). The social readjustment rating scale. *Journal of Psychosomatic Research*, *11*, 213–218. doi: 10.1016/0022-3999(67)90010-4

Horowitz, M., Wilner, N., & Alvarez, W. (1979). Impact of event scales: A measure of subjective stress. *Psychosomatic Medicine*, *41*, 209–218. 0033-3174/79/03020910/$0l .75

Kiecolt-Glaser, J. K., Loving, T. J., Stowell, J. R., Malarkey, W. B., Lemeshow, S., Dickinson, S. L., & Glaser, R. (2005). Hostile marital interactions, proinflammatory cytokine production, and wound healing. *Archives of General Psychiatry*, *62*, 1377–1384. doi:10.1001/archpsyc.62.12.1377

Layte, R., & Whelan, C. T. (2014). Who feels inferior? A test of the status anxiety hypothesis of social inequalities in health. *European Sociological Review, 30*, 10. doi: 10.1093/esr/jcu057

Lazarus, R. S., & Folkman, S. (1984). *Stress, appraisal, and coping*. New York: Springer.

Leonard, K. E., & Eiden, R. D. (2007). Marital and Family Processes in the Context of Alcohol Use and Alcohol Disorders. *Annual Review of Clinical Psychology*, *3*, 285–310. doi: 10.1146/annurev.clinpsy.3.022806.091424

Ng, D. M., & Jeffery, R. W. (2003). Relationships Between Perceived Stress and Health Behaviors in a Sample of Working Adults. *Health Psychology*, *22*, 638–642. doi:10.1037/0278-6133.22.6.638

O'Connor, D. B., Thayer, J. F., & Vedhana, K (2021). Stress and health: A review of psychobiological processes. *Annual Review of Psychology*, *72*, 663–688. doi: 10.1146/annurev-psych-062520-122331

Sani, F., Herrera, M., Wakefield, J. R. H., Boroch, O., & Gulyas, C. (2012). Comparing social contact and group identification as predictors of mental health. *British Journal of Social Psychology*, *51*, 781–790. doi: 10.1111/j.2044-8309.2012.02101.x

Sani, F., Madhok, V., Norbury, M., Dugard, P., & Wakefield, J. R. H. (2015). Greater number of group identifications is associated with lower odds of being depressed: Evidence from a Scottish community sample. *Social Psychiatry & Psychiatric Epidemiology*, *50*, 1389–1397. doi: 10.1007/s00127-15-1076-4

Sapolski, R. M. (2004). *Why zebras don't get ulcers* (3rd ed.). New York: Henry Holt.

Sarnyai, Z., Berger, M., & Jawan, I. (2016). Allostatic load mediates the impact of stress and trauma on physical and mental health in Indigenous Australians. *Australasian Psychiatry*, *24*, 72–75. doi: 10.1177/1039856215620025

Selye, H. (1956). *The stress of life*. New York: McGraw-Hill.

Slavich, G. M., Giletta, M., Helms, S. W., Hastings, P. D., Rudolph, K. D., Nock, M. K., & Prinstein, M. J. (2020). Interpersonal life stress, inflammation, and depression in adolescence: Testing Social Signal Transduction Theory of Depression. *Depression & Anxiety*, *37*, 179–193. doi: 10.1002/da.22987

Torres, S. J., & Nowson, C. A. (2007). Relationship between stress, eating behavior, and obesity. *Nutrition*, *23*, 887–894. doi: 10.1016/j.nut.2007.08.008

Totman, R., Kiff, J., Reed, S. E., & Craig, J. W. (1980). Predicting experimental colds in volunteers from different measures of recent life stress. *Journal of Psychosomatic Research*, *24*, 155–163. doi: 10.1016/0022-3999(80)90037-9

Walsh, D., McCartney, G., Smith, M., & Armour, G. (2019). Relationship between childhood socioeconomic position and adverse childhood experiences (ACEs): A systematic review. *Journal of Epidemiology & Community Health*, *73*, 1087–1093. doi: 10.1136/jech-2019-212738

Weyers, S., Dragano, N., Mobus, S., Beck, E. M., Stang, A., Mohlenkamp, S., Jockel, K. H., Erbel, R., & Siegrist, J. (2008). Low socio-economic position is associated with poor social networks and social support: Results from the Heinz Nixdorf Recall Study. *International Journal for Equity in Health*, *7*, 13. doi: 10.1186/1475-9276-7-13

6

Psychoneuroimmunology: Revisiting Kiecolt-Glaser, Marucha, Malarkey, Mercado, and Glaser (1995)

Kiecolt-Glaser, J. K., Marucha, P. T., Malarkey, W. B., Mercado, A. M., & Glaser, R. (1995). Slowing of wound healing by psychological stress. *The Lancet, 346*, 1194–1196.

John Weinman, Elizabeth Broadbent, and Roger Booth

BACKGROUND

THE BIRTH OF PSYCHONEUROIMMUNOLOGY (PNI)

In 1960, George Engel, a psychiatrist working at the University of Rochester, New York, published a far-sighted paper entitled 'A unified concept of health and disease', in which he pointed out that all disease is biopsychosocial in nature and highlighted the need to expand our traditional biomedical models to encompass that notion (Engel, 1960). This was at the beginning of two decades of significant expansion of knowledge and understanding of immunology and the immune system: the functions of subsets of lymphocytes were recognised, Major Histocompatibility Complex (MHC) molecules (HLA in humans) were identified as controlling elements for antigen recognition and response, and immune hormones (cytokines) were discovered as key players in inflammation and immune regulation. However, the concensus view among immunologists at the time was that the immune system was largely self-regulating and autonomous within the living body.

Nevertheless, on the periphery of conventional immunology were researchers whose studies indicated that immune responsiveness and immune regulation might be widely integrated with other body systems and behaviours. One of the most influential researchers at this time was George Solomon, often now referred to as 'the father of psychoneuroimmunology'. Solomon, a psychiatrist, had been studying psychological factors in patients with the autoimmune disease rheumatoid arthritis, and teamed up with a clinical psychologist colleague at the University of California, San Francisco, Rudolf Moos, to conduct systematic studies of the life histories and personality characteristics of arthritis patients in an effort to understand the observed association between emotional states and the onset and course of the disease. Among the publications resulting from this work was a paper entitled 'Emotions, immunity, and disease: A speculative theoretical integration' (Solomon & Moos, 1964), which foreshadowed many key areas in what was to become the interdisciplinary field of psychoneuroimmunology (PNI). It also highlighted for Solomon the need to understand immunology and immunological techniques, and resulted in his spending time at two leading centres of immunological research – the Scripps Research Institute in San Diego, California, and the Walter and Eliza Hall Institute in Melbourne, Australia.

Cross-disciplinary collaborations are often beneficial because 'outsiders' can make naïve suggestions about a discipline that were previously 'unthinkable' to those steeped in the dogma of that particular field. For PNI, being an inherently multidisciplinary area, interdisciplinary collaborations were almost essential until the discipline had matured sufficiently for university-based PNI training programmes to be established (see Sidebar 6.1 for an important pioneering example). Further, experimental models were required in which causal changes in medically-relevant variables could be established. In the 1980s, the emergence of Human Immunodeficiency Virus (HIV) infections and the accompanying Acquired Immunodeficiency Syndrome (AIDS) provided such a model and, in the absence of effective treatments, researchers began exploring whether psychological, social, and behavioural factors were related to the trajectory of the disease and whether any of these could be modified to improve prognosis. Two key indicators of infection progression and immune compromise – HIV viral load and CD4 T lymphocyte numbers – were readily measurable in blood and provided convincing evidence of psycho–immune linkages in HIV infection (Chida & Vedhara, 2009). Concurrently, several imaginative ways to investigate stress effects on human immune-related variables associated with infections were being developed by researchers interested in PNI. For example, Sheldon Cohen and colleagues at the University of Pittsburg, published an important large study showing that perceived stress directly correlated with incidence of infection following intranasal inoculation of volunteers with common cold viruses (Cohen et al., 1991; see Sani, Chapter 5, this volume).

From the early days of PNI research, another interdisciplinary collaborative team that made a huge contribution to the field was set up by Janice Kiecolt-Glaser (a psychologist) and her husband Ronald Glaser (a microbiologist) at Ohio State University, Columbus, Ohio. 'Jan and Ron', as they were affectionately known in the field, developed imaginative and innovative ways of exploring psycho–neuro–immune relationships in human subjects. For example, their research revealed effects of such factors as daily stresses, chronic caregiving, marital discord, and emotional expression on immune measures such as circulating lymphocyte populations, circulating antibody concentrations specific for latent herpes viruses such as Epstein-Barr virus, and antibody responses to hepatitis B vaccination

(Kiecolt-Glaser & Glaser, 1995). Their studies contributed to the growing body of work demonstrating the importance of psychosocial factors as modulators of immune responses, particularly those associated with susceptibility to and recovery from infections.

By the last decade of the 20th century, accumulated data from studies involving laboratory animals and human participants clearly showed that PNI wasn't simply an interesting curiosity but, instead, constituted an important set of bidirectional effects – psychosocial processes affecting immune responsiveness and vice versa (Dantzer & Kelley, 2007) – affecting illness and disease, with potential for novel interventions to improve outcomes. The medical community was beginning to take notice and to consider whether there might be applications of PNI to medical areas beyond infection. Following an interdisciplinary round-table discussion on possible future research directions at their university, 'Jan and Ron' hit on the idea of exploring the effects of psychosocial effects on wound healing – a process with important immune and inflammatory components and known also to involve nervous system and neuroendocrine pathways.

DETAILED OVERVIEW

Their first study of wound healing (Kiecolt-Glaser et al., 1995), the classic study which is the focus of this chapter, assessed whether stress caused by caring for a relative with Alzheimer's disease had an effect on wound healing. In it, they studied 13 women caring for relatives with dementia and compared them with 13 control women matched for age and family income. The ages of the women ranged from 47 to 81 with a mean of 62 for the caregivers and 60 for the control group. The caregivers had been providing care for husbands or mothers for an average of 7.8 years, averaging around seven hours per day on caring activities. Kiecolt-Glaser and colleagues studied wound healing by applying a 3.5 mm punch biospy to the forearm of each woman, then removing the disc of skin from the biopsy area and applying a sterile dressing. Beginning a week after biopsy, they photographed the wounds every 2–8 days depending on participant availability, and also applied a hydrogen peroxide solution to the wound and noted whether or not the wound foamed. Hydrogen peroxide foams when it interacts with peroxidase enzymes in the tissue of a healing wound and so when there was no longer any foaming after peroxide application, they defined the wound as being completely healed. The results were dramatic: wound healing took significantly longer in caregivers than in controls (49 versus 39 days). Also, the differences in wound size were greatest early in the process of wound repair.

They also assessed aspects of immune function in the two groups of women by taking a blood sample before the initial biopsy, purifying and culturing the blood mononuclear cells (lymphocytes and monocytes), and stimulating them with various mitogens to activate them to synthesise interleukin-1B (IL-1B), which is an important proinflammatory cytokine involved in the early activation of immune and inflammatory responses and a key regulator of several physiological processes required for wound healing. They then measured the concentration of IL-1B messenger RNA in the cells as an indicator or how much of the cytokine they were producing. Again the results were dramatic. Cultured immune cells from caregivers produced significantly less IL-B mRNA than did cultured cells from the control group. Finally, caregivers reported significantly more stress on a perceived stress scale than did controls, but did not differ significantly in medication use or health behaviours that might affect wound healing.

As a pilot to explore psychological effects on wound healing, this study only used a small number of participants, but the two groups were well matched and the cytokine data were consistent with other studies from this research group that had shown immunological differences between stressed dementia caregivers and well-matched controls. Further, the relatively large effects seen in this study not only revealed a previously unknown PNI effect with important clinical implications, they opened the way for extensive future research in wound healing (outlined below). Although not discussed in this paper, in retrospect, the choice of using a regular application of hydrogen peroxide to assess wound healing may well have been a fortuitous one for such a pilot study, as it is conceivable that it slightly impaired and slowed healing rates, thereby accentuating the difference between the caregivers and controls.

Sidebar 6.1. Classical Conditioning of Immunity

A collaboration in the 1970s between Robert Ader (a behavioural psychologist) and Nicholas Cohen (an immunologist) at the University of Rochester, New York, resulted in a serendipitous discovery that had a profound influence on the trajectory of PNI. They were studying conditioned taste aversion in laboratory rats by giving them a sweet-tasting saccharin solution accompanied by an injection of the noxious drug, cyclophosphamide, which induced gastrointestinal upset. They found that some of the animals that were subsequently forced to drink the saccharin solution later died. Further, the magnitude of the rats' taste avoidance response and their mortality rate were directly related to the volume of saccharin solution consumed. As an immunologist, Cohen knew that cyclophosphamide, as well as inducing nausea, was a potent immunosuppressive drug. Cohen hypothesised that, in addition to conditioning the taste aversion response, cyclophosphamide might have been conditioning immunosuppressive effects. In other words, it was predicted that after the saccharin and cyclophosphamide pairings, the taste of saccharin alone was sufficient, through some sort of neuro-immune pathway, to suppress the immune system just as if the rats had been dosed with the immunosuppressive drug. Ader and Cohen confirmed this hypothesis in a controlled experiment showing that the behavioural conditioning process could suppress antibody responses in their rats (Ader & Cohen, 1975).

This work opened up the field of behavioural immunology and, over the following decade, there were many demonstrations of conditioned immune changes (both positively and negatively) in laboratory animals using a variety of conditioning stimuli and immune responses (Ader & Cohen, 1993). Ader went on to become the founder of the Psychoneuroimmunology Research Society, and he and Cohen remained highly influential figures in PNI throughout their research careers. However, although the conditioning studies generated considerable excitement and enthusiasm within the fledgling PNI research community, the effects were not large, and so conventional immunologists mostly considered the findings to be biological curiosities of little or no relevance to the immune system's role in disease processes. To counter this argument, Ader and Cohen applied their immune conditioning paradigm to a strain of laboratory mice that, left untreated, normally develop the lethal autoimmune disease, systemic lupus erythematosus (SLE) at a high rate. They were able to use conditioning to suppress the pathological autoimmune responses in these mice and so extend their survival (Ader & Cohen, 1982).

IMPACT AND INFLUENCE

The seminal paper by Kiecolt-Glaser et al. (1995) inspired a branch of research on psychological factors and wound healing that has advanced our knowledge of psychoneuroimmunology. The idea sparked subsequent research into different types of wound, alternative methods of assessing healing, and the effects of psychological interventions on stress and healing. These studies have shed light on potential mediating mechanisms, and strengthened evidence of causal links, with implications for clinical care. These issues will be considered in the remainder of the chapter.

It is useful to organise the research evidence in terms of, first, experimental wound studies with healthy participants and, second, clinical wound studies with patient samples. Experimental wound studies are generally aimed at understanding underlying biological and psychological mechanisms, and clinical wound studies tell us more about the range of clinical areas where these findings can be applied. Within each of these areas, research has utilised a range of methods to assess healing, and tested a number of psychological interventions, as will be described in the next sections.

EXPERIMENTAL WOUND STUDIES

The creation of an experimental wound in a healthy participant enables researchers to study the effects of stress on healing in a live model that is uncomplicated by underlying illness. Researchers can study the effects of stress on the different stages of healing and on various immune parameters. To understand these effects, it is important to understand how the immune system is involved in wound healing (see Sidebar 6.2). Three main types of experimental wound models have been examined in PNI, each of which can give insights into different aspects of healing (see Sidebar 6.3). Sidebar 6.4 explains the mechanisms though which stress can affect wound healing.

Sidebar 6.2. A Brief Description of Wound Healing Stages

The skin forms a protective barrier that keeps foreign organisms out of the body and keeps moisture within it. When the skin is broken, healing progresses through four key stages, and cells in the wound recognise and secrete a range of factors that control the progression of these stages:

1. Immediately after wounding, the *haemostasis* stage begins, during which vasoconstriction occurs and platelets form a clot to stop blood loss and release growth-factors that attract immune cells to the wound.

2. Within about an hour, the *inflammation* stage begins, during which neutrophils and macrophages reduce infection by eliminating foreign material and produce cytokines and growth factors that attract fibroblasts. Inflammation typically lasts four to five days.

3. Fibroblasts initiate the *proliferation* stage, when epithelialisation occurs and the clot is replaced by granulation tissue. During this phase, fibroblasts create collagen and the extracellular matrix, endothelial cells promote re-epithelialisation, and keratinocytes promote re-vascularisation. This stage typically lasts two to three weeks, and errors during this stage or persistent foreign bodies can result in poor healing.

4. The final stage is *remodelling*, which involves the gradual removal of immature type III collagen and replacement with type I collagen, a process that can take months to years.

Prevalent immune cells in the epidermis include Langerhans cells (a form of macrophage), and CD8 tissue memory cells, and in the dermis are dendritic cells, natural killer cells, and CD8 tissue memory cells. Langerhans cells play a key role in connecting keratinocytes in the skin; they also collect foreign material from a wound site then migrate to the lymph nodes to present that material to lymphocytes and so activate immune responses (West & Bennett, 2018).

Sidebar 6.3.   Three Main Types of Experimental Wound in PNI Studies

1. Induced blister wounds have been used to assess the inflammatory stage of healing. Blisters can be induced using a vacuum technique on the arm, and the epidermal layer then removed to create uniform wounds. Exudate fluid can be collected from the wounds at various times during the first 24–48 hours and assayed for cytokines, neutrophils, and matrix metalloproteinases (important wound-healing enzymes). Trans-epidermal water loss can also be measured to assess epithelialisation (see below).

2. The tape-stripping model has been used to assess re-epithelialisation. The stratum corneum (the uppermost layer of the skin, which is mainly composed of keratinocytes) can be removed by applying adhesive tape repeatedly to a small section of skin, usually on the inner arm. Damage to the surface barrier allows water vapour to escape, which is measured as trans-epidermal water loss (TEWL) using a probe adjacent to the wound. As the wound repairs, the rate of water loss diminishes, providing a measure of re-epithelialisation. Healing can be assessed within minutes/hours, but a limitation of TEWL is that it is affected by ambient temperature and humidity. The presence of cytokines and other soluble proteins in the epidermis can also be assessed from the skin left on the tape.

3. Punch biopsies (typically 2–5 mm) have been taken from either the skin or inside the mouth on the oral hard palate (to study mucosal wound healing) under local anaesthesia. Healing is assessed by changes in the size of the surface wound over time, ratings of re-epithelialisation, or changes in the structure and dimensions of the wound bed using ultrasound. The removed skin sample can also be analysed for the presence of cells important in healing processes. Disadvantages of punch biopsies include the possibility of a small scar and the need for repeated assessments of healing, typically over seven to 14 days. Biopsies are most useful to assess the proliferative stage of healing.

Sidebar 6.4.   How Stress Affects Healing

Stress affects healing through the release of stress hormones and behavioural processes, both of which influence the regulation of the sympathetic adrenal medullary axis and hypothalamic pituitary axis. The resultant release of stress hormones (cortisol, epinephrine, norepinephrine) influence the function of the

(Continued)

(Continued)

immune cells through receptors on their surface and change their participation in wound healing processes. Psychological stress can also impact health behaviours, such as smoking and sleep, that are known to influence immune function and healing (see Sani, Chapter 5, this volume).

Overall, observational research subsequent to the classical paper by Kiecolt-Glaser et al. (1995) has supported the original finding that psychological stress impairs wound healing. A systematic review of 22 studies (15 experimental; 7 clinical) reported that, in 17 of these, stress impaired healing or dysregulated a biomarker associated with healing (Walburn et al., 2009). Meta-analysis of a subset of 11 of these studies found a negative effect of stress on healing with a moderate to large effect size (r = -.42). Some of these studies were on experimentally created wounds, and these studies are described in more detail below. Evidence from the clinical studies is presented in a later section.

In the review, four of the five studies on tape stripping found that brief laboratory stress, examination stress, and marital stress extended wound healing times. Paradoxically, the fifth study found that people with post-traumatic stress disorder had enhanced healing, suggesting that not all types of stress necessarily have the same physiological effects. Specifically, baseline abnormalities in glucocorticoids and sympatho-medullary activity in people with PTSD could trigger enhanced immune activation in response to a tape stripping wound. Five observational studies found negative effects of psychological variables on punch biopsy healing, including dysphoria (Bosch et al., 2007), depression and perceived stress (Ebrecht et al., 2004), examination stress (Marucha et al., 1998), and the original study on caregiving stress (Kiecolt-Glaser et al., 1995), although one study found that depression was not related to healing (in a surgical group; McGuire et al., 2006). Results across three studies on blister fluid in healing wounds found that higher perceived life stress was associated with lower production of inflammatory cytokines (Glaser et al., 1999), marital conflict resulted in slower healing (Kiecolt-Glaser at al., 2005), and examination stress resulted in slower healing and impaired neutrophil activation (Roy et al., 2005). One other study found depressive symptoms were not associated with metalloproteinase concentrations or tissue inhibitors of metalloproteinases in blister fluids (Yang et al., 2002). In summary, these observational studies suggest that psychological stress can influence inflammatory processes and impact subsequent wound healing.

Another important source of evidence comes from psychological intervention studies. A systematic review of studies into the effects of psychological interventions on healing synthesised 19 studies, six of which were conducted with experimentally induced wounds and had effect sizes (standardised mean differences) from small to large (.13 to .82), (Robinson, Norton, et al., 2017). Key interventions studied to date include relaxation, social support, and emotional disclosure, as detailed below.

Several blister and TEWL studies have investigated whether relaxation or mindfulness interventions can improve wound re-epithelialisation. Compared with quiet reading, 20 minutes of relaxation improved healing of a tape-stripping wound regardless of whether relaxation was performed before or after wounding (Robinson et al., 2015). However, another study did not find any significant effect of relaxation administered during the first eight hours after blister wounding on epithelialisation, as assessed by TEWL over eight days (Gouin et al., 2008). Compared to a wait-list control group, an 8-week mindfulness-based stress reduction (MBSR) course did not improve healing of a blister wound but did reduce levels of the cytokine interleukin-8 and placental growth factor in the wound 22 hours after wounding (Meesters et al., 2018). This provides mixed evidence overall, and it is important to consider whether the timing of the intervention coincides with the healing period, as well as the timing of the outcomes assessed.

Other research has assessed social support interventions. Participants who completed a laboratory stressor, the Trier Social Stress Test (TSST), in the presence of a supportive confederate did not have improved skin barrier recovery compared with participants without support (Robles, 2007). In contrast, in another study, participants who underwent a tape-stripping procedure alongside another participant with whom the participant completed a social closeness induction task had faster healing than did participants who went through the procedure alone, and the effect was mediated by self-reported stress reduction (Robinson, Ravikulan, et al., 2017) (see Jetten, Bentley, & Young, Chapter 9, this volume). Even social robots may be able to provide companionship and improve healing. After the TSST, participants randomised to interact with Paro, a pet-type robot, had improved skin barrier recovery compared with a control group who sat alone without any activity (Law et al., 2020b). However, there was no effect of Paro in a non-stressed population (Law et al., 2020a), suggesting that social support interventions may work best for stressed populations. The type of support and by whom it is best provided are critical considerations.

The effects of emotional disclosure interventions on the healing of punch biopsy wounds have also been studied (see Karl, Chapter 13, this volume). Emotional disclosure (expressive writing) compared with a control writing task (factually writing about daily activities) improved the healing of punch biopsy wounds, as assessed by ultrasound of the wound, in male students (Weinman et al., 2008). A similar study showed emotional disclosure improved ratings of epithelialisation among older adult men and women (Koschwanez et al., 2013). Analyses of skin biopsies demonstrated that stress was associated with fewer Langerhans cells and lower activation of immune cells, and these were associated with slower healing (Koschwanez et al., 2015). These studies provide promising evidence for benefits of expressive writing on the healing of experimental wounds.

The above studies have varied in their methods, which makes conclusions difficult, but overall there is promising preliminary evidence that healing of experimental wounds can be improved through psychological interventions. Differences in findings between studies may be due to several factors, including the level of baseline stress that participants are under, different sensitivities of wound healing parameters to changes over time, and the intervention timing and delivery method. Stress reduction interventions are likely to have the strongest effects in stressed populations, and when they are timed to coincide with critical healing periods.

CLINICAL WOUND HEALING STUDIES

There is a long tradition of research investigating the links between stress and the skin in different clinical contexts (Graubard et al., 2021). Much of this has focused on the possible role of stress and related emotions in either causing or exacerbating skin diseases, such as eczema or psoriasis (e.g., Evers & van Beugen, 2021). However, since the publication of the Kiecolt-Glaser et al. (1995) paper, there has been a growing interest in assessing the extent to which stress and related psychological factors might influence the healing of skin wounds, such as foot and leg ulcers, as well as those incurred by injury or surgical procedures. Kiecolt-Glaser and colleagues had anticipated the latter in their 1998 paper, in which they outlined a model to explain how stress and other bio-behavioural factors could influence post-operative wound healing and recovery.

Stress and recovery from surgical wounds.

Recovery from surgery has provided an important clinical context for studying the effects of stress on wound healing. High levels of pre-operative stress and negative mood states have long been known to influence many aspects of post-operative recovery, such as length of stay in hospital and quality of life (Weinman & Johnston, 1988 and, in recent years, this research has begun to investigate whether these effects could extend to the healing of surgical wounds.

The review by Walburn at al. (2009) mentioned earlier, identified seven studies which had been conducted in clinical settings, including five focusing on post-surgical recovery. These involved patients recovering from a range of surgical procedures, including coronary artery bypass grafting, hernia repair, and oral surgery. Even though very different measures of stress and healing were used, the overall pattern of results confirms the importance of stress and other negative mood states in slowing and/or complicating the wound healing process after surgery. Although interesting, these studies often lacked either accurate assessments of healing speed or measures of mediating psychological or physiological mechanisms. For example, in a recent large-scale study of factors influencing recovery from day surgery, Nilsson et al. (2019) assessed post-operative pain, reddening and swelling of the surgical wound but provided no direct evidence on healing speed.

Fortunately, there are now a small number of studies which have shown direct links between pre-operative psychological state and rate of wound healing. A good example is a study of recovery from hernia surgery (Broadbent et al., 2003), which showed that pre-operative self-reported worry about surgery predicted slower healing time as well as lower matrix metalloproteinase-9 (MMP-9) in the wound fluid. The latter finding is important since MMP-9 is regulated by cytokines

IL-1 and IL-6, facilitates cellular migration in the wound area, and aids in tissue re-modelling (Yang et al., 2002).

It is also important to note that the effects of stress on wound healing and surgical recovery may be compounded by the effects of the accompanying physical pain (McGuire et al., 2006). Not only does pain have an adverse effect on healing speed, but also the experience of pain is stressful and activates negative emotions, such as anxiety, which can then adversely affect the healing process. In addition to the effects of pain, there are other confounding factors since these post-operative studies have been carried out in diverse patient groups being treated for a range of problems with very different outcomes. The type of stress assessment varies considerably across studies and may involve measures of immediate pre-operative stress levels (e.g., state anxiety) and/or more long-term (i.e., chronic) life stress. To control for these sorts of factors, some recent work has investigated stress and post-operative recovery in heathy individuals, such as donors for various transplant procedures. As these individuals are in good health and because these surgical procedures are usually planned, it is possible to assess stress, wound healing, and recovery thoroughly before and after surgery with fewer confounds. For example, in a study of post-operative recovery of healthy kidney donors for renal transplant surgery, Maple et al. (2015) used high-resolution ultrasound scans of surgical wounds to assess post-operative wound size and tissue fluid. They found that higher pre-operative life stress, lower optimism, and lower conscientiousness were all associated with slower wound healing after controlling for factors such as age, BMI, smoking status, local anaesthetic use, and wound drain placement.

With accumulating evidence that pre-operative stress and related emotional states can slow down the wound healing process in surgical patients, it is not surprising that researchers have developed a range of interventions for trying to enhance post-operative recovery, including wound healing. Before the Kiecolt-Glaser et al. (1995) paper, many different types of psychological preparation for surgery had been investigated. In their review of randomised controlled trials of different methods for preparing patients for surgery, Johnston & Vögele (1993) showed that many improved different aspects of recovery, including mood, pain, length of stay, and clinical outcomes. While some of these methods did involve stress reduction components, such as relaxation and hypnosis, none attempted to examine the possible effects on speed of healing of the surgical wound.

Focusing specifically on studies which had examined possible impacts on healing, a review by Robinson, Norton et al. (2017) included five studies of clinical wounds, all of which found improved wound healing following pre-operative psychological intervention. Even though the studies varied in the patient groups, types of surgery, and both timing and type of wound healing measure, all five studies reported positive effects on healing, with effect sizes from 0.53 to 1.89. One study investigated the impact of a 15-minute intervention, targeting patient concerns about surgery, delivered one month before surgery (Pereira et al., 2016). Although there was a significant improvement in healing in the intervention group, the evidence is somewhat undermined by the rather weak wound healing measure, which was based on nurse ratings rather than precise assessments of wound size or mediating immune markers.

Two quite similar studies (Ginandes et al., 2003; Rao et al., 2008) compared relaxation-based interventions (e.g., hypnosis; yoga and breathing exercises) with more general support (e.g., education, social support) and found that both resulted in faster healing compared with usual care. Although both interventions improved recovery and wound healing, those involving the relaxation-based components were the most effective. In line with this, other studies have found that relaxation interventions were helpful for patients undergoing surgery. Broadbent et al. (2012) and Holden-Lund (1988) both conducted studies investigating the effects of relaxation on recovery from cholecystectomy surgery and had similar effect sizes (0.61 and 0.71) compared with standard care. Overall, these studies suggest that the healing of surgical wounds can be improved by psychological interventions, particularly those which are aimed at reducing patients' levels of stress and anxiety prior to surgery. The precise nature and timing of these interventions still need to be clarified.

Stress and the healing of skin wounds

Some of the commonest wounds seen in clinical practice are the foot ulcers that occur in patients with poorly controlled diabetes and venous leg ulcers (VLUs), both of which cause considerable discomfort for patients. Foot ulcers in people with diabetes are slow to heal and often re-occur even after they have healed, resulting in poorer quality of life, increased risk of amputation, and higher five-year mortality (Armstrong et al., 2017). Researchers have investigated the possible role of a range of clinical and psychosocial factors in either the cause or recurrence of these ulcers. Although there is some evidence that negative emotions, particularly depression, might play a causal role, the jury is still out on this (Holt, 2020). A comprehensive recent systematic review concluded that, while depression may increase risk only for first-time ulcers, it had no consistent effect on healing or recurrence (Westby et al., 2020).

Since the evidence for the role of psychosocial factors in the healing of diabetic foot ulcers is equivocal, it is hardly surprising to find that attempts to improve healing using psychological interventions have not been very successful. A recent review of 31 studies failed to show consistent evidence of the efficacy of interventions designed to prevent ulcer onset, healing, or recurrence (Norman et al., 2020). However, nearly all these studies made use of educational interventions, which were not specifically designed to target stress, and so there is certainly scope for future work to attempt this. More specifically, future studies will need to be more specific in defining the components of psychological interventions aimed at improving ulcer healing, and to differentiate those which are focused on stress reduction from those aimed at providing educational and/or behaviour change approaches.

Venous leg ulcers (VLUs) are a common, recurrent chronic wound, which increase in prevalence with age. They are usually painful and give off an unpleasant smell, both of which can have significant effects on the individual's quality of life

(Etufugh & Phillips, 2007). Studies of factors influencing VLU healing speed have mainly focused on clinical variables such as size and duration of the ulcer. However, there is now evidence to indicate that stress may play a role both via compromised immunity and behavioural factors, such as lower adherence to good bandaging and recommended self-care practices such as leg elevation. Thus, as with other clinical wounds, stress may directly affect healing via physiological changes associated with the stress response dysregulating immune function or indirectly as a result of unhealthy behaviours and poor adherence.

Earlier studies reported a negative relationship between stress, negative emotions, and rates of VLU healing (Cole-King & Harding, 2001; Wong & Lee, 2008), but these were limited by the use of cross-sectional designs and ratings of healing based on clinical judgement rather than objective measures. A more definitive longitudinal study by Walburn et al. (2017)used a wide range of validated measures to investigate predictors of VLU over 24 weeks. After controlling for sociodemographic and clinical variables, a slower rate of change in ulcer area was predicted by greater stress, depression, and having more negative beliefs about the VLU. Slower healing was found in those patients who had a more negative emotional response to the ulcer at baseline.

In their review of psychological interventions and wound healing, Robinson, Norton et al. (2017) identified two studies on VLUs, using very different interventions. One evaluated the effects of a socially supportive wound care group (Edwards et al., 2009) and the other assessed the efficacy of biofeedback-based relaxation training (Rice et al., 2001). Although both showed promising effects, they involved quite small samples and there is considerable scope for further work on this to compare different types of intervention and explore mediating processes. For example, one recent study has shown that an intervention based on enhancing patient expectations of wound healing had positive outcomes compared with standard care (Jockenhöfer et al., 2020).

These findings, showing beneficial effects of stress-reduction interventions on speed of wound healing, emphasise the impact and long-term translational influence of Kiecolt-Glaser et al.'s (1995) classic study. In another paper from the same group, Kiecolt-Glaser et al. (1998) provided a tentative model showing how stress could affect wound healing and recovery from surgery, and much of the research which has followed has provided support for the ideas that they presented at that time.

CONCLUSIONS

From its beginnings as an exploration of possible psychosocial influences on immunity and the physiological mediating pathways, PNI has evolved into a fully-fledged discipline encompassing the relationships between psycho-socio-cultural factors and neuroendocrine and immune processes. PNI research has progressed impressively over the years, and now extends into virtually all disciplines of clinical medicine, augmenting the understanding of illness and healing processes and contributing to innovative interventions and treatments. It is clear that Kiecolt-Glaser et al.'s (1995) study has played an important role in this. In developing a novel and ecologically valid paradigm for investigating mind–body interactions, their work has resulted in many experimental and clinical studies, which have provided accumulating evidence that different psychological states, especially stress, have significant effects on both immune function and wound healing. These findings have helped us to understand why skin wounds are slow to heal in stressed individuals, and have provided the impetus for psychological interventions for enhancing the wound healing process. There is now a need for carefully designed clinical trials using well-defined interventions not only to improve clinical care but also to generate a better understanding of the complex ways in which mind and body interact.

FURTHER READING

Solomon, G. F. (2000). *From psyche to soma and back: Tales of biopsychosocial medicine*. Bloomington, IN: Xlibris.

An interesting and very readable autobiographical account of the life and work of one of the pioneers of psychoneuroimmunology.

Segerstrom, S. C. (2012). *The Oxford handbook of psychoneuroimmunology*. Oxford: Oxford University Press.

A multi-author volume demonstrating how advances in psychological science can contribute to advancing knowledge in psychoneuroimmunology. It illustrates the best of PNI: cutting-edge models of how the outer and inner worlds interact with each other, and the complexity of both of those worlds.

Walburn, J., Vedhara, K., Hankins, M., Rixon, L., & Weinman, J. (2009). Psychological stress and wound healing in humans: a systematic review and meta-analysis. *Journal of Psychosomatic Research, 67*(3), 253–271.

Reviews the evidence for the effects of stress on healing.

Robinson, H., Norton, S., Jarrett, P., & Broadbent, E. (2017). The effects of psychological interventions on wound healing: A systematic review of randomized trials. *British Journal of Health Psychology, 22*(4), 805–835.

Reviews the effects of psychological interventions on healing.

O'Connor, D. B., Thayer, J. F., & Vedhara, K. (2021). Stress and health: A review of psychobiological processes. *Annual Review of Psychology, 72*(1), 663–688.

Presents an overview of the different biological systems that interact in the context of stress and health processes.

REFERENCES

Ader, R., & Cohen, N. (1975). Behaviorally conditioned immunosuppression. *Psychosomatic Medicine, 37*(4), 333–340.

Ader, R., & Cohen, N. (1982). Behaviorally conditioned immunosuppression and murine systemic lupus erythematosus. *Science, 215*(4539), 1534–1536.

Ader, R., & Cohen, N. (1993). Psychoneuroimmunology: Conditioning and stress. *Annual Review of Psychology*, *44*, 53–85.

Armstrong, D. G., Boulton, A. J. M., & Bus, S. A. (2017). Diabetic foot ulcers and their recurrence. *New England Journal of Medicine*, *376*, 2367–2375.

Beilin, B., Shavit, Y., Trabekin, E., Mordashev, B., Mayburd, E., Zeidel, A., & Bessler, H. (2003). The effects of postoperative pain management on immune response to surgery. *Anesthesia & Analgesia*, *97*, 822–827.

Bosch, J.A., Engeland, C.G., Cacioppo, J.T., Marucha, P.T. (2007). Depressive symptoms predict mucosal wound healing. *Psychosomatic Medicine*, 69, 597–605.

Broadbent, E., Petrie, K. J., Alley, P. G., & Booth, R. J. (2003). Psychological stress impairs early wound repair following surgery. *Psychosomatic Medicine*, *65*, 865–869.

Broadbent, E., Kahokehr, A., Booth, R. J., Thomas, J., Windsor, J. A., Buchanan, C. M., ... & Hill, A. G. (2012). A brief relaxation intervention reduces stress and improves surgical wound healing response: a randomised trial. *Brain, behavior, and immunity*, *26*(2), 212-217.

Chida, Y., & Vedhara, K. (2009). Adverse psychosocial factors predict poorer prognosis in HIV disease: A meta-analytic review of prospective investigations. *Brain, Behavior, and Immunity*, *23*(4), 434–445.

Cohen, S., Tyrrell, D. A., & Smith, A. P. (1991). Psychological stress and susceptibility to the common cold. *New England Journal of Medicine*, *325*(9), 606–612.

Cole-King, A., & Harding, K. G. (2001). Psychological factors and delayed healing in chronic wounds. *Psychosomatic Medicine*, *63*, 216–220.

Dantzer, R., & Kelley, K. W. (2007). Twenty years of research on cytokine-induced sickness behavior. *Brain, Behavior, and Immunity*, *21*(2), 153–160.

Ebrecht, M., Hextall, J., Kirtley, L.G., Taylor, A., Dyson, M., Weinman, J. (2004). Perceived stress and cortisol levels predict speed of wound healing in healthy male adults. *Psychoneuroendocrinology*, *29*, 798–809.

Edwards, H., Courtney, M., Finlayson, K., Shuter, P., & Lindsay, E. (2009). A randomised controlled trial of a community nursing intervention: Improved quality of life and healing for clients with chronic leg ulcers. *Journal of Clinical Nursing*, *18*, 1541–1549.

Engel, G. L. (1960). A unified concept of health and disease. *Perspectives in Biology and Medicine*, *3*, 459–485.

Etufugh, C. N., & Phillips, T. J. (2007). Venous ulcers. *Clinics in Dermatology*, *25*, 121–130.

Evers, A. W. M., & van Beugen, S. (2021). How stress affects the skin: From designs to mechanisms. *British Journal of Dermatology*, *185*, 130–138.

Ginandes, C., Brooks, P., Sando, W., Jones, C., & Aker, J. (2003). Can medical hypnosis accelerate post-surgical wound healing? Results of a clinical trial. *American Journal of Clinical Hypnosis*, *45*(4), 333–351.

Glaser, R., Kiecolt-Glaser, J.K., Marucha, P.T., MacCallum, R.C., Laskowski, B.F., Malarkey, W.B. (1999). Stress-related changes in proinflammatory cytokine production in wounds. *Archives of General Psychiatry*, *56*, 450–6.

Gouin, J. P., Kiecolt-Glaser, J. K., Malarkey, W. B., & Glaser, R. (2008). The influence of anger expression on wound healing. *Brain, Behavior, and Immunity*, *22*(5), 699–708.

Graubard, R., Perez-Sanchez, A., & Katta, R. (2021). Stress and the skin: An overview of mind–body therapies as a treatment strategy in dermatology. *Dermatology Practical & Conceptual*, *11*(4), e2021091.

Holden-lund, C. (1988). Effects of relaxation with guided imagery on surgical stress and wound healing. *Research in nursing & health*, *11*(4), 235-244.

Holt, R. I. G. (2020). Diabetes-related foot ulcers and the mind. *Diabetic Medicine*, *37*(8), 1223–1224.

Jockenhöfer, F., Knust, C., Benson, S., Schedlowski, M., & Dissemond, J. (2020). Influence of placebo effects on quality of life and wound healing in patients with chronic venous leg ulcers. *JDDG: Journal der Deutschen Dermatologischen Gesellschaft*, *18*(2), 103–109.

Johnston, M., & Vögele, C. (1993). Benefits of psychological preparation for surgery: A meta-analysis. *Annals of Behavioral Medicine*, *15*(4), 245–256.

Kiecolt-Glaser, J. K., & Glaser, R. (1995). Psychoneuroimmunology and health consequences: Data and shared mechanisms. *Psychosomatic Medicine*, *57*(3), 269–274.

Kiecolt-Glaser, J. K., Marucha, P. T., Malarkey, W. B., Mercado, A. M., & Glaser, R. (1995). Slowing of wound healing by psychological stress. *Lancet*, *346*(8984), 1194–1196.

Kiecolt-Glaser, J. K., Page, G. G., Marucha, P. T., MacCallum, R. C., & Glaser, R. (1998). Psychological influences on surgical recovery: Perspectives from psychoneuroimmunology. *American Psychologist*, *53*, 1209–1218.

Kiecolt-Glaser, J. K., Loving, T.J., Stowell, J.R., Malarkey, W.B., Lemeshow, S., Dickinson, S.L., Glaser, R. (2005). Hostile marital interactions, proinflammatory cytokine production and wound healing. *Archives of General Psychiatry*, *62*, 1377–84.

Koschwanez, H., Vurnek, M., Weinman, J., Tarlton, J., Whiting, C., Amirapu, S., Colgan, S., Long, D., Jarrett, P., & Broadbent, E. (2015). Stress-related changes to immune cells in the skin prior to wounding may impair subsequent healing. *Brain, Behavior, and Immunity*, *50*, 47–51.

Koschwanez, H. E., Kerse, N., Darragh, M., Jarrett, P., Booth, R. J., & Broadbent, E. (2013). Expressive writing and wound healing in older adults: A randomized controlled trial. *Psychosomatic Medicine*, *75*(6), 581–590.

Law, M., Jarrett, P., Nater, U. M., Skoluda, N., & Broadbent, E. (2020a). The effects of environmental enrichment on skin barrier recovery in humans: A randomised trial. *Scientific Reports*, *10*(1), 1–11.

Law, M., Jarrett, P., Nater, U. M., Skoluda, N., & Broadbent, E. (2020b). The effects of sensory enrichment after a laboratory stressor on human skin barrier recovery in a randomized trial. *Psychosomatic Medicine*, *82*(9), 877–886.

McGuire, L., Heffner, K. L., Glaser, R., Needleman, B., Malarkey, W. B., Dickinson, S., Lemeshow, S., Cook, C., Muscarella, P., Melvin, S., Ellison, C., & Kiecolt-Glaser, J. K. (2006). Pain and wound healing in surgical patients. *Annals of Behavioral Medicine*, *31*, 165–172.

Maple, H., Chilcot, J., Lee, V., Simmonds, S., Weinman, J., & Mamode, N. (2015). Stress predicts the trajectory of wound healing in living kidney donors as measured by high-resolution ultrasound. *Brain, behavior, and immunity*, *43*, 19–26.

Marucha, P.T., Kiecolt-Glaser, J.K., Favagehi, M. (1998). Mucosal wound healing is impaired by examination stress. *Psychosomatic Medicine*, *60*, 362–5.

Meesters, A., den Bosch-Meevissen, Y. M. I., Weijzen, C. A., Buurman, W. A., Losen, M., Schepers, J., Thissen, M. R., Alberts, H. J., Schalkwijk, C. G., & Peters, M. L.

(2018). The effect of mindfulness-based stress reduction on wound healing: A preliminary study. *Journal of Behavioral Medicine, 41*(3), 385–397.

Nilsson, U., Dahlberg, K., & Jaensson, M. (2019). Preoperative mental and physical health is associated with poorer postoperative recovery in patients undergoing day surgery: A secondary analysis from a randomized controlled study. *World Journal of Surgery, 43*, 1949–1956.

Norman, G., Westby, M. J., Vedhara, K., Game, F., & Cullum, N. A. (2020). Effectiveness of psychosocial interventions for the prevention and treatment of foot ulcers in people with diabetes: A systematic review. *Diabetic Medicine, 37*(8), 1256–1265.

Pereira, L., Figueiredo-Braga, M., & Carvalho, I. P. (2016). Preoperative anxiety in ambulatory surgery: The impact of an empathic patient-centered approach on psychological and clinical outcomes. *Patient education and counseling, 99*(5), 733–738.

Rao, R. M., Nagendra, H. R., Raghuram, N., Vinay, C., Chandrashekara, S., Gopinath, K. S., & Srinath, B. S. (2008). Influence of yoga on postoperative outcomes and wound healing in early operable breast cancer patients undergoing surgery. *International journal of yoga, 1*(1), 33.

Rice, B., Kalker, A. J., Schindler, J. V., & Dixon, R. M. (2001). Effect of biofeedback-assisted relaxation training on foot ulcer healing. *Journal of the American Podiatric Medical Association, 91*, 132–141.

Robinson, H., Jarrett, P., & Broadbent, E. (2015). The effects of relaxation before or after skin damage on skin barrier recovery: A preliminary study. *Psychosomatic Medicine, 77*(8), 844–852.

Robinson, H., Norton, S., Jarrett, P., & Broadbent, E. (2017). The effects of psychological interventions on wound healing: A systematic review of randomized trials. *British Journal of Health Psychology, 22*(4), 805–835.

Robinson, H., Ravikulan, A., Nater, U. M., Skoluda, N., Jarrett, P., & Broadbent, E. (2017). The role of social closeness during tape stripping to facilitate skin barrier recovery: Preliminary findings. *Health Psychology, 36*(7), 619–629.

Robles, T. F. (2007). Stress, social support, and delayed skin barrier recovery. *Psychosomatic Medicine, 69*(8), 807–815.

Roy, S., Khanna, S., Yeh, P., Rink, C., Malarkey, W.B., Kiecolt-Glaser, J.K., Laskowski, B., Glaser, R, Sen, C.K. (2005). Wound site neutrophil transcriptome in response to psychological stress in young men. *Gene Expression, 12*, 273–87.

Solomon, G. F., & Moos, R. H. (1964). Emotions, immunity and disease: A speculative theoretical integration. *Archives of General Psychiatry, 11*, 657–674.

Walburn, J., Vedhara, K., Hankins, M., Rixon, L., & Weinman, J. (2009). Psychological stress and wound healing in humans: A systematic review and meta-analysis. *Journal of Psychosomatic Research, 67*(3), 253–271.

Walburn, J., Weinman, J., Norton, S., Hankins, M., Dawe, K., Banjoko, B., & Vedhara, K. (2017). Stress, illness perceptions, behaviors, and healing in venous leg ulcers: findings from a prospective observational study. *Psychosomatic medicine, 79*(5), 585.

Weinman, J., Ebrecht, M., Scott, S., Walburn, J., & Dyson, M. (2008). Enhanced wound healing after emotional disclosure intervention. *British Journal of Health Psychology, 13*(Pt 1), 95–102.

Weinman, J., & Johnston, M. (1988). Stressful medical procedures: An analysis of the effects of psychological interventions and of the stressfulness of the procedures. In S.

Maes, C. D. Spielberger, P. B. Defares, & I. G. Sarason (Eds.), *Topics in Health Psychology* (pp. 205–217). London: Wiley.

West, H. C., & Bennett, C. L. (2018). Redefining the role of Langerhans cells as immune regulators within the skin. *Frontiers in Immunology*, *8*(1941).

Westby, M., Norman, G., Vedhara, K., Game, F., & Cullum, N. (2020). Psychosocial and behavioural prognostic factors for diabetic foot ulcer development and healing: A systematic review. *Diabetic Medicine*, *37*(8), 1244–1255.

Wong, I., & Lee, D. (2008) Chronic wounds: Why some heal and others don't? Psychosocial determinants of wound healing in older people. *Hong Kong Journal of Dermatology and Venereology*, *16*, 71–76.

Yang, E. V., Bane, C. M., MacCallum, R. C., Kiecolt-Glaser, J. K., Malarkey, W. B., & Glaser, R. (2002). Stress related modulation of matrix metalloproteinase expression. *Journal of Neuroimmunology*, *133*, 144–150.

7

Personality and Health: Revisiting Friedman and Rosenman (1959)

Friedman, M., & Rosenman, R. H. (1959). Association of specific overt behavior pattern with blood and cardiovascular findings: Blood cholesterol level, blood clotting time, incidence of arcus senilis, and clinical coronary artery disease. *Journal of the American Medical Association, 169*, 1286–1296.

Nick Haslam & Roderick D. Buchanan

BACKGROUND

This chapter explores the relationship between personality and health. The seminal paper by Friedman and Rosenman (1959) on 'Type A' personality, which was introduced as a possible risk factor for cardiovascular disease, serves as a stimulus and unique case study for the personality–health relationship. We place Friedman and Roseman's work within its historical context, and outline how their research explored early ideas on the role of personality in health and disease. We provide a detailed and critical analysis of their paper, and outline the promising early evidence implicating Type A personality in the etiology of cardiovascular disease. We next discuss how the early promise was later overturned in subsequent studies and research syntheses, and suggest some of the factors responsible for that change, which ultimately led to Type A being abandoned as a field of research in health psychology. In conclusion, Type A personality was a 'failed idea', but serves as a cautionary tale for researchers examining the personality–health relationship, showing how evidence and perspectives evolve as research methods become more precise. Despite the demise of 'Type A', this work nevertheless paved the way for modern research on personality and health, and a burgeoning body of research highlights the vital role that other personality characteristics play in understanding the psychology of health.

PERSONALITY AND HEALTH

The idea that people's personalities are linked to the diseases and health problems they experience has a long history. For the emerging disciplines of psychiatry and psychology in the early 20th century it seemed obvious that mental and physical states were connected, and that the ways people thought and felt were related to their physical health. However, early attempts to link personality and disease were problematic. They tended to invoke psychological dynamics that were outside individuals' awareness and were thus difficult to test. And they were often drawn from single case studies and lacked a broader and more reliable empirical basis (Buchanan et al., 2018).

The second half of the 20th century saw the development of a more systematic approach to the study of personality, and a more nuanced and scientific effort to determine whether personality characteristics correlated with particular illnesses. Personality psychologists constructed models of personality structure – the fundamental dimensions along which people differ in their ways of thinking, feeling, and behaving – and developed psychological tests to quantify them, with strict definitions and rigorous attempts to validate their structure and validity. Using these tests to assess large samples of people, psychologists examined how differences in personality traits predicted a vast range of other phenomena, including aspects of physical health. From these beginnings, a substantial body of knowledge has emerged on the associations between personality and health.

However, the early days of this more *scientific* approach to personality and health were not without problems. Some of the findings from this era have not stood the test of time and have had to be abandoned. Perhaps the most interesting of these findings concerns the so-called 'Type A' personality, which was first identified in the late 1950s and received broad attention in the scientific community and popular media alike. It made a huge impact because it addressed an urgent priority in public health. Heart disease had emerged as the most prominent threat to health and longevity in affluent Western societies – not least because it was affecting many successful people in their prime. It had become increasingly recognised as the most common cause of death in the US (Dalen et al., 2014).

DETAILED OVERVIEW

Friedman and Roseman's (1959) classic study in health psychology was carried out by two cardiologists who had no formal training in psychology. Meyer Friedman and Ray Rosenman worked together in the 1950s in a hospital treating patients with heart disease and became curious about the factors that contributed to it. They suspected that in addition to the main risk factors that were beginning to become well known at the time – such as diet, physical inactivity, and high blood cholesterol – other factors might be involved. Their hunch was that these factors had something to do with a particular personality style. They were not the first to think along these lines, and not the only ones to link psychological factors with heart health. What was new was the way in which they connected these dispositions to the challenges and pressures of modern life. To illustrate, the cardiologists cited historical case studies in which lifestyle and generalised dispositions seemed connected to the conditions that physicians' patients presented with. For example, they outlined the case of the famous Canadian physician Sir William Osler, who claimed in 1910 that his typical patient with chest pain was 'vigorous in mind and body, and the keen and ambitious man, the indicator of whose engines is always set at full speed ahead' (Chesney et al., 1980, p. 255).

Three lines of evidence supported Friedman and Rosenman's predictions about the behavioural tendencies associated with the risk of heart disease. First, they carried out a survey of business executives and doctors, many of whom expressed the opinion that excessive drive, competitiveness, and stress contributed to cardiac risk. Second, they conducted an experiment on a group of accountants, finding that their cardiovascular functioning was adversely affected by periods of life stress, even when their diets and levels of physical activity did not change. Finally, they noticed that the chairs in their waiting room showed unusual patterns of wear on the front edge, apparently due to their patients being jittery and prone to jump up frequently to ask when they could see their physician. This is no doubt the first upholstery-based medical advance!

Having decided that heart disease may be linked with how people responded to stress, Friedman and Rosenman designed a study that tried to specify the behaviour pattern or 'emotional complex' that is associated with coronary heart disease (CHD) – which they referred to as 'coronary artery disease' in their article – and test whether it is in fact associated with cardiovascular risk. In the first step of this classic study, they defined the behaviour pattern as having six features: (1) intense need for achievement; (2) deep-seated competitiveness; (3) a strong desire for recognition and career advancement; (4) chronic working to multiple deadlines; (5) a tendency to try to perform tasks quickly; and (6) high mental and physical alertness. Friedman and Rosenman dubbed this 'pattern A'. They also defined a 'pattern B', which was defined as the opposite of that pattern, 'characterized by relative absence of drive, ambition, sense of urgency, desire to compete, or involvement in deadlines' (1959, p. 1286), as well as a 'pattern C', which involved a chronic state of anxiety or insecurity. People exhibiting pattern A should be at greater risk of CHD than those exhibiting patterns B and C if their prediction was correct.

To test their prediction, Friedman and Rosenman recruited three groups of participants. To represent pattern A, they selected 83 men aged between 30 and 60 years who were nominated by co-workers in several companies and organisations after the pattern had been explained to them. Another 83 men in the same age bracket were nominated by people in a different set of workplaces – predominantly less corporate – to represent pattern B. Finally, to represent pattern C, 46 blind men were recruited with the rationale that they lacked ambition and drive like their pattern B peers, but also experienced chronic financial and physical insecurity. It should be clear that by the standards of modern health psychology research the methods of recruitment of the three samples left a lot to be desired!

The three groups were selected using an informal and unstandardised proce-dure and from markedly different settings. They also differed in a multitude of potentially systematic ways beyond the behavioural patterns that were the focus of the study. For example, all the men representing patterns A and B were employed, but all the blind men of pattern C were not. Such problematic selection meth-ods may raise questions on whether any observed differences between the three groups in cardiovascular response could be exclusively attributed to participants' differing levels of drive (high for A, low for B and C) and insecurity (low for A and B, high for C). Given that the size of each group was relatively small, it would also be difficult to detect an effect for Type A if this effect was also small. In addition, the modest group sizes might allow random differences between the groups to exert a misleading influence.

After they had been recruited into the study, all 212 participants were inter-viewed about their family history of CHD, their general health history, their normal time spent working and sleeping, and their smoking, physical activity, and dietary habits. The degree to which their respective behaviour pattern was completely developed was then evaluated by the researchers, except for those in group C, because of their 'ubiquitous general air of resignation, worry, and hopelessness'. Groups A and B then recorded their food and alcohol intake for a week using a daily diary, while group C had their intake evaluated in daily telephone calls or by inspecting the menus for the roughly half who lived in institutions. Note again how these measurements were not carried out systematically and identically for the different groups, another methodological limitation of the study that would be unlikely to be considered acceptable by contemporary standards. In addition to the interview and dietary intake evaluation, three physical health-related assessments were carried out. Blood was collected to assess the participants' cholesterol level and clotting (coagulation) time. The presence of any CHD was evaluated by asking participants about any experiences of chest pain (angina pectoralis) and admin-istering an electrocardiogram (ECG). Finally, *arcus senilis* – a pale-coloured fatty ring around the eye's cornea that is associated with having a family history of high cholesterol – was evaluated for the men in groups A and B.

Friedman and Rosenman opened their presentation of their study results by confirming that most members of each group showed the completely-developed behaviour pattern for that group. They also provided a short qualitative sketch of how participants in the three groups behaved. The men in group A appeared to be capable workers but they also felt over-committed, excessively driven by their ambitions, frustrated by the lack of time to get things done, and highly competitive at work and elsewhere. The group B men were starkly different. They lacked the group A men's sense of time urgency and seemed more content with life and less concerned about winning, personal advancement, and keeping busy with multiple goals. Finally, the men in group C seemed equally free of impatience, competitive-ness, or drive to excel, but were worried about their financial futures.

Friedman and Rosenman also revealed several differences between the groups based on the pre-study behavioural and physical measurements taken. Compared with the 'chilled-out' group B men, group A men were taller, more physically active, and worked six hours longer each week, although they did not sleep any less. Group A and B participants had a similar intake of calories and fat, although group A men were more likely to be restricting their diet. Group A and B members were equally likely to be smokers, although group A men smoked more excessively, and the two groups did not differ in their alcohol intake. Group A men reported a somewhat higher rate of parental CHD and had higher blood cholesterol levels. They showed no overall difference in blood clotting time but had a much higher rate of *arcus senilis* – although interestingly this was not associated with blood cholesterol levels. It is worth noting that, with rare exceptions, Friedman and Rosenman did not report statistical tests for most of these comparisons.

Results so far seemed to indicate notable differences between the participants with the two behaviour patterns A and B. Group A men had a few signs of increased health risk, notably more overwork, excessive smoking, cholesterol, and cholesterol-related eye problems, and a hint (albeit one that was not statistically significant) of an elevated family history of CHD. But what about the most crucial test of the research question: how did the groups differ on the rate of CHD signs? Here the findings were striking: 23 (28%) men in group A had diagnosable symptoms and/or ECG signs of CHD, compared to three (4%) in group B and two (4%) in group C.

Although Friedman and Rosenman raised the possibility that this very large group difference in CHD might be due to group differences in other risk factors, they then dismissed that possibility. For example, although group A men worked longer hours on average than the other men, no group B men who worked long hours received a CHD diagnosis, and rates of CHD had risen in the decades before the study while average working hours had declined. Group A men did not have worse dietary or sleep habits than the other men, so those habits could not account for their higher rate of CHD. Men in group A did smoke more heavily than those in the other groups, but CHD was just as common among lighter and heavier smokers in group A, and very few heavy smokers in group B developed CHD. Friedman and Rosenman used similar arguments to dismiss alcohol consumption, parental CHD history, and blood cholesterol levels as causes of the very large group differences in CHD rates. They proposed that long working hours, excessive smoking, heavy drinking, and high cholesterol *accompanied* behaviour pattern A, but did not cause people with that pattern to have elevated rates of CHD. They argued that the behaviour pattern itself was responsible for those elevated rates. Type A personality, Friedman and Rosenman concluded, put people at significant risk of CHD.

IMPACT

THE LEGACY OF FRIEDMAN AND ROSEMAN (1959): DOES TYPE A PERSONALITY CONTRIBUTE TO HEART DISEASE?

Early promise

Friedman and Rosenman's (1959) article linked the Type A behaviour pattern with CHD when people were evaluated at one point in time. This is what is known as a 'cross-sectional' study. Study findings provided some indication that perhaps Type A personality may play a *causal* role in CHD. But the design of the study was such that many other explanations were still plausible, and could not be ruled out. For example, this association might have been observed because the onset of CHD increased Type A behaviour, which would be the opposite of the proposed causal effect, even though such an alternative explanation did not chime with extant theory. Alternatively, the association between Type A and CHD might have been observed because both were associated with some third unmeasured factor or variable – colloquially known by scientists as the 'third variable' problem. For example, the health and lifestyle factors that Friedman and Rosenman so readily dismissed might still be the culprits. Thus, their initial study fell far short of supporting a causal developmental link between personality and heart disease risk. To do that, researchers would have to conduct studies with more robust designs: for example, carrying out prospective longitudinal studies to determine whether Type A personality, measured at an earlier time (e.g., at age 40), was associated with elevated rates of CHD at follow-up years later (e.g., at age 70). If personality predicted the subsequent development of CHD, researchers could be more confident in inferring that it may be a causal risk factor for the disease and rule out alternative explanations for the cross-sectional association of the two variables.

Inspired by Friedman and Rosenman's promising findings, several large-scale longitudinal studies were carried out to test whether Type A personality predicted elevated rate of CHD years later. The first of these was known as the Western Collaborative Group Study, in which Rosenman and Friedman were heavily involved. The initial results of this study seemed to support the earlier predictions. At an 8.5-year follow-up of a sample of more than 3500 men, participants who were classified as Type A had clinical levels of CHD at double the rate of Type B participants (Rosenman et al., 1975), a powerful effect that remained when other risk factors were statistically controlled. This finding led a gathering of experts to proclaim that 'this risk is greater than that imposed by age, elevated values of systolic blood pressure and serum cholesterol, and smoking and appears to be of the same order of magnitude as the relative risk associated with the latter three of these other factors' (Cooper et al., 1981, p. 1200). The Type A personality concept had, it seemed, shown itself to be a legitimate psychological risk factor on a par with well-established risk factors, and this positive message was reinforced by other studies carried out in the late 1970s. If true, such findings imply that public health professionals should intervene on personality with the same urgency with which they tackled smoking and high cholesterol diets.

The tide turns

Then something changed. Subsequent large-scale longitudinal studies started to find very little evidence of elevated CHD risk among participants exhibiting a Type A pattern. The Multiple Risk Intervention Trial (MRFIT), covering more than 3000 adults, for example, found no relationship at all between Type A personality and any expression of CHD (Shekelle et al., 1985). As these more extensive longitudinal studies accumulated, a different picture began to emerge. Literature reviews and meta-analyses – studies that statistically combine the results of multiple previous studies – began to suggest that the effect of Type A personality on subsequent CHD was so small as to be trivial or even no different from zero. For example, a meta-analysis of 25 longitudinal studies (Myrtek, 2001), with a combined sample size of 74,326 study participants, found no statistically significant association between Type A and CHD, and the correlation was *very* small ($r = .003$). Other reviews came to similar conclusions. For example, Kuper, Marmot, and Hemingway (2002) failed to find consistent evidence for a causal role for Type A personality in CHD. If anything, this evidence was weaker than evidence for other factors linked to CHD risk, such as depression, social support, and various aspects of people's work environments.

Some later research even found that Type A personality was associated with *decreased* risk of CHD, or with superior clinical outcomes among people who had CHD. For example, the 22-year follow-up of participants in the Western Collaborative Group Study (Ragland & Brand, 1988) was at odds with the earlier 8.5-year follow-up that had found strong evidence for Type A CHD risk (Rosenman et al., 1975). This long-term follow-up indicated that Type A participants who had CHD were less likely than Type B participants to subsequently experience a fatal heart attack, suggesting that Type A might actually be *protective* of the most serious outcomes of the disease. Similarly, a more recent study followed a large sample of elderly Finnish men over a 20-year period (Šmigelskas et al., 2015). They found that on some measures of Type A personality, high scorers were *less* likely than low scorers to die of cardiovascular disease, including CHD. Clearly, the promise of early research on the Type A–CHD link was not borne out by the consistently null findings of these later studies. This downward trend had already been highlighted by Miller et al. (1991), who showed that studies were significantly more likely to report positive findings about the Type A–CHD link before 1979 than after it.

Sidebar 7.1. Does Personality Cause Cancer?

Sadly, Type A personality was not the only failed idea in the personality and health field where evidence has been exaggerated or just plain incorrect. A similar but more shocking story can be told about other work by sociologist Ronald Grossarth-Maticek and psychologist Hans Eysenck, who claimed to find a relationship between personality and CHD, and personality and cancer. These prospective studies, critically evaluated by Buchanan (2010) and Pelosi (2019), produced risk estimates for CHD-prone and cancer-prone personalities that were absurdly high – far higher than any risk estimates found by 'Type A' researchers. Grossarth-Maticek and Eysenck's research also received tobacco industry funding, since it suggested that personality rather than smoking was the prime cause of these diseases. But even tobacco industry insiders had their reservations

(Continued)

(Continued)

because the obvious lack of credibility of this research limited its PR and legal value. The personality measures Grossarth-Maticek used were very verbose and clumsy, and there were insufficient controls put in place to ensure that these were genuinely predictive studies. If this research had been trustworthy, it would have amounted to an astonishing breakthrough in the understanding of personality and disease. But alas, it is now regarded as so scientifically questionable that many of Grossarth-Maticek and Eysenck's publications have been formally retracted – that is, retrospectively withdrawn – by scientific journals (Marks & Buchanan, 2020). This was an ignominious postscript to Eysenck's renowned career, driven by his dubious quest to downplay the risks of smoking. It involved many compromises on his part, including a commitment to a typological approach to personality when he had previously been a proponent of a dimensional framework that had helped pave the way for the Big Five.

WHY DID THE ASSOCIATION BETWEEN TYPE A AND HEART DISEASE 'DISAPPEAR'?

As we have seen, the apparently powerful link between Type A personality and CHD identified by Friedman and Rosenman (1959), and supported by early prospective research studies, diminished and ultimately 'disappeared' in later research. What could possibly account for this example of a 'decline effect', where a scientific finding initially seems full of promise and gradually fades away? Two main explanations have been offered, one psychological and one sociological.

Type A's 'toxic' component?

The psychological explanation for the 'vanishing' Type A personality effect suggested that the Type A concept was too broad. Friedman and Rosenman described the behaviour pattern as a cluster of six tendencies, ranging from ambition to alertness and from competitiveness to rapid performance of tasks. Perhaps only one or two of these tendencies is genuinely 'toxic' to people's cardiovascular health, while others are neutral or even beneficial to health. If so, it would be better for researchers to target the 'active ingredients' of Type A rather than the entire cluster. The quest for the 'toxic' content of Type A personality was on.

Some psychologists identified hostility as the pathological component of Type A. Being antagonistic and easily angered was seen by Friedman and Rosenman as a basic element of the Type A pattern. Their preferred way of assessing the pattern paid close attention to hostile behaviour. Using a specially designed interview procedure, Friedman and Rosenman's measure of Type A personality required the interviewer to note when the person used profanity, wore hostile facial expressions, and interrupted them. Their mostly female interviewers were also required to note when the person referred to them using condescending names like 'honey' or 'toots', or clenched their fists, as well as other less hostile but sped-up behav-ioural tendencies. Aware of the centrality of hostile behaviour in Friedman and Rosenman's interview measure, Dembrovski and Costa (1987) proposed that hostility might be the health-damaging aspect of the Type A pattern. They recom-mended that future researchers focus on this aspect rather than the pattern more broadly.

Some research supported Dembrovski and Costa's proposal. One meta-analysis, discussed earlier, found no increased risk of CHD associated with Type A personal-ity, but did find some increased risk associated with hostility (Myrtek, 2001). How-ever, even this finding was somewhat underwhelming, with a very small, albeit statistically significant, correlation of 0.022 between hostility and CHD. As Myrtek noted, this correlation was too small to have any practical or *clinical* significance in the prediction or prevention of CHD. Other research found somewhat larger rela-tionships between hostility and physical health. For example, Miller and colleagues' (1996) meta-analysis found a statistically significant correlation between hostility and CHD when controlling for other risk factors – although the effect size was still quite small ($r = 0.08$). Based on this evidence, hostility by itself does not appear to be an especially 'toxic' component of Type A personality, and no other component with larger or non-trivial effect sizes has been identified (see Sidebar 7.2).

Sidebar 7.2. Effect Sizes

Effect size is an index that is vitally important in health psychology and in many other fields. It is a way to represent the magnitude of the relationship between variables or of the difference between groups. For example, if researchers wish to assess the strength of the association between levels of a health behaviour and levels of a health outcome, or to evaluate the effectiveness of an interven-tion that is administered to a treatment group but not to a control group, they can quantify those effects into a simple, easily interpreted metric. That metric can be used to compare different effects (e.g., to see if intervention A is more effective than intervention B) and also to accurately estimate the size of an effect by combining the results of multiple studies in a so-called 'meta-analysis' (e.g., averaging the effect sizes from 20 studies of intervention A).

One common effect size metric is the correlation coefficient. In psychology, correlations of 0.1, 0.3, and 0.5 are conventionally judged to represent small, medium, and large effects, respectively. Small effects imply that the association or intervention being examined is relatively weak. For example, a 0.1 correla-tion only enables prediction of an outcome at slightly above chance levels (55% accuracy), whereas a 0.5 correlation enables much greater accuracy (75%). Small effects can sometimes be important, but often they suggest that the association of interest is too weak to be practically important, or that the intervention being tested is not sufficiently effective to be worthwhile.

The tobacco industry's role

The second, sociological, explanation for the decline of the apparent validity of Type A personality was that it occurred because the early positive studies may have been biased. Public health researchers Petticrew, Lee, and McKee (2012) investigated the role of the tobacco industry in funding and promoting research on Type A using a trove of previously unavailable documents. The industry's involvement in that research lasted around four decades, beginning in the 1950s. The Philip Morris company, one of the largest global tobacco producers, in particular, funded many university-based studies on the role of personality in CHD, which included at least US$11 million funnelled to the Meyer Friedman Institute. Research findings supporting a role for Type A personality and stress in CHD were actively promoted to the public by industry-funded public relations firms and Rosenman and Friedman took an active part in these PR efforts.

The reason why tobacco companies might have been keen to support and promote research linking personality and disease is not difficult to guess. In the second half of the 20th century smoking was increasingly implicated in a range of diseases, endangering the tobacco industry's profits by motivating people to quit and exposing it to potential litigation. If people's susceptibility to these diseases could be attributed to other aspects of their behaviour besides smoking, then the causal role of smoking in disease could be denied. For example, if Type A personality put people at risk of CHD and also made them more likely to smoke, then smoking would be an innocent correlate of CHD rather than a cause, consistent with the 'third variable' explanation alluded to earlier. Moreover, the tobacco industry's claim that personality dispositions might explain away the evidence of the damaging effects of smoking was not their only line of defence. Petticrew et al. (2012) noted that the industry also funded research on how people's genetics and or so-called 'addictive personalities' could provide alternative explanations for the links between smoking and cancer. In the damning words of a senior executive at Philip Morris:

> It is very valuable to the cigarette defense to establish firmly that unsuccessfully managed stress plays a dominating role in the etiology of cancer. Additionally, success for the Friedman project will have a strong tendency to discredit the major prospective mortality studies that appear to indict smoking but fail to discover, and adjust for, a very large effect on mortality from negative mental states. (Petticrew et al., 2012, p. 2020)

Of course, simply showing that 'Big Tobacco' funded and publicised research that favoured its financial interests does not provide unequivocal proof that this research arrived at incorrect conclusions or interpretations, or was biased. However, there is some evidence that this tobacco-funded research may have been biased. In a review of 14 studies of the possible causal effect of Type A personality on CHD, eminent public health researchers Kuper, Marmot, and Hemingway (2002) found that only four of these found evidence for such an effect, and three of these had direct or indirect tobacco industry funding. It seems plausible, therefore, that at least some of these positive findings may have been biased. In any case, as tobacco funding for research 'dried up' over the years, so did the evidence for the role of Type A personality in heart disease.

QUESTIONING THE TYPE A CONSTRUCT

The findings presented above, that only certain aspects of Type A personality may be health-damaging, raises two interesting points. First, if this personality pattern has some 'toxic' components and some innocuous ones, then the pattern itself may not be the best way to characterise the traits that place people at risk of heart disease. Hostility may be a more targeted trait for this purpose than Type A personality. Second, if Type A personality contains a cluster of characteristics with different implications for health – some problematic and health damaging, others quite healthy, such as ordinary achievement striving – then perhaps it is not a coherent, unitary pattern at all.

This second possibility is quite plausible. Recall that Friedman and Rosenman developed the Type A concept, defining six proposed elements of this 'emotional complex'. As cardiologists with no psychological training, they did not borrow an existing concept from the personality psychology literature, but instead built one from scratch based on their own clinical observations and speculations. Similarly, they did not use standard psychological approaches for developing a reliable and valid measure of Type A personality, but instead assessed it unsystematically by simply asking workers to nominate colleagues who fitted the proposed pattern. It is evident that this is a sub-optimal way to develop and assess a proposed new personality trait. In Friedman and Rosenman's defence, personality psychology at the time was not as far advanced in developing a widely accepted framework for describing personality as currently exists, which meant they could not rely on an established 'received' method in defining and measuring the Type A behaviour pattern. Such a framework was to follow, paving the way for a more systematic examination of personality and health.

THE 'BIG FIVE'

Research in the 1960s and 1970s began to find evidence that human personality traits could be organised along five fundamental dimensions, which came to be known as the 'Big Five' or 'Five Factor Model of Personality', comprising Agreeableness, Conscientiousness, Extraversion, Neuroticism, and Openness to Experience traits or *dimensions* (see Table 7.1) (John, 1990). These dimensions have since become the dominant means to describe and measure personality variation. Every personality trait can be located within this five-factor framework, either as related to a single 'Big Five' dimension, or to a blend of two or more dimensions. For example, the *self-esteem* trait is primarily related to (low) Neuroticism, whereas the *shyness* trait is related to (high) Neuroticism as well as (low) Extraversion. So, how does Type A personality relate to the Big Five?

Research on measures of Type A personality have found that its relationship with the Big Five is complex. One reason for this finding is that Type A itself

Table 7.1   Brief definitions of the 'Big Five' personality dimensions

'Big Five' dimension	Definition
Agreeableness	Tendency to be cooperative, trusting, warm and friendly
Conscientiousness	Tendency to be industrious, driven, persistent and self-controlled
Extraversion	Tendency to be outgoing, active and dominant
Neuroticism	Tendency to experience negative emotional states
Openness	Tendency to be imaginative, interested in ideas and having broad interests

is complex. Research by Edwards et al. (1990), for example, showed that a popular test of Type A contained three quite distinct underlying components or factors, the most important of which they dubbed Hard-Driving/Competitiveness and General/Speed Impatience. Subsequent research has shown that these factors have very different associations with other variables (Wilmot et al., 2019). The Hard-Driving/Competitiveness factor seems to have largely positive implications for people, correlating with greater job satisfaction and better academic performance. In contrast, the General/Speed Impatience factor has largely negative implications, associated with poorer physical and mental health.

The relationships these factors have with the Big Five make sense of these diverging implications. Hard-Driving/Competitiveness is associated with high Conscientiousness and Extraversion – two traits generally considered adaptive – whereas General/Speed Impatience is associated with two much less adaptive traits: high Neuroticism and low Agreeableness. Competitive people are driven, industrious, and active goal-seekers, whereas impatient ones are antagonistic and susceptible to negative emotions. In short, Friedman and Rosenman's (1959) Type A personality concept represented a 'shotgun' approach to characterising individuals' personality, wedding two very different personality traits, one 'healthy' and the other 'unhealthy'. For this reason, researchers such as Edwards et al. (1990) have proposed a 'divorce', arguing that researchers should abandon the Type A concept and instead examine its component factors separately.

TYPES OR DIMENSIONS?

Friedman and Rosenman seem to have been incorrect about 'Type A' personality in another way. They proposed that this personality style is a dichotomous or class variable: a 'type'. Just as a household pet may be either a cat or a dog, but is certainly not both to some degree, Friedman and Rosenman suggested that a person belonged either to Type A or to Type B – at least in theory. However, type concepts have fallen out of favour in psychology because there is no good evidence that any precise personality 'types' exist (Haslam, 2019). Decades of research have shown that personality varies by degrees along a set of dimensions, like the Big Five, rather than a set of categorical types. The limitation of the type concept in this instance was demonstrated by the finding that one third of people who had been classified as either Type A or B had apparently switched to the other 'type' 10 years later (Carmelli et al., 1987). Friedman and Rosenman cannot be 'blamed' for thinking in typological terms in the 1950s when they developed their intriguing idea, but as research and methods in personality have developed, it is evident that such ideas were misguided. Type A personality is not a type, nor is it even a single dimension.

CONCLUSIONS

The story of Type A personality is a sobering one for those interested in the possible role of personality in health and illness. Here was a behaviour pattern that initially seemed to be as powerful a risk factor for heart disease as any other, which half a century later has been abandoned as a way to predict or explain susceptibility to CHD. However, it would be a mistake to think that all links between personality and health are equally weak, dubious, or fake. There is robust evidence from numerous studies linking numerous personality traits and health. For example, Conscientiousness has been shown to predict longer life (Jokela et al., 2013), and Neuroticism is associated with a wide assortment of physical complaints (Lahey, 2009) and many mental health problems, such as depression (Kendler et al., 2004). Similarly, personality traits associated with perseverance and impulse control have been shown to be linked to people engaging in health-promoting behaviour (Bogg & Roberts, 2004). Such traits are also associated with avoidance of risky behaviours and adherence to treatment regimens, as well as eating well and exercising regularly. Thus, these traits should have positive, albeit indirect, effects on health behaviours and outcomes. Even if personality characteristics such as Type A do not mysteriously *cause* heart disease or cancer, some aspects of it may well be part of the complex web of influences that make disease less likely, less severe, or less lasting.

The key message gained from studying the legacy of Friedman and Rosenman's 'Type A' study is not that personality plays no role in health and disease, rather that there should be an awareness of exaggerated claims that it does. Many people, including some health professionals, firmly believe in the power of psychological factors in physical illness (Buchanan et al., 2018). That belief, sometimes travelling under the cover of mystical ideas about 'mind–body connections', is often expressed in claims that people can vanquish disease simply by adopting a positive mindset. Such claims are naïve, and they can also be harmful if they discourage sufferers from seeking treatments that *do* work. Likewise, such beliefs may increase the tendency to blame people for getting sick or not recovering beyond reasonable limits. Personality *is* implicated in health, but the case study of Type A should make people demand that evidence for its implications is strong, scientific, and unbiased, and that unitary, causal relations are seldom the case given that the causes of health and illness are complex and multifactorial.

FURTHER READING

Buchanan, R. (2010). *Playing with fire: The controversial career of Hans J. Eysenck.* Oxford: Oxford University Press.

This is a biography of Eysenck, with Chapter 9 detailing Eysenck's collaboration with Grossarth-Maticek and his role in the smoking and health debate.

Buchanan, R., Haslam, N., & Pickren, W. (2018). The enduring appeal of psychosocial explanations of physical illness. In C. Johansen (Ed.), *Personality and disease: Scientific proof vs wishful thinking* (pp. 205–222). New York: Springer.

A historical overview of the frequently dubious ways in which psychological explanations, including those invoking personality, have been used to explain disease.

Hampson, S. (2017). Personality and health. *Oxford research encyclopedia of psychology.* Retrieved from https://oxfordre.com/psychology/view/10.1093/acrefore/9780190236557.001.0001/acrefore-9780190236557-e-121

This article offers a useful and balanced contemporary overview of the role of personality in health and illness.

Pelosi, A. (2019) Personality and fatal diseases: Revisiting a scientific scandal. *Journal of Health Psychology, 24*, 421–439.

This article presents a forensic examination of the questionable work of Grossarth-Maticek and Eysenck on supposedly cancer-prone personalities.

Petticrew, M. P., Lee, K., & McKee, M. (2012). Type A behavior pattern and coronary heart disease: Philip Morris's 'crown jewel'. *American Journal of Public Health, 102*, 2018–2025.

Petticrew and colleagues lay out a detailed exposé of the role of 'big tobacco' in funding, promoting, and potentially distorting research on Type A personality and heart disease.

REFERENCES

Bogg, T., & Roberts, B. W. (2004). Conscientiousness and health-related behaviors: A meta-analysis of the leading behavioral contributors to mortality. *Psychological Bulletin, 130*(6), 887–919. https://doi.org/10.1037/0033-2909.130.6.887

Buchanan, R. (2010). *Playing with fire: The controversial career of Hans J. Eysenck.* Oxford: Oxford University Press.

Buchanan, R., Haslam, N., & Pickren, W. (2018). The enduring appeal of psychosocial explanations of physical illness. In C. Johansen (Ed.), *Personality and disease: Scientific proof vs wishful thinking* (pp. 205–222). New York: Springer. https://doi.org/10.1016/B978-0-12-805300-3.00011-6

Carmelli, D., Rosenman, R. H., & Chesney, M. A. (1987). Stability of the Type A structured interview and related questionnaires in a 10-year follow-up of an adult cohort of twins. *Journal of Behavioral Medicine, 10*(5), 513–525. https://doi.org/10.1007/BF00846148

Chesney, M. A., Eagleston, J. R., & Rosenman, R. H. (1980). The Type A structured interview: A behavioral assessment in the rough. *Journal of Behavioral Assessment, 2*(4), 255–272. https://doi.org/10.1007/BF01666785

Cooper, T., Detre, T., & Weiss, S. M. (1981). Coronary-prone behavior and coronary heart disease: A critical review. *Circulation*, *263*, 1199–1215. https://doi.org/10.1161/01.CIR.63.6.1199

Dalen, J. E., Alpert, J. S., Goldberg, R. J., & Weinstein, R. S. (2014). The epidemic of the 20th century: Coronary heart disease. *The American Journal of Medicine*, *127*(9), 807–812. https://doi.org/10.1016/j.amjmed.2014.04.015

Dembroski, T., & Costa, P. (1987). Coronary prone behavior: Components of the Type A pattern and hostility. *Journal of Personality*, *55*, 211–235. https://doi.org/10.1111/j.1467-6494.1987.tb00435.x

Edwards, J. R., Baglioni, A. J., Jr., & Cooper, C. L. (1990). Examining the relationships among self-report measures of the Type A behavior pattern: The effects of dimensionality, measurement error, and differences in underlying constructs. *Journal of Applied Psychology*, *75*, 440–454. http://dx.doi.org/10.1037/0021-9010.75.4.440

Friedman, M., & Rosenman, R. H. (1959). Association of specific overt behavior pattern with blood and cardiovascular findings; blood cholesterol level, blood clotting time, incidence of arcus senilis, and clinical coronary artery disease. *Journal of the American Medical Association*, *169*(12), 1286–1296. https://doi: 10.1001/jama.1959.03000290012005

Haslam, N. (2019). Unicorns, snarks, and personality types: A review of the first 102 taxometric studies of personality. *Australian Journal of Psychology*, *71*, 39–49. https://doi.org/10.1111/ajpy.12228

John, O. P. (1990). The 'Big-Five' factor taxonomy: Dimensions of personality in the natural language and in questionnaires. In L. A. Pervin (Ed.), *Handbook of personality theory and research* (pp. 66–100). New York: Guilford Press.

Jokela, M., Batty, G. D., Nyberg, S. T., Virtanen, M., Nabi, H., Singh-Manoux, A., & Kivimäki, M. (2013). Personality and all-cause mortality: Individual-participant meta-analysis of 3,947 deaths in 76,150 adults. *American Journal of Epidemiology*, *178*, 667–675. https://doi.org/10.1093/aje/kwt170

Kendler, K. S., Kuhn, J., & Prescott, C. A. (2004). The interrelationship of neuroticism, sex, and stressful life events in the prediction of episodes of major depression. *American Journal of Psychiatry*, *161*(4), 631–636. http://dx.doi.org/10.1176/appi.ajp.161.4.631.

Kuper, H., Marmot, M., & Hemingway, H. (2002). Systematic review of prospective cohort studies of psychological factors in the etiology and prognosis of coronary heart disease. *Seminars in Vascular Medicine*, *2*(3), 267–314. doi: 10.1055/s-2002-35401

Lahey, B. B. (2009). Public health significance of neuroticism. *American Psychologist*, *64*(4), 241–256. https://doi.org/10.1037/a0015309

Marks, D. F., & Buchanan, R. D. (2020). King's College London's enquiry into Hans J Eysenck's 'Unsafe' publications must be properly completed. *Journal of Health Psychology*, *25*, 3–6. https://doi.org/10.1177/1359105319887791

Miller, T. Q., Smith, T. W., Turner, C. W., Guijarro, M. L., & Hallet, A. J. (1996). A meta-analytic review of research on hostility and physical health. *Psychological Bulletin, 119*, 322–348. doi: 10.1037/0033-2909.119.2.322

Miller, T. Q., Turner, C. W., Tindale, R. S., Posavac, E. J., & Dugoni, B. L. (1991). Reasons for the trend toward null findings in research on Type A behavior. *Psychological Bulletin*, *110*(3), 469–485. https://doi.org/10.1037/0033-2909.110.3.469

Myrtek, M. (2001). Meta-analyses of prospective studies on coronary heart disease, Type A personality, and hostility. *International Journal of Cardiology*, *79*, 245–251. https://doi.org/10.1016/S0167-5273(01)00441-7

Pelosi, A. (2019) Personality and fatal diseases: Revisiting a scientific scandal. *Journal of Health Psychology*, *24*, 421–439. https://doi.org/10.1177/1359105318822045

Petticrew, M. P., Lee, K., & McKee, M. (2012). Type A behavior pattern and coronary heart disease: Philip Morris's 'crown jewel'. *American Journal of Public Health*, *102*, 2018–2025. https://doi.org/10.2105/AJPH.2012.300816

Ragland, D. R., & Brand, R. J. (1988). Type A behavior and mortality from coronary heart disease. *New England Journal of Medicine, 318*(2), 65–69. doi: 10.1056/NEJM198801143180201

Rosenman, R. H., Brand, R. J., Jenkins, C. D., Friedman, M., Straus, R., & Wurm, M. (1975). Coronary heart disease in the Western Collaborative Group Study: Final follow-up experience of 8½ years. *JAMA*, *233*(8), 872–877. doi:10.1001/jama.1975.03260080034016

Shekelle, R. B., Hulley, S., Neaton, J., Billings, J., Borhani, N., Gerace, T., Jacobs, D., Lasser, N., Mittlemark, M., & Stamler, J., and the MRFIT Research Group (1985). The MRFIT behavior pattern study: II. Type A behavior pattern and incidence of coronary heart disease. *American Journal of Epidemiology*, *122*, 559–570. https://doi.org/10.1093/oxfordjournals.aje.a114135

Šmigelskas, K., Žemaitienė, N., Julkunen, J., & Kauhanen, J. (2015). Type A behavior pattern is not a predictor of premature mortality. *International Journal of Behavioral Medicine*, *22*, 161–169. https://doi.org/10.1007/s12529-014-9435-1

Wilmot, M. P., Haslam, N., Tian, J., & Ones, D. S. (2019). Direct and conceptual replications of the taxometric analysis of Type A behavior. *Journal of Personality and Social Psychology*, *116*, e12–e26. https://doi.org/10.1037/pspp0000195

8 | Health Inequalities: Revisiting Marmot, Rose, Shipley, and Hamilton (1978)

Marmot, M. G., Rose, G., Shipley, M., & Hamilton, P. J. S. (1978). Employment grade and coronary heart disease in British civil servants. *Journal of Epidemiology and Community Health, 32*, 244–249.

Benjamin Schüz

BACKGROUND

When Marmot and colleagues (1978) published their seminal study on socioeconomic differences in coronary health, Britain was a country characterised by stark social class differences. Arguments can be made that these class differences have remained largely unchanged since, and that these differences more than ever determine people's chances for happiness, well-being, and health. However, the Whitehall studies, on which this classic paper was based, have, at least, influenced how scientists have studied and explained social differences in health, and this process has led to an increased recognition of *social inequality* in research in Psychology.

SOCIAL CLASS AND INEQUALITY

Social structure in the United Kingdom has been shaped by a class system that was based on hereditary titles and is now structured along access to tangible and intangible resources. The most current National Statistics socioeconomic classification system (Office for National Statistics (UK), 2020) distinguishes between eight hierarchical classes (with subgroups) ranging from '(1) Higher managerial, administrative, and professional occupations' to '(8) Never worked or long-term unemployed'. Here, class is defined mostly through occupation, with different professions implying differences in factors such as income, social prestige, and through employment status – that is, whether and how long someone has been employed at all or unemployed.

However, class is only one indicator of *social inequality* (see Sidebar 8.1): educational attainment, income, or less tangible indicators such as reputation continue to determine an individual's standing in most Western societies. This standing, in turn, determines access to resources, both tangible and intangible, and thus influences important end points such as health and well-being (Mielck, 2005). These social issues provided the context and backdrop of inequality for Marmot et al.'s classic study, and, more broadly, the Whitehall studies.

Sidebar 8.1. Social Inequality

Social inequality, in the most abstract sense, is the uneven distribution of resources or end points, such as health, in a society along socially defined groups. Sometimes, social inequality is further differentiated into *horizontal* and *vertical* inequality (see Figure 8.1). Vertical inequality describes an uneven distribution of resources along more or less objective qualitative differences between individuals, for example in skills or qualifications, whereas horizontal inequality describes an uneven distribution of resources along characteristics that should not be related to skills, output, or qualifications, such as age, gender, or ethnicity (Spallek et al., 2012). Put more bluntly, horizontal inequality is likely to result from procedural or other discrimination. By contrast, vertical inequality is patterned along indicators of some inherent quality of the individual and might therefore seem more equitable. Whenever such differences in health outcomes, or in access to health-related resources, are perceived as unjust, preventable, and systemic, they

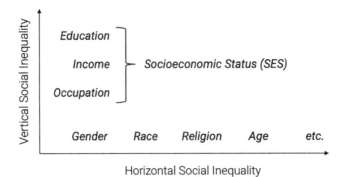

Figure 8.1 Horizontal and vertical dimensions of inequality (based on Mielck, 2005)

are often described as 'health inequities', which implies injustice, rather than unavoidable differences or inequalities (Arcaya et al., 2015).

However, such a differentiation of inequality dimensions remains silent as to which of these are most relevant for differences in health. There is considerable debate on how to operationalise and measure social inequality and socioeconomic position. For example, in a quite comprehensive handbook, Shaw et al. (2007) list no fewer than 83 indicators of socioeconomic position that range from individual-level indicators, such as years of formal education, to regionally aggregated indicators, such as the Scottish Index of Multiple Deprivation. These indicators also imply different resources – for example, formal education might indicate better orthographic skills, whereas differences in the index of multiple deprivation indicates, among others, the regional availability of resources such as jobs. Thus, the availability of one indicator or another, or the decision to examine inequalities based on one indicator over another, has considerable implications for understanding the mechanisms and pathways that link differences between people in the indicators to health outcomes (Galobardes, 2012).

INEQUALITY AND HEALTH

Social differences in health outcomes, such as morbidity and mortality, were of course not a new discovery when the Marmot et al. (1978) article was published. Knowledge about the social determinants of health informed the 1848 Public Health Act, which addressed social differences in the outbreaks of epidemics resulting from appalling sanitary conditions. Similarly, knowledge of differences in health care access informed the establishment of the National Health Service in the UK in 1948 to facilitate universal access. However, this has not necessarily resulted in improved health for all, as substantial inequalities in health persist, both in the United Kingdom and globally. For example, in England, a male child born today in one of the least deprived 10% areas can expect to live 9.7 years longer than a male child born in one of the 10% most deprived areas (Office for National Statistics, 2022). This difference is smaller for females (7.9 years), but is still unacceptably large. To a substantial degree, these social inequalities in life expectancy are due to social differences in the causes of death, such as cardiovascular disease: people living in the most deprived areas of England are more than four times as likely to die from cardiovascular disease (Public Health England, 2019). And while both cardiovascular mortality and inequalities in cardiovascular disease prevalence seem to be decreasing at least in European countries (Di Girolamo et al., 2020), the wider causes of health inequalities need further research. Marmot et al.'s (1978) study on occupational grade and mortality was a crucial initial step forwards in this regard.

DETAILED OVERVIEW

CORONARY MORTALITY AND OCCUPATIONAL GRADE: THE MARMOT ET AL. (1978) STUDY

The Marmot et al. (1978) study is the key publication arising from the Whitehall I study of employees in the British Civil Service. This study, commenced in 1967, screened and examined civil servants, and tracked their subsequent mortality. A key feature of the study is that it examined employees within the same organisation, working at the same location, but within the highly socially stratified environment of the British Civil Service.

In the study, more than 18,000 men, and, notably, no women, were initially screened and 17,530 were included in the final analyses. Participants' blood pressure, plasma cholesterol, blood glucose, height, and weight (for BMI computation) were assessed, and participants provided information on their grade of employment, smoking history, respiratory symptoms, medical history, and leisure-time activity. Employment grade was then classified into 'administrative professional', 'executive command clerical', and 'other' grades. The 'other' grade included mainly messengers and other unskilled manual workers and represents the lowest social status in the hierarchy within the civil service. These health data were then linked to the participants' records in the central registry of the National Health Service, and allowed extraction of mortality follow-up data across a period of seven and a half years.

Main results: Mortality risk and occupational grade

During the follow-up period, more than 1,000 of the originally-screened employees had died, of whom 462 had died of coronary heart disease (CHD). The main goal of all subsequent analyses was to find out whether these 462 individuals differed, in terms of their occupational grade, from those who survived. Because the population of public service workers could differ from the UK general population along factors relevant for mortality, such as age and smoking prevalence, the analyses adjusted for these potential differences. Four sets of analyses were conducted, as detailed below.

The researchers first examined the proportion of individuals who had died from coronary heart diseases, stratified by age group (40–49, 50–59, and 60–64), and then by occupational grade within each age group. In the youngest age group (40–49), six out of 280 employees (2.14%) in the lowest occupational grade, the 'other' group, had died from coronary heart disease over the study period. In the 'clerical' group, 12 out of 800 employees (1.5% of that group) had died from coronary heart disease. This proportion further decreased as occupational grade increased: 45 out of 5,733 (0.78%) participants in the 'professional/executive' group (representing 0.78%) had died from CHD, and none of the 470 in the 'administrative' group. The inverse relationship between grade of employment and risk of death by coronary heart disease was found in all age groups: the lower the employment grade, the higher the risk of dying from coronary heart disease. And this difference also increased with age such that in the youngest age group (40–49 years), men in the 'other' employment group were more than twice as likely to die from coronary heart disease than those in administrative professions. This difference increased to almost eightfold when comparing men in administrative positions to those in the 'other' employment grade in the 60–64 years of age group.

Marmot et al. then examined the prevalence of coronary risk factors (high blood pressure, high plasma cholesterol, smoking, high BMI, high blood glucose, low physical activity, and lower height) in the different occupational grades following a similar approach: they counted the proportion of employees in the different age groups who exhibited a specific risk factor and stratified this by occupational grade. What they found was remarkable. With the exception of plasma cholesterol, all of the risk factors examined (systolic blood pressure, smoking, BMI, blood glucose, physical activity), as well as height, followed the same distribution as mortality risk: the lower the occupational grade, the higher the prevalence of one or more major coronary risk factors (Figure 8.2).

In a third set of analyses, the authors examined whether the differences in the coronary risk factors shown in Figure 8.2 were related to the grade differences in mortality. Essentially, this was a question about underlying mechanisms: if the differences in mortality followed a pattern similar to the differences in risk factors, this could suggest two possible underlying causes: either that the differences in risk factors directly influenced the differences in mortality (a causal explanation) or that a third variable caused both the differences in risk factors and the differences in mortality to follow a similar pattern. To test the first possibility, the authors plotted CHD mortality in the different grades along risk factor levels, and then applied statistical techniques (see Sidebar 8.2) to examine the unique contribution of each risk factor in the different grade groups. The idea here was to

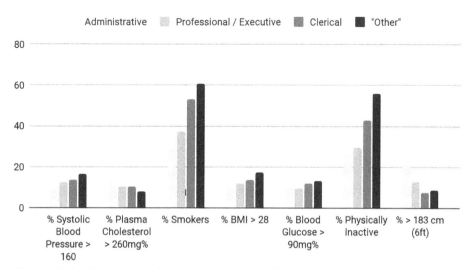

Figure 8.2 Prevalence of major coronary risk factors in occupational grade groups (based on data from Marmot et al., 1978)

examine whether the presence of a risk factor within a specific occupational group explained the association between occupational group and mortality.

Across all age groups, the risk of an employee in the 'other' occupational grade (lowest grade) dying from coronary heart disease was four times higher than that of an employee in the 'administrative' grade (highest grade). Once the grade differences in all risk factors were taken into account, this difference in mortality risk was reduced, indicating that these risk factors explained a proportion of the differences in mortality. This is remarkable because while the association between employment grade and mortality is partly attributable to the coronary risk factors, these factors alone do not fully explain the association. A logistic regression confirmed that the coronary risk factors explained only around 40% of the association between grade and mortality, leaving 60% of the association between employment grade and mortality unexplained. This means that while employees in the lower occupation grades did indeed smoke more, had higher systolic blood pressure and some other risk factors, as well as lower total cholesterol levels, these differences alone could not explain the observed grade-related mortality differences. In short, there must be some other factor or variable that explained these underlying grade differences in mortality. The key question was what these factors were.

Sidebar 8.2. Identifying Risk Factors for Mortality: Analysing Indirect Effects

To examine the contribution of risk factors to cardiovascular mortality, Marmot et al. (1978) used statistical methods that were considered 'state of the art' at the time, but have been modified and refined since. Questions about the quantifiable contribution of a particular risk factor, or a combination of risk factors, to socioeconomic differences in mortality imply so-called 'indirect effects', in which an exposure variable (e.g., social inequality) affects an outcome variable (e.g., mortality) via a set of intermediary or mediating variables (e.g., risk factors). The underlying assumption here is that variation in the exposure variable causes variation in the intermediary variables, which in turn cause variation in the outcome variable (the indirect effect). If all relevant intermediary or *mediating* variables are known, the effects of the exposure variable on the outcome variable could be fully accounted for. This is particularly interesting as some of these mediating variables could be modifiable (e.g., in interventions).

In psychology, and health psychology in particular, analysis of indirect effects has traditionally been employed more frequently than in other disciplines. Most current applications in psychology employ some form of conditional process analysis (Hayes, 2017), which involves the estimation of indirect effects within an ordinal least squares regression framework (process analysis), together with analyses to identify the boundary conditions for these indirect effects (conditional analysis). In epidemiology, however, there is an ongoing debate concerning the causal assumptions underlying such analyses and the biases that may arise from them. These include biases through confounding between the mediator and outcome (*collider bias*: e.g., in examining whether the effects of ambient noise on cardiovascular health are mediated through blood pressure, all variables that could affect both blood pressure and cardiovascular health, such as individual BMI, could act as confounders). Other sources of bias result from uncontrolled or difficult-to-estimate interactions between exposure and mediator (e.g., when effects of a behavioural intervention to improve cardiovascular health are mediated through physical activity, and the natural baseline rate of physical activity in the population cannot be accounted for). Finally, biases might result from confounding between the mediator and the outcome conditional on the exposure (e.g., when the effects of smoking on cardiovascular disease are mediated through atherosclerosis, which are both dependent on blood pressure, which in turn is dependent on smoking status: Richiardi et al., 2013).

The fourth set of analyses sought to test and rule out alternative explanations for the observed associations. In particular, Marmot et al. examined whether pre-existing illnesses might have determined the occupation in which someone was employed. The 'other' category in the study describes unskilled work, which might feasibly have been a solution for employees unfit for more demanding work. If this were the case, the increased CHD mortality risk found in the lower employment grades may not be attributable to social inequality *per se* but, rather, to the fact that employees in the lower grades had poorer health in the first place. Marmot et al. examined this by determining the association between occupational grade and mortality separately for those who had, and those who did not have, a pre-existing medical condition (cardiovascular, pulmonological, or diabetes) at the time of their employment. This analysis showed that the association between occupational grade and mortality was stronger in employees who had a pre-existing medical condition. In fact, there was a four-fold increase in mortality risk for employees in the 'other' occupations compared to those in administrative jobs. However, in employees without pre-existing conditions, a class gradient remained, with those in the 'other' category still about twice as likely to die from coronary heart disease than those in the 'administrative' category. The gradient was less clear for the other categories. Marmot et al. interpreted this as highlighting that, although selection might play a role, it could not explain the gradient in the symptom-free group.

DEVELOPMENTS

BEYOND THE CLASSIC STUDY: WHITEHALL II AND A SOCIAL-ECOLOGICAL FRAMEWORK OF HEALTH INEQUALITY

A key contribution of the Marmot et al. (1978) study, and of the multiple publications coming out of the Whitehall I and II studies, is the demonstration of a clear socioeconomic gradient in mortality, which is complex in its origins and not attributable to any single medical or behavioural risk factor, or to selection effects. Given that the study was conducted in the relatively controlled setting of employees of the British Civil Service in Whitehall, with most, if not all, participants employed in physically undemanding occupations with regular wages, allows a unique view into the effects of a socially determined stratification feature: occupational grade.

The Whitehall I study sparked debate about the causes and mechanisms underlying the grade differences in mortality, specifically the question of what caused the grade differences in mortality beyond the risk factors that were assessed. A second, even larger study of British Civil Servants, the Whitehall II study (Marmot et al., 1991), with a particular focus on work stress and social factors, was consequentially initiated and is still ongoing. The Whitehall II study initially recruited just over 10,000 men and women in 1985. In 2019–2020, its 13th wave of data collection was completed, with the initial participants now aged between 64 and 89. With more and more data on both work- and out-of-work influences on health, a more complex picture on the social gradient in health is beginning to emerge, although it is far from complete. Data from the Whitehall II study highlight a range of factors that explain occupational grade differences in health outcomes, from organisational structure and work climate (e.g., De Vogli et al., 2007), to social support provided through networks outside work (Fuhrer & Stansfeld, 2002; see Jetten, Bentley, & Young, Chapter 9, this volume), early childhood social influences (Bartley et al., 2007), and health behaviours (Stringhini et al., 2011). As the cohort reached its retiring age, the focus of recent studies has widened to include examining protective factors for health during retirement and the social gradient in dementia risk (e.g., Sommerlad et al., 2019). The inclusion of job control and social support in the study acknowledges psychological models of work stress (Demand-Control-Support model; Karasek & Theorell, 1990), which proposes that work stress results from the interaction of high demands at work, low control over how these work demands are being carried out, and low available social support either at the workplace or beyond (see Sani, Chapter 5, this volume).

Whitehall II also included a more detailed assessment of health-related behaviours and showed that differential engagement in these behaviours could explain the social gradient in health beyond the findings from Marmot et al. (1978). For example, Stringhini et al. (2011) showed that socioeconomic differences in key health behaviours (smoking status, alcohol consumption, fruit and vegetable consumption, physical activity) could explain a greater proportion of the variability in mortality rates attributable to socioeconomic differences than the analyses in Whitehall I, although it still did not explain the association fully.

The follow-up Whitehall studies suggest a more complex pattern of effects, whereby socioeconomic and risk indicators may interact in explaining disparities in health outcomes. For example, lower control over life at home was found to explain socioeconomic differences in coronary heart disease among women, but not among men (Chandola et al., 2004), which suggests gender-specific effects of risk and protective factors. In summary, the Whitehall studies contributed to a better understanding of health inequalities and have pointed to complex interactions between socioeconomic and risk factors on multiple levels.

Marmot subsequently chaired the World Health Organization's Commission on the Social Determinants of Health, which has produced an influential social-ecological framework integrating these findings (Commission on the Social Determinants of Health, 2008; Figure 8.3). This social-ecological framework integrates the structural determinants of health inequalities, which are socially determined, across multiple ecological levels. It outlines three spheres of influences on health, which, in themselves, might operate on multiple environmental levels: (1) a higher-order sphere outlining factors in the socioeconomic and political context that affect health, such as economic policies, governance factors, or cultural and social norms; (2) a sphere outlining how these higher-order factors determine an individual's standing within society, for example through educational attainment (which comes with access to resources and prestige), or through prestige assigned to specific occupations, or through societal gender norms (no distinction is made according to horizontal or vertical dimensions of inequality); and (3) intermediary and social determinants of health from more macro-level determinants, such as equal access to healthcare, to more micro-level determinants, such as individual health behaviours (see Ruiter, de Leeuw, Crutzen, and Kok, Chapter 4, this volume). The distinction between spheres of influence allows the identification of additional mechanisms through which social inequality might affect health (e.g., food outlets; Berger et al., 2019). The social-ecological framework can also outline courses for action to reduce inequalities (Solar & Irwin, 2008) and inform more systematic research into the causal mechanisms underlying socioeconomic differences in health.

SOCIAL INEQUALITY AND HEALTH PSYCHOLOGY

Since Marmot et al.'s (1978) study, psychologists working in health contexts have increasingly focused their research on issues of inequality, social class, intersectionality, and related phenomena. This research has eschewed an exclusive focus on socioeconomic indices and emphasised salient social-psychological and cognitive processes, and the interaction of factors from behavioural theories with socioeconomically-patterned differences in access to resources. Some findings are briefly worth highlighting here.

For example, experiencing acute shortages of material resources (i.e., being in a state of poverty) causes changes in cognitive processes (Mani et al., 2013), and affected individuals prioritise short-term gains over longer-term goals. Pepper and Nettle (2017) argue that such patterns are the result of a trade-off between distal positive consequences in the future (better health) against proximal positive consequences in the present (pleasure). They further propose the 'uncontrollable mortality risk' hypothesis that this cognitive shift is due to a lack of perceived control over mortality: they argue that if mortality is inevitable and attributable largely to external factors, it would not make sense to invest in health behaviours, as it is unlikely that any benefits of investing in health will be realised.

It is known that disadvantage and discrimination lead to experiencing more stress, which in turn can result in maladaptive behavioural coping, such as smoking (Jahnel et al., 2019). Jahnel and colleagues (2018) also showed that the time people spend in environments with differing health regulations (e.g., smoking bans vs. no smoking bans) is socially patterned and predicts health behaviour. In these examples, stress and the exposure to regulations serve as intermediary factors in explaining socioeconomic differences in health-related behaviours (i.e., act as *mediators*). However, the presence and intensity of social inequality might also change the effects of proximal determinants of behaviour such as attitudes or intentions (i.e., it may act as a *moderator*; e.g., Schüz, Conner, et al., 2021; see also Conner & Norman, Chapter 2, this volume). Unfortunately, socioeconomic influences on health behaviours are poorly specified in most theories of health behaviour (Schüz, 2017), which makes the relationships between proximal determinants of behaviour and socioeconomic factors difficult to ascertain: are there direct, indirect, interactive, or other complex relationships?

Theoretically, the answer is clear. Most social-cognitive theories, such as those subsumed in the reasoned action approach (Fishbein, 2008), assume that influences from more distal variables, such as age, sex, or socioeconomic factors, are mediated through a parsimonious set of social cognitions (see Sidebar 8.2). A recent multi-sample study (Hagger & Hamilton, 2021) provides some evidence for these indirect effects. In this study, age was found to predict attitudes, social norms, and perceived behavioural control towards binge drinking, which, in turn, predicted lower engagement in binge drinking. However, these indirect effects usually do not fully explain socioeconomic differences in health behaviours, and direct effects remain.

It is likely that the relationships between social-cognitive determinants and health behaviours are modified by socioeconomic factors. For example, a recent study on COVID-protective behaviours, such as hand hygiene, masking, maintaining social distancing, or reducing social contacts (Schüz, Conner, et al., 2021), indicated that the relationship between behavioural intentions and protective behaviours varied as a function of deprivation: for individuals living in more deprived areas, the relationship between intentions and behaviour was weaker than for those living in less deprived areas. As discussed above, socioeconomic status determines access to resources, opportunities, and barriers, and these differences in access determine whether and to what degree individual cognitions, such as intentions, can be translated into behaviour. The study also showed that these resources are located at the level of the individual (e.g., knowledge or skills), the immediate environment someone lives in (e.g., walkable neighbourhoods), everyday settings (e.g., workplaces), or on a societal level (e.g., access to healthcare; see also the socio-ecological framework in Figure 8.3).

From a theoretical viewpoint, such moderated effects imply that it is an overgeneralisation to assume that the effects of behavioural determinants are equal across socioeconomic backgrounds. Accordingly, theories in health psychology would profit from revision. The poor specification of socioeconomic influences potentially reflects a trend in psychology to overgeneralise findings from middle- and

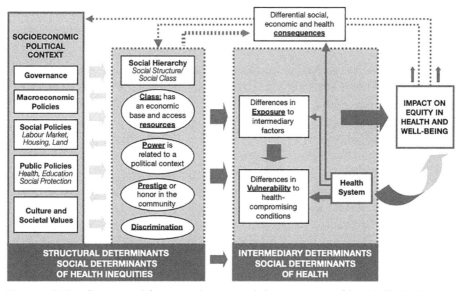

Figure 8.3 Conceptual framework on social determinants of health (Solar & Irwin, 2008)

higher-class samples (see APA Task Force on Socioeconomic Status, 2007). Particularly relevant for interventions, however, such differences in the effects of social-cognitive determinants also imply that interventions informed by determinants could be less effective in individuals from more deprived backgrounds. Such differential effects can result in differences in the effects of behaviour change interventions (Schüz & Webb Hooper, 2020), which in turn may increase health inequalities (so-called equity impacts of interventions: see Sidebar 8.3). For example, a systematic review (Schüz et al., 2017) showed that the relationships between behavioural intentions in physical activity are stronger in samples with higher educational attainment compared to samples with lower educational attainment. Interventions to increase physical activity that target individual intentions, such as through persuasive messages, even if effective in increasing intentions overall, could result in differences in changes in activity – as those with higher educational attainment might be better equipped to translate intentions into behaviour.

Sidebar 8.3. Equity Impact of Interventions to Promote Health and Well-being

Equity relates to whether differences in an outcome such as health are perceived as unjust. The so-called 'Sesame Street Effect' is a classic example of equity impacts of an intervention. Cook et al. (1975) found that watching the children's television show *Sesame Street* improved literacy and numeracy skills among all elementary school children who watched it, but these effects were stronger in less

(Continued)

(Continued)

disadvantaged children than in those children from disadvantaged backgrounds that the show was initially designed for. It was suggested that this was likely because parents from middle-class backgrounds engaged with the show more than parents from more deprived backgrounds. Moreover, this differential effect was found to increase inequalities between poor and middle-class children. Brown et al. (2014) demonstrated similar effects in public health smoking cessation interventions, where behavioural support for smoking cessation was found to disproportionly benefit smokers from less disadvantaged backgrounds (Brown et al., 2014).

Equity impacts are a considerable population health challenge, because such interventions may inadvertently increase health inequalities. Lehne et al.'s (2019) logic model for interventions to improve physical activity suggests that a negative equity impact of behavioural interventions could result from differences in reach, differences in the engagement with supposedly effective intervention components, differences in retention, or differential effects of intervention components.

To systematically examine the equity impact of interventions, the Equity Group within the Cochrane Collaboration has developed a framework (PRO-GRESS-Plus; O'Neill et al., 2014) that outlines some of the most relevant dimensions of social stratification for health. PROGRESS is an acronym and stands for 'Place of Residence', 'Race/Ethnicity/Culture/Language', 'Occupation', 'Gender/Sex', 'Religion', 'Education', 'Socioeconomic status', and 'Social capital', with 'plus' indicating additional factors such as age or sexual orientation – dimensions that are related to experiences of discrimination.

While PROGRESS-Plus has been employed relatively widely to examine differential effects of interventions to improve health, it only recently began to attract more attention in health psychology, indicating that the systematic exploration of the determinants underlying socioeconomic differences in health-related behaviours is a field ripe for further research. However, differential outcomes of interventions are still not routinely reported in research. For example, an equity-focused systematic review on physical activity interventions (Attwood et al., 2016) found that out of 171 intervention studies that assessed PROGRESS-Plus factors, only 25 actually reported analyses stratified by at least one of these dimensions.

Various mechanisms may underlie the differential effects of behaviour change interventions. If interventions require recipients to access cognitive or other resources in order to obtain, understand, and act on health-related information, these interventions are less likely to be effective in disadvantaged groups, as access to these resources is tied to social disadvantage (Adams et al., 2016). At the same time, however, even behavioural intervention techniques such as nudging, which supposedly require minimal resources, are likely to produce equity impacts, at least under some circumstances. For example, a recent review of real-world nudging interventions for dietary behaviours (Schüz, Meyerhof, et al., 2021) found that cognitively-oriented nudges such as a traffic-light nutrition score had more substantial effects among less deprived participants, whereas nudges that made access to healthy foods easier were more likely to profit participants regardless of their socioeconomic background.

However, most current trials of behavioural interventions are actually designed to detect effects of the intervention in the overall population rather than differential effects in socio-demographic subgroups. Methodological strategies, such as pooled coordinated re-analyses of multiple similar studies (Czwikla et al., 2021), or increasing power through propensity-score matched samples (Renneberg et al., 2022) could overcome some of these limitations, but consequently, more interventions need to be designed and powered to detect equity impacts and subsequently provide more realistic estimates of their effectiveness in different socioeconomic subgroups. However, the extra effort would be worth it, as this would allow the creation of a more reliable evidence base on socioeconomic effects of the components of behavioural interventions and, in turn, potentially more effective behavioural interventions.

CONCLUSIONS

Social inequalities in health were not unknown before the Whitehall studies, but Marmot et al.'s (1978) classic study contributed extensively to understanding the causes underlying the social patterning of health. Even though the classic study is based on a specific British social classification mechanism – the distinction of several occupational grades within the British Civil Service – social patterns in health have subsequently been established as universal: the more socially disadvantaged a person is, the worse their health. The Whitehall studies highlighted that in order to understand health inequalities, an integrative perspective on inequalities is needed in which neither a focus on the broader societal causes of inequalities nor a focus on individual behaviours suffices. A broader and more systematic examination of social inequalities and their role for individual psychological processes is still way out on the horizon and this probably has as much to do with the inherent focus of the field of health psychology on individual processes as it does with the social backgrounds of the majority of actors within academic psychology, which is still predominantly white and middle-class.

The notion that interventions to improve health and well-being could inadvertently increase health inequalities through equity impacts deserves further research and attention in health psychology, as the equity impacts of interventions are rarely reported (see Sidebar 8.3). Reducing unjust and unnecessary inequalities in health is a key societal challenge, and will require significant resources. However, clear direction is needed as to where to allocate resources, and the findings from the Whitehall studies, and subsequent reviews (Marmot et al., 2020), are an excellent starting point in this regard. Health psychology is well placed to pick up the baton, and, through its strong tradition in systematic research into behavioural interventions, provide some pathways towards the reduction of health inequalities.

FURTHER READING

For a detailed overview on international health inequalities, the OECD report *Health for everyone?* is highly recommended (OECD, 2019). A follow-up on the 2010 Marmot review with a focus on England is provided by Marmot et al. (2020). For a stimulating discussion on the social psychological implications of inequality, readers are directed to Manstead (2018). A regularly updated directory on activities of the American Psychological Association dealing with socioeconomic status can be found at www.apa.org/pi/ses. A highly accessible overview of inequality effects on psychological and behavioural processes is provided in Keith Payne's excellent book, *The broken ladder: How inequality affects the way we think, live, and die* (Payne, 2017).

The issues of intervention-generated inequities and how these might be particularly relevant for interventions that target health behaviours are introduced in Adams et al. (2016). As a general resource on issues relating to social epidemiology that health psychologists might want to consult, textbooks such as the one edited by Berkman, Kawachi, and Glymour (2014) provide good generalised overviews.

The Australian Broadcasting Corporation (ABC) has published a series of radio lectures by Sir Michael Marmot that provide an excellent overview on health inequalities (www.abc.net.au/radionational/programs/boyerlectures/series/2016-boyer-lectures/7802472) in four episodes:

1. Social justice and health: Making a difference (www.abc.net.au/radio-national/programs/boyerlectures/social-justice-and-health-making-a-difference/7804552)

2. Living and working (www.abc.net.au/radionational/programs/boyerlec-tures/boyer-lecture-living-and-working/7804514)

3. Give every child the best start (www.abc.net.au/radionational/programs/boyerlectures/boyer-lecture-give-every-child-the-best-start/7787486)

4. Health inequality and the causes of the causes (www.abc.net.au/radio-national/programs/boyerlectures/boyer-lecture-health-inequality-and-the-causes-of-the-causes/7763106)

REFERENCES

Adams, J., Mytton, O., White, M., & Monsivais, P. (2016). Why are some population interventions for diet and obesity more equitable and effective than others? The role of individual agency. *PLoS Medicine*, *13*(4), e1001990. https://doi.org/10.1371/journal.pmed.1001990

APA Task Force on Socioeconomic Status. (2007). *Report of the APA Task Force on Socioeconomic Status*. Washington, DC: American Psychological Association. https://doi.org/https://www.apa.org/pi/ses/resources/publications/task-force-2006.pdf

Arcaya, M. C., Arcaya, A. L., & Subramanian, S. V. (2015). Inequalities in health: Definitions, concepts, and theories. *Global Health Action*, *8*(1), 27106. https://doi.org/10.3402/gha.v8.27106

Attwood, S., van Sluijs, E., & Sutton, S. (2016). Exploring equity in primary-care-based physical activity interventions using PROGRESS-Plus: A systematic review and evidence synthesis. *International Journal of Behavioral Nutrition and Physical Activity*, *13*, 60. https://doi.org/10.1186/s12966-016-0384-8

Bartley, M., Head, J., & Stansfeld, S. (2007). Is attachment style a source of resilience against health inequalities at work? *Social Science and Medicine*, *64*(4), 765–775. https://doi.org/10.1016/j.socscimed.2006.09.033

Berger, N., Kaufman, T. K., Bader, M. D. M., Rundle, A. G., Mooney, S. J., Neckerman, K. M., & Lovasi, G. S. (2019). Disparities in trajectories of changes in the unhealthy food environment in New York City: A latent class growth analysis, 1990–2010. *Social Science and Medicine, 234*, Article 112362. https://doi.org/10.1016/j.socscimed.2019.112362

Berkman, L. F., Kawachi, I., & Glymour, M. M. (2014). *Social epidemiology* (2nd ed.). Oxford: Oxford University Press.

Brown, T., Platt, S., & Amos, A. (2014). Equity impact of population-level interventions and policies to reduce smoking in adults: a systematic review. *Drugs and Alcohol Dependency, 138*, 7–16. https://doi.org/10.1016/j.drugalcdep.2014.03.001

Chandola, T., Kuper, H., Singh-Manoux, A., Bartley, M., & Marmot, M. (2004). The effect of control at home on CHD events in the Whitehall II study: Gender differences in psychosocial domestic pathways to social inequalities in CHD. *Social Science and Medicine, 58*(8), 1501–1509. https://doi.org/10.1016/s0277-9536(03)00352-6

Commission on the Social Determinants of Health (Ed.). (2008). *Closing the gap in a generation: Health equity through action on the social determinants of health*. Geneva: World Health Organization.

Cook, T. D., Appleton, H., Conner, R. F., Shaffer, A., Tamkin, G., & Weber, S. J. (1975). *"Sesame Street" Revisited*. New York: Russell Sage Foundation.

Czwikla, G., Boen, F., Cook, D. G., de Jong, J., Harris, T., Hilz, L. K., ... & Bolte, G. (2021). Equity-specific effects of interventions to promote physical activity among middle-aged and older adults: Results from applying a novel equity-specific re-analysis strategy. *International Journal of Behavioral Nutrition and Physical Activity, 18*(1), 65. https://doi.org/10.1186/s12966-021-01131-w

De Vogli, R., Ferrie, J. E., Chandola, T., Kivimäki, M., & Marmot, M. G. (2007). Unfairness and health: Evidence from the Whitehall II study. *Journal of Epidemiology and Community Health, 61*(6), 513–518. https://doi.org/10.1136/jech.2006.052563

Di Girolamo, C., Nusselder, W. J., Bopp, M., Brønnum-Hansen, H., Costa, G., Kovács, K., Leinsalu, M., Martikainen, P., Pacelli, B., Rubio Valverde, J., & Mackenbach, J. P. (2020). Progress in reducing inequalities in cardiovascular disease mortality in Europe. *Heart, 106*(1), 40. https://doi.org/10.1136/heartjnl-2019-315129

Fishbein, M. (2008). A reasoned action approach to health promotion. *Medical Decision Making, 28*(6), 834–844. https://doi.org/10.1177/0272989x08326092

Fuhrer, R., & Stansfeld, S. A. (2002). How gender affects patterns of social relations and their impact on health: A comparison of one or multiple sources of support from 'close persons'. *Social Science and Medicine, 54*(5), 811–825. https://doi.org/10.1016/S0277-9536(01)00111-3

Galobardes, B. (2012). Socioeconomic inequalities in health: Individual or area level; does it matter? *BMC Public Health, 12*, 171. https://doi.org/10.1186/1471-2458-12-171

Hagger, M. S., & Hamilton, K. (2021). Effects of socio-structural variables in the theory of planned behavior: A mediation model in multiple samples and behaviors. *Psychology and Health, 36*(3), 307–333. https://doi.org/10.1080/08870446.2020.1784420

Hayes, A. F. (2017). *Introduction to mediation, moderation, and conditional process analysis: A regression-based approach*. New York: Guilford Press.

Jahnel, T., Ferguson, S. G., Shiffman, S., & Schüz, B. (2019). Daily stress as link between disadvantage and smoking: An ecological momentary assessment study. *BMC Public Health, 19*(1), 1284. https://doi.org/10.1186/s12889-019-7631-2

Jahnel, T., Ferguson, S. G., Shiffman, S., Thrul, J., & Schüz, B. (2018). Momentary smoking context as a mediator of the relationship between SES and smoking. *Addictive Behaviors, 83*, 136–141. https://doi.org/10.1016/j.addbeh.2017.12.014

Karasek, R., & Theorell, T. (1990). *Healthy work: Stress, productivity, and the reconstruction of working life*. New York: Basic Books.

Lehne, G., Voelcker-Rehage, C., Meyer, J., Bammann, K., Gansefort, D., Brüchert, T., & Bolte, G. (2019). Equity impact assessment of interventions to promote physical activity among older adults: A logic model framework. *International Journal of Environmental Research and Public Health*, *16*(3), 420. https://doi.org/10.3390/ijerph16030420

Mani, A., Mullainathan, S., Shafir, E., & Zhao, J. (2013). Poverty impedes cognitive function. *Science*, *341*(6149), 976–980. https://doi.org/10.1126/science.1238041

Manstead, A. S. R. (2018). The psychology of social class: How socioeconomic status impacts thought, feelings, and behaviour. *British Journal of Social Psychology*, *57*(2), 267–291. https://doi.org/https://doi.org/10.1111/bjso.12251

Marmot, M. G., Allen, J., Boyce, T., Goldblatt, P., & Morrison, J. (2020). *Health equity in England: The Marmot Review 10 years on*. London: Institute of Health Equity. www.health.org.uk/publications/reports/the-marmot-review-10-years-on

Marmot, M. G., Rose, G., Shipley, M., & Hamilton, P. J. (1978). Employment grade and coronary heart disease in British civil servants. *Journal of Epidemiology and Community Health*, *32*(4), 244–249. https://doi.org/10.1136/jech.32.4.244

Marmot, M. G., Smith, G. D., Stansfeld, S., Patel, C., North, F., Head, J., White, I., Brunner, E., & Feeney, A. (1991). Health inequalities among British civil servants: The Whitehall II study. *Lancet*, *337*(8754), 1387–1393. https://doi.org/10.1016/0140-6736(91)93068-k

Mielck, A. (2005). *Soziale Ungleichheit und Gesundheit. Einführung in die aktuelle Diskussion*. Bern, Switzerland: Hans Huber.

O'Neill, J., Tabish, H., Welch, V., Petticrew, M., Pottie, K., Clarke, M., ... Tugwell, P. (2014). Applying an equity lens to interventions: Using PROGRESS ensures consideration of socially stratifying factors to illuminate inequities in health. *Journal of Clinical Epidemiology*, *67*(1), 56–64. https://doi.org/10.1016/j.jclinepi.2013.08.005

OECD. (2019). *Health for everyone?* Paris: OECD. https://doi.org/doi:https://doi.org/10.1787/3c8385d0-en

Office for National Statistics (UK). (2020). *SOC 2020 Volume 3: The National Statistics Socio-economic Classification (NS-SEC rebased on the SOC 2020)*. London: Office for National Statistics. Available at: www.ons.gov.uk/methodology/classificationsand standards/standardoccupationalclassificationsoc/soc2020/soc2020volume3 thenationalstatisticssocioeconomicclassificationnssecrebasedonthesoc2020 (retrieved 9 August 2022).

Office for National Statistics (UK). (2022). *Health state life expectancies by national deprivation deciles, England: 2018 to 2020*. London: Office for National Statistics. Available at: www.ons.gov.uk/peoplepopulationandcommunity/healthandsocialcare/ healthinequalities/bulletins/healthstatelifeexpectanciesbyindexofmultipledeprivationimd/ 2018to2020 (retrieved 11 August 2022).

Payne, K. (2017). *The broken ladder: How inequality affects the way we think, live, and die*. London: Viking.

Pepper, G. V., & Nettle, D. (2017). The behavioural constellation of deprivation: Causes and consequences. *Behavioral and Brain Sciences*, *40*, Article e314. https://doi.org/10.1017/S0140525X1600234X

Public Health England. (2019). *Health matters: Preventing cardiovascular disease*. London: Public Health England. Available at: www.gov.uk/government/publications/ health-matters-preventing-cardiovascular-disease/health-matters-preventing-cardiovascular-disease#health-inequalities (retrieved 7 January 2022).

Renneberg, B., Schulze, J., Böhme, S., West, S. G., & Schüz, B. (2022). Effectiveness and equity evaluation of an insurance-wide telephone-counseling program for self-management of chronic diseases: The Health Coach Study. *Applied Psychology: Health and Well-Being*. Online first, 18 November 2021. https://doi.org/10.1111/aphw.12322

Richiardi, L., Bellocco, R., & Zugna, D. (2013). Mediation analysis in epidemiology: Methods, interpretation and bias. *International Journal of Epidemiology*, *42*(5), 1511–1519. https://doi.org/10.1093/ije/dyt127

Schüz, B. (2017). Socio-economic status and theories of health behaviour: Time to upgrade a control variable. *British Journal of Health Psychology*, *22*(1), 1–7. https://doi.org/10.1111/bjhp.12205

Schüz, B., Conner, M., Wilding, S., Alhawtan, R., Prestwich, A., & Norman, P. (2021). Do socio-structural factors moderate the effects of health cognitions on COVID-19 protection behaviours? *Social Science and Medicine*, *285*, 114261. https://doi.org/10.1016/j.socscimed.2021.114261

Schüz, B., Li, A. S.-W., Hardinge, A., McEachan, R. R. C., & Conner, M. (2017). Socioeconomic status as a moderator between social cognitions and physical activity: Systematic review and meta-analysis based on the Theory of Planned Behavior. *Psychology of Sport and Exercise*, *30*, 186–195. https://doi.org/10.1016/j.psychsport.2017.03.004

Schüz, B., Meyerhof, H., Hilz, L. K., & Mata, J. (2021). Equity effects of dietary nudging field experiments: Systematic review. *Frontiers in Public Health*, *9*, 668998. https://doi.org/10.3389/fpubh.2021.668998

Schüz, B., & Webb Hooper, M. (2020). Addressing underserved populations and disparities in behavior change. In K. Hamilton, L. D. Cameron, M. S. Hagger, N. Hankonen, & T. Lintunen (Eds.), *The handbook of behavior change* (pp. 385–400). Cambridge: Cambridge University Press. https://doi.org/DOI: 10.1017/9781108677318.027

Shaw, M., Galobardes, B., Lawlor, D. A., Lynch, J., Wheeler, B., & Davey Smith, G. (2007). *The handbook of inequality and socioeconomic position: Concepts and measures*. Bristol: Policy Press.

Solar, O., & Irwin, A. (2008). *A conceptual framework for action on the social determinants of health* [pdf]. Geneva: World Health Organization. www.who.int/sdhconference/resources/ConceptualframeworkforactiononSDH_eng.pdf

Sommerlad, A., Sabia, S., Singh-Manoux, A., Lewis, G., & Livingston, G. (2019). Association of social contact with dementia and cognition: 28-year follow-up of the Whitehall II cohort study. *PLoS Medicine*, *16*(8), Article e1002862. https://doi.org/10.1371/journal.pmed.1002862

Spallek, J., Kuntz, B., & Schott, T. (2012). Sozialepidemiologie. *Public Health Forum*, *20*(3), 4–8. https://doi.org/doi:10.1016/j.phf.2012.06.015

Stringhini, S., Dugravot, A., Shipley, M., Goldberg, M., Zins, M., Kivimäki, M., Marmot, M., Sabia, S., & Singh-Manoux, A. (2011). Health behaviours, socioeconomic status, and mortality: Further analyses of the British Whitehall II and the French GAZEL prospective cohorts. *PLoS Medicine*, *8*(2), Article e1000419. https://doi.org/10.1371/journal.pmed.1000419

9

Social Networks and Health: Revisiting Berkman and Syme (1979)

Berkman, L. F., & Syme, S. L. (1979). Social networks, host resistance, and mortality: A nine-year follow-up study of Alameda County residents. *American Journal of Epidemiology, 109*, 186–204.

Jolanda Jetten, Sarah V. Bentley & Tarli Young

BACKGROUND

Currently, there is an ardent interest among health researchers in the way that both social connectedness and social isolation can affect health and well-being. However, this interest in the *social* determinants of health is only relatively recent: for decades, when researchers set out to examine predictors of health, they focused mostly on behavioural factors *other than* social connectedness. They would, for instance, explore the extent to which certain behaviours were associated with living longer, such as eating regular meals, receiving adequate sleep, maintaining an optimum weight, not smoking, limiting alcohol consumption, and participating in regular physical activity (Houseman & Dorman, 2005). While all of those personal health habits are important when predicting who will live longer, the work by Lisa Berkman and Leonard Syme (1979) was one of the first studies that convincingly showed not only that people who lacked social connectedness were more likely to die younger, but also that this relationship held when accounting for the more established personal health behaviours, such as over-eating, lack of physical exercise, alcohol consumption, and smoking. In short, Berkman and Syme demonstrated that social connectedness is a unique and strong predictor of health and mortality.

The work by Berkman and Syme has been of particular importance in advancing our knowledge of the important role that social factors, such as social connectedness, play when understanding health outcomes. As we outline in the next sections, this demonstration that social behaviours uniquely predict health was a profoundly new insight at the time, and its practical implications have been enormous. In particular, it has since led researchers and practitioners to consider the ways in which people's social connectedness can be boosted and their social contact enhanced in order to harness these powerful health benefits. Before unpacking these implications further, we provide an overview of the details of this classic study.

DETAILED OVERVIEW

STUDYING ALAMEDA COUNTY RESIDENTS OVER NINE YEARS

Berkman and Syme (1979) begin their article with the observation that, even though the relationship between social connectedness and better health has often been theorised, most of these studies have been limited in two ways. First, these studies typically do not directly measure social connectedness and, second, they mostly focus on specific groups, such as widows. An example of such research is a study conducted in the US and Australia demonstrating that 375 widows in the first year after the death of their husband reported more complaints about their health than a matched control group (Maddison & Viola, 1968).

Berkman and Syme argue that such findings only indirectly support the social connectedness hypothesis because social connection itself was not measured, thus preventing any conclusions that health decline among widows, compared to the control group, was directly due to the loss of social connectedness following bereavement. Furthermore, given the specificity of the sample and the distinct social connectedness challenge (i.e., the death of a husband), it remained to be seen whether these findings generalised to the general population. Berkman and Syme's study aimed to improve on these two methodological shortcomings. Using a random sample of thousands of Americans living in the community, their study demonstrated that those who reported fewer social and community ties at the start of the study were more likely to die in the proceeding nine years than those who were better socially connected at the start. Let us explain in greater detail how the study was conducted and what the findings show.

In 1965, the American Human Population Laboratory within the California Department of Health conducted a survey based on a stratified systematic sample in Alameda County. The sampling resulted in the selection of 4,452 households, in which all adults were invited to complete a survey. Out of the 8,023 adults that were eligible to take part in the study, 6,928 (86%) returned a completed survey. Even though non-responders were more likely to be white, male, older, and either single or widowed people, the skew was relatively small, and the researchers concluded that they had been successful in recruiting a representative sample of adults in the county. Berkman and Syme's analysis was restricted to those between the ages of 30 and 69, leaving them with a total sample of 4,725, including 2,496 women and 2,229 men.

Sidebar 9.1. Other Findings from the Alameda
County Residents Study

The study by Berkman and Syme was only one of many papers published
from the Alameda County Resident data. For instance, Wingard, Berkman
and Brand published a paper in the *American Journal of Epidemiology* in 1982
showing that nine-year mortality was independently predicted by five health-
related practices, such as never smoking, taking regular physical exercise, low
alcohol consumption, average weight status, and sleeping seven to eight hours
per night. Mortality was not predicted by eating breakfast and not snacking
between meals. Interestingly, too, further data were collected in 1973, 1985,
1988, 1994, and 1999, and analyses of these data further corroborated these
earlier conclusions. For instance, exploring 17-year mortality rates among participants in the 1965 data collection wave (who were then 65+ years of age),
Kaplan and colleagues (1987) found that the same behavioural risk factors as
identified by Wingard and colleagues (1982) remained predictors of mortality
even at older ages.

A wide range of measures were used and data from this large longitudinal study
formed the basis of many papers (see Sidebar 9.1). In their research, Berkman and
Syme (1979) focused on two measures in particular: degree of social connectedness
and mortality data in the nine-year period following the completion of the survey.
Social connectedness was measured in four different ways. Specifically, survey-
takers were asked (a) whether they were married or not, (b) to quantify the number
of close friends and relatives they saw frequently, (c) whether they were a member
of a church or temple, and (d) the degree to which they reported being part of informal or formal group associations. Mortality over the nine-year period was assessed
by matching participants' data with the California Death Registry from 1965 to 1974.

Berkman and Syme (1979) conducted a series of analyses in which they determined whether mortality rates within a particular age bracket differed between
those with higher or lower levels of social connectedness. In all analyses, they
controlled for other variables that could affect mortality, notably age, health practices, and socioeconomic status. Unsurprisingly, mortality increased with age and
mortality was also higher for men than it was for women across all age brackets
(see Sidebar 9.2 for the most noteworthy gender differences). More interesting to
Berkman and Syme was the relationship between various indicators of social connectedness and mortality. So, what did they find?

On the first indicator of social connectedness, marital status, there was clear
evidence that the mortality rate was lower for those who were married than for
those who were not married. Specifically, in the nine-year follow-up period, the
chances of dying were 9.86% for those who were married compared to 13.13%
for those who were not married. The differences between those who were married
and those who were not were found within each age group (see Figure 9.1).

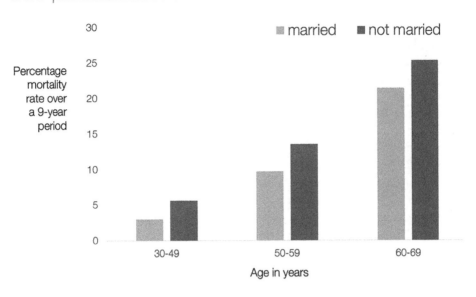

Figure 9.1   Mortality rate over a nine-year period by age group as a function of marital status

Similar findings were observed on the second indicator of social connectedness. In every age bracket, mortality was higher among participants who reported low levels of contact with friends and relatives (i.e., fewer relationships and less frequent contact) compared with those who reported high levels of social contact. When examining the whole sample, those who reported the highest level of contact with friends and family had a mortality rate of 6.60%. The mortality rate was similar for those who reported medium levels of contact (6.18%), but significantly higher for those who reported the lowest levels of contact with friends and relatives (11.25%).

The third indicator of social connectedness was church or temple attendance. While the effects of this indicator were less pronounced, across all age groups, there was a significant difference in mortality rates between those who identified themselves as a church or temple attender and those who did not. More specifically, people regularly attending a place of worship were less likely to die in the nine years following the survey (6.28%) compared to those who did not (8.54%).

Finally, when exploring the relationship between belonging to formal and informal groups and mortality (the fourth indicator of social connectedness), there was again an effect showing that belonging to groups was associated with a lower mortality rate (6.96%) compared to not belonging to such groups (9.68%). Note, however, that there was no significant difference in mortality between members and non-members for the highest age group (see Figure 9.2). When gender was taken into account, there were no differences between men who were members of formal and informal groups and men who were not (in particular, for men in the oldest age group), but there were significant differences for women across all age groups (see also Sidebar 9.2).

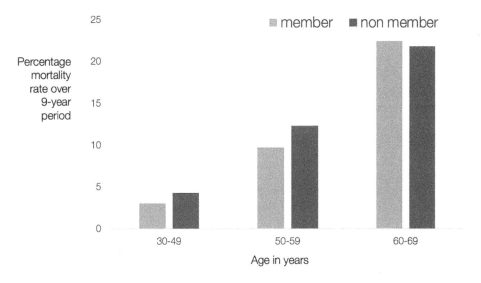

Figure 9.2 Mortality rate over a nine-year period by age group as a function of membership in formal or informal groups

Further analysis showed that even though all four categories of social connectedness significantly predicted mortality, the more intimate the social ties were (e.g., marriage and contact with friends and relatives), the stronger the effect was of social connectedness on mortality over the following nine-year period. Put differently, when the type of social connection was taken into account, social connectedness became an even stronger predictor of mortality. This is a point to which we will return later in this chapter.

Sidebar 9.2. The Relationship between Social Connectedness for Women and Men

Berkman and Syme (1979) observed several gender differences that are worth noting. First, and unsurprisingly given that women generally live longer, across all age groups, women had lower mortality rates than men. Second, the mortality risks associated with not being married were greater for men than for women – i.e., men's health benefitted more from marriage than women's health. Third, low levels of contact with friends and relatives posed a greater risk for women than for men. Fourth, compared to women, men did not benefit as much from membership in informal and formal groups. That is, for men, belonging to such groups did not reduce their mortality rate while it did for women.

The researchers also then calculated a 'social network' index by combining the total number of social ties, and with a higher weighting placed on closer contacts, such as family. They found that people low on the index were twice as likely to die from various causes than people high on the index, and again, this analysis controlled for other contributors to mortality, such as socioeconomic status, physical health, and healthy behaviours. In conclusion, the evidence that better social connectedness prevents an early death was strong. Berkman and Syme (1979) summarised this as follows:

> the most isolated group of men was found to have an age-adjusted mortality rate 2.3 times higher than men with the most connections; for women who were isolated, the rate was 2.8 times higher than the rate for women with the most social connections. (p. 1085)

ALTERNATIVE EXPLANATIONS: ILLNESS PREVENTING SOCIAL CONNECTEDNESS

Despite overwhelming support for the hypothesis that social connectedness predicted mortality, Berkman and Syme cautioned against inferring causality. They stated that it was not possible to argue that participants had a reduced chance of dying over nine years *because* they were well connected socially in 1965. Indeed, they suggested that it might well be the case that the causal relationship goes in the other direction – when the survey was conducted in 1965, sickness or poor health may have caused participants to be less well connected. It may thus be possible that the participant's death was not so much due to their lack of social connections, but because of underlying health issues that also prevented them from having an active social life.

Even though it is not possible to completely rule out this alternative explanation, Berkman and Syme (1979) conducted two analyses that suggest that this account cannot fully explain the mortality data. First, they controlled for the physical health status of the participants at baseline in 1965, and found that the relationship between social connectedness and mortality remained strong and significant. This suggests that initial health status may be relevant when predicting an early death, but it does not explain the observed effect that those who are better socially connected were less likely to die in the nine years following the survey.

Second, the researchers reasoned that if poor health at baseline was a major factor, one would predict that those who are ill in 1965 would be more likely to die in the first years following the survey. In other words, we would not expect to see an even distribution of deaths across the nine years, but data showing more deaths earlier rather than later in this nine-year period. However, results of this analysis show little evidence for an uneven distribution. All in all, the researchers summarise these results by saying that:

> though not conclusive, these findings suggest that physical illness alone does not appear capable of accounting for the association between social disconnection and increased mortality rates. (Berkman & Syme, 1979, p. 1075)

ALTERNATIVE EXPLANATIONS: SOCIOECONOMIC STATUS

Berkman and Syme (1979) also proposed that there might be another factor accounting for the observed relationship between social connectedness and mortality. They proposed that socioeconomic status (SES) might be such a factor, due to evidence that (a) poorer people die younger, and (b) poorer people are less well socially connected than their wealthier counterparts. There is certainly considerable research backing up their reasoning with a large body of work showing that lower SES is both associated with an early death (Marmot, 2015) and with less well-developed social networks (Iyer et al., 2009; Jetten et al., 2013; see also C. Haslam, Jetten, et al., 2018).

To rule out the role of SES in predicting mortality, Berkman and Syme conducted further analyses of their data whereby they controlled for SES in the relationship between social connectedness and mortality. Based on those analyses, they went on to conclude that social connectedness predicts mortality *independently* of SES. Unfortunately, however, Berkman and Syme do not provide much detail on the findings of their analyses, and they do not answer the questions of whether social connectedness is related to SES or whether mortality is related to SES. Nevertheless, in their paper, they do include data on mortality rates according to (a) level of social connectedness (those with fewest social connections versus those with most social connections) and (b) different SES levels as determined by income and education. These data demonstrate that mortality is higher for those with fewest compared to most social connections, and across *all* SES groups.

In order to assess the magnitude of the social connectedness versus SES effect, we had a closer look at these data. Re-analysing the Berkman and Syme data, we found that those in the upper SES groups had a lower mortality rate than those from middle or lower SES backgrounds (see Figure 9.3). However, the mortality rates of upper SES participants with the fewest social connections was higher than the mortality rates of lower SES participants with most social connections (8.61% versus 6.81%, respectively). Thus, social connectedness seemed to offset the negative health consequences of low SES status.

ALTERNATIVE EXPLANATIONS: HEALTH BEHAVIOURS VERSUS SOCIAL CONNECTEDNESS

One could argue that the beneficial impact of being socially connected may not be greater than other behaviours that are good for our health (e.g., not smoking). Berkman and Syme (1979) certainly considered this possibility and – to assess the unique predictive power of social connectedness on mortality – they conducted several analyses controlling for other health behaviours. Importantly, their analyses showed that the relationship between social connectedness and mortality holds when controlling for a number of important health factors: smoking status, diet, alcohol consumption, physical activity, and low utilisation of preventative health services.

The implications of these findings are important; however, again, Berkman and Syme did not analyse their data in depth and questions remain. For example, if one

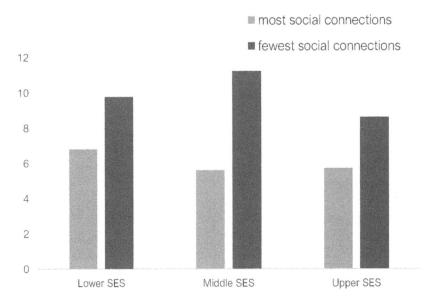

Figure 9.3 Mortality rate over a nine-year period as a function of fewest versus most social connections and socioeconomic status (SES)

Note: We collapsed the 'lower' and 'lower-middle' into 'lower SES' and the 'upper middle' and 'upper' into 'upper SES'.

would want to live longer, is it better to have good and many social connections or should one just give up smoking? Likewise, is being physically active and not obese a better predictor of a long life, or does social connectedness trump the effects of these health factors? Fortunately, Berkman and Syme included detailed information in the tables in their publication that allow us to provide answers to these questions.

Specifically, when it comes to smoking, the negative effect of not being socially connected is higher than the effect of smoking (never smoking was associated with a 5.10% death rate, and currently smoking with a 10.25% death rate, whereas having the fewest social connections was associated with a 13.51% death rate, and most social connections with a 2.43% death rate). As can be seen in Table 9.1, not smoking and having higher levels of social connectedness was associated with a 2.89% death rate whereas never having smoked and having the fewest social connections was associated with a 9.09% chance of dying. This trend continued even when examining people who currently smoked. Participants who were currently smoking but had high levels of social connection, had slightly lower mortality rates (8.17%) than those who had never smoked but had few social connections (9.09%) – highlighting further the powerful buffering effect of social connection.

When it came to the negative effects of being overweight relative to the lack of social connections, as for smoking, having poor social connections was a greater risk than being overweight. Specifically, among those who were 30% overweight, the chance of dying for those who were poorly socially connected was 15.90%,

Table 9.1 Risk factors associated with smoking, being overweight, alcohol consumption and being physically inactive pitted against having the fewest or most social connections

	Fewest social connections	Fewest social connections	Most social connections	Most social connections
Smoking	Currently smoking: 15.82%	Never smoked: 9.09%	Currently smoking: 8.17%	Never smoked: 2.89%
Overweight (yes>30% overweight)	Yes: 15.90%	No: 12.32%	Yes: 5.06%	No: 5.54%
Alcohol consumption	Higher: 16.86%	Lower: 12.73%	Higher: 11.26%	Lower: 4.97%
Physically active	Least active: 15.80%	Moderately active: 11.54%	Least active: 7.24%	Moderately active: 6.02%
Preventative health measures	No checks: 10.46%	Checks: 8.40%	No checks: 4.94%	Checks: 4.69%

Note: This table summarises the original data which was split by gender. Risk rates reflect the collapsed rates across gender and may differ slightly from age-adjusted rates that would be calculated if we had access to the full data set. No male participants are represented in the overweight/fewest connections category and the high preventative healthcare/fewest connections category as there were insufficient numbers in the original study for analysis (fewer than 30).

while it was 5.06% of those who were overweight but better socially connected. As Table 9.1 shows, the death rate for those who were overweight but had good social connections was lower than for those who were not overweight but had fewer social connections (5.06% versus 12.32%, respectively). When participants had good social connections, it made little difference if they were overweight or not. Specifically, the death rate was 5.06% for those who were overweight and well connected and it was 5.54% for those who were not overweight and had many connections.

Analysis of alcohol consumption leads to similar findings, with data showing that those who consumed more than 46 drinks per month were at higher risk of dying when they were poorly socially connected (16.86%) than when they were well connected socially (11.26%). As Table 9.1 shows, death rates were generally lower for those who consumed 0 to 16 drinks per month, but here too it was clear that the death rate was higher for those with poorer social connections (12.73%) than those with better social connections (4.97%).

When participants were physically inactive, death rates were more favourable for those who had more social connections (7.24%) than those who had fewer social connections (15.80%). In fact, the death rate for those who were moderately physically active but had few social connections was higher than it was for those who were physically inactive but had the most social connections (11.54% versus 7.24%, respectively).

Finally, among participants who did not undertake preventative health measures (medical and dental check-ups in the year prior to the survey), mortality rates were higher for those who were not socially connected (10.46%), than those who had many social connections (4.94%). In fact, the mortality rates were much higher among those who had undertaken preventative health practices but were socially disconnected, compared to participants who undertook no preventative health practices but had many social connections (8.40% versus 4.94%).

All in all, it appears that the negative effect of being poorly connected outweighs the risk of smoking, being overweight, alcohol consumption, being physically inactive and undertaking few preventative healthcare practices. While this certainly does not suggest that we should downplay the negative health effects of these non-social behaviours, it does suggest that the negative effects of being poorly socially connected are on par with these well-known health risk factors.

DEVELOPMENTS

BEYOND THE BERKMAN AND SYME STUDY: FOLLOW-UPS

Even though the study by Berkman and Syme is impressive in several respects, one clear weakness is its reliance on self-report data of health indicators (e.g., alcohol consumption and physical activity). Fortunately, subsequent studies have overcome this limitation, and in so doing have also provided further – and more robust – evidence for the link between social connectedness and mortality. For instance, House, Robbins, and Metzner (1982) collected data from a sample of 2,754 individuals from the Tecumseh community in Michigan. The study included both social integration measures and biomedical measures of morbidity (e.g., coronary heart disease, hypertension, cholesterol, blood glucose levels) at baseline. Statistical analyses of mortality rates 9–12 years later showed that, after controlling for age and standard biomedical risk, isolated people were more likely to die than those involved in meaningful social relationships (e.g., with their spouse, friends, and relatives) and in social activities (e.g., going to meetings and church attendance). Schoenbach, Kaplan, Fredman, and Kleinbaum (1986) conducted a similar study among 2,059 residents in Georgia and confirmed that social ties predicted mortality risk, and that this was particularly true for white men and older people.

Even though many of these studies were conducted in North America, in the decades after the study by Berkman and Syme (1979), evidence for the link between social connectedness and mortality has also emerged in large longitudinal studies conducted in Europe (e.g., in Denmark by Barefoot et al., 2005), Asia (e.g., in Japan by Nakanishi & Tatara, 2000), and Australia (e.g., Giles et al., 2005). More recently still, a longitudinal analysis of data from a nationally representative sample in the UK showed that the number of social groups a person is a member of following retirement predicts mortality (Steffens et al., 2016). Retirees who had two group memberships before retirement had a 2% risk of death over the first six years of retirement if they maintained these memberships, a 5% risk if they lost membership of one group, or a 12% risk if they lost membership of both.

Some studies have also provided evidence that social integration protects against specific illnesses, such as cardiovascular disease (Orth-Gomér & Johnson, 1987), or mortality after being diagnosed with breast cancer (Kroenke et al., 2006). Interestingly, too, social connectedness has been found to decrease the risk of developing certain types of illness. For instance, Wilson and colleagues (2007) studied older people in the Chicago area and found that the risk of developing Alzheimer's disease doubled among those with smaller social networks and lower levels of social participation. Likewise, Glass et al. (2006) found that social engagement among retirees in New Haven (e.g., volunteering in the community) predicted lower levels of depressive symptoms over time.

Importantly, evidence that social connectedness protects a person's health has been obtained from research methodologies other than longitudinal studies. Most impressive is a study by Cohen, Doyle, Skoner, Rabin, and Gwaltney (1997), in which they invited participants to the laboratory and measured their participation in 12 types of social relationships (e.g., with a spouse, close neighbours, workmates). This allowed them to calculate a social connectedness index. After this, participants were given nasal drops containing a rhinovirus (associated with the common cold). Results revealed that participants with a wider range of social relationship were subsequently less likely to go on to develop the common cold after exposure to the virus.

Noteworthy, too, is an influential meta-analysis reported by Holt-Lunstad, Smith, and Layton (2010). This analysis integrated findings from 148 studies involving over 300,000 participants and found that reduced mortality was strongly associated with two key social factors: *social integration* and *social support*. Indeed, the effect sizes of these social factors in predicting mortality was higher than effect sizes associated with nine important physical factors previously documented in the research literature, including not smoking, low alcohol consumption, having flu vaccination, being physically active, not being obese, and not being exposed to air pollution. These data provide robust support for Berkman and Syme's findings, showing again that the relation between social connectedness and mortality is evident even when controlling for a range of demographic factors (including age, gender, initial health status, follow-up period, and cause of death).

In summary, the relationship between social connectedness and health has now been observed across many countries, in many social contexts, using different methodologies, and over many decades. However, one of the questions that remains is why social connectedness would protect health? What is the underlying mechanism?

BEYOND THE ALAMEDA COUNTY RESIDENTS' STUDY: WHY DOES SOCIAL CONNECTEDNESS PROTECT HEALTH?

Even though the classic study by Berkman and Syme (1979) provides compelling evidence for the relationship between social connectedness and health, the two researchers acknowledged that the reason for the relationship was unclear. A similar observation was made by House and colleagues (1982) three years after publication of the Berkman and Syme study. While they largely replicated Berkman and Syme's findings, House and colleagues also concluded that 'our understanding of the mechanisms through which social relationships and activities affect mortality is incomplete' (p. 140). Both teams of researchers end their papers with a call for more research that would elucidate the underlying mechanism of the relationship between social connectedness and health – a task that both teams argued is important given the robust impact of social connectedness on health.

Recently, important progress has been made in answering these questions. Of particular relevance has been work that has theorised this relationship from a social identity perspective (also known as 'social cure' research, see C. Haslam, Jetten et al. 2018.; Jetten, Haslam, & Haslam, 2012; Jetten et al., 2017). The term *social identity* refers to that part of a person's sense of self that derives from their membership in one or more social groups. This can be contrasted with personal identity, which refers to a person's sense of themselves as a unique individual (Tajfel & Turner, 1979; Turner et al., 1987). Whereas personal identity defines a sense of 'I' and 'me' that sets a person apart from others, social identity defines the self in terms of 'we' and 'us' in ways that psychologically connect the person to other members of their group. The social identity approach draws on well-established social psychological theories of group processes – social identity theory (Tajfel & Turner, 1979) and self-categorisation theory (Turner et al., 1987) – and these perspectives are increasingly used to understand health outcomes in response to illness, disease, and trauma. For instance, this theoretical framework has been used to understand trajectories in adjustment to acquired brain injury, as well as recovery from addictions. It has also been used to explain both the expression and experience of stress and depression. Furthermore, in addition to informing health treatments (e.g., Groups4Health, as elaborated further below), social identity theorising has been applied to advance an understanding of the trajectories and outcomes of major life changes, including the transition from school to university, working to retirement, and moving from independent living to residential care (for an overview, see C. Haslam, Jetten et al. 2018.).

The social identity approach to health allows us to answer the question of how social connection impacts on health. As discussed above, social identity relates to the sense of self people gain from connection to groups. These social group connections unlock a range of psychological resources. In particular, research has shown that social identification with one or more groups provides people with resources such as a sense of (a) self-esteem (Jetten et al., 2015), (b) personal control (Greenaway et al., 2015), and (c) meaning and purpose (Steffens et al., 2017). Similarly, social identification is also a basis for the provision and receipt of social support (Bowe et al., 2020; Haslam, Reicher, & Levine, 2012). A lack of social connectedness therefore negatively impacts on individuals because it cuts them off from these important resources. It is the provision of these fundamental psychological 'cures' that explains the association between social connection and positive health.

However, it is important to bear in mind that not all group memberships are protective of health. As is clear from the Berkman and Syme study, social connections had a stronger effect on longevity when the social relationships were more intimate or meaningful (e.g., marriage or with family and friends). This qualification has also been central in the social identity analysis of health and well-being

(C. Haslam, Jetten et al. 2018; Jetten et al., 2017). Indeed, it has been recognised that there are many groups that we belong to that have very little impact on our health and well-being. This is because, when we do not identify highly with these groups, these memberships are not internalised as an important part of self, and hence the group in question will have little or no impact on health (Turner et al., 1987, see also Jetten et al., 2014). There is now considerable evidence that the power of these psychological resources is only unlocked through the quality of social connections, with several meta-analyses demonstrating a strong relationship between the level of social identification and various indicators of well-being (e.g., Cruwys et al., 2014; Greenaway et al., 2015; Jetten et al., 2015; Steffens et al., 2017).

WHY IS THE FINDING THAT SOCIAL CONNECTEDNESS PROTECTS HEALTH SO IMPORTANT?

In summary, this classic study by Berkman and Syme (1979) was the first to show convincingly that being better socially connected predicts survival. So, why is this such an important finding? To answer this question, two issues should be considered. The first relates to the sheer magnitude of this effect. Referring back to the work of Holt-Lunstad and colleagues (2010), their meta-analysis compellingly showed that social connectedness (in terms of social integration and social support) was not only predictive of mortality, but that it was a stronger predictor of mortality than well-researched physical risk factors (a fact that is not readily recognised; see C. Haslam, Jetten et al. 2018). Consider the following conclusion by Putnam (2000) after he reviewed research into the relationship between social connectedness and health:

> As a rough rule of thumb, if you belong to no group but decide to join one, you cut your risk of dying over the next year *in half*. If you smoke and belong to no groups, it's a toss-up statistically whether you should stop smoking or start joining. (p. 331)

Practically speaking, then, if one would like to know where to focus to improve public health, it would be wise to focus on people's social connectedness. This leads on to a second reason why these findings are so important: that if we know just how important social connection is for health, we can focus on social connectedness in our health interventions. That is, it makes good sense to consider ways to boost people's social connectedness because interventions that focus on enhancing social connectedness can have profound consequences for health and mortality. And, in many ways, interventions that focus on enhancing social connectedness may be easier for some people than other behaviours they might be asked to engage in to improve their health. As Putnam (2000, p. 331) put it: 'it's easier to join a group than to lose weight, exercise regularly, or quit smoking'.

Having said that, while it may be easier to join a group than to engage in other health behaviours, this does not mean that joining a new group is straightforward and many people might benefit from assistance with connecting. For this reason, social identity-informed interventions have recently been developed that aim to target the question, and improvement, of social connectedness (Bentley et al., 2021; Cruwys et al., 2022; Haslam et al., 2016; Haslam et al., 2019). One flagship programme, known as Groups4Health (also referred to as G4H), has now been tested across three clinical trials. G4H is a group-based intervention that aims to empower people to assess, manage, and strengthen their social networks. Results from these trials have demonstrated its utility in reducing loneliness, as well as significantly improving social connectedness, mental health, and well-being outcomes. By targeting social identity as the mechanism, these studies show that it is possible not only to harness but also to build on the strong relationship that Berkman and Syme uncovered between social connectedness and health.

CONCLUSIONS

The classic study by Berkman and Syme (1979) has been important in opening our eyes to the notion that social relations are just as important (and sometimes more so) for our health than other well-known lifestyle factors, such as physical activity, smoking, and alcohol consumption. The implications of this insight are far-reaching. If we can become healthier and live longer by boosting and expanding our social connectedness, it then becomes possible to consider new socially-informed pathways to enhance health. Recent social cure interventions have built on the key insights of the original study by Berkman and Syme (1979), showing that by enhancing social connectedness we can provide a promising route to better health and longer life.

FURTHER READING

(Marked with * in references)

To get a better feeling for the findings of this classic study, you may want to start by reading Berkman and Syme's paper. The paper is quite accessible and the statistics they use are quite straightforward and easy to understand. If you are interested in the way that the social identity approach is relevant to understanding why there is a relationship between social connectedness and health, then you may want to read Jetten et al. (2012) or the more recent comprehensive overview of the literature by C. Haslam, Jetten et al. 2018).

The recent book by C. Haslam, Jetten et al. (2018) is also a good starting point for anyone interested in interventions that harness and build social connectedness. The final chapter of this book is dedicated to outlining the G4H programme and provides suggestions on how practitioners might use it in their work. Finally, for readers who are interested in a comprehensive and up-to-date review of social identity interventions to improve health, we refer you to a recent publication by Steffens and colleagues (2021, in *Health Psychology Review*). This meta-analysis of 27 studies examines the positive impact of interventions that build social identification on quality of life, physical health, self-esteem, well-being, anxiety, depression, cognitive health, and stress.

REFERENCES

(* = further reading)

Barefoot, J. C., Grønbaek, M., Jensen, G., Schnohr, P., & Prescott, E. (2005). Social network diversity and risks of ischemic heart disease and total mortality: Findings from the Copenhagen City Heart study. *American Journal of Epidemiology*, *161*, 960–967. https://doi.org/10.1093/aje/kwi128

*Berkman, L. F., & Syme, S. L. (1979). Social networks, host resistance, and mortality: A nine-year follow-up study of Alameda County residents. *American Journal of Epidemiology*, *109*, 186–204. https://doi.org/10.1093/oxfordjournals.aje.a112674

Bowe, M., Gray, D., Stevenson, C., McNamara, N., Wakefield, J. R., Kellezi, B., … & Costa, S. (2020). A social cure in the community: A mixed-method exploration of the role of social identity in the experiences and well-being of community volunteers. *European Journal of Social Psychology*. https://doi.org/10.1002/ejsp.2706

Cohen, S., Doyle, W. J., Skoner, D. P., Rabin, B. S., & Gwaltney, J. M. (1997). Social ties and susceptibility to the common cold. *Journal of the American Medical Association*, *277*(24), 1940–1944. https://doi.org/10.1001/jama.1997.03540480040036

Cruwys, T., Haslam, S. A., Dingle, G. A., Haslam, C., & Jetten, J. (2014). Depression and social identity: An integrative review. *Personality and Social Psychology Review*, *18*(3), 215–238. https://doi.org/10.1177/1088868314523839

Cruwys, T., Haslam, C., Rathbone, J. A., Williams, E., Haslam, S. A., & Walter, Z. (2022). Groups 4 Health versus cognitive-behavioural therepy for depression and loneliness in young people: Randomised phase 3 non-inferiority trial with 12-month follow-up. *The British Journal of Psychiatry*, *220*(3), 140–147. https://doi.org/10.1192/bjp.2021.128

Giles, L. C., Glonek, G. F. V., Luscz, M. A., & Andrews, G. R. (2005). Effect of social networks on 10 year survival in very old Australians: The Australian longitudinal study of aging. *Journal of Epidemiology and Community Health*, *59*, 574–579. http://dx.doi.org/10.1136/jech.2004.025429

Glass, T. A., De Leon, C. F., Bassuk, S. S., & Berkman, L. F. (2006). Social engagement and depressive symptoms in late life: Longitudinal findings. *Journal of Aging and Health*, *18*(4), 604–628. https://doi.org/10.1177/0898264306291017

Greenaway, K. H., Haslam, S. A., Branscombe, N. R., Cruwys, T., Ysseldyk, R., & Heldreth, C. (2015). From 'we' to 'me': Group identification enhances perceived personal control with consequences for health and well-being. *Journal of Personality and Social Psychology*, *109*, 53–74. https://doi.org/10.1037/pspi0000019

Haslam C, Cruwys T, Haslam SA, Dingle GA, Chang MX-L. (2016). GROUPS 4 HEALTH: Evidence that a social-identity intervention that builds and strengthens social group membership improves health. Journal of Affective Disorders, 194, 188-195. DOI: 10.1016/j.jad.2016.01.010

Haslam C, Cruwys T, Chang M, Bentley SV, Haslam SA, Dingle G, Jetten J. (2019). GROUPS 4 HEALTH reduces loneliness and social anxiety in adults with psychological distress: Findings from a randomised controlled trial. Journal of Consulting and Clinical Psychology, 87(9), 787–801. https://doi.org/10.1037/ccp0000427

*Haslam, C., Jetten, J., Cruwys, T., Dingle, G. A., & Haslam, S. A. (2018). *The new psychology of health: Unlocking the social cure*. London: Routledge. https://doi.org/10.4324/9781315648569

Haslam, S. A., McMahon, C., Cruwys, T., Haslam, C., Jetten, J., & Steffens, N. K. (2018). Social cure, what social cure? The propensity to underestimate the importance of social factors for health. *Social Science & Medicine, 198*, 14–21. https://doi.org/10.1016/j.socscimed.2017.12.020

Haslam, S. A., Reicher, S. D., & Levine, M. (2012). When other people are heaven, when other people are hell: How social identity determines the nature and impact of social support. In J. Jetten, C. Haslam, & S. A. Haslam (Eds.), *The social cure: Identity, health, and well-being* (pp. 157–174). London: Psychology Press.

Holt-Lunstad, J., Smith, T. B., & Layton, J. B. (2010). Social relationships and mortality risk: A meta-analytic review. *PLoS Medicine, 7*(7), 2–20. https://doi.org/10.1371/journal.pmed.1000316

House, J. S., Robbins, C., & Metzner, H. L. (1982). The association of social relationships and activities with mortality: Prospective evidence from the Tecumseh community health study. *American Journal of Epidemiology, 116*, 123–140. https://doi.org/10.1093/oxfordjournals.aje.a113387

Houseman, J., & Dorman, S. (2005). The Alameda county study: A systematic, chronological review. *American Journal of Health Education, 36*, 5. https://doi.org/10.1080/19325037.2005.10608200

Iyer, A., Jetten, J., Tsivrikos, D., Postmes, T., & Haslam, S. A. (2009). The more (and the more compatible) the merrier: Multiple group memberships and identity compatibility as predictors of adjustment after life transitions. *British Journal of Social Psychology, 48*, 707–733. https://doi.org/10.1348/014466608X397628

Jetten, J., Branscombe, N. R., Haslam, S. A., Haslam, C., Cruwys, T., Jones, J. M., Cui, L., Dingle, G., Liu, J., Murphy, S. C., Thai, A., Walter, Z., & Zhang, A. (2015). Having a lot of a good thing: Multiple important group memberships as a source of self-esteem. *PLoS ONE, 10*(6), e0131035. https://doi.org/10.1371/journal.pone.0131035

*Jetten, J., Haslam, C., & Haslam, S. A. (Eds.). (2012). *The social cure: Identity, health and well-being*. London: Psychology Press. https://doi.org/10.4324/9780203813195

Jetten, J., Haslam, C., Haslam, S. A., Dingle, G., & Jones, J. M. (2014). How groups affect our health and well-being: The path from theory to policy. *Social Issues and Policy Review, 8*, 103–130. https://doi.org/10.1111/sipr.12003

Jetten, J., Haslam, S. A., & Barlow, F. (2013). Bringing back the system: One reason why conservatives are happier than liberals is that higher socio-economic status gives them access to more group memberships. *Social Psychological and Personality Science, 4*, 6–13. https://doi.org/10.1177/1948550612439721

Jetten, J., Haslam, S. A., Cruwys, T., Greenaway, K. H., Haslam, C., & Steffens, N. K. (2017). Advancing the social identity approach to health and well-being: Progressing the social cure research agenda. *European Journal of Social Psychology, 47*, 789–802. https://doi.org/10.1002/ejsp.2333

Kaplan, G., Seeman, T., Cohen, R., et al. (1987). Mortality among the elderly in the Alameda County Study: Behavioral and demographic risk factors. *American Journal of Public Health, 77*(3), 307–312. https://doi.org/10.2105/AJPH.77.3.307

Kroenke, C. H., Kubzansky, L. D., Schernhammer, E. S., Holmes, M. D., & Kawachi, I. (2006). Social networks, social support, and survival after breast cancer diagnosis. *Journal of Clinical Oncology, 24*(7), 1105–1111. https://doi.org/10.1200/JCO.2005.04.2846

Maddison, D., & Viola, A. (1968). The health of widows in the year following bereavement. *Journal of Psychosomatic Research, 12*, 297–306. https://doi.org/10.1016/0022-3999(68)90084-6

Marmot, M. (2015). *The health gap: The challenge of an unequal world*. London: Bloomsbury.

Nakanishi, N., & Tatara, K. (2000). Relationship between social relations and mortality of older Japanese people living alone. *Journal of Clinical Geropsychology*, *6*, 213–222. https://doi.org/10.1023/A:1009593216851

Orth-Gomér, K., & Johnson, J. V. (1987). Social network interaction and mortality: A six year follow-up study of a random sample of the Swedish population. *Journal of Chronic Disease*, *40*(10), 949–957. https://doi.org/10.1016/0021-9681(87)90145-7. PMID: 3611293

Putnam, R. D. (2000). *Bowling alone: The collapse and revival of American community*. New York: Simon & Schuster.

Schoenbach, V. J., Kaplan, B. H., Fredman, L., Kleinbaum, D. G. (1986). Social ties and mortality in Evans County, Georgia. *American Journal of Epidemiology*, *123*, 577–591. https://doi.org/10.1093/oxfordjournals.aje.a114278

Steffens, N. K., Cruwys, T., Haslam, S. A., Haslam, C., & Jetten, J. (2016). Maintaining and developing social group memberships in retirement reduces the risk of premature death: Evidence from a nationally representative longitudinal cohort study. *BMJ Open*, *6*, e010164. https://doi.org/10.1136/bmjopen-2015-010164

Steffens, N. K., Haslam, S. A., Schuh, S. C., Jetten, J., & van Dick, R. (2017). A meta-analytic review of social identification and health in organizational contexts. *Personality and Social Psychology Review*, *21*, 303–335. https://doi.org/10.1177/10888683 16656701

*Steffens, N. K., La Rue, C. J., Haslam, C., Walter, Z. C., Cruwys, T., Munt, K. A., Haslam, S. A., Jetten, J., & Tarrant, M. (2021). Social identification-building interventions to improve health: A systematic review and meta-analysis. *Health Psychology Review*, *15*, 85–112. https://doi.org/10.1080/17437199.2019.1669481

Tajfel, H., & Turner, J. C. (1979). An integrative theory of intergroup conflict. In W. G. Austin & S. Worchel (Eds.), *The social psychology of intergroup relations* (pp. 33–48). Pacific Grove, CA: Brooks/Cole.

Turner, J. C., Hogg, M. A., Oakes, P. J., Reicher, S. D., & Wetherell, M. (1987). *Rediscovering the social group: A self-categorization theory*. Oxford: Blackwell.

Wilson, R. S., Krueger, K. R., Arnold, S. E., Schneider, J. A., Kelly, J. F., Barnes, L. L., Tang, Y., & Bennett, D. A. (2007). Loneliness and risk of Alzheimer disease. *Archives of General Psychiatry*, *64*(2), 234–240. https://doi.org/10.1001/archpsyc.64.2.234

Wingard, D. L., Berkman, L. F., & Brand, R. J. (1982). A multivariate analysis of health-related practices. *American Journal of Epidemiology*, *116*, 765–775. https://doi.org/10.1093/oxfordjournals.aje.a113466

10 | Fear Appeals and Illness Perceptions: Revisiting Leventhal, Singer, and Jones (1965)

Leventhal, H., Singer, R., & Jones, S. (1965). Effects of fear and specificity of recommendation upon attitudes and behavior. *Journal of Personality and Social Psychology*, 2, 20–29.

Linda D. Cameron

BACKGROUND

A major challenge in the fields of health psychology, public health, and behavioural medicine is to identify ways to motivate people to engage in protective behaviours such as getting vaccinations, eating healthy diets, exercising regularly, taking medication, and avoiding use of unhealthy substances such as tobacco. How can people be motivated to take these actions to protect themselves from illnesses and other health harms? Should they be 'scared into action' through messages that convey the frightening consequences of illnesses such as cancer or heart disease? Or would such scare tactics 'boomerang' and instead cause people to 'switch off' and avoid the health risk issue altogether? Should messages instead avoid the use of fear arousal and simply inform people about the objective health risks and benefits of protective action so that they can make reasoned decisions that are based purely on knowledge? These are questions that health psychologists interested in behaviour change have faced for decades, and controversies over them continue to abound (Borland, 2018; Kok et al., 2018; Peters & Shoots-Reinhard, 2018). Yet scientific breakthroughs on this topic emerged over 60 years ago, including the advances in research on this topic led by Howard Leventhal.

Leventhal, a social and health psychologist, has made indelible contributions on how psychologists and behavioural medicine scientists understand health-related decisions and behaviours. In particular, his early theoretical and empirical work on attitudes, behaviour change, and emotions within the context of illness control were foundational to the inception of the field of health psychology. This chapter focuses on a classic study conducted by Leventhal and his colleagues Robert Singer and Susan Jones at Yale University, which was published in 1965. It begins with a detailed description of the study, which includes an overview of the scientific context that motivated the study aims and hypotheses, and a summary of the study methods and main findings. The chapter then reviews significant theoretical and empirical advances stimulated by these study findings over the subsequent decades. Highlights of these advances include the parallel-process model, the common-sense model of illness self-regulation, the extended parallel-process model, and implementation intention strategies for promoting protective actions.

DETAILED OVERVIEW

STUDY RATIONALE, AIMS, AND HYPOTHESES

Leventhal et al.'s classic study was designed to address a growing conundrum in the field regarding the influence of fear arousal on individuals' attitudes about a health threat and the responses and behaviours they undertake to alleviate that threat. At the time, it was well established that merely providing individuals with factual information about the risks of a health threat, such as heart disease, and the protective action, such as regular physical activity, was not sufficient to motivate attitude and behaviour change; rather, the message must also activate motivational forces that persuade people about the seriousness of the threat and the benefits of the action (Berkowitz & Cottingham, 1960; Janis & Feshbach, 1953).

Researchers turned their attention to testing the motivational effects of fear arousal, given that fear is a primary reaction to danger and can mobilise protective 'flight or fight' responses (e.g., attempts to escape a threatening situation or attack an aggressor). Dollard and Miller (1950) formulated an early perspective, the fear-drive model, proposing that fear is a motivational state that drives protective behaviours which, if successful in reducing fear, are reinforced and learned. Yet experiments testing the impact of fear-arousing messages on health attitudes and behaviours had produced conflicting evidence on the motivational drive of fear arousal. On the one hand, studies by Janis and colleagues (Janis & Feshbach, 1953, 1954; Janis & Terwilliger, 1962) demonstrated that high-fear messages induced defensive reactions of avoidance and resistance to the validity of the message, which undermined changes in attitudes and health-protective actions. In these studies, high fear-inducing messages with vivid descriptions and graphic photographs conveying disease consequences of unhealthy behaviour (i.e., dental decay and poor oral hygiene; lung cancer and cigarette smoking) were *less* persuasive relative to messages designed to induce milder levels of fear. In effect, it was the messages that aroused mild fear rather than those that aroused high fear that led to the greatest attitude and behaviour change. In contrast, other studies had provided evidence that messages inducing higher fear arousal are instead more persuasive than those inducing milder levels of fear (Berkowitz & Cottingham, 1960; Leventhal & Niles, 1964; Niles, 1964). Further, these effects were obtained in studies that utilised more graphic and frightening communications relative to the communications tested by Janis and colleagues; with their communications conveying vivid depictions of car accidents and lung cancer, they found higher levels of attitude and behaviour motivation change with increasing fear arousal. Their findings therefore supported the hypothesis that fear drives message acceptance even at higher ranges of fear arousal.

The discrepancy in the two sets of research findings led Leventhal and his colleagues to consider the conditions under which fear arousal would have a persuasive effect on attitudes and actions and the conditions under which it would not. They proposed that fear arousal will motivate attitude and behaviour change when the recommended action seems highly feasible and available. For example, participants in the Leventhal and Niles (1964) study could easily and immediately take the recommended actions: they could go directly to get a lung X-ray in a room down the hall, and they could immediately refrain from smoking a cigarette. However, fear arousal in the absence of a clearly-specified plan for taking action would be insufficient to promote protective behaviour.

The primary aims of Leventhal et al.'s classic study were to systematically test the independent and combined effects of fear arousal and the availability of a clear and easily achievable plan for taking protective action on attitude change and behaviour, which, in this study, was obtaining a tetanus vaccination. They predicted that high-fear communications about tetanus would induce more positive attitudes about the importance of tetanus vaccines, higher vaccination intentions, and higher vaccination rates when compared with low-fear communications. Further, they predicted that the provision of a specific *action plan* for obtaining the vaccine would elicit higher vaccination rates when compared to no provision of an action plan. Finally, they predicted an interaction effect of fear arousal and action plan, such that participants receiving the combination of a high-fear communication and an action plan would have the highest levels of positive attitudes, intentions, and behaviour and the effect of the combination of these two manipulations would be greater than the sum of their separate main effects.

The study had an additional aim: to determine which emotional sequelae of fear arousal might be responsible for the effects on attitudes and behaviour. Frightening and gruesome health messages can arouse a variety of emotional reactions, including tension, anxiety, discomfort, and even anger and nausea. The researchers measured a variety of emotional reactions to the communications to gather information about which reactions are associated with persuasion and protective behaviour.

STUDY METHOD: DESIGN, MANIPULATIONS, PROCEDURE, AND MEASURES

This study utilised a 2 × 2 experimental design with fear arousal (high versus low) and action plan (detailed plan versus general recommendations) as the independent variables, with an additional control condition added later in which 30 participants received only the action plan message. Seniors at Yale University were recruited to participate in a study described as an evaluation of a public health pamphlet. Each participant arrived for an individual session and received a pamphlet about tetanus vaccines along with instructions to read it carefully and, when finished, complete a questionnaire.

The pamphlet first presented a 'fear section' detailing the causes of tetanus and a case history of a person who contracted tetanus, with the contents designed to induce either high or low levels of fear. The two versions presented the same facts, but they varied in the use of frightening details (e.g., high incidence and tetanus bacteria being everywhere, including under fingernails and in the mouth) versus non-frightening details (e.g., non-dramatic presentation of information about the prevalence and incidence of tetanus); emotional language and outcomes (e.g., the case history patient died) versus non-emotional language (e.g., the case history patient survived), and photographs that were in colour and graphic (e.g., a child in a tetanic convulsion, a gaping tracheotomy wound, patients with urinary catheters and nasal tubes) versus black-and-white line drawings of facial grimaces induced by tetanus.

The pamphlet next presented the 'recommendation section', with details about the importance of tetanus vaccinations, statistics demonstrating their high effectiveness in protecting against the disease, and a statement that students can obtain tetanus vaccinations free of charge from the University Health Services. This information was identical in both versions of the recommendation section, although the action plan version also provided detailed suggestions for how to obtain the shot during the course of one's daily activities. This version described the location of the University Health Services, provided times when the shots were available, and the steps needed to schedule a shot. It also included a map depicting the location and a suggestion that readers identify a time during the week when they would pass by the building and have time to get the vaccination. In contrast, the version with no action plan did not include these details. As seniors, all participants were familiar with the location of the building but only those reading the action plan version would be guided to develop a detailed plan for obtaining the tetanus shot when it was convenient for them to do so.

In summary, the 141 participants in the first phase of the study received one of four pamphlets: (1) High fear/action plan; (2) High fear/no action plan; (3) Low fear/action plan; and (4) Low fear/no action plan. In a subsequent phase, the researchers added a fifth condition in which 30 participants received a pamphlet that contained only the action plan section. This fifth condition enabled the researchers to test the independent effects of action planning in the absence of any fear arousal. As reflected in the findings, this condition provided crucial information about the importance of even low levels of fear in motivating protective action.

The questionnaire completed after reviewing the pamphlet included measures of prior tetanus vaccinations; fear arousal, or experience of fear-related emotions while reading the pamphlet; attitudes about the likelihood and severity of tetanus and the importance of obtaining a vaccine; vaccine intentions; and reactions to the pamphlet contents. For the fear arousal measure, participants rated their feelings of multiple facets: fear, tension, nervousness, anxiety, discomfort, anger, and nausea. Reactions to the pamphlet included ratings of the effectiveness of the pictures in enhancing the messages and worry when thinking about the possibility of getting tetanus. As the primary measure of behaviour, the researchers obtained health services records of tetanus vaccinations for all participants over the six weeks following their participation.

MAIN STUDY FINDINGS

Overall, 59 participants reported that they had not received a tetanus shot in the past two years and thus a tetanus vaccination was deemed medically warranted for them based on recommendations for tetanus vaccinations at that time. Most analyses tested for differences as a function of vaccination status in addition to the main independent variables of fear arousal and action plan.

Analyses of the ratings of fear-related emotions confirmed that the fear arousal manipulation was successful: participants who read the pamphlet section designed to induce high fear reported substantially higher levels of fear, tension, anxiety, nervousness, discomfort, anger, and nausea relative to participants who read the section designed to induce low fear. Importantly, these fear arousal differences held for both participants who had received tetanus vaccines in the past two years and those who had not and, with the exception of nausea, regardless of the action plan manipulation.

High fear arousal also induced more positive attitudes about the tetanus vaccine, such that recipients of the high fear section gave higher ratings of their importance relative to recipients of the low fear section. These fear arousal effects held regardless of vaccination status and action plan provision. Fear arousal had similar effects on tetanus vaccine intentions for the 59 participants who were eligible for the vaccine. Because the intention ratings were highly skewed, since most participants gave high ratings, the researchers divided scores into strong intentions (i.e., the top scale rating of 13; $N = 27$) versus weak intentions (i.e., 12 or lower; $N = 32$). As hypothesised, more participants reported strong intentions to obtain the vaccine in the high fear arousal condition than in the low fear arousal condition. In contrast, there were no differences as a function of action plan conditions. Thus, fear arousal influenced positive attitudes and intentions whereas action planning did not.

A contrasting pattern of fear arousal and action plan effects emerged for behaviour. For the 59 participants who were eligible for tetanus vaccines, those in the action plan condition were over eight times more likely than those in the no-action-plan condition to obtain a vaccination, a statistically significant difference (27.6% versus 3.3%, respectively; $p < .01$). Yet fear arousal had no impact on tetanus vaccine behaviour; the action planning effect on behaviour was equivalent across the high and low fear arousal conditions, suggesting that action plans motivate behaviour regardless of the level of fear arousal.

Whereas the behavioural effects of action planning were clear, the potential influence of fear arousal remained uncertain because both high and low fear arousal conditions induced some level of fear. Could the arousal of lower levels of fear be necessary and sufficient to exert an impact on behaviour, with its impact comparable to that of higher fear arousal? To clarify whether fear arousal – even at low levels – is a necessary condition for motivating action, the researchers added a condition in which participants who had not received a tetanus shot in the previous two years received a pamphlet containing only the information about developing an action plan for obtaining the tetanus vaccine and a recommendation to do so. Of these 30 participants, not one went to get a tetanus vaccination in the subsequent weeks. Action planning was insufficient on its own to motivate protective behaviour.

Finally, analyses of the emotion items and reactions to the pamphlets revealed important insights into specific fear-related factors that are differentially associated with changes in attitudes and with actions. Feelings associated with attitude change included worry about contracting tetanus and irritation or anger over the illustrations. Importantly, the pattern of associations for attitude change with irritation and anger runs counter to arguments that fear-arousing communications induce defensive reactance and resistance to messages. Yet worry and anger were not associated with action. Instead, comparisons of the action plan conditions revealed that the action plan reduced feelings of nausea. Nausea can be regarded as an inhibitory fear state that suppresses striving to achieve goals such as disease prevention (Kollar, 1961). That the action plan suppressed nausea induced by the high-fear message highlights one potential pathway through which specific planning can promote action in response to fear arousal – by reducing inhibitory facets of fear.

IMPACT

THEORETICAL AND EMPIRICAL IMPACTS AND ADVANCES

Leventhal et al.'s (1965) classic study was instrumental in reconciling the conflicting findings on the role of fear arousal in motivating protective actions, and it was the first to demonstrate that fear arousal is necessary but not sufficient for the enactment of protective behaviour. Instead, a *combination* of fear arousal and action planning is needed for behaviour change. Yet the study was not without limitations. For example, it might have lacked sufficient statistical power due to the small sample sizes, and particularly for analyses that included only participants who were eligible for tetanus vaccines. In addition, the use of a sample of college students limits the potential generalisability of the findings. Other methodological limitations include the addition of the control condition in which participants received only the action plan at a later point in time which, as the authors note, confounds this control manipulation with the passage of one year in comparisons of this condition with the other four conditions. Further, the measure of vaccine intentions had problematic psychometric properties, such as the use of a single item and a ceiling effect that led the authors to categorise ratings of 1 to 12 as 'weak intentions' and a rating of 13 as 'strong intentions'. More valid and sensitive measures of behavioural intentions are now standard in the field (e.g., Courneya et al., 2006). Nevertheless, the findings were replicated and extended in further studies (e.g., Leventhal & Watts, 1966; Leventhal et al., 1967) and together, these studies set the foundation for numerous theoretical and empirical advances in health psychology research, as described in the following sections.

The parallel-process model

Leventhal et al.'s classic research on fear arousal and action plans directly informed the development of an influential model of how individuals process and respond to fear-inducing messages, and, more broadly, threats to health, which became known as the parallel-process model (see Figure 10.1; Leventhal, 1970). This model of health and illness behaviour proposes that perceptions of stimuli or messages indicative of health threats (e.g., symptoms or unusual sensations in the body, health communications, or diagnoses) activate emotions such as fear and distress, which, in turn, elicit actions for managing and reducing them (fear control). Simultaneously, these perceptions of stimuli elicit a cognitive representation of the health threat and, in turn, actions or procedures for coping with and reducing the threat (danger control). Fear control and danger control processes operate in parallel and in partial independence of each other, and the outcomes of each set of actions are appraised to determine their efficacy in reducing the negative emotions (fear control) and health threat (danger control). The model thus delineates the critical roles of fear arousal and action plans in generating responses to health threat information. Further, the model incorporates the roles of cognitive representations of the health threat and the dynamics involving appraisals of outcomes and their use in revising representations, fear-related emotions, and action plans or coping procedures. The parallel-process model emphasises the dynamic, problem-solving nature of the processes through which individuals perceive and interpret health threat stimuli, experience fear and distress, take actions to simultaneously manage the emotional distress and the objective health danger, and appraise outcomes of those actions to determine whether they should be continued or revised.

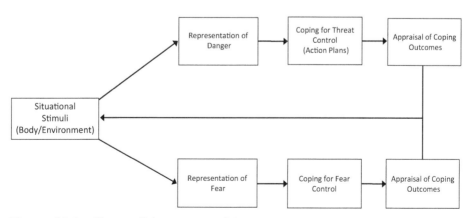

Figure 10.1 The parallel-process model

The parallel-process model was arguably the first to propose not only how cognitions and emotions interactively influence health behaviours and outcomes, but also to provide a *self-regulatory* theory of illness cognition and behaviour. Self-regulation is construed as a dynamic motivational system of setting goals, developing and enacting strategies to achieve them, appraising outcomes of those actions, and revising goals and strategies to further improve outcomes as needed (see also Conner and Norman, Chapter 2, this volume). This perspective contrasts sharply with other dominant perspectives of health behaviour and personality at the time. For example, health cognition models (e.g., the health belief model; Rosenstock, 1974) offered only a static view of cognitive beliefs guiding health behaviours, such that beliefs are regarded as stable and unchanging over time rather than as dynamic and shifting in response to appraisals of behavioural outcomes. This self-regulatory perspective also contrasts with the prevailing learning and conditioning perspectives, which largely ignored the roles of conscious cognitions and problem-solving dynamics (e.g., Skinner, 1974).

The common-sense model of illness self-regulation

Over the subsequent decades, the parallel-process model evolved into the more elaborated common-sense model of the self-regulation of health and illness behaviour (Leventhal et al., 1980; Leventhal et al., 2012). The common-sense model incorporates several new sets of features and processes (see Figure 10.2). First, drawing on advances in cognitive neuroscience (see Epstein, 1994; Stacy et al., 2004), it delineates abstract-conceptual and concrete-experiential levels of information processing. Abstract-conceptual processing involves conceptual reasoning that generally takes the form of linguistic and linear ways of thinking (e.g., considering the likelihood of developing skin cancer and its potential causes). Concrete-experiential processing involves perceptions and memories of events, images, and other perceptual stimuli (e.g., feeling a raised lump on one's arm and having images of skin

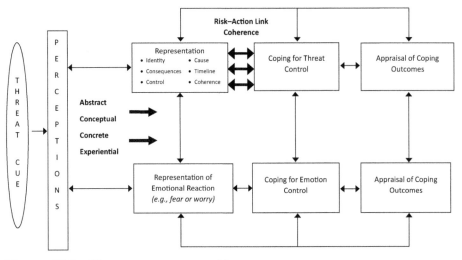

Figure 10.2 The common-sense model

cancer moles and sores 'pop' into mind). Abstract processing leads to relatively cool, deliberative appraisals and decisions, whereas concrete-experiential processing activates 'hot' reactions and impulsive responses (Epstein, 1994; Metcalfe & Mischel, 1999). This distinction captures the common experience of having a 'cool' understanding of an event (e.g., 'This bump is likely from an insect bite') while also having a 'hot' and even contradictory impulse (e.g., rushing to ask one's partner if it looks like skin cancer). The common-sense model thus emphasises the central roles of both perceptual stimuli, such as bodily symptoms and visual cues (e.g., images of skin cancer in health messages), and action plans, or the behavioural procedures for controlling danger and fear. These perceptual and behavioural features are central to motivation and self-regulation. For example, fear arousal is the product of perceptions and cognitive interpretations of what they mean. For example, a lump on one's arm might generate a fear response when it is seen and felt, *and* then is interpreted as a potential sign of cancer.

Another key feature of the common-sense model is the elaboration of the structure and contents of mental representations of health threats. According to the model, people act as common-sense scientists to generate mental schema or representations of illnesses and other health threats. These representations might not be medically accurate (and, in fact, they often diverge substantially from medical accuracy), but they are coherent understandings that make sense to the individual. These representations are structured to include specific beliefs about five features: (1) identity, including the label (e.g., 'skin cancer') and symptoms (e.g., blackened moles, large lumps); (2) causes (e.g., excessive sun exposure, family history of skin cancer); (3) timeline or duration (e.g., it is chronic and won't go away); (4) consequences (e.g., painful death); and (5) control (e.g., surgery to remove the tumor, chemotherapy to kill any remaining cancer cells). Anthropological research with people from cultures around the world reveals that these mental models or representations of illness invariably incorporate these five sets of beliefs (Kleinman, 1980, 1988), suggesting that humans possess an inherent, universal drive to seek out information about these attributes of illness: What is it? Why did I get it? How long will it last? What's going to happen to me? How do I treat it?

Finally, the common-sense model highlights the role of coherence in the connections or links between the illness representation and coping actions. These links must be understandable and 'make sense' to optimally motivate the protective action and reduce emotional distress. For example, if a person's abdominal pain is diagnosed as an ulcer and the doctor prescribes antibiotics to treat it, the person will feel more reassured and motivated to take the antibiotics if that person has a clear understanding of how the ulcer is caused by a helicobacter pylori bacterial infection. If the person believes that ulcers are largely caused by stress, then the antibiotics prescription will seem puzzling and likely go unfilled or unfinished.

The common-sense model has been used extensively in research on how people respond to and manage a wide variety of illnesses and other health threats, including heart disease (e.g., Horowitz et al., 2004), cancer (e.g., Kelly et al., 2005), diabetes (e.g., Keogh et al., 2011), and risks of serious illnesses (e.g., Cameron, 2008). This large body of research has led to significant advances in the development of applications of the model in the design of health communications and interventions for improving adherence to protective behaviours and reducing distress. For example, the common-sense model has been used to guide the development of skills training programmes for clinicians that are designed to improve communications during consultations with patients (de Ridder et al., 2007; Elliott et al., 2008). These programmes train clinicians to ask about illness representations to identify and address inaccurate beliefs. Other interventions directly target individuals with illness conditions or those at risk for particular illnesses. These programmes focus on addressing inaccurate illness beliefs, instilling a coherent understanding of how protective behaviours work to control risk of illness consequences, and developing action plans to engage in protective behaviours (Lee et al., 2011; Petrie et al., 2002).

The common-sense model has continued to evolve and spur variations of the model to address specific health contexts and incorporate additional psychosocial factors. For example, it has been modified to specifically address fear arousal and action plans within the contexts of cancer survivorship (Durazo & Cameron, 2019); specific behaviours, such as adherence to medications (Horne et al., 2019); and personality factors, such as dispositional optimism and perfectionism (Hagger et al., 2017; Hagger & Orbell, 2021). The common-sense model has even been applied to address risk beliefs, fear arousal, and protective actions in other domains, including environmental risks such as exposure to arsenic in well water (Severtson et al., 2006).

The extended parallel-process model

Research guided by the parallel-process model and the common-sense model stimulated additional directions of advancement on understanding the roles of fear arousal and action plans in health-related behaviours. One key direction was the development of the extended parallel-process model (Witte, 1992a), which specifically addresses people's responses to fear appeals – that is, messages designed to arouse fear in order to persuade people to adopt a recommended behaviour. This model elaborates on danger control process by delineating the roles of efficacy appraisals in determining behaviour engagement. If a recommended behaviour is appraised as personally feasible (self-efficacy) and effective in controlling the threat (response efficacy), then fear arousal will lead to acceptance of the message and, in turn, protective action. If either self-efficacy or response efficacy is low, however, then fear control processes will lead to defensive responses such as denial, avoidance, and reactance; as a consequence, the message is rejected and no behaviour change occurs. Nevertheless, the extended parallel-process model highlights the crucial role of fear arousal. If the message recipient has no feelings of threat, then the message is rejected as unimportant.

The extended parallel-process model has guided the use of fear appeals in numerous health contexts. For example, it has been used extensively in the design and evaluation of HIV/AIDS prevention campaigns (e.g., Witte, 1992b; Witte & Morrison, 1995) as well as in the context of prevention behaviours for skin cancer

(Stephenson & Witte, 1998), meningitis (Gore & Bracken, 2005), and adolescent pregnancy (Witte, 1997). Yet debate over the efficacy of fear appeals continues, with many researchers continuing to argue that they are ineffective and can even lead to maladaptive responses when they induce avoidance or rejection of the validity of a health threat (Hardcastle et al., 2016; Kok et al., 2018; see Sidebar 10.1). Nevertheless, well over 100 studies have supported the fundamental propositions of the extended parallel-process model that fear arousal motivates attitude and behaviour change and particularly when both self-efficacy and response efficacy are high (Tannenbaum et al., 2015; Witte & Allen, 2000). The model's principles are widely used in public health messages. For example, close to 75% of public service announcements about alcohol use between 2007 and 2010 incorporated the message features of fear arousal and efficacy (Niederdeppe et al., 2018).

Sidebar 10.1. Pictorial Warnings for Tobacco Products: Do These Fear Appeals Deter Use?

The use of pictorial warnings on tobacco products and in advertisements represents one area of controversy surrounding the application of fear appeals to motivate behaviour change. Over 110 countries have implemented tobacco regulation policies requiring these pictorial warnings, which depict graphic images of the health consequences of smoking, such as blackened lungs, mouth cancer ulcers, corpses, and premature infants in neonatal intensive care units. Interested readers can view a gallery of pictorial warnings from numerous countries provided by the Tobacco Labelling Resource Centre (https://tobacco labels.ca/healthwarningimages/). These warnings are designed to inform users of the harms of smoking through graphic and emotionally-evocative images, and the fear-related reactions elicited by these warnings are expected to discourage use and, for regular users, motivate attempts to quit.

Not surprisingly, these policies have met with strong opposition from the tobacco industry which, through aggressive litigation efforts, has successfully stalled or blocked their implementation in many countries, including the United States (R.J. Reynolds Tobacco Co.V. Food and Drug Admin.: D.C. Cir., 2012.). Yet opposition to their use also resides in the health psychology field, where it has stimulated lively debates over their efficacy at scientific meetings and in the pages of scientific journals. For example, Kok and colleagues (2018) published an article in which they criticise the evidence on the efficacy of fear appeals and, in particular, pictorial warnings in changing tobacco use. They argue that methodologically-sound research on these behavioural effects remains lacking. Further, the authors contend that these initiatives fail to apply theory appropriately because they ignore the critical roles of self-efficacy and response-efficacy, both of which must be high for fear appeals to be effective. This article was followed by a series of commentaries in which scientific experts dispute the assertions made by

(Continued)

(Continued)

Kok et al. They argue, for example, that Kok and colleagues mischaracterise and misinterpret both the evidence and the application of theory to the implementation of pictorial tobacco warnings and other fear appeals (e.g., Borland, 2018; Peters et al., 2018). They note that these warning campaigns apply theory appropriately by including messages designed to enhance self-efficacy and response efficacy, along with links to sources of help. Commentators (e.g., Brewer et al., 2018; Peters et al., 2018) also point to evidence from rigorous trials demonstrating that pictorial warnings can increase quitting behaviour (e.g., Brewer et al., 2016). Further, they note that whereas the demonstrated effects of pictorial warnings on behaviour may be relatively modest given the difficulties of cessation and limited exposure to warnings in trials, the warnings have been demonstrated to exert appreciably stronger effects on attention, knowledge, emotional processes, behavioural intentions, and other cognitive and affective factors guiding behaviour change decisions (e.g., Noar et al., 2016). As with many stimulating scientific debates, the Kok et al. article and the commentaries highlighted important directions for further research to bring these controversial issues to resolution.

Implementation intentions

Whereas the *fear arousal* component of the Leventhal et al. (1965) classic study has been central to the theoretical, empirical, and intervention advances stimulated by the extended parallel-process model, the *action plan* component has informed a robust body of research leading to the development of strategies for translating behavioural motivations or intentions into behaviour. One such strategy is an implementation intention (Gollwitzer, 1999), which is a self-regulatory tool for bridging the all-too-common 'gap' between one's intentions to engage in a protective action (e.g., desires to engage in regular physical activity) and actual behaviour (e.g., maintaining a physical activity programme). As with the action planning procedure in the classic study by Leventhal and colleagues, this strategy involves the specification of situational cues that will prompt awareness that it is time to engage in the behaviour along with concrete plans as to exactly what one will do at that moment. An implementation intention commonly takes the linguistic form of, '*If* [I am in a specific situation, such as a place, or have a certain sensation, such as hunger], *then* [I will take a specific action]'. For example, a person who is motivated to go for a walk on most days might develop and mentally rehearse the implementation intention, '*If* I am arriving home from work and passing the shoe rack in the hallway, *then* I will put on my sneakers and head out the door for a walk'. Importantly, even several minutes of mentally rehearsing an implementation intention can substantially increase the likelihood of taking action (Brandstätter et al., 2001). Briefly rehearsing implementation intentions can increase adherence to a diverse range of behaviours, including improvements in dietary intake (Vila et al., 2017), physical activity (Bélanger-Gravel et al., 2013), and medication adherence (Brown et al., 2009), as well as reductions in the use of substances such as alcohol and tobacco (Malaguti et al., 2020).

CONCLUSIONS

This classic study by Leventhal et al. (1965) significantly advanced the science of fear arousal and health behaviour. The findings were among the first from a series of studies that lay to rest the predominant fear-drive model proposing that eliciting fear alone was sufficient to motivate protective action, and were instrumental in reconciling the conflicting findings on whether extreme fear arousal was counter-productive due to its elicitation of defensive responses. The study clearly demonstrated that it is the combination of fear arousal, even at modest levels, and an action plan that results in health-protective behaviours. This classic study was a catalyst for many fruitful avenues of theory development and empirical advances, including the parallel-process model, the common-sense model of illness self-regulation, the extended parallel-process model, and implementation intention strategies. This generativity in theoretical advances and its fruitful translation to health communications, interventions, and practices, speaks to the scientific power of the research spurred by this classic study. While theoretical developments, particularly with the common-sense model, and applications to communications and interventions continue at pace, the future is likely to witness rapid growth in theory-guided social media interventions that provide information about health threats, tools for developing action plans, strategies for the adaptive management of fear-related emotions, and feedback tools for appraising progress in managing illnesses and illness risk. For example, the Adolescent Adherence Patient Tool (ADAPT; Kosse, Bouvy, de Vries, & Koster, 2019) provides self-regulation aids for managing asthma during the adolescent years. They include tools to adjust worry levels so that they motivate medication adherence, symptom monitors to inform appraisals of progress in managing asthma, and prompts to take protective action. These social media interventions have the potential to reach large populations around the globe and provide easy and affordable access to effective self-regulation support and resources. Leventhal's theoretical and empirical contributions have been, and continue to be, instrumental in the development of a wide array of communication and intervention strategies to promote motivation and enactment of health-protective behaviours.

FURTHER READING

Cameron, L. D., Fleszar-Pavlović, S., & Khachikian, T. (2020). Changing behavior using the common-sense model of self-regulation. In M. Hagger, L. D. Cameron, K. Hamilton, N. Hankonen, & T. Lintunen (Eds.), *Handbook of behavior change* (pp. 60–76). Cambridge: Cambridge University Press. https://doi.org/10.1017/9781108677318.005

This chapter provides a broad overview of research on interventions based on the common-sense model of self-regulation. It reviews a variety of approaches for applying the model to develop and implement strategies to change health-related behaviours as well as behaviours in other domains, such as climate change mitigation and education.

Leventhal, H., Bodnar-Deren, S., Breland, J. Y., Gash-Converse, J., Phillips, L. A., Leventhal, E., & Cameron, L. D. (2012). Modeling health and illness behavior: The approach of the common-sense model. In A. Baum, T. Revenson, & J. Singer (Eds.), *Handbook of health psychology* (2nd ed., pp. 3–36). Hoboken, NJ: Psychology Press.

This chapter reviews the theoretical principles underlying the common-sense model of self-regulation, the dynamics of common-sense self-regulation, and research guided by the common-sense model. It provides an excellent review of research on the roles of illness perceptions and action plans in shaping responses to health threats.

REFERENCES

Bélanger-Gravel, A., Godin, G., & Amireault, S. (2013). A meta-analytic review of the effect of implementation intentions on physical activity. *Health Psychology Review, 7,* 23–54. https://doi.org/10.1080/17437199.2011.560095

Berkowitz, L., & Cottingham, D. (1960). The interest value and relevance of fear arousing communications. *Journal of Abnormal and Social Psychology, 60,* 37–43. https://doi.org/10.1037/h0045247

Borland, R. (2018). Misinterpreting theory and ignoring evidence: Fear appeals can actually work: A comment on Kok et al. (2018). *Health Psychology Review, 12,* 126–128. https://doi.org/10.1080/17437199.2018.1445545

Brandstätter, V., Lengfelder, A., & Gollwitzer, P. M. (2001). Implementation intentions and efficient action initiation. *Journal of Personality and Social Psychology, 81,* 946–960. https://doi.org/10.1037/0022-3514.81.5.946

Brewer, N. T., Hall, M. G., & Noar, S. M. (2018). Pictorial cigarette pack warnings increase quitting. *Health Psychology Review, 12,* 129–132. https://doi.org/10.1080/17437199.2018.1445544

Brewer, N. T., Hall, M. G., Noar, S. M., Parada, H., Stein-Seroussi, A., Bach, L. E., ... Ribisl, K. M. (2016). Impact of pictorial cigarette pack warnings on changes in smoking behavior: A randomized clinical trial. *JAMA Internal Medicine, 176,* 905–912. https://doi.org/10.1001/jamainternmed.2016.2621

Brown, I., Sheeran, P., & Reuber, M. (2009). Enhancing antiepileptic drug adherence: A randomized controlled trial. *Epilepsy & Behavior, 16,* 634–639. https://doi.org/10.1016/j.yebeh.2009.09.014

Cameron, L. D. (2008). Illness risk representations and motivations to engage in protective behavior: The case of skin cancer risk. *Psychology & Health, 23,* 91–112. https://doi.org/10.1080/14768320701342383

Courneya, K. S., Conner, M., & Rhodes, R. E. (2006). Effects of different measurement scales on the variability and predictive validity of the 'two-component' model of the theory of planned behavior in the exercise domain. *Psychology & Health, 21,* 557–570. doi:10.1080/14768320500422857

de Ridder, D. T., Theunissen, N. C., & Dulmen, S. M. (2007). Does training general practitioners to elicit patients' illness representations and action plans influence their communication as a whole? *Patient Education and Counseling, 66,* 327–336. https://doi.org/10.1016/j.pec.2007.01.006

Dollard, J., & Miller, N. E. (1950). *Personality and psychotherapy: An analysis in terms of learning, thinking, and culture.* New York: McGraw-Hill. https://doi.org/10.1177/004057365100800323

Durazo, A., & Cameron, L. D. (2019). Representations of cancer recurrence risk, recurrence worry, and health-protective behaviours: An elaborated, systematic review. *Health Psychology Review*, *13*(4), 447–476. https://doi.org/10.1080/17437199.2019.1618725

Elliott, R. A., Barber, N., Clifford, S., Horne, R., & Hartley, E. (2008). The cost effectiveness of a telephone-based pharmacy advisory service to improve adherence to newly prescribed medicines. *Pharmacy World & Science*, *30*, 17–23. https://doi.org/10.1007/s11096-007-9134-y

Epstein, S. (1994). Integration of the cognitive and the psychodynamic unconscious. *American Psychologist*, *49*, 709–724. http://dx.doi.org/10.1037/0003-066X.49.8.709

Gollwitzer, P. M. (1999). Implementation intentions: Strong effects of simple plans. *American Psychologist*, *54*, 493–503. https://doi.org/10.1037/0003-066X.54.7.493

Gore, T. D., & Bracken, C. (2005). Testing the theoretical design of a health risk message: Reexamining the major tenets of the extended parallel process model. *Health Education and Behavior*, *32*, 27–41. https://doi.org/10.1177/1090198104266901

Hagger, M. S., Koch, S., Chatzisarantis, N. L. D., & Orbell, S. (2017). The common sense model of self-regulation: Meta-analysis and test of a process model. *Psychological Bulletin*, *143*, 1117–1154. http://dx.doi.org/10.1037/bul0000118

Hagger, M. S., & Orbell, S. (2021). The common-sense model of illness self-regulation: A conceptual review and proposed extended model. *Health Psychology Review*, *16*(3), 347–377. https://doi.org/10.1080/17437199.2021.1878050

Hardcastle, S. J., Chan, D. K. C., Caudwell, K. M., Sultan, S., Cranwell, J., Chatzisarantis, N. L. D., & Hagger, M. S. (2016). Larger and more prominent graphic health warnings on plain-packaged tobacco products and avoidant responses in current smokers: A qualitative study. *International Journal of Behavioral Medicine*, *23*, 94–101. https://doi.org/10.1007/s12529-015-9487-x

Horne, R., Cooper, V., Wileman, V., & Chan, A. (2019). Supporting adherence to medicines for long-term conditions: A perceptions and practicalities approach based on an extended common-sense model. *European Psychologist*, *24*, 82–96. http://dx.doi.org/10.1027/1016-9040/a000353

Horowitz, C., Rein, S., & Leventhal, H. (2004). A story of maladies, misconceptions and mishaps: Effective management of heart failure. *Social Science and Medicine*, *58*, 631–643. https://doi.org/10.1016/s0277-9536(03)00232-6

Janis, I. L., & Feshbach, S. (1953). Effects of fear-arousing communications. *Journal of Abnormal and Social Psychology*, *48*, 78–92. https://doi.org/10.1037/h0060732

Janis, I. L., & Feshbach, S. (1954). Personality differences associated with responsiveness to fear-arousing communications. *Journal of Personality*, *23*, 54–166. https://doi.org/10.1111/j.1467-6494.1954.tb01145.x

Janis, I. L., & Terwilliger, R. F. (1962). An experimental study of psychological resistances to fear arousing communications. *Journal of Abnormal and Social Psychology*, *65*, 403–410. https://doi.org/10.1037/h0047601

Kelly, K., Leventhal, H., Andrykowski, M., Toppmeyer, D., Much, J., Dermody, J., Marvin, M., Baran, J., & Schwalb, M. (2005). Using the common-sense model to understand perceived cancer risk in individuals testing for BRCA1/2 mutations. *Psychooncology*, *14*, 34–48. https://doi.org/10.1002/pon.805

Keogh, K. M., Smith, S. M., White, P., McGilloway, S., Kelly, A., Gibney, J., & O'Dowd, T. (2011). Psychological family intervention for poorly controlled type 2 diabetes. *American Journal of Managed Care*, *17*, 105–113.

Kleinman, A. (1980). *Patients and healers in the context of culture: An exploration of the borderland between anthropology, medicine, and psychiatry* (Vol. 3). Los Angeles, CA: University of California Press.

Kleinman, A. (1988). *The illness narratives: Suffering, healing, and the human condition*. New York: Basic Books.

Kok, G., Peters, G. Y., Kessels, L. T. E., ten Hoor, G. A., & Ruiter, R. A. C. (2018). Ignoring theory and misinterpreting evidence: The false belief in fear appeals. *Health Psychology Review*, *12*, 111–125. https://doi.org/10.1080/17437199.2017.1415767

Kollar, E. J. (1961). Psychological stress: A re-evaluation. *Journal of Nervous and Mental Disease*, *132*, 382–396. https://doi.org/10.1037/h0022089

Kosse, R. C., Bouvy, M. L., de Vries, T. W., & Koster, S. (2019). Effect of a mHealth intervention on adherence in adolescents with asthma: A randomized controlled trial. *Respiratory Medicine*, *149*, 46–51. https://doi.org/10.1016/j.rmed.2019.02.009

Lee, T. J., Cameron, L. D., Wünsche, B., & Stevens, C. (2011). A randomized trial of computer-based communications using imagery and text information to alter representations of heart disease risk and motivate protective behaviour. *British Journal of Health Psychology*, *16*, 72–91. https://doi.org/10.1348/135910710X511709

Leventhal, H. (1970). Findings and theory in the study of fear communications. In L. Berkowitz (Ed.), *Advances in experimental social psychology* (Vol. 5, pp. 119–186). New York: Academic Press. https://doi.org/I0.1016/S0065-2601(08)60091-X

Leventhal, H., Bodnar-Deren, S., Breland, J. Y., Gash-Converse, J., Phillips, L. A., Leventhal, E., & Cameron, L. D. (2012). Modeling health and illness behavior: The approach of the common-sense model. In A. Baum, T. Revenson, & J. Singer (Eds.), *Handbook of health psychology* (2nd ed., pp. 3–36). Hoboken, NJ: Psychology Press.

Leventhal, H., & Niles, P. A. (1964). A field experiment on fear arousal with data on the validity of questionnaire measures. *Journal of Personality*, *32*, 459–479. https://doi.org/10.1111/j.1467-6494.1964.tb01352.x

Leventhal, H., Meyer, D., & Nerenz, D. (1980). The common sense model of illness danger. In S. Rachman (Ed.), *Medical Psychology* (Vol. II, pp. 7-30). New York: Pergamon Press.

Leventhal, H., Singer, R., & Jones, S. (1965). Effects of fear and specificity of recommendation upon attitudes and behavior. *Journal of Personality and Social Psychology*, *2*, 20–29.

Leventhal, H., & Watts, J. C. (1966). Sources of resistance to fear-arousing communications on smoking and lung cancer. *Journal of Personality*, *34*, 155–175. https://doi.org/10.1111/j.1467-6494.1966.tb01706.x

Leventhal, H., Watts, J. C., & Pagano, F. (1967). Effects of fear and instructions on how to cope with danger. *Journal of Personality and Social Psychology*, *6*, 313–321. https://doi.org/10.1037/h0021222

Malaguti, A., Ciocanel, O., Sani, F., Dillon, J. F., Eriksen, A., & Power, K. (2020). Effectiveness of the use of implementation intentions on reduction of substance use: A meta-analysis. *Drug and Alcohol Dependence*, *214*, https://doi.org/10.1016/j.drugalcdep.2020.108120

Metcalfe, J., & Mischel, W. (1999). A hot/cool-system analysis of delay of gratification: Dynamics of willpower. *Psychological Review*, *106*, 3–19. https://doi.org/10.1037/0033-295X.106.1.3

Niederdeppe, J., Avery, R. J., Miller, E. E. N. (2018). Theoretical foundations of appeals in alcohol-abuse and drunk-driving public service announcements in the United States, 1995–2010. *American Journal of Health Promotion*, *32*, 887–896. https://doi.org/10.1111/risa.13140

Niles, P. (1964). Two personality measures associated with responsiveness to fear-arousing communications. Unpublished doctoral dissertation, Yale University, New Haven, CT.

Noar, S. M., Hall, M. G., Francis, D. B., Ribisl, K. M., Pepper, J. K., & Brewer, N. T. (2016). Pictorial pack warnings: A meta-analysis of experimental studies. *Tobacco Control*, *25*, 342–354. http://dx.doi.org/10.1136/tobaccocontrol-2014-051978

Peters, E., & Shoots-Reinhard, B. (2018). Don't throw the baby out with the bath water: Commentary on Kok, Peters, Kessels, ten Hoor, and Ruiter (2018). *Health Psychology Review*, *12*, 140–143. https://doi.org/10.1080/17437199.2018.1445542

Petrie, K. J., Cameron, L. D., Ellis, C. J., Buick, D., & Weinman, J. (2002). Changing illness perceptions after myocardial infarction: An early intervention randomized controlled trial. *Psychosomatic Medicine*, *64*, 580–586. http://dx.doi.org/10.1097/00006842-200207000-00007

R. J. Reynolds Tobacco Co. V. Food and Drug Administration-402 U.S. App. D.C. 438, D.C. 696 F.3d 1205 (2012). www.lexisnexis.com/community/casebrief/p/casebrief-r-j-reynolds-tobacco-co-v-fda

Rosenstock, I. M. (1974). The health belief model and preventative health behavior. *Health Education Monographs*, *2*, 354–386. https://doi.org/10.1177/109019817400200405

Severtson, D. J., Baumann, L. C., & Brown, R. L. (2006). Applying a health behavior theory to explore the influence of information and experience on arsenic risk perceptions, policy beliefs, and protective behavior. *Risk Analysis*, *26*, 353–368. https://doi.org/10.1111/j.1539-6924.2006.00737.x

Skinner, B. F. (1974). *About behaviorism*. New York: Knopf.

Stacy, A. W., Ames, S. L., & Knowlton, B. J. (2004). Neurologically plausible distinctions in cognition relevant to drug use etiology and prevention. *Substance Use and Misuse*, *39*, 1571–1623. https://doi.org/10.1081/ja-200033204

Stephenson, M., & Witte, K. (1998). Fear, threat, and perception of efficacy from frightening skin cancer messages. *Public Health Review*, *26*, 147–174.

Tannenbaum, M. B., Hepler, J., Zimmerman, R. S., Saul, L., Jacobs, S., Wilson, K., & Albarracín, D. (2015). Appealing to fear: A meta-analysis of fear appeal effectiveness and theories. *Psychological Bulletin*, *141*(6), 1178–1204. https://doi.org/10.1037/a0039729

Vila, I., Carrero, I., & Redondo, R. (2017). Reducing fat intake using implementation intentions: A meta-analytic review. *British Journal of Health Psychology*, *22*, 281–294. https://doi.org/10.1111/bjhp.12230

Witte, K. (1992a). Putting the fear back into fear appeals: The extended parallel process model. *Communication Monographs*, *59*, 329–349. https://doi.org/10.1080/03637759209376276

Witte, K. (1992b). The role of threat and efficacy in AIDS prevention. *International Quarterly of Community Health Education*, *12*, 225–249. https://doi.org/10.2190/U43P-9QLX-HJ5P-U2J5

Witte, K. (1997). Preventing teen pregnancy through persuasive communications: Realities, myths, and hard-fact truths. *Journal of Community Health*, *22*, 137–154. https://doi.org/10.1023/a:1025116923109

Witte, K., & Allen, M. (2000). A meta-analysis of fear appeals: Implications for effective public health campaigns. *Health Education & Behavior*, *27*, 591–615. https://doi.org/10.1177/109019810002700506

Witte, K., & Morrison, K. (1995). The use of scare tactics in AIDS prevention: The case of juvenile detention and high school youth. *Journal of Applied Communication Research*, *23*, 128–142. https://doi.org/10.1080/00909889509365419

11 | Placebo Effects: Revisiting Kirsch (1985)

Kirsch, I. (1985). Response expectancy as a determinant of experience and behavior. *American Psychologist, 40,* 1189–1202.

Felicity L. Bishop

BACKGROUND

Placebo effects are positive and measurable effects that result from the administration of a placebo intervention; a placebo intervention is defined as being biologically inert for the symptom in question (Grünbaum, 1981; but see also Howick, 2017). As discussed in detail in Sidebar 11.1, there are numerous challenges around terminology and definitions in this field.

Sidebar 11.1. Terminology and Definitions

The terms 'placebo effect' and 'placebo response' are sometimes used interchangeably but this is imprecise and inaccurate. The distinction between them can best be illustrated by considering randomised placebo-controlled clinical trials. In a three-arm placebo-controlled trial testing a new drug, patients report their symptoms at baseline before being randomly assigned to one of three groups. The 'drug group' receives a course of capsules containing the drug under investigation. The 'placebo group' receives a course of capsules that appear identical to those in the drug group but that actually contain an inert substance (e.g., flour; see Golomb et al., 2010, for

(Continued)

(Continued)

more on the contents of placebos). The 'natural history control group' does not receive any capsules. After a pre-established period of taking the capsules, patients in all three groups again report their symptoms. The *placebo response* is the change in symptoms from baseline in the group taking the placebo. Multiple factors might contribute to this response, including not only the administration of the placebo but also 'Hawthorne effects' (the effect of being observed; Landsberger, 1958), natural history (e.g., spontaneous remission), and regression to the mean (a statistical arte-fact). The *placebo effect* is a subcomponent of the placebo response – the difference between the outcomes reported by the placebo group and the natural history group. In other words, the placebo effect is the effect that can be attributed to the administration of the placebo (Zhang & Doherty, 2018). It is important to be aware of this distinction, particularly when reading claims about placebos that are based on analyses of clinical trials, because clinical trials often only include two arms (drug and placebo), and so while they can document placebo responses, they cannot, by design, measure the magnitude of placebo effects. An elaborated definition can be applied across clinical trials testing placebos and laboratory studies of placebo effects, where underpinning mechanisms may also be invoked. For example, an expert consensus group from the Society of Interdisciplinary Placebo Studies offers this definition: 'Placebo and nocebo effects[1] refer to the beneficial or adverse effects that occur in clinical or laboratory medical contexts, respectively, after administra-tion of an inert treatment or as part of active treatments, due to mechanisms such as expectancies of the patient' (Evers et al., 2018, p. 205). As well as invoking the underpinning mechanisms (note it is expectancies that are explicitly mentioned, building on Kirsch (1985)), this definition also allows for placebo effects to occur alongside active treatments. And so now the placebo effect is not only part of a pla-cebo response but may also be part of a larger overall response to active treatment.

The following scenario depicts an archetypal placebo effect in a clinical practice scenario:

James goes to see Doctor Smith because he has some acute knee pain. Doctor Smith listens empathetically to James' description of his pain and the impact it is having on him. Doctor Smith then examines him and decides that James' pain is musculoskeletal and not caused by any serious underlying pathology. Doctor Smith knows there is nothing seriously wrong with James and expects he will probably recover in his own time without medical intervention. In an attempt to help James without risking the side-effects that may be associated with treatments such as ibuprofen, Doctor Smith prescribes James some pills and says that they are powerful painkillers that will help to reduce his pain. The pills are placebos, made from starch and water. James takes the pills and finds that his pain decreases as Doctor Smith's advice indicated.

---

[1] Nocebo effects are adverse placebo effects (i.e., symptoms such as itch, nausea, headache) that may result from placebo administration.

The above scenario illustrates some of the features of placebo effects that make them so fascinating for scientists, clinicians, and the public alike, not least the suggestion of mysterious mind–body interactions. From a scientific perspective, placebo effects raise fascinating issues, including, for example, the veracity of the patient-reported pain relief, the ethics of the deception enacted by the doctor, and last, but certainly not least, the mechanisms of action of the placebo. Does the patient's pain really decrease, or do they just say it does to please the doctor? Is it OK for the doctor to lie to the patient if doing so decreases the patient's pain? How can ingesting a small amount of substances like sugar or starch reduce a patient's pain? These questions themselves rest on certain assumptions and in turn raise more questions. What is 'real' pain reduction and how can it be measured? What happens if the patient is informed and consents to receiving a placebo? Instead of focusing on the substance of the placebo, what if explanations for placebo effects are sought in the context and process of the interaction between doctor, patient, and intervention?

The scientific study of placebo effects is undoubtedly multifaceted and multidisciplinary, with significant contributions from not only health and other psychologists but also neurobiologists, bioethicists, epidemiologists, and clinical scientists, among others. Within this broader context, this chapter will critically review Kirsch's (1985) paper outlining Response Expectancy Theory. While Kirsch drew on three substantive research areas to explicate his theory – placebo effects, fear reduction, and hypnosis – this chapter focuses on the contribution of Response Expectancy Theory to the understanding of placebo effects. The chapter begins by outlining Kirsch's (1985) seminal *American Psychologist* paper in which he first detailed Response Expectancy Theory. It will then examine the impact of Response Expectancy Theory in terms of how placebo effects are understood, drawing on research into depression and other conditions. The chapter then considers how the learning mechanisms underpinning placebo effects have been theorised and, finally, how the science of placebo effects can be translated into clinical applications.

DETAILED OVERVIEW

KIRSCH (1985): RESPONSE EXPECTANCY THEORY

Kirsch (1985) positioned his work as an extension of learning theory, wherein expectancy was already a well-established concept with nuanced variations. For example, Rotter's (1954) social learning theory proposed that the potential for a behaviour to be performed is a function of the perceived likelihood that the behaviour will result in a specific outcome (i.e., expectancy) and the perceived value of that outcome (i.e., reinforcement value). Bolles (1972, as cited in Kirsch, 1985) further specified S-S expectancies (that certain stimuli predict the occurrence of other stimuli) and R-S expectancies (that certain behaviours will have certain consequences). Bandura (1977) distinguished between outcome expectancies (about the likelihood that a specific behaviour will have specific consequences) and self-efficacy expectancies (about one's personal ability to perform a specific behaviour). Against this backdrop, Kirsch (1985) defined response expectancies as expectations concerning *non-volitional* responses. Non-volitional responses are experienced as occurring automatically, and include, for example, pain, anxiety, itch, happiness, nausea, and sadness. These responses themselves have positive (e.g., happiness) and negative (e.g., pain) reinforcing properties that can influence the extent to which people undertake voluntary behaviours that trigger them. The key point that Kirsch (1985) developed in Response Expectancy Theory is that non-volitional responses are also 'elicited and/or enhanced by the expectancy of their occurrence' (Kirsch, 1985, p. 1189). In other words, the extent to which people expect to experience non-volitional responses not only makes them more or less likely to engage in associated behaviours, but also has a direct causal role in triggering the non-volitional responses themselves and determining their magnitude.

When Kirsch published Response Expectancy Theory in 1985, expectancies were thought to be involved in placebo effects (e.g., see Frank, 1973), but classical conditioning was a leading alternative explanatory mechanism. In arguing for response expectancies, Kirsch (1985) drew on specific conditioning studies as well as Wickramasekera's (1980) articulation of a classical conditioning theory of placebo effects. According to Wickramasekera (1980), drugs should be considered unconditioned stimuli (US) whose effects are unconditioned responses (UR): drugs elicit drug effects because their pharmacological ingredients have specific biological actions. Placebos can be considered conditioned stimuli (CS) whose effects are conditioned responses (CR): placebos elicit placebo effects because of conditioned, or learnt, associations between superficial or incidental characteristics that are shared between placebos and drugs. For example, a placebo analgaesic (CS) may elicit pain relief (CR) because it looks like an effective analgaesic, such as morphine, because it is administered by qualified medical personnel known to administer powerful drugs, and/or because it is administered in a hospital or a doctor's surgery.

To be a credible theory of placebo effects, Response Expectancy Theory needed not only to account for the extant evidence from classical conditioning studies of placebo effects, but also to explain findings that were inconsistent with classical conditioning theory. Kirsch (1985) presented his argument in three parts: (1) placebo effects which can be accounted for by classical conditioning; (2) placebo effects which cannot be accounted for by classical conditioning but can be accounted for by Response Expectancy Theory; and (3) evidence that should lead to the rejection of specific hypotheses derived from the classical conditioning model of placebo.

In relation to placebo effects which can be accounted for by classical conditioning, Kirsch (1985) discussed a series of studies purporting to demonstrate placebo effects elicited by classical conditioning procedures. Kirsch argued that while conditioning procedures may elicit some placebo effects in laboratory animals and humans, findings were inconsistent: not all studies purporting to show conditioning effects had successfully implemented classical conditioning procedures and evidence suggested that classical conditioning inhibited (i.e., reduced) or reversed (i.e., increased alertness) rather than increased responses to placebo tranquilizers.

Thus, Kirsch (1985) established that there might be a need for an additional explanation of placebo effects beyond classical conditioning.

The next step in Kirsch's (1985) argument was to strengthen the need for a new theory of placebo effects, by presenting evidence of placebo effects which cannot be accounted for by classical conditioning. He argued that there are placebo effects that classical conditioning cannot account for but that can be accounted for by Response Expectancy Theory. In other words, he presented evidence that expectancy effects and conditioning effects can be dissociated. Kirsch argued that for placebo effects to be underpinned by classical conditioning mechanisms, the placebo effect should map back to the effect of the drug; this is because, according to classical conditioning accounts, the conditioned response (the placebo effect) is the result of a learned association between the placebo and the unconditioned response (the drug effect). And he presented multiple studies illustrating placebo effects that diverge from drug effects, some of which had used a balanced placebo design (see Sidebar 11.2) to demonstrate differences between placebo and drug effects. For example, Kirsch described evidence that the drug effect of alcohol is to decrease sexual arousal, but the placebo effect of alcohol is to increase sexual arousal; these effects may derive from commonly held beliefs about alcohol's effects.

Sidebar 11.2. Balanced Placebo Design and the Open-Hidden Paradigm

The balanced placebo design enables researchers to tease apart different factors that contribute to placebo and drug responses in experimental settings. Specifically, it enables researchers to isolate the effect of verbal instruction (as a means of shaping response expectancies) from the effect of the imbibed substance. This design was developed for alcohol studies partly to address concerns about relying on blinding as a manipulation of expectancies, given that participants had consented in advance to the possibility of receiving a drug or placebo (Rohsenow & Marlatt, 1981). In the balanced placebo design, participants are randomly assigned to one of four groups, defined by every combination of two factors: what they receive and what they are told they are receiving. Group A receive a drug and are told it is a drug ('open-label' drug condition, similar to usual clinical practice). Group B receive a placebo and are told it is a drug (deceptive placebo condition). Group C receive a drug and are told it is a placebo (deceptive drug condition). Group D are given a placebo and are told it is a placebo ('open-label' placebo condition). Consistent with Kirsch's (1985) Response Expectancy Theory, a recent systematic review of studies using the balanced placebo design found evidence of interactions, including divergence between drug and placebo effects (Boussageon et al., 2022).

(Continued)

(Continued)

The open-hidden experimental design was developed to separate out the placebo effect from the drug response. It differs from the balanced placebo design in that now all participants are given a drug and no participants receive a placebo. Instead, participants are randomly assigned to one of two conditions: the open condition, in which they are aware of when they are receiving the drug, or the hidden condition, in which they are unaware of when they are receiving the drug. The distinction between the open and hidden condition can be achieved, for example, by having an intravenous analgaesic administered automatically by a machine that is (open), or is not (hidden), visible and audible to participants. Studies using this design show that treatments are less effective when patients are not aware of treatment administration compared to when they are aware (Colloca et al., 2004).

Finally, Kirsch (1985) argued that a hypothesis derived from Wickramasekera's (1980) classical conditioning model of placebo effects – concerning the relative magnitude of drug and placebo effects – can be rejected based on the evidence. The classical conditioning model assumed that placebo and drug effects are additive, and that the drug response includes two components – a drug effect and a placebo effect. The subsequent prediction, or hypothesis, was that the drug effect would make a larger contribution than the placebo effect to overall drug response. In other words, if the overall drug response was to be separated into drug effect and placebo effect components, the drug effect component would be larger than the placebo effect component. Kirsch cited three studies in which the drug effect was either similar to or smaller than the placebo effect, thus providing evidence to reject Wickramasekera's (1980) hypothesis.

Having established the need for response expectancies in addition to classical conditioning models of placebo effects, Kirsch (1985) proceeded to discuss putative mechanisms underpinning response expectancies. He offered three propositions. The first was that response expectancies have a direct, unmediated, effect on subjective experience. For example, this would mean that expecting to experience pain relief from a placebo analgaesic does itself directly cause the experience of pain relief, without any intervening psychological or biological processes. The second proposition was that the psychological state of holding response expectancies has a corresponding physiological state. This is how Response Expectancy Theory accounts for what, at the time, was new evidence suggesting a role for endorphins in producing placebo analgesia (Fields & Levine, 1984): Kirsch argued that endorphin release is the physiological substrate of the subjective experience of placebo analgesia induced by response expectancies. The final proposition was that, in addition to directly changing the subjective experience of non-volitional responses, response expectancies will trigger behavioural changes in a way that is consistent with Rotter's (1954) social learning theory and associated models. Here, it is important to again consider the notion that response expectancies are one type of a broader class of expectancies (expectancies concerning non-volitional responses), all of which have reinforcement values that influence the potential for behaviour. For example, response expectancies for analgesia likely have a positive reinforcement value (i.e., pain relief is a good thing), and it is this positive reinforcement value that drives associated behaviours (e.g., taking analgaesics).

In summary, Kirsch (1985) drew on animal and human studies of classical conditioning to argue that the classical conditioning model was at best an incomplete account of placebo effects and at worst may be misleading. In comparison, Kirsch argued that Response Expectancy Theory could account for extant findings and response expectancies may themselves mediate the effects of conditioning. And according to Response Expectancy Theory, changes in the subjective experience of non-volitional responses following placebo administration (e.g., pain relief) are a direct, unmediated consequence of response expectancies; physiological changes (e.g., endorphin release) represent the physical counterparts of subjective experience; and behavioural changes (e.g., analgaesic consumption) are the reinforced consequences of subjective experience. At the time of first publication, Response Expectancy Theory accounted for findings from classical conditioning studies and offered novel insight into findings that were inconsistent with the classical conditioning model of placebo effects. Response Expectancy Theory has undoubtedly influenced current theories and applications of placebo effects, which will now be discussed in turn. Sidebar 11.3 highlights an important strand of Kirsch's own research on Response Expectancy Theory – his work on placebo effects in anti-depressants.

Sidebar 11.3. Placebo Effects and Anti-depressant Medications

Kirsch's work on placebo effects in anti-depressants, and his interpretation of this evidence, has been one of the more controversial strands of research within the Response Expectancy Theory paradigm. Kirsch applied and extended the logic of Response Expectancy Theory to question commonly held assumptions about the relative contribution of drug and placebo effects to patients' overall response to anti-depressants. A series of meta-analytic studies each pooled data from randomised, placebo-controlled clinical trials of anti-depressants to investigate the difference between drug and placebo responses using more data than possible in any single trial. These meta-analytic methods, which are now well accepted and often considered to be the pinnacle of evidence hierarchies, were themselves controversial when this series of studies began. Kirsch and Sapirstein's (1998) meta-analysis of 19 double-blind, placebo-controlled trials of anti-depressant medication was accompanied by an editor's note, which, among other things, cautioned readers about the controversial nature and application

(Continued)

(Continued)

of meta-analysis. In this early meta-analysis, Kirsch and Sapirstein (1998) pooled data from 19 trials involving 2,318 patients. Because the trials did not include the no-treatment control arms necessary to directly estimate the magnitude of placebo effects, the researchers had to find another way to do this. Baseline and post-treatment self-reported depression scores were available, and so they used these data to calculate standardised improvement from baseline among medication and placebo groups from all included trials. They reported a weighted mean effect size of 1.55 SDs for medication and 1.16 for placebo and argued that this meant only 25% was a drug response ((1.55-1.16)/1.55) and the remaining 75% was a placebo response. Kirsch and Sapirstein (1998) investigated the extent to which this large placebo response might itself be attributable to placebo effects rather than confounders such as natural history and Hawthorne effects, which also contribute to the placebo response. However, they did this by comparing their effects to effects computed from a separate set of trials of psychotherapy for depression that had included a no-treatment control group, which makes the results challenging to interpret as the two sets of trials may be different in important respects that render questionable any comparisons between effect sizes.

Subsequent meta-analyses sought to address the limitations of the earlier work. Kirsch et al. (2002) meta-analysed anti-depressant efficacy data submitted to the US Food and Drug Administration (FDA). By analysing data submitted to the FDA, they could address criticisms of the earlier work, including that it had been subject to publication bias and had pooled trials that had used different response measures. In an even more pronounced result than the earlier meta-analysis, Kirsch et al. (2002) found that only 18% of the drug response could be attributed to the drug effect. A third – larger and more methodologically sophisticated – meta-analysis was also consistent with the earlier two meta-analyses: across 35 trials of anti-depressants submitted to the FDA, placebo responses had a magnitude 80% of that of drug responses (Kirsch et al., 2008). While the main finding appears to be robust, Kirsch's interpretation and the findings from additional secondary analyses was controversial. He argued that not only did the findings suggest that commonly prescribed anti-depressants had limited efficacy for patients with mild to moderate depression, but that the benefits for patients with more severe depression might be largely attributable to placebo effects and that, seen in this light, the benefits might not outweigh the harms (i.e., adverse effects, including vulnerability to future episodes of depression) associated with anti-depressants (Kirsch, 2014). Unsurprisingly, this prompted scientific and other responses and interest from within and beyond psychiatry, psychology, and placebo studies: Kirsch (2008) provides a fascinating account of these reactions to his work in the wider scientific and medical communities and the popular media.

DEVELOPMENTS

ALTERNATIVE THEORIES

As outlined above, Kirsch explicitly presented his Response Expectancy Theory in relation to a classical conditioning model of placebo effects. This debate, between expectancy and conditioning, has continued since the publication of the 1985 paper. For example, Stewart-Williams and Podd (2004) reviewed the literature while considering two distinct issues – the factors that shape placebo effects and the learning that mediates these effects. They argued that (1) classical conditioning is one possible input to placebo effects (others being, for example, verbal suggestion, observational learning), (2) classical conditioning can lead to either nonconscious learning or conscious, expectancy-based learning, and (3) both nonconscious learning and conscious expectancy-based learning can produce physiological and subjective placebo effects. In his comments on this attempted integration, Kirsch (2004) pointed out that classical conditioning was already acknowledged as one possible factor that can generate expectations, and that expectancies are not required to be held consciously (although they can be when attention is thus directed). The debate between conditioning and expectancy continues today (e.g., see Bąbel et al., 2017) and the relationship between and relative importance of these processes may differ across symptoms (Wolters et al., 2019). Research on the neurophysiological underpinnings of placebo effects has also contributed extensively to knowledge of the different effects that placebos have in different systems and on different symptoms (Benedetti et al., 2022).

It is worth noting that other theories of placebo effects have also been proposed but have not gained the widespread evidence base or acceptance of Response Expectancy Theory and conditioning. The 'common factors' framework was developed as an alternative way of thinking about placebo effects in psychotherapy. This framework proposed that components that are shared across (or common to) diverse forms of psychotherapy, such as empathy and therapeutic alliance, may largely drive patient outcomes (Horvath, 1988; Wampold, 2015). Meaning response theory was proposed as an alternative to both response expectancy and classical conditioning. This framework proposed that the subjective meaning a recipient attaches to a placebo is responsible for its effects (Hutchinson & Moerman, 2018; Moerman & Jonas, 2002). More promising is an integrative framework for understanding placebo effects. It suggests that multiple, different aspects of the psychosocial context (including conditioning, communication and therapeutic ritual, and social observation) should be conceptualised as inputs to neurobiologically mediated processes, through which expectancies produce placebo effects (Colloca & Miller, 2011b).

APPLICATIONS: FROM THE PSYCHOLOGIST'S LAB TO THE DOCTOR'S CLINIC

Historically, debates about clinical applications of placebo effects have been dominated by ethical concerns stemming from archetypal placebo scenarios like the one at the start of this chapter. Such deceptive prescribing of placebos, in which the doctor does not tell the patient that they are prescribing a placebo, takes away the patient's right to choose, makes it impossible for patients to give informed consent, and violates the core bioethical principle of respect for the patient's autonomy (Miller & Colloca, 2009). However, more recently, researchers have questioned the need for deception and explored other ways of using placebo effects in practice. In particular, the last 10 years or so have seen growing interest in translating the science of placebo effects from the laboratory to the clinic (Colloca & Miller, 2011a). And a translational science of placebo effects is now developing, as scientists and clinicians learn more about how different placebo effects work, for whom, and in what clinical practice contexts. In addition to needing a solid foundation in theory and evidence – part of which is provided by Response Expectancy Theory – a core part of this endeavour will be continuing to explore and address not only ethical issues but also patients' and clinicians' perspectives. Promisingly, surveys and qualitative studies suggest that patients and clinicians are potentially interested in ethically appropriate clinical applications of placebo effects (Hardman et al., 2020; Linde et al., 2018).

Many different approaches to harnessing placebo effects to improve patient outcomes have been discussed in the literature. Three will be discussed here in relation to Response Expectancy Theory: open-label placebos, dose extender placebos, and positive messages from an empathetic clinician. In a first example, Kaptchuk and colleagues (2010), at the Harvard Program in Placebo Studies, published a ground-breaking study demonstrating clinically meaningful placebo effects from placebo tablets given openly and honestly without deception to patients with Irritable Bowel Syndrome. Other similar studies from the Harvard group and others have since been published demonstrating open-label placebo effects in multiple conditions, including back pain, migraine, and cancer-related fatigue. A recent meta-analytic review of 11 trials concluded that, while further work is needed in this relatively new research area and the studies had methodological limitations, the results overall were promising and suggest a moderate effect size of open-label placebos compared to no treatment controls (von Wernsdorff et al., 2021). In all the trials in the meta-analysis, the patients in the open-label placebo arm received instructions including positive messages about the likely effects of the placebo. These instructions could reasonably be expected to increase patients' response expectancies, indicating that response expectancies might have a causal role in eliciting open-label placebo effects. However, further work is needed to determine the extent to which expectancies underpin different open-label placebo effects and other mechanisms, including conditioning, may be involved (Colloca & Howick, 2018; Ongaro & Kaptchuk, 2019).

A quite different type of open-label placebo is a placebo used openly and honestly as a 'dose-extender' to enable patients to reduce their consumption of medication. Reducing the consumption of medication might, in turn, bring benefits such as reduced occurrence or severity of side effects and reduced financial costs. In comparison to recent open-label placebo studies, in which placebos are prescribed instead of medication, open-label placebos as dose-extenders involve placebos being prescribed alongside medication. For example, Sandler and Bodfish (2008) demonstrated the effectiveness of a classical conditioning protocol in which placebos were paired with the individually optimised dose of mixed amphetamine salts for children with ADHD for one month, after which placebos were paired with half of the individually optimised dose of mixed amphetamine salts. The effects were maintained in the latter phase, despite halving the dose of mixed amphetamine salts. Given the conditioning protocols involved in generating placebo effects from dose-extenders in ADHD and other conditions, it would seem appropriate that classical conditioning forms part of theoretical accounts of these placebos (Colloca et al., 2016), although the possible role of response expectancies should also be examined.

The two examples above of clinical applications of placebo effects both involve the use of placebos. However, it is also possible to harness placebo effects in clinical practice without using placebos. This possibility flows directly from Response Expectancy Theory, which would predict that response expectancies can cause non-volitional responses to established medical interventions as well as to placebo interventions. Evidence from the open-hidden paradigm supports this (see Sidebar 11.2). In a clinical setting, modifying patients' response expectancies could be done within the context of the doctor–patient therapeutic relationship: trials have demonstrated the contribution of warm and positive doctor–patient interactions to placebo effects (Kaptchuk et al., 2008) and findings from doctor–patient communication studies demonstrate the beneficial effects of factors such as clinical empathy (Bensing & Verheul, 2010; Mercer et al., 2016). Evidence suggests that training clinicians in clinical empathy and positive messages may have small but significant effects on some clinical outcomes, including pain (Howick et al., 2018). But translating these findings into something that clinicians can implement in routine practice is not straightforward and researchers are exploring current practice (e.g., van Vliet et al., 2019) and developing new approaches to training clinicians to deliver clinically appropriate positive messages within the context of empathic interactions; Sidebar 11.4 provides an example.

Sidebar 11.4. Developing a Clinical Intervention to Modify Patients' Response Expectancies

Smith et al. (2021) developed a very brief digital training programme in clinical empathy and positive messages for primary care clinicians. This work illustrates the complexities of translating findings from placebo effects studies into clinical practice, where the wider clinical, psychological, interpersonal, and institutional contexts within which any intervention occurs all need to be considered. The study used a person-based approach to developing interventions (Yardley et al., 2015). This approach is resource-intensive but is designed to ensure

(Continued)

(Continued)

interventions are not only evidence- and theory-based, but also optimally engaging for their target users – and therefore likely to be implemented by busy clinicians with many competing demands on their time and skills. Placebo evidence and theory – including Response Expectancy Theory (Kirsch, 1985) – were reviewed and integrated with extensive qualitative work on patients' and clinicians' perspectives and a behavioural analysis to identify relevant behaviour change techniques. Work is underway to test the effects and mechanisms of action of the digital training programme, including the extent to which response expectancies mediate any symptom changes.

One critical issue for researchers developing clinical applications of placebo effects is the need to carefully consider the differences between the well-controlled laboratory settings of many placebo and response expectancy studies and the inherently messier and more complex nature of clinical settings. Laboratory-based studies that induce acute pain and present a novel treatment may constitute a more straightforward psychosocial context within which to generate response expectancies. In clinical settings, patients with chronic or recurrent pain are likely to have existing response expectancies based on a history of trying multiple treatments with limited success. Values and goals may also be more salient for patients with chronic pain in clinical settings (compared to experimentally induced acute pain) and can interact with expectancies (Geers et al., 2005; Hyland et al., 2007). Related concepts, such as 'hope', may better reflect how some patients with chronic pain conceptualise and evaluate treatment effects (Eaves et al., 2016). Among other things, these differences highlight the importance of developing and testing theory about how expectancies are formed and modified in clinical contexts (Geers et al., 2019).

CONCLUSIONS

Kirsch's (1985) Response Expectancy Theory articulated a coherent theory of placebo effects that was grounded in wider learning theory and accounted for the extant evidence of placebo effects. Response Expectancy Theory states that changes in the subjective experience of non-volitional responses following placebo administration (e.g., pain relief) are a direct, unmediated consequence of response expectancies; physiological changes (e.g., endorphin release) represent the physical counterparts of subjective experience; and behavioural changes (e.g., analgaesic consumption) are the reinforced consequences of subjective experience. Since Kirsch's original article, there have been extensive methodological developments that have deepened and extended understanding of the mechanisms underpinning placebo effects, not least a proliferation of neuroimaging and related techniques that have generated neurophysiological models of placebo effects in diverse conditions. Despite this, and while conditioning remains relevant to some placebo effects, expectancies remain at the centre of leading integrative theories. In the future, while more work is needed to fully understand the mechanisms underpinning placebo effects, the ongoing development and maturation of a translational science of placebo effects represents a new and vital endeavour for placebo studies that could see expectancy theory being applied clinically for patient benefit.

FURTHER READING

Kirsch, I. (2009). *The emperor's new drugs:* Exploding the antidepressant myth. London: The Bodley Head.

For Kirsch's engaging account of expectancies and placebo effects in depression, and the implications for anti-depressants.

Benedetti, F., Frisaldi, E., & Shaibani, A. (2022). Thirty years of neuroscientific investigation of placebo and nocebo: The interesting, the good, and the bad. *Annual Review of Pharmacology and Toxicology, 62*(1), 323–340. https://doi.org/10.1146/annurev-pharmtox-052120-104536

For a comprehensive review of the neuroscience of placebo effects across diverse symptoms.

Colloca, L. (Ed.). (2018). *Neurobiology of the placebo effect, Volume I–II*. Cambridge, MA: Elsevier/Academic Press.

For a wide-ranging and forward-looking collection of articles on placebo effects.

Peerdeman, K. J., van Laarhoven, A. I. M., Peters, M. L., & Evers, A. W. M. (2016). An integrative review of the influence of expectancies on pain. *Frontiers in Psychology, 7*, 1270. https://doi.org/10.3389/fpsyg.2016.01270

For a clinically oriented review of response expectancies, other types of expectations, and how they relate to the experience of pain.

REFERENCES

Bąbel, P., Bajcar, E. A., Adamczyk, W., Kicman, P., Lisińska, N., Świder, K., & Colloca, L. (2017). Classical conditioning without verbal suggestions elicits placebo analgesia and nocebo hyperalgesia. *PLoS ONE, 12*(7), e0181856. https://doi.org/10.1371/journal.pone.0181856

Bandura, A. (1977). Self-efficacy: Toward a unifying theory of behavioral change. *Psychological Review, 84*(2), 191–215. https://doi.org/10.1037/0033-295X.84.2.191

Benedetti, F., Frisaldi, E., & Shaibani, A. (2022). Thirty years of neuroscientific investigation of placebo and nocebo: The interesting, the good, and the bad. *Annual Review of Pharmacology and Toxicology, 62*(1), 323–340. https://doi.org/10.1146/annurev-pharmtox-052120-104536

Bensing, J. M., & Verheul, W. (2010). The silent healer: The role of communication in placebo effects. *Patient Education and Counseling, 80*(3), 293–299. https://doi.org/10.1016/j.pec.2010.05.033

Boussageon, R., Howick, J., Baron, R., Naudet, F., Falissard, B., Harika-Germaneau, G., Wassouf, I., Gueyffier, F., Jaafari, N., & Blanchard, C. (2022). How do they add up? The interaction between the placebo and treatment effect: A systematic review. *British Journal of Clinical Pharmacology*, *88*(1), 3638–3656. https://doi.org/10.1111/bcp.15345

Colloca, L., Enck, P., & DeGrazia, D. (2016). Relieving pain using dose-extending placebos: A scoping review. *Pain*, *157*(8), 1590–1598. https://doi.org/10.1097/j.pain.0000000000000566

Colloca, L., & Howick, J. (2018). Placebos without deception: Outcomes, mechanisms, and ethics. *International Review of Neurobiology*, *138*, 219–240. https://doi.org/10.1016/bs.irn.2018.01.005

Colloca, L., Lopiano, L., Lanotte, M., & Benedetti, F. (2004). Overt versus covert treatment for pain, anxiety, and Parkinson's disease. *The Lancet Neurology*, *3*(11), 679–684. https://doi.org/10.1016/S1474-4422(04)00908-1

Colloca, L., & Miller, F. G. (2011a). Harnessing the placebo effect: The need for translational research. *Philosophical Transactions of the Royal Society B: Biological Sciences*, *366*(1572), 1922–1930. https://doi.org/10.1098/rstb.2010.0399

Colloca, L., & Miller, F. G. (2011b). How placebo responses are formed: A learning perspective. *Philosophical Transactions of the Royal Society B: Biological Sciences*, *366*(1572), 1859–1869. https://doi.org/10.1098/rstb.2010.0398

Eaves, E. R., Nichter, M., & Ritenbaugh, C. (2016). Ways of hoping: Navigating the paradox of hope and despair in chronic pain. *Culture, Medicine and Psychiatry*, *40*(1), 35–58. https://doi.org/10.1007/s11013-015-9465-4

Evers, A. W. M., Colloca, L., Blease, C., Annoni, M., Atlas, L. Y., Benedetti, F., Bingel, U., Büchel, C., Carvalho, C., Colagiuri, B., Crum, A. J., Enck, P., Gaab, J., Geers, A. L., Howick, J., Jensen, K. B., · Kirsch, I., Meissner, K., Napadow, V., Peerdeman, K. J., Raz, A., Rief, W., Vase, L., Wager, T. D., Wampold, B. E., Weimer, K., Wiech, K., Kaptchuk, T. J., Klinger, R., & Kelley, J. M. (2018). Implications of placebo and nocebo effects for clinical practice: Expert consensus. *Psychotherapy and Psychosomatics*, *87*(4), 204–210. https://doi.org/10.1159/000490354

Fields, H. L., & Levine, J. D. (1984). Placebo analgesia – a role for endorphins? *Trends in Neurosciences*, *7*(8), 271–273. http://dx.doi.org/10.1016/S0166-2236(84)80193-9

Frank, J. D. (1973). *Persuasion and healing: A comparative study of psychotherapy* (Revised ed.). Baltimore, MD: Johns Hopkins University Press.

Geers, A. L., Briñol, P., & Petty, R. E. (2019). An analysis of the basic processes of formation and change of placebo expectations. *Review of General Psychology*, *23*(2), 211–229. https://doi.org/10.1037/gpr0000171

Geers, A. L., Weiland, P. E., Kosbab, K., Landry, S. J., & Helfer, S. G. (2005). Goal activation, expectations, and the placebo effect. *Journal of Personality and Social Psychology*, *89*(2), 143–159. https://doi.org/10.1037/0022-3514.89.2.143

Golomb, B. A., Erickson, L. C., Koperski, S., Sack, D., Enkin, M., & Howick, J. (2010). What's in placebos: Who knows? Analysis of randomized, controlled trials. *Annals of Internal Medicine*, *153*(8), 532–535. https://doi.org/10.7326/0003-4819-153-8-201010190-00010

Grünbaum, A. (1981). The placebo concept. *Behaviour Research and Therapy*, *19*(2), 157–167. https://doi.org/10.1016/0005-7967(81)90040-1

Hardman, D. I., Geraghty, A. W., Lewith, G., Lown, M., Viecelli, C., & Bishop, F. L. (2020). From substance to process: A meta-ethnographic review of how healthcare professionals and patients understand placebos and their effects in primary care. *Health: An Interdisciplinary Journal for the Social Study of Health, Illness and Medicine*, *24*(3), 315–340. https://doi.org/10.1177/1363459318800169

Horvath, P. (1988). Placebos and common factors in two decades of psychotherapy research. *Psychological Bulletin*, *104*(2), 214–225. https://doi.org/10.1037/0033-2909.104.2.214

Howick, J. (2017). The relativity of 'placebos': Defending a modified version of Grünbaum's definition. *Synthese*, *194*(4), 1363–1396. https://doi.org/10.1007/s11229-015-1001-0

Howick, J., Moscrop, A., Mebius, A., Fanshawe, T. R., Lewith, G., Bishop, F. L., Mistiaen, P., Roberts, N. W., Dieninytė, E., Hu, X. Y., Aveyard, P., & Onakpoya, I. J. (2018). Effects of empathic and positive communication in healthcare consultations: A systematic review and meta-analysis. *Journal of the Royal Society of Medicine*, *111*(7), 240–252. https://doi.org/10.1177%2F0141076818769477

Hutchinson, P., & Moerman, D. E. (2018). The meaning response, 'placebo,' and methods. *Perspectives in Biology and Medicine*, *61*(3), 361–378. https://doi.org/10.1353/pbm.2018.0049

Hyland, M. E., Whalley, B., & Geraghty, A. W. A. (2007). Dispositional predictors of placebo responding: A motivational interpretation of flower essence and gratitude therapy. *Journal of Psychosomatic Research*, *62*(3), 331–340. https://doi.org/10.1016/j.jpsychores.2006.10.006

Kaptchuk, T. J., Friedlander, E., Kelley, J. M., Sanchez, M. N., Kokkotou, E., Singer, J. P., Kowalczykowski, M., Miller, F. G., Kirsch, I., & Lembo, A. J. (2010). Placebos without deception: A randomized controlled trial in Irritable Bowel Syndrome. *PLoS ONE*, *5*(12), e15591. https://doi.org/10.1371/journal.pone.0015591

Kaptchuk, T. J., Kelley, J. M., Conboy, L. A., Davis, R. B., Kerr, C. E., Jacobson, E. E., Kirsch, I., Schyner, R. N., Nam, B. H., Nguyen, L. T., Park, M., Rivers, A. L., McManus, C., Kokkotou, E., Drossman, D. A., Goldman, P., & Lembo, A. J. (2008). Components of placebo effect: Randomised controlled trial in patients with irritable bowel syndrome. *British Medical Journal*, *336*, 999–1003. https://doi.org/10.1136/bmj.39524.439618.25

Kirsch, I. (1985). Response expectancy as a determinant of experience and behavior. *American Psychologist*, *40*(11), 1189–1202. https://doi.org/10.1037/0003-066X.40.11.1189

Kirsch, I. (2004). Conditioning, expectancy, and the placebo effect: Comment on Stewart-Williams and Podd (2004). *Psychological Bulletin*, *130*(2), 341–343. https://psycnet.apa.org/doi/10.1037/0033-2909.130.2.341

Kirsch, I. (2008). Challenging received wisdom: Antidepressants and the placebo effect. *McGill Journal of Medicine: MJM: An International Forum for the Advancement of Medical Sciences by Students*, *11*(2), 219–222.

Kirsch, I. (2014). Antidepressants and the placebo effect. *Zeitschrift fur Psychologie*, *222*(3), 128–134. https://doi.org/10.1027/2151-2604/a000176

Kirsch, I., Deacon, B. J., Huedo-Medina, T. B., Scoboria, A., Moore, T. J., & Johnson, B. T. (2008). Initial severity and antidepressant benefits: A meta-analysis of data submitted to the Food and Drug Administration. *PLoS Medicine*, *5*(2), e45. https://doi.org/10.1371/journal.pmed.0050045

Kirsch, I., Moore, T. J., Scoboria, A., & Nicholls, S. S. (2002). The emperor's new drugs: An analysis of antidepressant medication data submitted to the U.S. Food and Drug Administration. *Prevention & Treatment*, *5*(1), Article 23. https://psycnet.apa.org/doi/10.1037/1522-3736.5.1.523a

Kirsch, I., & Sapirstein, G. (1998). Listening to Prozac but hearing placebo: A meta-analysis of antidepressant medication. *Prevention & Treatment*, *1*(2), Article 2a. https://doi.org/10.1037/1522-3736.1.1.12a

Landsberger, H. A. (1958). *Hawthorne revisited: Management and the worker: Its critics, and developments in human relations in industry.* Ithaca, NY: Cornell University Press.

Linde, K., Atmann, O., Meissner, K., Schneider, A., Meister, R., Kriston, L., & Werner, C. (2018). How often do general practitioners use placebos and non-specific interventions? Systematic review and meta-analysis of surveys. *PLoS ONE, 13*(8), e0202211. https://doi.org/10.1371/journal.pone.0202211

Mercer, S. W., Higgins, M., Bikker, A. M., Fitzpatrick, B., McConnachie, A., Lloyd, S. M., Little, P., & Watt, G. C. M. (2016). General practitioners' empathy and health outcomes: A prospective observational study of consultations in areas of high and low deprivation. *Annals of Family Medicine, 14*(2), 117–124. https://doi.org/10.1370/afm.1910

Miller, F. G., & Colloca, L. (2009). The legitimacy of placebo treatments in clinical practice: Evidence and ethics. *The American Journal of Bioethics, 9*(12), 39–47. https://doi.org/10.1080/15265160903316263

Moerman, D. E., & Jonas, W. B. (2002). Deconstructing the placebo effect and finding the meaning response. *Annals of Internal Medicine, 136*(6), 471–476. https://doi.org/10.7326/0003-4819-136-6-200203190-00011

Ongaro, G., & Kaptchuk, T. J. (2019). Symptom perception, placebo effects, and the Bayesian brain. *Pain, 160*(1), 1–4. https://doi.org/10.1097/j.pain.0000000000001367

Rohsenow, D. J., & Marlatt, G. A. (1981). The balanced placebo design: Methodological considerations. *Addictive Behaviors, 6*(2), 107–122. https://doi.org/10.1016/0306-4603(81)90003-4

Rotter, J. B. (1954). *Social learning and clinical psychology.* Englewood Cliffs, NJ: Prentice-Hall.

Sandler, A. D., & Bodfish, J. W. (2008). Open-label use of placebos in the treatment of ADHD: A pilot study. *Child: Care, Health and Development, 34*(1), 104–110. https://doi.org/10.1111/j.1365-2214.2007.00797.x

Smith, K. A., Vennik, J., Morrison, L., Hughes, S., Steele, M., Tiwari, R., Bostock, J., Howick, J., Mallen, C., Little, P., Ratnapalan, M., Lyness, E., Misurya, P., Leydon, G. M., Dambha-Miller, H., Everitt, H. A., & Bishop, F. L. (2021). Harnessing placebo effects in primary care: Using the person-based approach to develop an online intervention to enhance practitioners' communication of clinical empathy and realistic optimism during consultations. *Frontiers in Pain Research, 2.* Article 721222. https://doi.org/10.3389/fpain.2021.721222

Stewart-Williams, S., & Podd, J. (2004). The placebo-effect: Dissolving the expectancy versus conditioning debate. *Psychological Bulletin, 130*(2), 324–340. https://doi.org/10.1037/0033-2909.130.2.324

van Vliet, L. M., Francke, A. L., Meijers, M. C., Westendorp, J., Hoffstädt, H., Evers, A. W. M., van der Wall, E., de Jong, P., Peerdeman, K. J., Stouthard, J., & van Dulmen, S. (2019). The use of expectancy and empathy when communicating with patients with advanced breast cancer: An observational study of clinician–patient consultations. *Frontiers in Psychiatry, 10.* Article 464. https://doi.org/10.3389/fpsyt.2019.00464

von Wernsdorff, M., Loef, M., Tuschen-Caffier, B., & Schmidt, S. (2021). Effects of open-label placebos in clinical trials: A systematic review and meta-analysis. *Scientific Reports, 11*(1), 3855. https://doi.org/10.1038/s41598-021-83148-6

Wampold, B. E. (2015). How important are the common factors in psychotherapy? An update. *World Psychiatry, 14*(3), 270–277. https://doi.org/10.1002/wps.20238

Wickramasekera, I. (1980). A conditioned response model of the placebo effect predictions from the model. *Biofeedback and Self Regulation*, *5*(1), 5–18. https://doi.org/10.1007/BF00999060

Wolters, F., Peerdeman, K. J., & Evers, A. W. M. (2019). Placebo and nocebo effects across symptoms: From pain to fatigue, dyspnea, nausea, and itch. *Frontiers in Psychiatry*, *10*, 470–470. https://doi.org/10.3389/fpsyt.2019.00470

Yardley, L., Morrison, L., Bradbury, K., & Muller, I. (2015). The person-based approach to intervention development: Application to digital health-related behavior change interventions. *Journal of Medical Internet Research*, *17*(1). https://doi.org/10.2196/jmir.4055

Zhang, W., & Doherty, M. (2018). Efficacy paradox and proportional contextual effect (PCE). *Clinical Immunology*, *186*, 82–86. https://doi.org/10.1016/j.clim.2017.07.018

12 | Behaviour Change: Revisiting Michie et al. (2013)

Michie, S., Richardson, M., Johnston, M., Abraham, C., Francis, J., Hardeman, W., Eccles, M. P., Cane, J., & Wood, C. E. (2013). The Behavior Change Technique Taxonomy (v1) of 93 hierarchically clustered techniques: Building an international consensus for the reporting of behavior change interventions. *Annals of Behavioral Medicine, 46*, 81–95.

Marie Johnston

BACKGROUND

HOW CAN BEHAVIOUR BE CHANGED?

Knowing how to change behaviour is crucial to addressing many global problems. For example, in the health domain, behaviour patterns cause many of the main diseases that result in death and disability. In addition, research has shown that numerous behaviours, such as dietary behaviours, physical activity, use of alcohol and drugs, smoking, and activities resulting in injury, feature prominently among the common risk factors for the leading causes of disability in the world (Lim et al., 2012) (see Figure 12.1).

Early in the 21st century, a UK Government Health Department asked behavioural scientists what were the best methods of changing dietary and activity behaviours to reduce obesity. Sadly, the question was met with a collective concern among scientists that very little was known despite over a quarter of a century of research on these topics. Could reviews of the current evidence from this research offer insight on the advice requested? Unfortunately, this proved very difficult

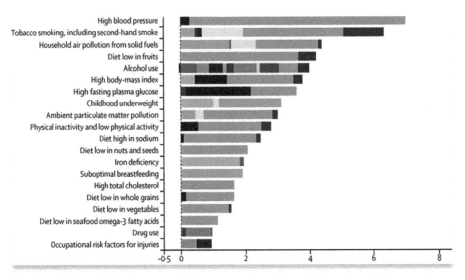

Figure 12.1 Global burden of disease attributable to 20 leading risk factors in 2010, expressed as a percentage of global disability-adjusted life-years for both sexes (adapted from Lim et al., 2012)

given the lack of an agreed terminology for describing the methods used, precluding a clear-cut synthesis of research across studies. Behaviour change intervention reports used the same words to describe different interventions or different words to describe similar interventions – often referred to as the 'jingle-jangle' fallacy (Block, 1995; Kelley, 1927). For example, 'behavioural counselling' had been used in one report of a study to mean education and suggesting changes (Steptoe & Wardle, 2001), and in another to refer to feedback on self-monitoring and reinforcement as well as recommendations for change (Tate et al., 2003). Thus, despite the large number of well-controlled studies showing interventions to be effective, pinpointing and replicating the content of interventions that were effective proved extremely challenging.

The field was in a similar state as botany prior to Linnaeus in lacking a shared 'language', or, more specifically, a system of terms and descriptions, to describe the essential components being studied. How could the field of botany develop if there was no agreement on the terms and ways of describing the plants being studied? Similarly, in the domain of behaviour change, summarising research on what is likely to be effective is likely to be a fruitless task without a systematic, shared means to describe behaviour change interventions. In addition, the absence of the common 'language' would make it difficult to tell whether or not interventions that people thought were effective in changing behaviour were truly effective and could be used in practice. Moreover, it would be difficult to replicate effective interventions if the descriptions were incomplete or unclear.

To answer the original policy question posed by the Health Department, groups of behavioural scientists began to systematically search published reports of intervention studies to identify the 'active content' of interventions that had been used to change diet and activity. The resulting organised structure, or *taxonomy*, of 26 'behaviour change techniques' (BCTs) was a major step forward as independent coders could identify the BCTs with good agreement (Abraham & Michie, 2008). The taxonomy provided the first attempt at producing a shared 'language' to describe the interventions, which included a formal definition of each BCT. The taxonomy provided a tool for researchers to make sense of the content of interventions without having to rely on the authors' idiosyncratic descriptions of the change techniques, making it possible to synthesis of evidence across studies that had used different terms for their methods. Others followed by creating BCT taxonomies for other behaviours, such as smoking and alcohol consumption (Michie, Abraham et al., 2009; Michie, Whittington et al., 2012), and others searched textbooks used in training behaviour change practitioners and made a preliminary attempt to link BCTs to theory (Michie, Johnston et al., 2008). However, despite these important advances, there was clearly a need for a taxonomy that could bring all of this work together, and that could be applied to any behaviour, as these taxonomies had demonstrable utility beyond answering health policy questions.

DETAILED OVERVIEW

THE CLASSIC STUDY: DEVELOPMENT OF THE BEHAVIOR CHANGE TECHNIQUE TAXONOMY V1

The aim of developing the Behavior Change Technique Taxonomy v1 (BCTTv1) was to create a taxonomy of BCTs that could be used to systematically describe and classify the 'active content' of any behaviour change intervention, that would be acceptable to the scientific, practitioner, and policy communities, and that would achieve sufficient agreement between users in specifying intervention content. Otherwise, it would be extremely difficult to extract the necessary useful elements of effective interventions for implementation in practice and all the effort of conducting studies of effectiveness would go to waste. Given the lack of an agreed standard methodology for developing and evaluating a taxonomy, researchers had to develop novel, fit-for-purpose methods of doing so. The methods adopted started by developing a clear definition of a BCT and differentiating these 'active ingredients' of behaviour change interventions from the supportive components that enabled the BCT to be delivered (see Sidebar 12.1). Next, the goal was to accumulate these definitions in a comprehensive list of BCTs from all the existing taxonomies. More than 50 experts in behaviour change were involved in several linked stages to ensure that likely users had a say in the taxonomy development. The extent of agreement between these users was assessed statistically.

Sidebar 12.1. Definition of a Behaviour Change Technique (BCT)

- A component of an intervention designed to change a specified behaviour

- The smallest (or smallest for the particular purpose) component that can be postulated to be an active ingredient within the intervention

- An observable activity

- Replicable

- Specified by an active verb and clarity about the desired behaviour change targeted with enough detail to achieve good agreement between experts

A BCT is the smallest component of an intervention compatible with retaining the postulated active ingredients, and can be used alone or in combination with other BCTs. (Michie, Johnston, & Carey, 2016)

The first step was to bring together BCTs from previous taxonomies and from a textbook search. Some of these BCTs were composites, such as 'stress management' or 'motivational interviewing', which could vary in the precise content included and so could not be used as BCTs as the specification of their content was not sufficiently precise. In the next stages, international experts in behaviour change generated labels and definitions for each technique and engaged in a series of *Delphi* consensus rounds to make these labels and definitions clear, distinct, non-overlapping, and usable in practice. Further experts then assessed the reliability of agreement achieved with this provisional taxonomy, followed by further adjustments to labels and definitions, consultations with stakeholders, and repetitions of these steps. The resulting list comprised 93 BCTs – an unwieldy number to negotiate without further structure. In the final stage, experts engaged in an open-sort clustering of the 93 BCTs, resulting in the hierarchical structure of 16 groups of BCTs (Figure 12.2), making it easier to locate each BCT. One such group is illustrated in Figure 12.3. Each of the 93 BCTs is included in a group and, in addition to the label and definition, has examples and some notes on using the BCT. At this stage, the project's International Advisory Group recommended publication of the BCTTv1 rather than continuing with further developmental work. The title included 'v1' to indicate that the taxonomy would require future additions and improvements. The process of the development of the BCTTv1 is also summarised in a video, which can be found at: www.youtube.com/watch?v=TJXUkSPNihc

Workshops held at the launch of the BCTTv1 made it clear that users would require training in its use. There were two main problems. First, despite being

Figure 12.2   The BCT Taxonomy v1: labels of 16 groups and 93 BCTs

Source: Michie, Richardson et al. (2013), by permission of Oxford University Press. www.ncbi.nlm.nih.gov/pubmed/23512568

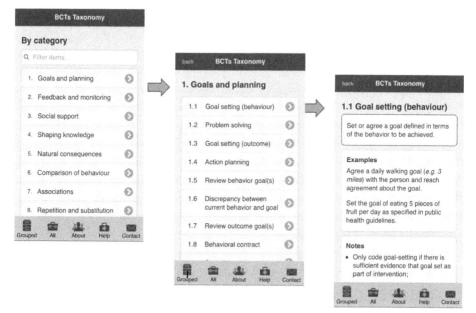

Figure 12.3   Screenshots from the BCTTv1 App. The first screen shows eight of the 16 groupings; the second screen shows the BCTs for grouping 1(Goals and Planning); and the third screen shows the definition, examples and notes for BCT1.1 (Goal setting behaviour). https://apps.apple.com/us/app/bct-taxonomy/id871193535

experts in behaviour change, users frequently found it difficult to identify the behaviour targeted by the BCT; for example, they sometimes thought of the target for the BCT as a thought, an emotion, or a health outcome, such as obesity, rather than a behaviour, such as eating or walking. Second, they were not used to following precise definitions and tended simply to use the label, wasting the opportunity for the shared, agreed specification of BCTs, which could only be achieved by using the full definition. Two forms of training were developed and evaluated: workshops involving between 10 and 40 participants, and smaller tutorials comprising three or four individuals (Michie, Wood et al., 2015; Wood, Richardson et al., 2015). Subsequently, three resources were added: online training in the use of the BCTTv1, an app to make it easier to use (see Figure 12.3), and a card game that has been helpful in introducing the BCTTv1 to potential users in a wide variety of settings and countries (see Figure 12.4, and the online resource at: www.m crimpsci.org/education-and-training-e-learning/).

HOW HAS THE BCTTV1 BEEN USED?

The BCTTv1 did not provide an 'answer' to the health policy question. While it specified more BCTs than any previous versions, it only provided behavioural scientists with an expert-agreed system to identify the BCTs and their defnitions, and gave no information on which were effective in changing behaviour. However, BCTs could be specified reliably, and several authors recommend using the taxonomy to

Figure 12.4 Cards for change used in training in the BCTTv1 techniques across 29 countries and five continents (www.mcrimpsci.org/change-exchange/cards-for-change/)

improve intervention reporting (Byrne, 2020; Knittle, 2015). Moreover, the taxonomy made it possible to identify BCTs that were included in behaviour change interventions which were effective. Using the original 26 BCT taxonomy, Michie and colleagues (2009) investigated the BCTs used in 122 studies and found that interventions which included the BCT 'self-monitoring' were more effective in changing physical activity and dietary behaviours than interventions that lacked this BCT. Further studies identified BCTs in effective interventions for physical activity, smoking, and dietary behaviours in a variety of populations (e.g., Black, Johnston et al., 2020; Bull et al., 2018; Caperon et al., 2018; French et al., 2014), for clinical behaviours (Cotterill et al., 2020), for cardiovascular risk behaviours (Suls et al., 2020), and in digital apps (Direito et al., 2014). Evidence for the effectiveness of several frequently used BCTs is reviewed by Hennessy and colleagues (2019). In addition, the BCTTv1 has been used to identify the BCTs used in intervention control groups (Black, Eisma et al., 2020), and the BCTs included in intervention protocols, which tend to be under-reported in published studies (de Bruin et al., 2021).

In addition to the use of the BCTTv1 to answer questions on effectiveness, it has been used to give public health guidance (NICE, 2014; Public Health England, 2018), and to facilitate behaviour change approaches in low- and middle-income countries (Byrne-Davis et al., 2017). The Scottish Government Department of Health used the early version of BCTTv1 as a basis for its Health Behaviour Change Competency Framework (www.healthscotland.com/documents/4877.aspx), while Public Health England (PHE) has adopted the BCT Taxonomy in numerous contexts, including: (a) coding national and research interventions; (b) assessing the effectiveness of PHE initiatives and interventions in terms of tackling the drivers of behaviour and identifying gaps and opportunities; and (c) the design and delivery of interventions in a number of interventions and campaigns across a number of topics, including antibiotic prescribing and screening programmes (personal communication with 'First Partner').

IMPACT

ASSESSING THE IMPACT OF MICHIE ET AL. (2013) AND THE BCTTv1: STRENGTHS AND LIMITATIONS

Sidebar 12.2. How 'Good' is the BCTTv1?

STRENGTHS

- Labels and definitions provide a shared language which improves communication between researchers and practitioners about interventions.

(Continued)

(Continued)

- There is good agreement between users on the presence or absence of BCTs in published reports.

- There is consensus internationally and across disciplines that it is useful.

- It is 'theory neutral' and so can be used within many different theoretical frameworks.

- It is being used more and more frequently and so provides a basis for a cumulative science of behaviour change.

- It is used to investigate the active components of effective interventions.

LIMITATIONS

- Additional BCTs have been identified (e.g., 'commanding') and BCTs have been used in different forms of delivery (e.g., groups, gamification).

- Some BCTs include two BCTs and need to be divided into two BCTs.

- The effectiveness of interventions may be determined by other factors than the BCTs, e.g., how the BCTs are delivered or the context of the population and setting in which they are delivered.

- The structure of the BCTTv1 makes it difficult to add BCTs to the groupings without repeating the sorting tasks with experts.

- The structure of the BCTTv1 is based on how the BCTs work, but a simple logical structure would be simpler to use and would be less dependent on the opinions of experts.

- The methods used to identify BCTs in effective interventions does not prove that the BCT *caused* the intervention to be effective – only that the BCT was included in effective interventions.

- The absence of evidence for a BCT does not constitute evidence that the BCT is ineffective.

- BCTs need to be linked to theoretical constructs in designing theory-based interventions and in understanding why a BCT may have an effect on behaviour.

The main strength of the BCTTv1 is that it provided a shared 'language' of labels with definitions for the BCTs in behavioural interventions, and those trained in its use could reach satisfactory agreement about the presence or absence of specific BCTs in published reports of behaviour change interventions – at least for commonly used BCTs. The BCTTv1 labels were designed to avoid alignment with any particular theory so that they could be used by researchers and practitioners from diverse disciplines, and it achieved a degree of consensus from the international interdisciplinary committee. By building on the work that had gone before, it served to unite research efforts to foster a cumulative rather than splintered approach to the science of behaviour change interventions. The BCTTv1 has been cited many times, demonstrating that it was clearly relevant to key issues in behaviour change.

But it was also clear that further development was needed, and the taxonomy was labelled 'v1' for a reason. There was an expectation that it would be advanced and developed further. Quite soon it was apparent that there were more BCTs than just these 93. For example, there was no BCT 'tell, order or instruct the person to do it' despite this being a 'favourite' BCT used by parents with their children, for example by imposing rules to protect from COVID-19 (Markowska-Manista & Zakrzewska-Olędzka, 2020), and the essential BCT, 'command', is used with considerable frequency in many contexts, such as by the military. Some BCTs in the BCTTv1 are really two or more BCTs. For example, the 'provide practical social support' BCT includes both giving support *and* advising the person to seek social support themselves. BCTs that need to be implemented by oneself are quite different procedures from those that are implemented by someone else (Hankonen, 2021).

In addition, several authors emphasised the need to take account of various other factors influencing the use of BCTs (Black, Williams et al., 2019). Figure 12.5 proposes several additional factors affecting the delivery and effectiveness of BCTs, including the dose of BCT delivered, the schedule and mode of delivery, and the source or who delivers the BCT (Michie, West et al., 2021). There is also research pointing to the style of delivery, which may make it more or less acceptable to the recipient (Hagger & Hardcastle, 2014), and that variations in the fidelity of delivery and quality of delivery may determine the effectiveness of BCTs in changing behaviour (Lorencatto et al., 2016; O'Carroll, 2020). BCTs appear to be more effective if delivered person-to-person rather than by written delivery (Black, Johnston et al., 2020), and there is increasing emphasis on establishing the competence of the person delivering the BCTs (Dixon & Johnston, 2021; Guerreiro et al., 2021).

Others have questioned the structure of the groups of techniques in the BCTTv1 – why are some BCTs placed within one group when they might fit better in another? The original 2013 groups were based on cluster analyses of open-sort groupings by experts, but similar groups have also been found using top-down groupings of BCTs to theoretical domains (Cane et al., 2015). Both methods result in an amalgam of the views of different experts and, as a result, may not fit a particular individual's intuitive grouping of the BCTs. A simple logical structure could overcome these problems. In addition, the structure of the groups presents problems, as it negates the possibility of adding newly-defined BCTs to the structure without repeating the original empirical grouping procedure. In developing the groups, experts were asked to consider how the BCT might work – its mechanism of action, rather than being a simple logical structure which might be easier to understand and to which BCTs could be easily added. For example, in the BCTTv1, some BCTs which involve reward are in the 'reward and threat' group, while others are in the 'scheduled consequences' group; a logical structure might place all BCTs that reward behaviour in the same class rather than in separate groups, and any newly defined BCTs that involved reward could simply be added to the group, based on logically belonging to the group, without further cluster analyses. For future developments, a logical structure would enable the development of an ontology of BCTs, i.e., a formal, logically structured, computer-readable method of representing the definitions and relationships between BCTs. Researchers in the Human Behavior Change Project are developing an ontology of BCTs and for several of the other components of a behaviour change intervention included in Figure 12.5, as illustrated in this video: www.youtube.com/watch?v=27tS-ToH7R0 (Wright et al., 2020).

Importantly, the BCTTv1 makes no claims as to the effectiveness of each BCT in changing behaviour. One can also be critical of how the BCTTv1 has been used to try to answer the question posed by the government policy makers; studies which review evidence to identify BCTs included in effective interventions run the risk of drawing unjustified conclusions. First, a BCT may appear to be effective because it is included in many interventions, and other BCTs which have scarcely been investigated may appear less effective – the absence of evidence supporting the effectiveness of a BCT does not constitute evidence that it is ineffective. Second, while the reviews aggregate evidence from well-controlled randomised controlled trials, the meta-regression methodology that has tended to be used to evaluate effectiveness of BCTs in synthesised research produces correlational rather than causal evidence as there is no randomisation to different BCTs. Third, this approach does not provide clear, formal evidence of how each BCT may interact or work synergistically together (or not) with one (or more) other BCTs to change behaviour. Critics of these methods have suggested that other types of research design are necessary to establish a causal effect (Peters et al., 2015), and others have proposed that a systematic programme of trials is necessary to assess which are effective (Armitage et al., 2021; Collins et al., 2007). A further set of questions surrounds the relationship of the BCTTv1 techniques to theories of behaviour change, and it is to this issue that the chapter now turns.

HOW DOES THE BCTTV1 RELATE TO BEHAVIOUR CHANGE THEORY?

The BCTTv1 explicitly avoided any alignment with theories so that it could be usable for those working within any framework, and some BCTs are relevant to multiple theories. In the *Handbook of behavior change*, Hagger, Cameron et al. (2020) identify 17 theories that have been applied to the development of behaviour change interventions and present helpful guidance on how to develop theory- and evidence-based behaviour change interventions (see also Hagger, Moyers

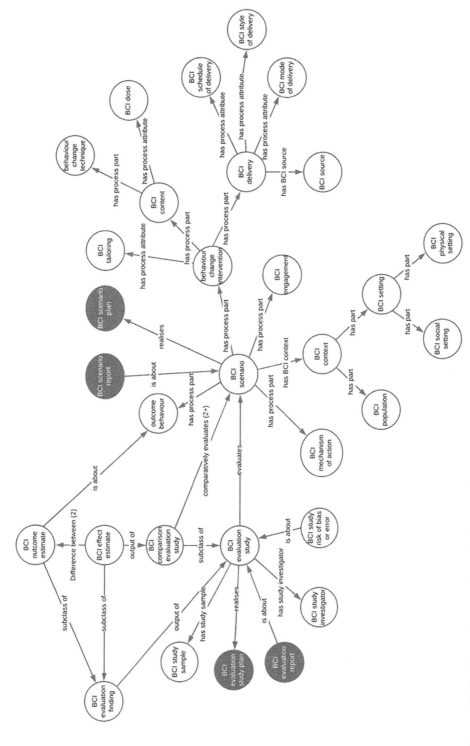

Figure 12.5 Part of an ontology of change techniques in the context of a behaviour change intervention scenario (reproduced from Michie, West et al., 2021)

et al., 2020). Several of these theoretical approaches use the same BCTs from the BCTTv1, demonstrating the value of a theory-neutral taxonomy.

The BCTTv1 notes indicate theory-based labels for BCTs, e.g., the notes for the BCT 'action planning' make the link with 'implementation intentions'. However, it would clearly be useful to identify the links between BCTs and theory in order to answer questions such as: if lack of self-efficacy is the cause of the behaviour, which BCTs might be effective in increasing the behaviour? Or if the BCT has been effective in changing the behaviour – was it effective because it changed attitudes, or was it because the feedback on behaviour was clearer? For example, Gardner, Whittington et al. (2010) used Control Theory to explain how the BCTs involved in audit and feedback changed clinical behaviours (see also Mansell, Chapter 3, this volume).

To systematically link BCTs with theoretical constructs, a series of studies investigated how BCTs might be linked to 'mechanisms of action' (Carey et al., 2017; Connell et al., 2017). These are the theoretical constructs, such as self-efficacy, attitudes, and feedback, that mediate the effects of BCTs on behaviour (Hagger, Moyers et al., 2020). Chapters 2 and 3 of this volume give a fuller account of these theoretical constructs (see Conner and Norman, Chapter 2, this volume; Mansell, Chapter 3, this volume). First, the published literature was systematically reviewed to identify links between BCTs, and mechanisms of action made by the authors of behaviour change interventions. Second, experts participated in a consensus exercise to reach agreement about potential links. A third study in the series showed agreement between the findings of the first two studies and went on to reconcile remaining discrepancies, resulting in 92 links between 55 BCTs and 26 theoretical mechanisms of action (Johnston et al., 2021). The full results can be accessed in an interactive online tool that enables users to explore evidence for 1,456 possible links between 26 theoretical constructs and BCTs, as introduced in this video: www.youtube.com/watch?v=V3xpnm0s8jw.

While these studies link BCTs to individual theoretical constructs, there have also been attempts to group BCTs in line with theory. For example, Tarrant and coworkers (2020) propose links between BCTs and constructs from social identity theory. In another example, Black and colleagues identified and grouped BCTs according to _reflective_ and _associative_ systems, two separate but interacting systems purported to underpin behaviour change in prominent dual-processing theories of behaviour (Black, Johnston et al., 2020; Dixon & Johnston, 2021). Two BCT groupings target mechanisms consistent with the first reflective, effortful processes, one identifying BCTs that are designed to increase motivation. These include techniques such as providing information about consequences, or incentives to change behaviour. The second grouping also includes BCTs that target change through change in reflective processes, and include techniques aimed at enhancing the effectiveness of self-regulatory processes in achieving one's goals, such as self-monitoring and action planning. A third grouping consists of BCTs that may target change through more impulsive processes, without engaging constructs indicating effortful conscious processing and change behaviour via association between the behaviour of interest and features of the context that serve as cues for the behaviour. These include techniques such as prompts or cues to perform the target behaviour (Borek et al., 2019).

A further theoretical challenge is to assess how BCTs work in combination. Several studies have examined whether the more BCTs delivered, the more behaviour change is achieved, but the results have thus far been inconclusive. This might be because adding more BCTs confuses those performing the intervention, adds inefficiency, interferes with delivery, or serves to dilute or lower the dose of each included BCT. Or it might be because BCTs were added to an intervention without considering how they might interact. For example, BCTs which increase fear may be ineffective or even counter-productive unless accompanied by BCTs which increase self-efficacy or action planning (see Kok et al., 2018). Kok et al. (2016) emphasise the need to specify the parameters, including the combination of BCTs that enable BCTs to be effective.

ALTERNATIVE APPROACHES TO DESCRIBING AND DEFINING BEHAVIOUR CHANGE METHODS

In contrast to the BCTTv1, following an extensive programme of research, Kok et al. (2016) have defined over 80 behaviour change methods targeting the behaviours of individuals, which are explicitly theory-based and 'have been shown to be able to change one or more determinants of behavior' (p. 299). The methods are organised according to the theoretical determinants of the behaviour, i.e., potential mechanisms of action, including knowledge, risk perception, skills and capability, and social norms. Each method is defined, linked to a theory, and has parameters as specified by the theory. Importantly, in further publications, evidence is provided demonstrating the effectiveness of each method in changing behaviour. By contrast, and as noted above, the BCTTv1 does not present evidence of effectiveness but only asserts that the BCTs have the potential to change behaviour and that the BCTTv1 is explicitly theory-neutral. The definitions of Kok et al.'s behaviour change methods are less prescriptive than the BCTTv1 in describing the actions needed to deliver the change methods, but they are embedded in the process of *intervention mapping*, a systematic series of steps for theory-based intervention development that begin with a description of the problem and end with the implementation and evaluation of the behaviour change intervention (Bartholomew et al., 2011).

While the BCTTv1 defines techniques that are delivered to the person whose behaviour must change, Knittle et al. (2020) have developed a compendium of techniques that can be used by the person themselves. It goes beyond the BCTTv1 in including techniques to enable increases in motivation as well as techniques to change behaviour. The 123 self-enactable techniques are presented as a list rather than in groupings; they were derived by a careful process of adapting previous BCT classifications, reviewing relevant literature, and gaining feedback from experts and members of the public on how easy the techniques would be to use. The final compendium has examples to aid application in practice and guidance for members of the public who may wish to use the compendium to change their own behaviour. Like the BCTTv1, the compendium is theory-neutral and does not provide evidence of effectiveness of the techniques.

These two alternative approaches complement the BCTTv1 by addressing the limitations of the BCTTv1, but lack some of its features. Further, researchers are seeking to identify additional BCTs that are delivered to groups of people, adding to the BCTs delivered to individuals (Borek et al., 2019). Other techniques are being identified in gamification delivery of behaviour change interventions (Krath et al., 2021). All of these approaches aim to gain better definition of the essential components of behaviour interventions, reflecting the urgent need for improved practical methods of changing behaviour, and the stage of progress in behaviour science.

CONCLUSIONS

Returning to the initial question posed by policy makers, it would appear that researchers in the field of behaviour change are still far from providing a comprehensive answer to the question about methods that would be effective in changing behaviour. But since that question was posed, research in disciplines relevant to behaviour change, including health psychology and behavioural science, has prompted significant advances in the 'science' of behaviour change, including a systematic means of describing intervention content, and linking that content with theory and the factors that may enhance or reduce their effectiveness. The field now has the means to provide more careful, systematic definitions of intervention content through a clear, shared, common unambiguous 'language' that has been developed through rigorous processes – reaching a situation analogous to the position of botany following Linnaeus's work! One can anticipate further elaborated definitions of techniques and mechanisms of action embedded within _ontologies_ that will be computer-readable and so applied more consistently than by human readers.

Importantly, more work is being done to delineate the factors, in addition to BCTs, that influence the effectiveness of behaviour change interventions. Figure 12.5 illustrates the elements needed to define the context and delivery of BCTs within a behaviour change intervention, and researchers in the Human Behavior Change Project are working to develop ontologies for each of these elements. The initial question has increased in complexity, beyond seeking to understand just 'what works?' to understanding 'what works, compared with what, for what behaviours, how well, for how long, with whom, in what setting, and why?' (Michie, Thomas et al., 2021, p. 1). Extensive programmes of research are planned to investigate which BCTs are effective in changing behaviour (Armitage et al., 2021) and to improve measures of the mechanisms of action (Sumner et al., 2018). In sum, the initial policy question may not have been answered, but researchers have since propelled the science of behaviour change interventions on the road to a promising future.

FURTHER READING

Kaplan, R. M., & Beatty, A. S. (Eds.). (2022). _Ontologies in the behavioral sciences: Accelerating research and the spread of knowledge._ Washington, DC: National Academies Press. https://doi: 10.17226/26464

This document from the US National Academies of Science, Engineering and Medicine discusses the role of ontologies in advancing behavioural science and indicates the potential of ontologies in domains such as behaviour change interventions.

Michie, S., Wood, C. E., Johnston, M., Abraham, C., Francis, J. J., & Hardeman, W. (2015). Behaviour change techniques: The development and evaluation of a taxonomic method for reporting and describing behaviour change interventions (a suite of five studies involving consensus methods, randomised controlled trials and analysis of qualitative data). *Health Technology Assessment, 19*(99), 1–88. https://doi: 10.3310/hta19990

This monograph gives a full account of the studies involved in the development of BCCTv1.

Peters, G.-J. Y., de Bruin, M., & Crutzen, R. (2015). Everything should be as simple as possible, but no simpler: Towards a protocol for accumulating evidence regarding the active content of health behaviour change interventions. *Health Psychology Review, 9*(1), 1–14. https://doi: 10.1080/17437199.2013.848409

This paper (and the published) responses offers a critique of how BCTs have been used in aggregating evidence from trials of behaviour change interventions.

REFERENCES

Abraham, C., & Michie, S. (2008). A taxonomy of behavior change techniques used in interventions. *Health Psychology*, *27*(3), 379. https://doi.org/10.1037/0278-6133.27.3.379

Armitage, C. J., Conner, M., Prestwich, A., de Bruin, M., Johnston, M., Sniehotta, F., & Epton, T. (2021). Investigating which behaviour change techniques work for whom in which contexts delivered by what means: Proposal for an international collaboratory of Centres for Understanding Behaviour Change (CUBiC). *British Journal of Health Psychology*, *26*(1), 1–14. https://doi.org/10.1111/bjhp.12479

Bartholomew, L. K., Parcel, G. S., Kok, G., Gottlieb, N. H., & Fernández, M. E. (2011). *Planning health promotion programs: An intervention mapping approach* (3rd ed.). San Francisco, CA: Jossey-Bass.

Black, N., Eisma, M. C., Viechtbauer, W., Johnston, M., West, R., Hartmann-Boyce, J., Michie, S., de Bruin, M. (2020). Variability and effectiveness of comparator group interventions in smoking cessation trials: A systematic review and meta-analysis. *Addiction*, *115*(9), 1607–1617. https://doi.org/10.1111/add.14969

Black, N., Johnston, M., Michie, S., Hartmann-Boyce, J., West, R., Viechtbauer, W., Eisma, M. C., Scott, C., & de Bruin, M. (2020). Behaviour change techniques associated with smoking cessation in intervention and comparator groups of randomized controlled trials: A systematic review and meta-regression. *Addiction*, *115*(11), 2008–2020. https://doi.org/10.1111/add.15056

Black, N., Williams, A. J., Javornik, N., Scott, C., Johnston, M., Eisma, M. C., Michie, S., Hartmann-Boyce, J., West, R., Viechtbauer, W., & de Bruin, M. (2019). Enhancing behavior change technique coding methods: Identifying behavioral targets and delivery styles in smoking cessation trials. *Annals of Behavioral Medicine*, *53*(6), 583–591. https://doi.org/10.1093/abm/kay068

Block, J. (1995). A contrarian view of the five-factor approach to personality description. *Psychological Bulletin*, *117*, 187–215. https://doi.org/10.1037/0033-2909.117.2.187

Borek, A. J., Abraham, C., Greaves, C. J., Gillison, F., Tarrant, M., Morgan-Trimmer, S., McCabe, R., & Smith, J. R. (2019). Identifying change processes in group-based health behaviour-change interventions: Development of the mechanisms of action in group-based interventions (MAGI) framework. *Health Psychology Review*, *13*(3), 227–247. https://doi.org/10.1080/17437199.2019.1625282

Bull, E. R., McCleary, N., Li, X., Dombrowski, S. U., Dusseldorp, E., & Johnston, M. (2018). Interventions to promote healthy eating, physical activity and smoking in low-income groups: A systematic review with meta-analysis of behavior change techniques and delivery/context. *International Journal of Behavioral Medicine*, *25*(6), 605–616. https://doi.org/10.1007/s12529-018-9734-z

Byrne, M. (2020). Gaps and priorities in advancing methods for health behaviour change research. *Health Psychology Review, 14*(1), 165–175. https://doi.org/10.1080/17437199.2019.1707106

Byrne-Davis, L. M., Bull, E. R., Burton, A., Dharni, N., Gillison, F., Maltinsky, W., Mason, C., Sharma, N., Armitage, C. J., Johnston, M., Byrne, G. J., & Hart, J. K. (2017). How behavioural science can contribute to health partnerships: The case of the change exchange. *Global Health*, *13*(1), 30. https://doi.org/10.1186/s12992-017-0254-4

Cane, J., Richardson, M., Johnston, M., Ladha, R., & Michie, S. (2015). From lists of behaviour change techniques (BCTs) to structured hierarchies: Comparison of two methods of developing a hierarchy of BCTs. *British Journal of Health Psychology*, *20*(1), 130–150. https://doi.org/10.1111/bjhp.12102

Carey, R. N., Connell, L. E., Johnston, M., Rothman, A. J., de Bruin, M., Kelly, M. P., & Michie, S. (2019). Behavior change techniques and their mechanisms of action: A synthesis of links described in published intervention literature. *Annals of Behavioral Medicine*, *53*(8), 693–707. https://doi.org/10.1093/abm/kay078

Caperon, L., Sykes-Muskett, B., Clancy, F., Newell, J., King, R., & Prestwich, A. (2018). How effective are interventions in improving dietary behaviour in low- and middle-income countries? A systematic review and meta-analysis. *Health Psychology Review*, *12*(3), 312–331. https://doi.org/10.1080/17437199.2018.1481763

Collins, L. M., Murphy, S. A., & Strecher, V. (2007). The multiphase optimization strategy (MOST) and the sequential multiple assignment randomized trial (SMART): New methods for more potent eHealth interventions. *American Journal of Preventive Medicine*, *32*, S112–S118. https://doi.org/10.1016/j.amepre.2007.01.022

Connell, L. E., Carey, R. N., De Bruin, M., Rothman, A. J., Johnston, M., Kelly, M. P., & Michie, S. (2018). Links between Behavior Change Techniques and Mechanisms of Action: An Expert Consensus Study. *Annals of Behavioral Medicine*, *53*(8), 708-720. https://doi.org/10.1093/abm/kay082

Cotterill, S., Tang, M. Y., Powell, R., Howarth, E., McGowan, L., Roberts, J., Brown, B., & Rhodes, S. (2020). Social norms interventions to change clinical behaviour in health workers: A systematic review and meta-analysis. *Health Services and Delivery Research*, *8*(41). htps://doi.org/10.3310/hsdr08410

de Bruin, M., Black, N., Javornik, N., Viechtbauer, W., Eisma, M. C., Hartman-Boyce, J., & Johnston, M. (2021). Underreporting of the active content of behavioural interventions: A systematic review and meta-analysis of randomised trials of smoking cessation interventions. *Health Psychology Review*, *15(2)*, 195–213. https://doi.org/10.1080/17437199.2019.1709098

Direito, A., Dale, L. P., Shields, E., Dobson, R., Whittaker, R., & Maddison, R. (2014). Do physical activity and dietary smartphone applications incorporate evidence-based behaviour change techniques? *BMC Public Health*, *14*(1), 1–7. https://doi.org/10.1186/1471-2458-14-646

Dixon, D., & Johnston, M. (2021). What competences are required to deliver person-person behaviour change interventions: Development of a health behaviour change competency framework. *International Journal of Behavioral Medicine, 28*(3), 308–317. https://doi.org/10.1007/s12529-020-09920-6

French, D. P., Olander, E. K., Chisholm, A., & Mc Sharry, J. (2014). Which behaviour change techniques are most effective at increasing older adults' self-efficacy and physical activity behaviour? A systematic review. *Annals of Behavioral Medicine, 48*(2), 225–234. https://doi.org/10.1007/s12160-014-9593-z

Gardner, B., Whittington, C., McAteer, J., Eccles, M. P., & Michie, S. (2010). Using theory to synthesise evidence from behaviour change interventions: The example of audit and feedback. *Social Science and Medicine, 70*, 1618–1625. https://doi.org/10.1016/j.socscimed.2010.01.039

Guerreiro, M. P., Strawbridge, J., Cavaco, A. M., Félix, I. B., Marques, M. M., & Cadogan, C. (2021). Development of a European competency framework for health and other professionals to support behaviour change in persons self-managing chronic disease. *BMC Medical Education, 21*(1), 1–14. https://doi.org/10.1186/s12909-021-02720-w

Hagger, M. S., Cameron, L. D., Hamilton, K., Hankonen, N., & Lintunen, T. (Eds.). (2020). *Handbook of behavior change*. Cambridge: Cambridge University Press.

Hagger, M. S., & Hardcastle, S. J. (2014). Interpersonal style should be included in taxonomies of behavior change techniques. *Frontiers in Psychology, 5*(254), 1–2. https://doi.org/10.3389/fpsyg.2014.00254

Hagger, M. S., Moyers, S., McAnally, K., & McKinley, L. E. (2020). Known knowns and known unknowns on behavior change interventions and mechanisms of action. *Health Psychology Review, 14*(1), 199–212. https://doi.org/10.1080/17437199.2020.1719184

Hankonen, N. (2021). Participants' enactment of behavior change techniques: A call for increased focus on what people do to manage their motivation and behavior. *Health Psychology Review, 15*(2), 185–194. https://doi.org/10.1080/17437199.2020.1814836

Hennessy, E. A., Johnson, B. T., Acabchuk, R. L., McCloskey, K., & Stewart-James, J. (2019). Self-regulation mechanisms in health behaviour change: A systematic meta-review of meta-analyses, 2006–2017. *Health Psychology Review, 14*(1), 6–42. https://doi.org/10. 1080/17437199.2019.1679654

Johnston, M., Carey, R. N., Connell Bohlen, L. E., Johnston, D. W., Rothman, A. J., de Bruin, M., Kelly, M. P., Groarke, H., & Michie, S. (2021). Development of an online tool for linking behavior change techniques and mechanisms of action based on triangulation of findings from literature synthesis and expert consensus. *Translational Behavioral Medicine, 11*(5), 1049–1065. https://doi.org/10.1093/tbm/ibaa050

Kelley, T. L. (1927). *Interpretation of educational measurements*. London & Chicago, IL: World Book.

Knittle, K. (2015). We cannot keep firing blanks – yet another appeal for improved RCT reporting: Commentary on Peters, de Bruin and Crutzen. *Health Psychology Review, 9*(1), 34–37. https://doi.org/10.1080/17437199.2014.900721

Knittle, K., Heino, M., Marques, M. M., Stenius, M., Beattie, M., Ehbrecht, F., … & Hankonen, N. (2020). The compendium of self-enactable techniques to change and self-manage motivation and behaviour v. 1.0. *Nature Human Behaviour, 4*(2), 215-223. https://doi.org/10.1038/s41562-019-0798-9

Kok, G., Gottlieb, N. H., Peters, G.-J. Y., Mullen, P. D., Parcel, G. S., Ruiter, R. A., & Bartholomew, L. K. (2016). A taxonomy of behaviour change methods: An intervention mapping approach. *Health Psychology Review, 10*(3), 297–312. https://doi.org/10.10 80/17437199.2015.1077155

Kok, G., Peters, G. J. Y., Kessels, L. T., Ten Hoor, G. A., & Ruiter, R. A. (2018). Ignoring theory and misinterpreting evidence: The false belief in fear appeals. *Health Psychology Review*, 12(2), 111-125. https://doi.org/10.1080/17437199.2017.1415767

Krath, J., Schürmann, L., & von Korflesch, H. F. (2021). Revealing the theoretical basis of gamification: A systematic review and analysis of theory in research on gamification, serious games and game-based learning. *Computers in Human Behavior, 125*, 106963. htps://doi.org/10.1016/j.chb.2021.106963

Lim, S. S., Vos, T., Flaxman, A. D., Danaei, G., Shibuya, K., Adair-Rohani, H., & Pelizzari, P. M. (2012). A comparative risk assessment of burden of disease and injury attributable to 67 risk factors and risk factor clusters in 21 regions, 1990–2010: A systematic analysis for the global burden of disease study 2010. *The Lancet, 380*(9859), 2224–2260. https://doi.org/10.1016/S0140-6736(12)61766-8

Lorencatto, F., West, R., Bruguera, C., Brose, L. S., & Michie, S. (2016). Assessing the quality of goal setting in behavioural support for smoking cessation and its association with outcomes. *Annals of Behavioral Medicine, 50*(2), 310–318. https://doi.org/10.1007/s12160-015-9755-7

Markowska-Manista, U., & Zakrzewska-Olędzka, D. (2020). Family with children in times of pandemic – what, where, how? Dilemmas of adult-imposed prohibitions and orders. *Society Register, 4*(3), 89–110. htps://doi.org/10.14746/sr.2020.4.3.05

Michie, S., Abraham, C., Whittington, C., McAteer, J., & Gupta, S. (2009). Effective techniques in healthy eating and physical activity interventions: A meta-regression. *Health Psychology, 28*, 690–701. https://doi.org/10.1037/a0016136

Michie, S., Whittington, C., Hamoudi, Z., Zarnani, F., Tober, G., & West, R. (2012). Identification of behaviour change techniques to reduce excessive alcohol consumption. *Addiction, 107*(8), 1431-1440.

Michie, S., Johnston, M., & Carey, R. (2016). Behavior change techniques. *Encyclopedia of behavioral medicine*. New York: Springer. https://doi.org/10.1007/978-1-4614-6439-6_1661-2

Michie, S., Johnston, M., Francis, J., Hardeman, W., & Eccles, M. (2008). From theory to intervention: Mapping theoretically derived behavioural determinants to behaviour change techniques. *Applied Psychology, 57*(4), 660–680. https://doi.org/10.1111/j.1464-0597.2008.00341.x

Michie, S., Richardson, M., Johnston, M., Abraham, C., Francis, J., Hardeman, W., Eccles, M. P., Cane, J., & Wood, C. E. (2013). The Behavior Change Technique Taxonomy (v1) of 93 hierarchically clustered techniques: Building an international consensus for the reporting of behavior change interventions. *Annals of Behavioral Medicine, 46*(1), 81–95. https://doi.org/10.1007/s12160-013-9486-6

Michie, S., Thomas, J., Johnston, M., Aonghusa, P. M., Shawe-Taylor, J., Kelly, M. P., Deleris, L. A., Finnerty, A. N., Marques, M. M., Norris, E., O'Mara-Eves, A., & West, R. (2017). The Human Behaviour-Change Project: Harnessing the power of artificial intelligence and machine learning for evidence synthesis and interpretation. *Implementation Science, 12*(1), 1–12. htps://doi.org/10.1186/s13012-017-0641-5

Michie, S., West, R., Finnerty, A. N., Norris, E., Wright, J. J., Marques, M. M., Johnston, M., Kelly, M. P., Thomas, J., & Hastings, J. (2021). Representation of behaviour change interventions and their evaluation: Development of the upper level of the behaviour change intervention ontology. *Wellcome Open Research, 5*, 123. https://doi.org/10.12688/wellcomeopenres.15902.2

Michie, S., Whittington, C., Hamoudi, Z., Zarnani, F., Tober, G., & West, R. (2012). Identification of behaviour change techniques to reduce excessive alcohol consumption. *Addiction*, 107(8), 1431-1440. https://doi.org/10.1111/j.1360-0443.2012.03845.

Michie, S., Wood, C. E., Johnston, M., Abraham, C., Francis, J., & Hardeman, W. (2015). Behaviour change techniques: The development and evaluation of a taxonomic method for reporting and describing behaviour change interventions (a suite of five studies involving consensus methods, randomised controlled trials and analysis of qualitative data). *Health Technology Assessment*, *19*(99), 1–188. https://doi.org/10.3310/hta19990

NICE. (2014). *Behaviour change: Individual approaches*. NICE Public Health Guideline [PH49]. London: National Institute for Health and Care Excellence.

O'Carroll, R. E. (2020). Self-regulation interventions: What do we know and where should we go? *Health Psychology Review*, *14*(1), 159–164. https://doi.org/10.1080/17437199.2019.1709529

Peters, G.-J. Y., de Bruin, M., & Crutzen, R. (2015). Everything should be as simple as possible, but no simpler: Towards a protocol for accumulating evidence regarding the active content of health behaviour change interventions. *Health Psychology Review, 9*(1), 1–14. https://doi.org/10.1080/17437199.2013.848409.

Public Health England. (2018). Strategy document: *Improving people's health: Applying behavioural and social sciences to improve population health and wellbeing in England*. PHE Publications Gateway Number 2018478. London: Public Health England.

Steptoe, A., & Wardle, J. (2001). Locus of control and health behaviour revisited: A multivariate analysis of young adults from 18 countries. *British Journal of Psychology*, *92*, 659–672. htps://doi.org/10.1348/000712601162400

Suls, J., Mogavero, J. N., Falzon, L., Pescatello, L. S., Hennessy, E. A., & Davidson, K. W. (2020). Health behaviour change in cardiovascular disease prevention and management: Meta-review of behaviour change techniques to affect self-regulation. *Health Psychology Review*, *14*(1), 43–65. https://doi.org/10.1080/17437199.2019.1691622

Sumner, J. A., Carey, R. N., Michie, S., Johnston, M., Edmondson, D., & Davidson, K. W. (2018). Using rigorous methods to advance behaviour change science. *Nature Human Behaviour*, *2*, 797–799. https://doi.org/10.1038/s41562-018-0471-8

Tarrant, M., Haslam, C., Carter, M., Calitri, R., & Haslam, S. A. (2020). Social identity interventions. In M. S. Hagger, L. D. Cameron, K. Hamilton, & T. Lintunen (Eds.), *Handbook of behavior change* (pp. 649–660). Cambridge: Cambridge University Press.

Tate, D. F., Jackvony, E. H., & Wing, R. R. (2003). Effects of internet behavioral counseling on weight loss in adults at risk for type 2 diabetes: A randomized trial. JAMA: *The Journal of the American Medical Association*, *289*(14), 1833–1836. https://doi.org/10.1001/jama.289.14.1833

Wood, C. E., Richardson, M., Johnston, M., Abraham, C., Francis, J., Hardeman, W., & Michie, S. (2015). Applying the behaviour change technique (BCT) taxonomy. *Translational Behavioral Medicine*, *5*(2), 134–148. https://doi.org/10.1007/s13142-014-0290-z

Wright, A. J., Norris, E., Finnerty, A. N., Marques, M. M., Johnston, M., Kelly, M. P., Hastings, J., West, R., & Michie, S. (2020). Ontologies relevant to behaviour change interventions: A method for their development. [version 3; peer review: 2 approved, 1 approved with reservations]. *Wellcome Open Research*, *5*, 126. https://doi.org/10.12688/wellcomeopenres.15908.3

13

Psychotherapeutic Interventions: Revisiting Pennebaker, Kiecolt-Glaser, and Glaser (1988)

Pennebaker, J. W., Kiecolt-Glaser, J. K., & Glaser, R. (1988). Disclosure of traumas and immune function: Health implications for psychotherapy. *Journal of Consulting and Clinical Psychology, 56*, 239–245.

Anke Karl

BACKGROUND

With the introduction of George Engel's biopsychological model (Engel, 1977), the 1980s saw increased research interest in the association between stress and mental health. The biopsychosocial model suggested a holistic perspective that includes biological, psychological, and social factors when considering a person's health (Engel, 1977). The model was informed by Engel's work on chronic pain and depression, which pointed to a close link between mental and physical health. Considering physiological aspects, psychological factors (thoughts, emotions, and behaviours) and socioeconomical, socio-environmental and cultural circumstances together is important for a better understanding of the underlying mechanisms of stress and mental health. The biopsychosocial model is therefore also important for informing the development of effective psychological interventions. It is in this context that Pennebaker's classic study (Pennebaker et al., 1988), which concurrently assessed psychological and biological effects of a novel psychological intervention, expressive writing, can be understood. The chapter will first review the development of expressive writing and the classic study. It will then assess the impact of the study for understanding the effects of expressive writing as a therapeutic tool with a focus on physical and mental health benefits. Finally, the chapter will consider how the study contributed to the understanding of therapeutic mechanisms of action of expressive writing and describe how the research inspired by the classic study had ripple effects for psychology research and the biopsychosocial understanding of mental and physical health.

DEVELOPMENT OF EXPRESSIVE WRITING AS A THERAPEUTIC TOOL

Expressive writing is a brief intervention in which participants are instructed to focus on their own traumatic or stressful experience and to express their deepest thoughts and feelings. Typically, participants write every day for 15–20 minutes for three or four consecutive days. The approach was developed by Pennebaker and colleagues in the mid-late 1980s (Pennebaker & Beall, 1986; Pennebaker et al., 1988) and has since been studied extensively and applied in mental and physical health settings.

Pennebaker's interest in the role of expressive writing as a health intervention came from personal experience. His mother's frequent health problems and the observation that individuals who have experienced psychological trauma early in life tended to keep those experiences secret, informed the hypothesis that expressing emotional experiences may reduce distress. This hypothesis inspired his first experiment (Pennebaker & Beall, 1986), in which he invited university students to the lab to write about personal trauma to see if this had a positive effect on their well-being. Interestingly, he found that those who were instructed to write about their most traumatic experience for four consecutive days for 15 minutes a day subsequently reported significantly fewer illness days and fewer visits to the student health centre than participants instructed to write about non-personal topics. Encouraged by this, Pennebaker et al. (1988) conducted a second study, the classic study that forms the focus of this chapter. An overview of the study, its theoretical context, and seminal contribution is provided below. A critical appraisal of the study is also presented, including consideration of its impact on subsequent research and theory into psychological interventions.

DETAILED OVERVIEW

THE IMMUNE FUNCTION STUDY

Drawing on Freud's idea of catharsis and work in the field of psychosomatics and health psychology, Pennebaker hypothesised that releasing strong feelings associated with upsetting memories should reduce distress via several mechanisms: first, through reduced suppression of thoughts and feelings, and thus physiological arousal (Gross & Levenson, 1993); second, through reframing the meaning of the event (Horowitz, 1986); and, third, through direct influence on the immune system. This third hypothesis was based on earlier findings by the paper's co-authors (Kiecolt-Glaser et al., 1984), in which central nervous system processes, such as (exam) stress or loneliness, were found to be associated with adverse immune functioning (Kiecolt-Glaser et al., 1984) and, conversely, that relaxation interventions improved immune functions (Kiecolt-Glaser et al., 1986).

Pennebaker et al. predicted that these immune improvements are associated with stress reduction and fewer health centre visits (see Weinman, Broadbent, and Booth, Chapter 6, this volume).

STUDY METHODS

Fifty healthy students (36 females, 14 males) participated in the study. Prior to the intervention, participants were assessed for their levels of subjective distress, weekly exercise, and daily intake of caffeine, alcohol, pain or sleep medication, and cigarettes. Participants were then randomised into two conditions that involved writing either about a personal traumatic event or a non-personal topic, for 20 minutes on each of four consecutive days. Those in the trauma writing condition received the following instruction:

> During each of the four writing days, I want you to write about the most traumatic and upsetting experiences of your entire life. You can write on different topics each day or on the same topic for all four days. The important thing is that you write about your deepest thoughts and feelings. Ideally, whatever you write about should deal with an event or experience that you have not talked with others about in detail. (Pennebaker et al., 1988, p. 240)

Participants in the control writing condition were asked to write on an assigned topic each day of the writing days and to describe the topic in detail but without discussing their own thoughts and feelings. Immediately before and after writing, participants completed questions about their current mood using negative mood words (e.g., frustrated) and current physical state using common symptoms (e.g., headache). Post-writing, participants evaluated their day's essay on a 7-point Likert scale regarding how personal they considered their essay to be, the degree to which they revealed emotions, and the degree to which they had previously refrained from telling others about the subject-matter of the writing task. Psychophysiological assessment included resting blood pressure, heart rate, and skin conductance during a 10-minute resting period. Participants also gave a blood sample, which was used to assess immune functioning.

The assessments were repeated on the last day of writing and again six weeks later. Additionally, participants completed a follow-up questionnaire at three months post intervention about the perceived effects of the writing experiment, including how valuable and meaningful they found it and how their health-related behaviour had changed. In addition, participants' health centre visits for two time periods were assessed, including one record for the four months from the beginning of the school year to the beginning of study and a second record for the time from the beginning of the study to the six-week follow-up.

To determine the cellular immune response, lymphocyte proliferation assays were processed from participants' blood. For this, lymphocytes, white blood cells important for the cell's immune defence, were separated from the whole blood and stimulated with two different mitogens (substances that facilitate cell division), phytohemagglutinin (PHA) and concanavalin A (ConA) at 37°C. This resulted in a process of lymphocyte transformation (blastogenesis), in which small, resting lymphocytes are transformed into large, active lymphocytes (lymphoblasts). The stimulating mitogens were used at three different concentrations and the result was quantified from the harvested cells using radioactivity with a scintillation counter which provided the counts per minute. The mean stimulation value was then determined relative to the control baseline value. A higher count indicates greater lymphocyte response, which signifies a more effective cellular immune response. Lymphocytes support the cellular immune response in fighting infection by actively destroying infected cells or by signalling other immune cells to participate in the immune response.

RESULTS

Compared to controls, participants who wrote about their traumatic experience showed an overall higher mitogen response immediately post-writing, which suggested better cellular immune functioning. They also reported significantly fewer health centre visits. Moreover, participants who wrote about their trauma used more self-referential and emotion words in their writing. Notably, those who wrote about their trauma reported higher levels of negative mood and physical symptoms immediately following the writing. However, at three-months follow-up, participants who wrote about their traumatic experience reported significantly higher levels of happiness, even though they initially reported feeling more depressed on the last day of writing. Unfortunately, relief was not explicitly assessed at any time point, although this was one of the hypothesised mechanisms.

Contrary to the hypotheses, no significant effects were observed for any of the health-related behaviours, suggesting that the intervention did not lead to behaviour change. Likewise, no treatment effects were found for the psychophysiological parameters of blood pressure, heart rate, and skin conductance. Finally, individuals in the trauma writing condition who reported to have written more about topics they had previously held back wrote more words on each essay, perceived their essays to be more personal, and benefitted more in their immune response by showing higher lymphocyte count and reduced blood pressure than low disclosers.

The authors concluded that disclosing traumatic experiences and expressing related emotions through a writing intervention confers potential health benefits as indicated by improved immune responses, that it facilitates change in emotional appraisal and meaning of the experience, and that it encourages them to develop their own solutions to the problem, which can be empowering.

CRITICAL APPRAISAL OF THE STUDY

The study immediately elicited critical discussion among the scientific community (Neale et al., 1988). Three key points included the size and significance of the immune functioning improvement in the trauma writing group, the apparent contradiction of Pennebaker's hypotheses of emotional relief effects by the observed higher levels of negative affect immediately after the writing in the trauma group, and the absence of an immediate post-writing association between affect and immune functioning. Specifically, it was suggested that the group interaction effect for immune functioning could have been driven by the control group's large drop in immune functioning rather than an improvement of immune functioning in the trauma writing group. Indeed, the immune function improvement was small and since no post-hoc tests for the mixed ANOVA were reported in the paper, it was not clear whether the group differences at post-writing were significant or, more importantly, if the pre-post increase within the trauma writing group was significant. Together with a p value of .04 for the day-by-condition interaction, and considering the sample size, post-hoc tests may not have revealed significant effects. The functional benefit of an increase of about .03 log-transformed points per minute was also unclear.

Beyond these issues, it might also be suggested that, rather than improving immune functioning, writing about the trauma could have protected those individuals from normally expected exam-term stress effects and prevented an immune function deterioration, as seen in controls. Participants' relief/catharsis as a major hypothesised mechanism was not assessed in the study, thus preventing direct conclusions about the relief hypothesis. The timing of the measurements could also be important. The trajectory of distress observed in the study seems to point to a short-term increase in distress during and immediately following the writing, before any longer-term benefits were observed. Future studies could assess the time course and longitudinal associations of physiological and psychological responses to expressive writing using ambulatory, ecological monitoring. Another discussion point is that the instructions left it to participants if they wanted to write repeatedly about the same issue or a different issue every day. It is conceivable that thorough processing of one event may actually be more beneficial but no analyses were reported to study whether processing the same or different events carried greater benefit.

A few additional methodological and ethical issues are noteworthy. The functional relevance of the observed immune change has been raised earlier and other, potentially more ecologically valid approaches for assessing immune functioning and health benefits of expressive writing are available, as discussed below. Furthermore, the study did not investigate long-term effects of the intervention, no information about inclusion and exclusion criteria were provided, and no sample size considerations were stated. The study effects were small-to-medium and the sample size of 50 participants could explain why some hypotheses were not confirmed.

Ethically, concerns include the failure to exclude potentially highly vulnerable individuals from the study (e.g., those with recent severe trauma, chronic post-traumatic stress disorder or severe depression and/or suicidal ideation). Although no adverse effects of the writing intervention were reported, the inclusion of those individuals who may have limited capacity to process their traumatic experience in such short time and/or without support from trained healthcare professionals in the most stressful exam period may have put them at risk for symptom deterioration.

IMPACT

The study stimulated several hundred papers on expressive writing. By focusing on potential biomarkers of psychological interventions and by inspiring decades of research into the mechanisms of action of the intervention (see below), the study was ahead of its time: only fairly recently have there been calls for more systematic research into complex psychological and physiological mechanisms that underlie psychological disorders and their successful treatment (Holmes et al., 2014; Holmes et al., 2018). The following section summarises current understanding of the effectiveness of expressive writing and what impact the original study had on research about the mechanisms of action of expressive writing.

HOW BENEFICIAL IS EXPRESSIVE WRITING FOR HEALTH AND WELL-BEING?

Frattaroli's (2006) meta-analysis of 146 studies, which included healthy and clinical samples, and studied a comprehensive set of psychological and physiological outcome measures, indicated a small effect of emotional disclosure ($r = .075$). This suggests that the benefits of expressive writing are rather negligible, e.g., being considerably smaller than the effect size for psychotherapy ($r = .322$: Smith & Glass, 1977). Frattaroli argued that in order to evaluate the effectiveness of expressive writing it needs to be remembered that psychotherapy is associated with considerably higher costs requiring a highly qualified therapist for many hours over months or even years. In light of this cost–benefit analysis, Frattaroli suggested that emotional disclosure should still be considered a worthwhile intervention because it is free and non-invasive, shows a small positive effect (and a medium effect for some specific populations: see below), and is experienced as helpful by most participants. Since this meta-analysis, hundreds of more experimental studies and randomised controlled trials for different specific clinical populations have been published, and to date approximately 15 meta-analyses on the effects of expressive writing have been published with findings largely mirroring those of Frattaroli.

FOR WHOM IS EXPRESSIVE WRITING PARTICULARLY BENEFICIAL?

Interestingly, Frattaroli's meta-analysis pointed to larger effects in specific samples or when administered under optimal conditions. For example, when allowing privacy during sessions and providing more specific disclosure instructions, the average effect size can be bigger ($r = .200$). The most consistent effects of expressive writing have been reported for trauma survivors with posttraumatic stress disorder (PTSD). PTSD is the inability to recover from psychological trauma, and is characterised by intrusive recollections of the experience, avoidance of related thoughts, emotions and trigger situations, altered cognitive and emotion processing, and elevated arousal (American Psychiatric Association, 2013). Kuester et al. (2016) revealed medium effect sizes for PTSD intrusion and hyperarousal improvement at follow-up when compared against active control conditions. Riddle and colleagues (2016) reported significant benefits for posttraumatic stress and general psychological health but not for depression and anxiety.

An extended version of the intervention, written exposure therapy, comprising five 30-minute sessions, was developed by Marx, Sloan and colleagues (Sloan, Marx et al., 2018; Thompson-Hollands et al., 2018; Thompson-Hollands et al., 2019). In a randomised controlled trial with 126 patients, Marx et al. found that the therapy was no less effective in reducing PTSD symptoms than cognitive processing therapy (Resick, 1993, 2008) immediately post-treatment (Sloan, Unger, et al., 2018) and also at 60-week follow-up (Thompson-Hollands et al., 2018). Both treatments had large effect sizes of PTSD symptom severity reduction and the majority of the sample in each condition no longer met PTSD diagnostic status at 60 weeks. In addition, written exposure therapy also had considerably lower treatment drop-out (6%) as compared to 39% in the cognitive processing condition. The benefits of expressive writing, especially when enhanced with additional therapist contact or individualised writing assignments, were also highlighted in a meta-analysis by Gerger et al. (2021). It can be recommended as a low-cost self-help intervention that can reach populations with limited access to mental healthcare, or where capacity to deliver traditional models of psychological intervention is limited.

UNINTENDED CONSEQUENCES AND SAFETY OF ONLINE EXPRESSIVE WRITING

For some samples, expressive writing interventions have been unhelpful or stressful, for example with increased illness-related doctor's visits in men receiving treatment for posttraumatic stress disorder (Gidron et al., 2002), higher levels of physical symptoms in childhood abuse survivors (Batten et al., 2002), and increased stress during COVID-19 in a Serbian community sample (Vukčević Marković et al., 2020). Also, individuals from collectivist cultures, in which expressing emotions is less socially acceptable (Wei et al., 2013) because the focus is on social harmony (Markus & Kitayama, 1991), have been shown to experience adverse outcomes, such as increased PTSD in Chinese American cancer survivors (Gallagher et al., 2018). It has therefore been suggested that culturally adapted writing instructions that emphasise cognitive reappraisal of the stressful event and reduce the focus on emotion disclosure should be used in individuals from collectivist cultures (Knowles et al., 2011).

Overall, expressive writing has been described as a safe intervention that can even be delivered online, which can increase accessibility for populations who cannot access in-person treatments. This has, for example, been beneficial for war and torture survivors (Knaevelsrud et al., 2015). However, it is important to address a current gap in expressive writing studies – the routine reporting of adverse events. Where the intervention has worsened the symptom experience, it is important to look into mechanisms that drive these adverse effects (Bonell et al., 2015). While drop-out rates in PTSD patients have been much lower than with conventional trauma-focused therapy (Sloan, Unger et al., 2018), it is acknowledged that the intervention can be intense and elicit strong negative emotions, which some individuals may find challenging to deal with on their own without the support of a therapist. These include individuals with complex PTSD, a new diagnostic category acknowledged in the ICD-11 (Brewin, 2020), characterised by impaired emotion regulation, high levels of self-criticism, and interpersonal difficulties. This pattern of disturbed self-organisation (Shevlin et al., 2018) is associated with higher treatment drop-out rates, less positive response to established trauma-focused therapies, and potentially adverse effects to expressive writing in its classic, unguided format (Batten et al., 2002). Expressive writing protocols that are suitable for individuals with PTSD after repeated, interpersonal trauma have been developed (Sloan, Unger et al., 2018; Thompson-Hollands et al., 2018; Thompson-Hollands et al., 2019).

To summarise, the original expressive writing instruction introduced by Pennebaker can be beneficial for mild to moderate presentations, and can be made safer and more effective by giving specific writing instructions that go beyond emotional disclosure (see below) and by increasing the number of sessions and adding guided support from a healthcare professional.

DOES THE CLAIM THAT EXPRESSIVE WRITING IMPROVES IMMUNE FUNCTIONING HOLD?

Frattaroli's meta-analysis (2006) suggested small significant immune effect across all studies and different immune functioning measures ($r = .099$). The functional importance of the immune response, as measured by the classic study, has been called into question, and other approaches to study immune functioning that are more closely linked with health effects have been used, such as vaccinations or wound healing.

Because psychological factors, such as stress or thought suppression, can negatively impact vaccination response (Petrie et al., 1998), it has been hypothesised that expressive writing could facilitate its effectiveness. In support, Petrie et al. (1995) found higher levels of antibodies against the hepatitis B vaccine. The importance of chronic stress has also been discussed for the success of the COVID-19 vaccination programme (Peters et al., 2021). Therefore, individualised expressive writing may be beneficial to address vaccination-related fears or other factors that could affect the vaccination success, such as burnout or chronic stress related to the pandemic, or individuals' life circumstances, such as frontline exposure to death and life threat, unemployment, lockdown, and social isolation. This could be a focus of future research.

An alternative paradigm to study whether a person's immune functioning is compromised by stress or depression, or is improved by expressive writing, is wound healing. For this, a person receives a punch biopsy or blister wound and the subsequent recovery of skin barrier function over time is monitored. A longer healing process signifies compromised immune functioning. The effect of stress on wound healing has been explained by decreased proinflammatory cytokines in the wound bed (see Weinman, Broadbent, and Booth, Chapter 6, this volume). These cytokines are key mediators in infection protection and wound repair. Hormones released during stressful situations, such as glucocorticoids and catecholamines, suppress the immune system and thus delay wound healing. Consequently, interventions designed to reduce psychological stress, such as expressive writing, have been shown to improve dermal wound healing (Koschwanez et al., 2013; Robinson et al., 2017). Vaccination and wound healing can be considered as two valid approaches to study the immune effects of expressive writing.

With respect to the role of the classic study, Pennebaker et al. (1988) and subsequent research have helped to give prominence to the role of the biological stress axis – the hypothalamic–pituitary–adrenal (HPA) axis – and related immune functioning in trauma survivors. This contributes understanding of why conditions such as PTSD are often associated with higher physical health problems, including high blood pressure, diabetes, and chronic pain (O'Donnell et al., 2021; Peruzzolo et al., 2022; Shapiro et al., 2022). The HPA axis regulates physiological mechanisms of stress reactions and immunity through a complex feedback system of neurohormones that are sent between the hypothalamus, pituitary gland, and adrenal glands. Narrative exposure therapy, a well-established trauma-focused CBT that includes creating a coherent written narrative of the traumatic experience, can improve immune functioning (Morath et al., 2014).

WHAT ARE THE MECHANISMS OF ACTION OF EXPRESSIVE WRITING?

Pennebaker's paper stimulated further research about the mechanisms through which expressive writing confers health benefits. One novel research avenue it inspired was the investigation of the link between language and recovery from trauma, which ultimately led to the development of a computerised text analysis program (Linguistic Inquiry and Word Count (LIWC) (Pennebaker, 1999). LIWC helped to identify specific linguistic features of improvement in mental and physical health (see Sidebar 13.1). Individuals who benefitted from the intervention showed increases in negative and positive emotion words and used greater amounts of cognitive words that indicate causal reasoning and insight (Pennebaker et al., 1997; Pennebaker & Seagal, 1999).

Sidebar 13.1. Linguistic Inquiry and Word Count Software

The LIWC software reveals the percentage of words in any given text that fall into one or more of over 80 linguistic (e.g., first-person singular pronouns, conjunctions), psychological (e.g., anger, achievement), and topical (e.g., leisure, money) categories. LIWC-based research has demonstrated a predominance of negative self-referential words in individuals who experience high levels of stress and negative emotionality (Tackman et al., 2019). Negative self-referential processing is a known vulnerability marker of depressive relapse (LeMoult et al., 2017). Recent advances in machine learning have extended understanding of mental and physical health and mechanisms of action of psychological therapies through LIWC-informed natural language processing (Bantum et al., 2017; Pulverman et al., 2015).

Several theories for mechanisms of action of expressive writing have been formulated and examined since 1988. The originally suggested Inhibition Theory (Pennebaker et al., 1988) posited that the participant experiences a cathartic effect by disclosing a previously undisclosed traumatic event and by acting out rather than inhibiting the associated emotions. This theory has since been challenged and research has suggested that emotion expression alone may not be enough; rather, it is the way the individual processes the event that is important. Cognitive Processing Theory (Horowitz, 1986) hypothesised that writing about feelings and thoughts associated with trauma can help the individual to process and reappraise the event and form a coherent narrative of the experience. This theory has been widely supported (Sidebar 13.2) and is also relevant for therapies focusing on evidence-based trauma. Related to this, Exposure Theory (Foa & Kozak, 1986) postulates that, through writing, the individual will be repeatedly exposed to negative emotions, which elicits habituation, fear extinction, and trauma memory updating. This theory has been especially supported for altering anxiety and fear-based emotions but has been questioned for emotions like anger, guilt, and shame. There was additional support for improved emotion regulation and self-perception and facilitating social integration as mechanisms (Sidebar 13.2).

Sidebar 13.2. Evidence for Expressive Writing Theories

Inhibition Theory. Although there has been evidence that inhibition and emotion suppression have negative health effects (Glenk et al., 2020; Lam et al., 2009), the number of emotion words expressed were either not associated with the outcome (Pennebaker et al., 1988) or very high levels of negative emotion words were negatively associated with the outcome (Hoyt et al., 2021). Rather than providing immediate relief, participants reported higher levels of negative emotions immediately post writing. Research also suggested that whether or not trauma had been previously disclosed did not appear to be associated with the outcome (Greenberg & Stone, 1992; Greenberg et al., 1996).

Cognitive Processing Theory. Participants described how the writing allowed them to gain a better understanding of what had happened to them (Pennebaker, 1993). Expressive writing was associated with an increased use of causation words (e.g., because, cause, effect) and insight words (e.g., consider, know). That expressive writing increases insight and meaning-making of the event and supports trauma memory integration is also reflected in cognitive models of PTSD (Brewin, 2001; Brewin et al., 1996; Ehlers & Clark, 2000) and trauma-focused cognitive behavioural therapies, such as Narrative Exposure Therapy (Schauer et al., 2012) or Written Exposure Therapy (Thompson-Hollands et al., 2019).

Exposure Theory. The goal of exposure is to build new inhibitory learning pathways in which fear is no longer associated with reminders and memories of the traumatic event (Craske et al., 2014). In PTSD patients, written exposure treatment was effective in reducing PTSD symptoms through the initial activation of the fear network, which is indicated by higher heart rate followed by a gradual between-session reduction of self-reported arousal (Wisco et al., 2016). Exposure works well for fear and anxiety but is insufficient to address anger, guilt, or shame (Grunert et al., 2007; Grunert et al., 2003), which could explain the potential adverse effects discussed earlier in this chapter (Batten et al., 2002).

Improved Emotion Regulation and Self-perception. Expressive writing can facilitate more effective emotion regulation and self-perception through a number of processes, such as reducing emotion suppression (Gortner et al., 2006), cognitive processing/reappraisal (discussed above), labelling emotions (Lieberman et al., 2011), self-affirmations (Creswell et al., 2007), and problem solving (Cameron & Nicholls, 1998). For this, the original writing instruction should be extended to invite participants to engage in these processes for better effects.

Social Integration Theory. Writing about a traumatic event may motivate an individual to share their experience more readily with others (Kovac & Range, 2000) and introduce positive changes within their social networks (Leung et al., 2019). The resulting validation and social support have been widely acknowledged as beneficial for recovery from trauma and preventing posttraumatic stress disorder (Brewin et al., 2000; Ozer et al., 2003). Another interesting perspective for future research is offered by the social identity approach to health (Haslam et al., 2018; see also Jetten, Bentley, and Young, Chapter 9, this volume), which holds that positive identification and integration with social groups support well-being and recovery from trauma (Cruwys et al., 2014; Muldoon et al., 2017). A writing intervention that makes salient shared social identities could facilitate a so-called 'social cure' effect.

CONCLUSIONS

Despite some methodological and ethical concerns, the classic study has been and still is of great importance, not only for the field of health psychology. It stimulated a number of novel research avenues and has had important implications for clinical psychology and psychotherapy. The study highlighted the close link between mental and physical health, thus supporting the biopsychosocial model for the understanding of many mental health conditions. It contributed to informing the development of new evidence-based psychological interventions, particularly for the treatment of post-traumatic stress disorder, and has stimulated much research that has explored the mechanisms of effect. Another important legacy of the research is how it inspired investigations into the role of linguistic markers of symptom reduction and increased well-being, and the development of a software that enables natural language processing.

Studying the effects of expressive writing has given important impetus for a better understanding of recovery from psychological trauma and treating PTSD. Research indicating how expressive writing may help people come to terms with traumatic events has synergies with contemporary recommended trauma-focused treatments (Guideline Development Panel for the Treatment of PTSD in Adults, American Psychological Association 2019; The National Institute for Health and Care Excellence (NICE) 2018) (Guideline Development Panel for the Treatment of PTSD in Adults, American Psychological Association, 2019; the National Institute for Health and Care Excellence (NICE), 2018). Within the trauma field, expressive writing has been applied as a standalone intervention (Thompson-Hollands et al., 2019) or as a complementary component in face-to-face or digital trauma-focused cognitive behaviour therapy (TF-CBT) (Kuester et al., 2016; Schauer et al., 2012). However, it has been shown that not all trauma survivors benefit from the original, short expressive writing intervention and the effects of the classic intervention can be small. Tailoring the writing intervention to patients' needs and cultural background in order to trigger the 'right' mechanisms (cognitive processing and meaning making, memory updating, improving self-perception, emotion regulation and growth) can lead to larger beneficial effects.

FURTHER READING

Pennebaker, James W., & Smyth, J. M. (2016). *Opening up by writing it down: How expressive writing improves health and eases emotional pain* (3rd ed.). New York: Guilford Press.

This is one of Pennebaker's seminal books on expressive writing, written for the general population as a self-help guide, where the authors describe the expressive writing approach, how it has been applied in different settings and for different populations, making links with supporting scientific research.

The Weekend University. (2021). *Using expressive writing to heal trauma – Dr James Pennebaker, PhD* [Interview], 19 January. Available at: www.youtube.com/watch?v=CjErOxiXqio

This is an interview with Pennebaker on his research on expressive writing and his journey as a researcher.

Irwin, M. R., & Slavich, G. M. (2017). Psychoneuroimmunology. In G. G. Berntson, J. T. Cacioppo, & L. G. Tassinary (Eds.), *Handbook of psychophysiology* (4th ed., pp. 377–397). Cambridge: Cambridge University Press.

An introductory chapter about psychoneuroimmunology in a key psychophysiology textbook that provides a detailed overview and understanding of the key immune function markers relevant for studying health and behaviour.

Shields, G. S., Spahr, C. M., & Slavich, G. M. (2020). Psychosocial interventions and immune system function: A systematic review and meta-analysis of randomized clinical trials. *JAMA Psychiatry, 77*(10), 1031–1043. https://doi.org/10.1001/jamapsychiatry.2020.0431

This study provides a meta-analysis about the effects of psychosocial interventions on immune system functions.

Slavich, G. M. (2020). Social safety theory: A biologically based evolutionary perspective on life stress, health, and behavior. *Annual Review of Clinical Psychology, 16*, 265–295. https://doi.org/10.1146/annurev-clinpsy-032816-045159

This paper provides an interesting new theory about the role of social threat and safety in understanding health and behaviour.

REFERENCES

American Psychiatric Association. (2013). *Diagnostic and statistical manual of mental disorders (5th ed.)*. Washington, DC: APA.

Bantum, E. O., Elhadad, N., Owen, J. E., Zhang, S., Golant, M., Buzaglo, J., Stephen, J., & Giese-Davis, J. (2017). Machine learning for identifying emotional expression in text: Improving the accuracy of established methods. *Journal of Technology in Behavioral Science, 2*(1), 21–27. https://doi.org/10.1007/s41347-017-0015-5

Batten, S. V., Follette, V. M., Rasmussen Hall, M. L., & Palm, K. M. (2002). Physical and psychological effects of written disclosure among sexual abuse survivors. *Behavior Therapy, 33*(1), 107–122. https://doi.org/10.1016/S0005-7894(02)80008-9

Bonell, C., Jamal, F., Melendez-Torres, G. J., & Cummins, S. (2015). "Dark logic": theorising the harmful consequences of public health interventions. *Journal of Epidemiology and Community Health, 69*(1), 95–98. https://doi.org/10.1136/jech-2014-204671

Brewin, C. R. (2001). A cognitive neuroscience account of posttraumatic stress disorder and its treatment. *Behaviour Research and Therapy, 39*(4), 373–393. https://doi.org/10.1016/s0005-7967(00)00087-5

Brewin, C. R. (2020). Complex post-traumatic stress disorder: A new diagnosis in ICD-11. *BJPsych Advances, 26*, 145–152. https://doi.org/10.1192/bja.2019.48

Brewin, C. R., Andrews, B., & Valentine, J. D. (2000). Meta-analysis of risk factors for posttraumatic stress disorder in trauma-exposed adults. *Journal of Consulting and Clinical Psychology, 68*(5), 748–766. https://doi.org/10.1037//0022-006x.68.5.748

Brewin, C. R., Dalgleish, T., & Joseph, S. (1996). A dual representation theory of posttraumatic stress disorder. *Psychological Review, 103*(4), 670–686. https://doi.org/10.1037/0033-295X.103.4.670

Cameron, L. D., & Nicholls, G. (1998). Expression of stressful experiences through writing: effects of a self-regulation manipulation for pessimists and optimists. *Health Psychology, 17*(1), 84–92. https://doi.org/10.1037//0278-6133.17.1.84

Craske, M. G., Treanor, M., Conway, C. C., Zbozinek, T., & Vervliet, B. (2014). Maximizing exposure therapy: an inhibitory learning approach. *Behaviour Research and Therapy, 58*, 10–23. https://doi.org/10.1016/j.brat.2014.04.006

Creswell, J. D., Lam, S., Stanton, A. L., Taylor, S. E., Bower, J. E., & Sherman, D. K. (2007). Does self-affirmation, cognitive processing, or discovery of meaning explain cancer-related health benefits of expressive writing? *Personality and Social Psychology Bulletin, 33*(2), 238–250. https://doi.org/10.1177/0146167206294412

Cruwys, T., Haslam, S. A., Dingle, G. A., Jetten, J., Hornsey, M. J., Desdemona Chong, E. M., & Oei, T. P. S. (2014). Feeling connected again: Interventions that increase social identification reduce depression symptoms in community and clinical settings. *Journal of Affective Disorders, 159*, 139–146. https://doi.org/10.1016/j.jad.2014.02.019

Ehlers, A., & Clark, D. M. (2000). A cognitive model of posttraumatic stress disorder. *Behaviour Research and Therapy*, *38*(4), 319–345. https://doi.org/10.1016/s0005-7967(99)00123-0

Engel, G. L. (1977). The need for a new medical model: A challenge for biomedicine. *Science*, *196*(4286), 129–136. https://doi.org/10.1126/science.847460

Foa, E. B., & Kozak, M. J. (1986). Emotional processing of fear: Exposure to corrective information. *Psychological Bulletin*, *99*(1), 20–35.

Frattaroli, J. (2006). Experimental disclosure and its moderators: A meta-analysis. *Psychological Bulletin*, *132*(6), 823–865. https://doi.org/10.1037/0033-2909.132.6.823

Gallagher, M. W., Long, L. J., Tsai, W., Stanton, A. L., & Lu, Q. (2018). The unexpected impact of expressive writing on posttraumatic stress and growth in Chinese American breast cancer survivors. *Journal of Clinical Psychology*, *74*(10), 1673–1686. https://doi.org/10.1002/jclp.22636

Gerger, H., Werner, C. P., Gaab, J., & Cuijpers, P. (2021). Comparative efficacy and acceptability of expressive writing treatments compared with psychotherapy, other writing treatments, and waiting list control for adult trauma survivors: A systematic review and network meta-analysis. *Psychological Medicine*, 1–13. https://doi.org/10.1017/S0033291721000143

Gidron, Y., Duncan, E., Lazar, A., Biderman, A., Tandeter, H., & Shvartzman, P. (2002). Effects of guided written disclosure of stressful experiences on clinic visits and symptoms in frequent clinic attenders. *Family Practice*, *19*(2), 161–166. https://doi.org/10.1093/fampra/19.2.161

Glenk, L. M., Kothgassner, O. D., Felnhofer, A., Gotovina, J., Pranger, C. L., Jensen, A. N., Mothes-Luksch, N., Goreis, A., Palme, R., & Jensen-Jarolim, E. (2020). Salivary cortisol responses to acute stress vary between allergic and healthy individuals: the role of plasma oxytocin, emotion regulation strategies, reported stress and anxiety. *Stress (Amsterdam, Netherlands)*, *23*(3), 275–283. https://doi.org/10.1080/10253890.2019.1675629

Gortner, E.-M., Rude, S. S., & Pennebaker, J. W. (2006). Benefits of expressive writing in lowering rumination and depressive symptoms. *Behavior Therapy*, *37*(3), 292–303. https://doi.org/10.1016/j.beth.2006.01.004

Greenberg, M. A., & Stone, A. A. (1992). Emotional disclosure about traumas and its relation to health: effects of previous disclosure and trauma severity. *Journal of Personality and Social Psychology*, *63*(1), 75–84. https://doi.org/10.1037//0022-3514.63.1.75

Greenberg, M. A., Wortman, C. B., & Stone, A. A. (1996). Emotional expression and physical health: revising traumatic memories or fostering self-regulation? *Journal of Personality and Social Psychology*, *71*(3), 588–602. https://doi.org/10.1037/0022-3514.71.3.588

Gross, J. J., & Levenson, R. W. (1993). Emotional suppression: Physiology, self-report, and expressive behavior. *Journal of Personality and Social Psychology*, *64*(6), 970–986. https://doi.org/10.1037/0022-3514.64.6.970

Grunert, Brad K, Weis, J. M., Smucker, M. R., & Christianson, H. F. (2007). Imagery rescripting and reprocessing therapy after failed prolonged exposure for post-traumatic stress disorder following industrial injury. *Journal of Behavior Therapy and Experimental Psychiatry*, *38*(4), 317–328. https://doi.org/10.1016/j.jbtep.2007.10.005

Grunert, B K, Smucker, M. R., Weis, J. M., & Rusch, M. D. (2003). When prolonged exposure fails: Adding an imagery-based cognitive restructuring component in the treatment of industrial accident victims suffering from PTSD. *Cognitive and Behavioral Practice*, *10*(4), 333–346.

Guideline Development Panel for the Treatment of PTSD in Adults, American Psychological Association. (2019). Summary of the clinical practice guideline for the treatment of posttraumatic stress disorder (PTSD) in adults. *The American Psychologist*, *74*(5), 596–607. https://doi.org/10.1037/amp0000473

Haslam, C., Jetten, J., Cruwys, T., Dingle, G. A., & Haslam, S. A. (2018). *The new psychology of health: Unlocking the social cure*. London: Routledge. https://doi. org/10.4324/9781315648569

Holmes, E. A., Craske, M. G., & Graybiel, A. M. (2014). Psychological treatments: A call for mental-health science. *Nature*, *511*(7509), 287–289. https://doi. org/10.1038/511287a

Holmes, E. A., Ghaderi, A., Harmer, C. J., Ramchandani, P. G., Cuijpers, P., Morrison, A. P., Roiser, J. P., Bockting, C. L. H., O'Connor, R. C., Shafran, R., Moulds, M. L., & Craske, M. G. (2018). The Lancet Psychiatry Commission on psychological treatments research in tomorrow's science. *The Lancet: Psychiatry*, *5*(3), 237–286. https://doi. org/10.1016/S2215-0366(17)30513-8

Horowitz, M. J. (1986). Stress-response syndromes: A review of posttraumatic and adjustment disorders. *Hospital & Community Psychiatry*, *37*(3), 241–249.

Hoyt, M. A., Darabos, K., & Llave, K. (2021). Emotional processing writing and physiological stress responses: Understanding constructive and unconstructive processes. *Cognition & Emotion*, *35*(6), 1187–1194. https://doi.org/10.1080/0269993 1.2021.1929083

Kiecolt-Glaser, J. K., Garner, W., Speicher, C., Penn, G. M., Holliday, J., & Glaser, R. (1984). Psychosocial modifiers of immunocompetence in medical students. *Psychosomatic Medicine*, *46*(1), 7–14. https://doi.org/10.1097/00006842-198401000-00003

Kiecolt-Glaser, J. K., Glaser, R., Strain, E. C., Stout, J. C., Tarr, K. L., Holliday, J. E., & Speicher, C. E. (1986). Modulation of cellular immunity in medical students. *Journal of Behavioral Medicine*, *9*(1), 5–21. https://doi.org/10.1007/BF00844640

Knaevelsrud, C., Brand, J., Lange, A., Ruwaard, J., & Wagner, B. (2015). Web-based psychotherapy for posttraumatic stress disorder in war-traumatized Arab patients: Randomized controlled trial. *Journal of Medical Internet Research*, *17*(3), e71. https:// doi.org/10.2196/jmir.3582

Knowles, E. D., Wearing, J. R., & Campos, B. (2011). Culture and the health benefits of expressive writing. *Social Psychological and Personality Science*, *2*(4), 408–415. https://doi.org/10.1177/1948550610395780

Koschwanez, H. E., Kerse, N., Darragh, M., Jarrett, P., Booth, R. J., & Broadbent, E. (2013). Expressive writing and wound healing in older adults: A randomized controlled trial. *Psychosomatic Medicine*, *75*(6), 581–590. https://doi.org/10.1097/PSY.0b013e31829b7b2e

Kovac, S. H., & Range, L. M. (2000). Writing Projects: Lessening Undergraduates' Unique Suicidal Bereavement. *Suicide and Life-Threatening Behavior*.

Kuester, A., Niemeyer, H., & Knaevelsrud, C. (2016). Internet-based interventions for posttraumatic stress: A meta-analysis of randomized controlled trials. *Clinical Psychology Review*, *43*, 1–16. https://doi.org/10.1016/j.cpr.2015.11.004

Lam, S., Dickerson, S. S., Zoccola, P. M., & Zaldivar, F. (2009). Emotion regulation and cortisol reactivity to a social-evaluative speech task. *Psychoneuroendocrinology*, *34*(9), 1355–1362. https://doi.org/10.1016/j.psyneuen.2009.04.006

LeMoult, J., Kircanski, K., Prasad, G., & Gotlib, I. H. (2017). Negative self-referential processing predicts the recurrence of major depressive episodes. *Clinical Psychological Science: A Journal of the Association for Psychological Science*, 5(1), 174–181. https://doi.org/10.1177/2167702616654898

Leung, Y. W., Maslej, M. M., Ho, C., Razavi, S., Uy, P., Hosseini, M.-A., Avery, J., Rodin, G., & Peterkin, A. (2019). Cocreating meaning through expressive writing and reading for cancer caregivers. *Journal of Palliative Care*, 825859719871538. https://doi.org/10.1177/0825859719871538

Lieberman, M. D., Inagaki, T. K., Tabibnia, G., & Crockett, M. J. (2011). Subjective responses to emotional stimuli during labeling, reappraisal, and distraction. *Emotion*, 11(3), 468–480. https://doi.org/10.1037/a0023503

Markus, H. R., & Kitayama, S. (1991). Culture and the self: Implications for cognition, emotion, and motivation. *Psychological Review*, 98(2), 224–253. https://doi.org/10.1037/0033-295X.98.2.224

Morath, J., Gola, H., Sommershof, A., Hamuni, G., Kolassa, S., Catani, C., Adenauer, H., Ruf-Leuschner, M., Schauer, M., Elbert, T., Groettrup, M., & Kolassa, I.-T. (2014). The effect of trauma-focused therapy on the altered T cell distribution in individuals with PTSD: Evidence from a randomized controlled trial. *Journal of Psychiatric Research*, 54, 1–10. https://doi.org/10.1016/j.jpsychires.2014.03.016

Muldoon, O. T., Acharya, K., Jay, S., Adhikari, K., Pettigrew, J., & Lowe, R. D. (2017). Community identity and collective efficacy: A social cure for traumatic stress in post-earthquake Nepal. *European Journal of Social Psychology*, 47(7), 904–915. https://doi.org/10.1002/ejsp.2330

Neale, J. M., Cox, D. S., Valdimarsdottir, H., & Stone, A. A. (1988). The relation between immunity and health: Comment on Pennebaker, Kiecolt-Glaser, and Glaser. *Journal of Consulting and Clinical Psychology*, 56(4), 636–637. https://doi.org/10.1037//0022-006x.56.4.636

O'Donnell, C. J., Schwartz Longacre, L., Cohen, B. E., Fayad, Z. A., Gillespie, C. F., Liberzon, I., Pathak, G. A., Polimanti, R., Risbrough, V., Ursano, R. J., Vander Heide, R. S., Yancy, C. W., Vaccarino, V., Sopko, G., & Stein, M. B. (2021). Posttraumatic stress disorder and cardiovascular disease: State of the science, knowledge gaps, and research opportunities. *JAMA Cardiology*, 6(10), 1207–1216. https://doi.org/10.1001/jamacardio.2021.2530

Ozer, E. J., Best, S. R., Lipsey, T. L., & Weiss, D. S. (2003). Predictors of posttraumatic stress disorder and symptoms in adults: a meta-analysis. *Psychological Bulletin*, 129(1), 52–73. https://doi.org/10.1037/0033-2909.129.1.52

Pennebaker, J W. (1993). Putting stress into words: health, linguistic, and therapeutic implications. *Behaviour Research and Therapy*, 31(6), 539–548. https://doi.org/10.1016/0005-7967(93)90105-4

Pennebaker, J. W. (1999). *Linguistic Inquiry and Word Count: LIWC* (R. J. Booth & M. E. Francis, Trans.). Erlbaum Publishers.

Pennebaker, J. W., & Beall, S. K. (1986). Confronting a traumatic event: Toward an understanding of inhibition and disease. *Journal of Abnormal Psychology*, 95(3), 274–281. https://doi.org/10.1037//0021-843x.95.3.274

Pennebaker, J. W., Kiecolt-Glaser, J. K., & Glaser, R. (1988). Disclosure of traumas and immune function: Health implications for psychotherapy. *Journal of Consulting and Clinical Psychology*, 56(2), 239–245. https://doi.org/10.1037/0022-006X.56.2.239

Pennebaker, J. W., Mayne, T. J., & Francis, M. E. (1997). Linguistic predictors of adaptive bereavement. *Journal of Personality and Social Psychology*, 72(4), 863–871. https://doi.org/10.1037/0022-3514.72.4.863

Pennebaker, J. W., & Seagal, J. D. (1999). Forming a story: The health benefits of narrative. *Journal of Clinical Psychology, 55*(10), 1243–1254. https://doi.org/10.1002/(SICI)1097-4679(199910)55:10<1243::AID-JCLP6>3.0.CO;2-N

Peruzzolo, T. L., Pinto, J. V., Roza, T. H., Shintani, A. O., Anzolin, A. P., Gnielka, V., Kohmann, A. M., Marin, A. S., Lorenzon, V. R., Brunoni, A. R., Kapczinski, F., & Passos, I. C. (2022). Inflammatory and oxidative stress markers in post-traumatic stress disorder: A systematic review and meta-analysis. *Molecular Psychiatry, 27*(8), 3150–3163. https://doi.org/10.1038/s41380-022-01564-0

Peters, E. M. J., Schedlowski, M., Watzl, C., & Gimsa, U. (2021). To stress or not to stress: Brain-behavior-immune interaction may weaken or promote the immune response to SARS-CoV-2. *Neurobiology of Stress, 14*, 100296. https://doi.org/10.1016/j.ynstr.2021.100296

Petrie, K. J., Booth, R. J., & Pennebaker, J. W. (1998). The immunological effects of thought suppression. *Journal of Personality and Social Psychology, 75*(5), 1264–1272. https://doi.org/10.1037/0022-3514.75.5.1264

Petrie, K. J., Booth, R. J., Pennebaker, J. W., Davison, K. P., & Thomas, M. G. (1995). Disclosure of trauma and immune response to a hepatitis B vaccination program. *Journal of Consulting and Clinical Psychology, 63*(5), 787–792. https://doi.org/10.1037//0022-006x.63.5.787

Pulverman, C. S., Lorenz, T. A., & Meston, C. M. (2015). Linguistic changes in expressive writing predict psychological outcomes in women with history of childhood sexual abuse and adult sexual dysfunction. *Psychological Trauma: Theory, Research, Practice and Policy, 7*(1), 50–57. https://doi.org/10.1037/a0036462

Resick, P. A. (1993). *Cognitive processing therapy for rape victims: A treatment manual* (M. Schnicke, Trans.). Thousand Oaks, CA: Sage.

Resick, P. A. (2008). *Cognitive processing therapy: Veteran/military version* (C. M. Monson & K. M. Chard, Trans.). Washington, DC: Department of Veterans' Affairs.

Riddle, J. P., Smith, H. E., & Jones, C. J. (2016). Does written emotional disclosure improve the psychological and physical health of caregivers? A systematic review and meta-analysis. *Behaviour Research and Therapy, 80*, 23–32. https://doi.org/10.1016/j.brat.2016.03.004

Robinson, H., Jarrett, P., Vedhara, K., & Broadbent, E. (2017). The effects of expressive writing before or after punch biopsy on wound healing. *Brain, Behavior, and Immunity, 61*, 217–227. https://doi.org/10.1016/j.bbi.2016.11.025

Schauer, M., Neuner, F., & Elbert, T. (2012). *Narrative exposure therapy: A short-term treatment for traumatic stress disorders*. Oxford: Hogrefe.

Shapiro, M. O., Short, N. A., Raines, A. M., Franklin, C. L., True, G., & Constans, J. I. (2022). Pain and posttraumatic stress: Associations among women veterans with a history of military sexual trauma. *Psychological Trauma: Theory, Research, Practice and Policy*. https://doi.org/10.1037/tra0001272

Shevlin, M., Hyland, P., Roberts, N. P., Bisson, J. I., Brewin, C. R., & Cloitre, M. (2018). A psychometric assessment of Disturbances in Self-Organization symptom indicators for ICD-11 Complex PTSD using the International Trauma Questionnaire. *European Journal of Psychotraumatology, 9*(1), 1419749. https://doi.org/10.1080/20008198.2017.1419749

Sloan, D. M., Marx, B. P., Lee, D. J., & Resick, P. A. (2018). A brief exposure-based treatment vs cognitive processing therapy for posttraumatic stress disorder: A randomized noninferiority clinical trial. *JAMA Psychiatry, 75*(3), 233–239. https://doi.org/10.1001/jamapsychiatry.2017.4249

Sloan, D. M., Unger, W., Lee, D. J., & Beck, J. G. (2018). A randomized controlled trial of group cognitive behavioral treatment for veterans diagnosed with chronic posttraumatic stress disorder. *Journal of Traumatic Stress*, *31*(6), 886–898. https://doi.org/10.1002/jts.22338

Smith, M. L., & Glass, G. V. (1977). Meta-analysis of psychotherapy outcome studies. *The American Psychologist*, *32*(9), 752–760. https://doi.org/10.1037/0003-066X.32.9.752

Tackman, A. M., Sbarra, D. A., Carey, A. L., Donnellan, M. B., Horn, A. B., Holtzman, N. S., Edwards, T. S., Pennebaker, J. W., & Mehl, M. R. (2019). Depression, negative emotionality, and self-referential language: A multi-lab, multi-measure, and multi-language-task research synthesis. *Journal of Personality and Social Psychology*, *116*(5), 817–834. https://doi.org/10.1037/pspp0000187

The National Institute for Health and Care Excellence (NICE). (2018, December 5). *Guidance for Post-traumatic Stress Disorder*. www.Nice.Org.Uk/Guidance/Ng116/Evidence

Thompson-Hollands, J., Marx, B. P., Lee, D. J., Resick, P. A., & Sloan, D. M. (2018). Long-term treatment gains of a brief exposure-based treatment for PTSD. *Depression and Anxiety*, *35*(10), 985–991. https://doi.org/10.1002/da.22825

Thompson-Hollands, J., Marx, B. P., & Sloan, D. M. (2019). Brief novel therapies for PTSD: Written Exposure Therapy. *Current Treatment Options in Psychiatry*, *6*(2), 99–106. https://doi.org/10.1007/s40501-019-00168-w

Vukčević Marković, M., Bjekić, J., & Priebe, S. (2020). Effectiveness of expressive writing in the reduction of psychological distress during the COVID-19 pandemic: A randomized controlled trial. *Frontiers in Psychology*, *11*, 587282. https://doi.org/10.3389/fpsyg.2020.587282

Wei, M., Su, J. C., Carrera, S., Lin, S.-P., & Yi, F. (2013). Suppression and interpersonal harmony: A cross-cultural comparison between Chinese and European Americans. *Journal of Counseling Psychology*, *60*(4), 625–633. https://doi.org/10.1037/a0033413

Wisco, B. E., Baker, A. S., & Sloan, D. M. (2016). Mechanisms of change in written exposure treatment of posttraumatic stress disorder. *Behavior Therapy*, *47*(1), 66–74. https://doi.org/10.1016/j.beth.2015.09.005

14 | Positive Psychology: Revisiting Seligman, Steen, Park, and Peterson (2005)

Seligman, M. E. P., Steen, T. A., Park, N., & Peterson, C. (2005). Positive psychology progress: Empirical validation of interventions. *American Psychologist, 60*, 410–421.

Ryan J. Goffredi, Christopher A. Sanders, Kennon M. Sheldon, and Laura A. King

BACKGROUND

Philosophers, scholars, theologians, and laypeople alike have pondered the question of how to live in a way that ultimately leads to happiness, thriving, and optimal functioning. What factors, actions, or material *things* (if any) promise to enhance happiness, not just temporarily but in the long run? This broad question has been approached in a multitude of ways over millennia, from the writings of Aristotle and religious scriptures to the more contemporary self-help movement. However, often lacking from these perspectives are prescriptions for happiness based on scientific evidence. Only relatively recently have some answers been provided by empirical research, particularly in the domain of positive psychology.

What is positive psychology?

Positive psychology is a sub-field of psychology that is concerned with 'understanding and building the qualities that make life worth living' (Seligman, 1999, p. 3). More specifically, positive psychology is the study of positive emotions and experiences, the personality characteristics linked to these, and the institutions that foster them (Seligman & Csikszentmihalyi, 2000).

As a discipline, positive psychology encompasses the work of researchers studying topics such as happiness, joy, gratitude, love, hope, optimism, forgiveness, flow, mastery, self-compassion, mindfulness, and meaning in life (Lopez & Snyder, 2009; Peterson, 2006). The focus of researchers working in this discipline extends beyond the individual to include relationships, families, communities, and societies (Peterson, 2006). Furthermore, positive psychology should be considered as capturing more than the study of happiness or well-being alone, but happiness is certainly a central focus.[1]

Interestingly, meta-analyses reveal that happiness is not only an outcome but also a *predictor* of positive outcomes in life: happier people are more creative and productive, more likely to be hired and promoted, have more friends and social support, experience greater relationship satisfaction, engage in more prosocial behaviours, and make better leaders (Lyubomirsky, King, & Diener, 2005; Walsh et al., 2018). Happier people tend to be physically healthier, more resilient to stress, have stronger immune systems, and live longer (Diener et al., 2017; Lyubomirsky, King, & Diener, 2005). In general, perspectives from positive psychology seem to emphasise the general point: *Whatever the good in life, happiness may foster it.*

Taken together, this research indicates that happiness tends to be a valuable experience and is linked to many adaptive outcomes and consequences. However, key questions remain: Can happiness be intentionally enhanced or increased? Or is a person's happiness an immutable quality determined at birth? Answering these questions were a key early goal of positive psychology – to identify interventions that could effectively increase happiness and well-being in a sustainable way.

DETAILED OVERVIEW

SELIGMAN, STEEN, PARK, AND PETERSON (2005)

In their seminal article, Seligman and colleagues (2005) coined the term 'positive psychology intervention' (PPI) to describe any treatment or programme aimed at enhancing well-being (for a further discussion of definitions see Schueller et al., 2014; Carr et al., 2020). This article reported on five interventions that were tested for efficacy for two outcomes in a randomised controlled trial: alleviating depression and enhancing happiness. Participants were told that they would engage in an activity designed to increase happiness, but that it was not guaranteed to do so, or that they might be given a 'placebo' exercise. Participants completed baseline measures of happiness and depression prior to being randomly assigned to one of the two conditions. Next, we summarise the five PPIs employed by Seligman and colleagues.

THE INTERVENTIONS

1. Gratitude Visit: Participants were given one week to write a letter expressing their gratitude to someone and then read that letter out aloud and in person to the recipient.

---

[1] Going forward, we use the terms happiness and well-being interchangeably (although see Jayawickreme et al., 2012 and Martela & Sheldon, 2019 for further discussion on the various definitions of well-being).

2. Three Good Things: Each night for one week, participants wrote down three things that went well that day, whether large (I got engaged), or small (my friend and I had a good conversation over coffee), or even pleasantly mundane (I didn't burn the toast). They then wrote about why that good thing happened.

3. You at Your Best: Participants wrote about a time when they were at their best – perhaps overcoming a challenge or making someone else's life better. Then, they reread the story they had written once a day for a week to identify and reflect on the personal strengths expressed therein.

4. Identifying Signature Strengths: Participants completed an online personality assessment. Feedback provided them with their top five 'signature' strengths and some ways those strengths could be expressed in daily activities. Participants were asked to use these strengths more often than usual throughout the week.

5. Using Signature Strengths in a New Way: Participants in this group took the online assessment and received their top five strengths, as in the Identifying Signature Strengths intervention. They were then instructed to use one of their strengths in a new and different way, as opposed to simply using the strengths more often, every day for one week.

Participants assigned to the 'placebo' group wrote about their earliest memories each night for one week. Depression and well-being were measured again immediately after the week-long activity period, and again one week, one month, three months, and six months post-intervention. Follow-up assessments were crucial to test the longevity of changes immediately following each intervention. Results showed that all conditions, including the placebo control condition, led to immediate salutary effects. The *you at your best* and *identifying signature strengths* interventions, and the *'placebo'* intervention showed benefits that lasted less than a week. The *gratitude visit* produced the largest immediate increases in happiness and decreases in depression, but these effects dissipated before the three-month follow-up. Only the *three good things* and *using signature strengths in a new way* led to benefits lasting up to six months. Notably, these effects were moderate or large in size, demonstrating that these PPIs promoted meaningful changes in happiness and symptoms of depression.

Taken together, results of this study demonstrated that sustainable increases in happiness, and decreases in depression, are possible through intervention. The two consistently effective strategies were the *reflecting on three good things* and the *using signature strengths in a new way* strategies. One caveat to these findings is that being happier for up to six months after an intervention does not necessarily entail 'living happily ever after' (Seligman et al., 2005, p. 10), but the study stands as an important catalyst of hundreds of studies testing the efficacy of various PPIs. In addition to the five exercises already discussed, researchers have evaluated PPIs involving acts of kindness (e.g., Lyubomirsky, Sheldon, & Schkade, 2005; Otake et al., 2006), optimism (e.g., King, 2001; Loveday et al., 2018), savouring (e.g., Bryant et al., 2005), mindfulness (e.g., Nyklíček & Kuijpers, 2008), humour (e.g., Wellenzohn et al., 2016), forgiveness (e.g., Akhtar & Barlow, 2018), setting highly valued goals (e.g., Cheavens et al., 2006; Sheldon & Houser-Marko, 2001), and writing about peak experiences (e.g., Burton & King, 2009), among others, which have demonstrated significant positive effects on happiness. Outcomes have also been expanded to include anxiety, stress, quality of life, and physical health (Carr et al., 2020; Kushlev et al., 2020).

Like all good scientific research, Seligman et al.'s study gave rise to many further questions to be answered in subsequent studies. Before addressing these, it is worth mentioning that recent meta-analyses and systematic reviews of PPI efficacy trials consistently show small-to-moderate effects of PPIs across studies on well-being, depression, and anxiety (Bolier et al., 2013; Carr et al., 2020; Chakhssi et al., 2018; Hendriks et al., 2020; Sin & Lyubomirsky, 2009). Even more promising, most meta-analyses find that the positive effects of PPIs tend to persist several months after the administration of the interventions, lending further support to Seligman and colleagues' findings (Bolier et al., 2013; Carr et al., 2020; Weiss et al., 2016). Following Seligman et al.'s study, however, several salient questions remained about the effects of PPIs, such as for whom, when, and why these strategies might work (see also Sidebar 14.1 summarising concerns over the self-selection of participants to psychological studies). Next, we explore these questions in depth.

DEVELOPMENTS

MODERATORS OF INTERVENTION EFFICACY

Research testing the efficacy of psychological interventions rarely show that 'one-size-fits-all' in their effects on outcomes, and PPIs are no different. Many factors may affect how a person experiences an intervention and benefits from it. These include individual difference factors, aspects of the interventions, and the fit between the person and the intervention. Below we summarise research on several such factors.

INDIVIDUAL DIFFERENCES IN BASELINE STATUS

Seligman et al. (2005) noted that their sample was, on average, mildly depressed at baseline. Much recent literature supports the notion that, compared to those who are relatively psychologically healthy at baseline, people with clinical levels of depression and anxiety and other psychological disorders are particularly likely to benefit from PPIs (Bolier et al., 2013; Carr et al., 2020; Weiss et al., 2016). The enhanced efficacy of PPIs in clinical populations may be due to a 'floor' effect, meaning that these individuals simply had more room for improvement in their levels of well-being (Sin & Lyubomirsky, 2009). Similarly, PPIs have also been shown to be effective in raising the well-being and lowering depression and anxiety in those with physical disorders such as chronic heart disease and cancer (Chakhssi et al., 2018).

Seligman et al. (2005) tentatively suggested that PPIs could be used by mental health professionals alongside typical treatment programmes in clinical settings.

Since that time, a number of psychotherapeutic models have been created that explicitly incorporate PPIs into counselling sessions, including positive psycho-therapy (PPT; Seligman et al., 2006) and strengths-centred therapy (SCT; Wong, 2006), among others. These approaches focus on identifying and utilising a client's strengths towards finding solutions to relevant issues as well as enhancing posi-tive emotions and life satisfaction. There is evidence that PPT and SCT are at least as effective, if not more so, in treating major depressive disorders (Seligman et al., 2006) and increasing well-being than standard therapies (Rashid, 2015). However, while many practitioners endorse psychotherapeutic models that incorporate PPIs, a survey of 480 counselling psychologists demonstrated that fewer than half of respondents reported incorporating PPIs into regular practice (Magyar-Moe et al., 2015).

Sidebar 14.1. Self-selection Bias

Much of the research testing PPI effects, including Seligman et al.'s (2005) study, faces a methodological limitation – participants *self-select* with respect to their participation in the intervention, that is, they volunteer to participate in the intervention, presumably because they are motivated to become happier and/ or less depressed. Such self-selection recruitment procedures are ubiquitous in research health psychology and other disciplines, and may result in bias. For example, the volunteer participants may be more likely to show cognitive bias, that is, they expect to become happier because they already have faith that such interventions may work. They might report being happier after the interven-tion when in reality this is not true. Similarly, self-selecting people may be more motivated to engage with the interventions and to improve their well-being than others. These factors make it difficult to tease out how effective PPIs truly are, since the effects may be significantly enhanced by the characteristics of those self-selecting into studies. This bias can be somewhat remedied by randomising participants to conditions, a tactic that several researchers have employed.

CULTURE

Seligman et al. (2005) did not find that race/ethnicity moderated PPI effects, although their sample comprised largely white and Anglo-American participants. While most PPI studies have been conducted in Western European contexts, typi-cally encompassing industrialised countries in North America and Western Europe, positive psychology research now has less reliance on samples drawn from North American/Western European contexts than studies conducted in other areas of psychology (Kim et al., 2018). Meta-analyses have generally concluded that effect sizes of PPIs on well-being and depression are larger in samples recruited from non-Western European contexts (Hendriks et al., 2018, 2020). It should be noted, however, that these findings might be due to differences in how interventions are administered in different regions of the globe (Hendriks et al., 2018, 2020). Broad conclusions regarding the efficacy of PPIs in different cultures are difficult to make, but there is some evidence that the match between ethnicity, national group, or culture and PPI content can affect outcomes.

To illustrate, results of individual studies support the notion that cultures that are more collectivistic in their generalised values, such as Chinese and South Korean contexts, are more likely to benefit from interventions that centre around helping others and are aligned with interdependent values (e.g., acts of kindness), whereas cultures that tend to be more individualistic in their values, such as those in Western European contexts, like the US, may benefit more from interventions focused on the pursuit of personal happiness. For example, Anglo-Americans gained a larger boost to their life satisfaction after engaging in gratitude or optimism interventions than a group of predominantly foreign-born Asian-Americans (Boehm et al., 2011). Additionally, university students in the US reported higher well-being than university students from South Korea after a gratitude exercise, but both groups benefitted equally from an intervention involving acts of kindness for others (Layous et al., 2013). Priming bilingual Chinese university students with Chinese, but not English, language elicited higher positive affect when recalling helping close others as opposed to strangers (Shin et al., 2021), with Chinese students benefitting more from recalling kind acts towards close others, while US students benefitted equally from recalling kind acts performed for both close others and strangers. Across these studies numerous examples emerge of the ways in which a person's culture and national identity influence the emotions that they experience when performing a PPI. In combination, these findings highlight the importance of matching PPIs to cultural values.

INTERVENTION FEATURES

Duration and administration

Seligman et al. (2005) administered interventions for one week. Unsurprisingly, interventions with a longer duration, lasting several weeks to several months, tend to show increased positive effects on outcomes like well-being and depression (Bolier et al., 2013; Carr et al., 2020; Sin & Lyubomirsky, 2009). In addition, mode of administration also plays a role in PPI efficacy. Seligman et al. (2005) found that three of their interventions of varying duration had a moderate impact on happiness and depressive symptoms even when delivered online with no in-person guidance. They surmised that greater effects might emerge if interventions were guided by skilled clinicians and educators. While there are examples in the literature of PPIs delivered online exhibiting equal effectiveness compared to in-person delivery (e.g., Heintzelman et al., 2020), recent meta-analyses show that individual, face-to-face delivery generally results in better outcomes, followed by in-person group administration, and then online self-help administration (Boiler et al., 2013; Carr et al., 2020; Chakhssi et al., 2018; Weiss et al., 2016).

Dose and variety

Evidence suggests that PPIs should be given in specific doses for optimal efficacy depending on the intervention itself. For example, performing five acts of kindness in a single day boosts happiness compared to performing a single act each day for five days, suggesting that a single act of kindness may be insufficient to boost happiness (Lyubomirsky, Sheldon, & Schkade, 2005). Conversely, 'counting one's blessings' once per week is more effective in enhancing well-being compared to doing the same activity three times per week, perhaps because the higher frequency robs the activity of its meaning and sincerity (Lyubomirsky, Sheldon, & Schkade, 2005). Of course, the dose–response relationships for any single intervention also likely depend on the fit between that intervention and the interests, needs, and other aspects of personality of those participating in it (Lyubomirsky & Layous, 2013).

Finally, variety in PPIs promotes more sustainable increases in well-being (Lyubomirsky, 2011; Sheldon & Lyubomirsky 2012, 2019). Research shows that people have a remarkable ability to adapt to a variety of positive and negative life changes, a characteristic known as *hedonic* adaptation (Frederick & Loewenstein, 1999). On the plus side, this means that humans are able to recover from many negative life events over time (Mancini et al., 2011). However, it also means that the initial rush of exhilaration after a positive event is likely to fade, returning people to baseline levels of happiness (Lucas et al., 2003). One way to combat the waning effects of hedonic adaptation is to introduce variety into positive events, keeping them novel and stimulating (Lyubomirsky, 2011). Interventions that intentionally imbue exercises with variety should be most likely to enhance well-being. In support of this prediction, students randomly assigned to perform varied acts of kindness over 10 weeks experienced greater happiness than a group assigned to perform the same act of kindness each week (Sheldon et al., 2012).

Single vs. multiple components

Seligman and colleagues posed the question of whether administering multiple PPIs in an intervention package might provide more well-being benefits than a single intervention. Subsequently, Seligman, Rashid, and Parks (2006) showed that a multi-component, multi-week PPI significantly reduced depressive symptoms among mildly to severely depressed people, compared to a neutral control and treatment-as-usual. Recently, Heintzelman and colleagues (2020) designed and implemented a comprehensive multi-modal PPI called ENHANCE, which incorporated 'modules' on gratitude, savouring, values, mindfulness, and social interaction aimed at improving well-being and physical health (Heintzelman et al., 2020; Kushlev et al., 2020). Further, a meta-analysis including 50 randomised controlled trials of multiple component PPIs found positive effects on well-being, depression, anxiety, and stress (Hendriks et al., 2020). Note that these studies did not compare multiple component interventions to single component interventions. Providing support to the notion that 'more is better', a meta-analysis showed multiple component interventions to be significantly more effective for alleviating depression than programmes using a single PPI (Carr et al., 2020). Finally, is there a limit to how many PPIs should be given? Schueller and Parks (2012) showed a curvilinear pattern, such that four exercises led to larger reductions in depressive symptoms than two, but six exercises led to less depression relief than four, suggesting potentially diminishing returns, although it remains to be seen if these findings are replicated, and to which PPIs this applies.

Person–activity fit

Another variable influencing the effectiveness of PPIs is person–activity fit. Seligman et al. (2005) acknowledged that individual differences might influence PPI effectiveness, but lacked data to address this issue. People have different personalities, values, needs, interests, and motivations for self-improvement, all of which might influence which PPIs are most effective for them. On a general level, the match between a person's goals and autonomous motives predicts more sustained effort over time, achievement of those goals, and increased well-being when those goals are completed (Sheldon & Elliot, 1999; Sheldon & Houser-Marko, 2001). Similar findings have emerged for PPIs. People who choose their own PPIs, that is, who are more motivated at baseline to participate, and those who put in higher effort over the duration of the intervention, evidence greater benefits to well-being and depression (Sheldon & Lyubomirsky, 2006; Sin & Lyubomirsky, 2009; Lyubomirsky et al., 2011; Proyer at al., 2015).

Lyubomirsky and Layous's (2013) Positive Activity Model (see Figure 14.1) captures this notion of person–activity fit. The model incorporates features of a particular PPI and aspects of the person engaging with it, along with the interaction of these. The model proposes that, while some features of any PPI may be broadly effective across people, each PPI will also be better suited to particular people. Research supports this prediction. People with a high preference for a particular PPI are more likely to complete it (Schueller, 2010). Further, preference for an intervention has been associated with increased happiness 3.5 years later (Proyer, et al., 2015). Personality traits can also moderate PPI effects. People high in trait openness and extraversion, for example, benefitted more from a gratitude intervention (Senf & Liau, 2013). In sum, PPIs are likely to be more effective when they are personally chosen and personally consistent.

HOW DO PPIS WORK?

Seligman et al.'s (2005) study inspired a substantial body of work supporting the overall effectiveness of several PPIs for enhancing well-being and decreasing anxiety and depression. A fundamental question arising from this research, then, is not *whether* PPIs work, but *how* they work. What, specifically, accounts for the effects of PPIs on well-being? The Positive Activity Model (Lyubomirsky & Layous, 2013; Sheldon & Lyubomirsky, 2019) gives some guidance on factors that might mediate the effects of PPIs on well-being. PPIs increase positive cognitions and emotions, and foster participation in adaptive behaviours that may ultimately lead

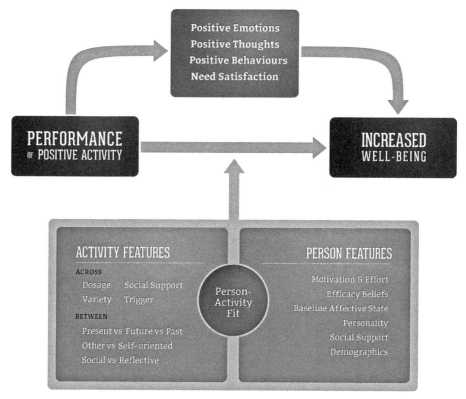

Figure 14.1   The Positive Activity Model (Lyubomirsky & Layous, 2013)

Note: Potential mediators and moderators of PPI efficacy are shown.

to increased happiness. The model also posits that PPIs contribute to satisfaction of basic psychological needs as described in Self Determination Theory (SDT; see Conner & Norman, Chapter 2, this volume; Ryan & Deci, 2000).

Evidence for these mediational effects is accumulating. In terms of positive cognitions, participants construe experiences more positively after a PPI compared to a control condition, even when their objective circumstances were no better (Dickerhoof, 2007). Further, studies have shown increases in optimistic thinking, self-compassionate thoughts, and the discovery of new personal insights were important mediating factors leading to increased well-being (Gander et al., 2018; Schotanus-Dijkstra et al., 2019). Similarly, studies show that positive emotions explain the well-being benefits of diverse PPIs, including a meditation intervention (Fredrickson et al., 2008), the three good things intervention (Gander et al., 2018), and a multi-component PPI (Hendriks et al., 2021). PPIs may also enhance various aspects of emotion regulation through encouraging the use of strategies such as situation modification and attentional deployment (Quoidbach et al., 2015).

Fewer studies have investigated the mediational role of positive behaviours. However, one study showed that a gratitude intervention led participants to engage in more physical exercise outside the intervention, which the authors argued could be one reason for their enhanced well-being at the end of the study (Emmons & McCullough, 2003).

Finally, at the motivational level, studies have employed constructs from SDT as candidate mediators of PPIs on happiness outcomes. Specifically, SDT proposes that all people have three basic psychological needs (autonomy, competence, and relatedness), and the fulfilment of these needs facilitates optimal functioning, personal growth, and overall health (Ryan & Deci, 2000). Several studies, often involving individuals striving for personally-valued goals, show that the need satisfaction that accompanies goal progress and achievement ultimately leads to increased well-being (Sheldon et al., 2010; Sheldon & Elliot, 1999; see also Martela & Sheldon, 2019).

In summary, PPIs are effective at increasing positive cognitions, emotions, and behaviours, and enhance the satisfaction of fundamental psychological needs, all of which contribute to increasing happiness. The work covered in this section builds on Seligman and colleagues' original research by identifying the mechanisms or mediators by which PPIs affect outcomes. This paves the way for researchers and practitioners to devise interventions that directly target the variables implicated in increasing happiness and mental health.

CONCLUSIONS

PPIs have been implemented in myriad settings, populations, and behaviours. PPI efficacy in promoting adaptive outcomes has been demonstrated in various populations, including teachers, healthcare workers, children and adolescents, police officers, service industry workers, individuals with chronic pain and physical and psychological disorders, prison inmates, government workers, and employees in dozens of other workplaces (Chakhssi et al., 2018; Donaldson et al., 2019; Huynh et al., 2015; Iddon et al., 2016; Meyers et al., 2013; Tejada-Gallardo et al., 2020).

In hindsight, the efficacy of programmes to increase well-being may seem relatively obvious and expected. However, progress in developing these interventions required an initial 'eureka' moment early in the short history of positive psychology – strong evidence that increasing happiness through intervention is possible. Seligman et al., in their seminal work in the area, together with many other prominent 'positive psychologists', have contributed to developing tools that are effective in producing sustained gains in well-being. Although the application of PPIs does not promise eternal euphoria, and ceaseless happiness is neither healthy nor adaptive, evidence suggests that their use in interventions can lead to small-to-moderate increases in happiness that have clear benefits to health and functioning and may contribute to long-term, adaptive outcomes.

Where is the field of positive psychology headed when it comes to future interventions? Research has only begun to uncover the mediating factors that 'do the work' in increasing participants' happiness and mental health. In addition, the identified mediators may be specific to particular interventions, populations, contexts, and behaviours. In addition, many underlying variables may be implicated in explaining PPI effects, and future research is needed to identify them (for a more generalised discussion on mechanisms, see Johnston, Chapter 12, this volume).

There is increasing evidence identifying the moderating variables that interact with PPIs and modulate their effectiveness, but these elements have generally been studied in groups of participants. In other words, there is considerable knowledge of the *average* effects of moderators like culture or mental health status, but there is, by contrast, little evidence of how these factors may affect individual responses. Each person has unique desires, motivations, experiences, backgrounds, and personality traits that may make a particular PPI more, or less, effective for their happiness and well-being. It could be that personalised interventions aimed at promoting happiness and positive outcomes may be necessary just as there is a trend towards personalised medicine (Chan & Ginsburg, 2011). Although in the case of medicine this means using information on a person's genetics and pharmacokinetic profiles to tailor treatments to maximise effectiveness, positive psychology may use factors such as person–activity fit, personal beliefs about well-being, and personality traits to optimise interventions (Schork, 2015).

With rates of anxiety and depression still on the rise around the globe (World Health Organization, 2017), it is likely that the healthcare and public health systems in many countries could benefit from implementing PPI interventions, and workplaces and businesses could positively affect their workers' health through occupational health programmes that incorporate PPIs. Moreover, recent research continues to show that PPIs genuinely help those who suffer in addition to helping those who might just need small 'boosts' in their happiness. Thus, PPIs have the potential to better individuals' lives in many settings.

FURTHER READING

Seligman, M. E., & Csikszentmihalyi, M. (2000). Positive psychology. An introduction. *The American Psychologist*, *55*(1), 5–14.

For those who are interested in the origins of positive psychology, this special issue of *American Psychologist* details its beginnings as a formal branch of psychology.

Lyubomirsky, S., King, L., & Diener, E. (2005). The benefits of frequent positive affect: Does happiness lead to success? *Psychological Bulletin*, *131*(6), 803–855.

An article highlighting evidence that happiness is more than merely a pleasant feeling; happiness can lead to success in many areas of life. In this light, readers can appreciate just how powerful positive psychology interventions can be.

Carr, A., Cullen, K., Keeney, C., Canning, C., Mooney, O., Chinseallaigh, E., & O'Dowd, A. (2020). Effectiveness of positive psychology interventions: A systematic review and meta-analysis. *Journal of Positive Psychology*, *16*(6), 749–769.

This is the largest meta-analysis of PPI effectiveness to date with 347 studies and over 72,000 participants included. The authors demonstrate the beneficial effects of PPIs on a large range of well-being outcomes and that these effects last several months. Numerous moderating factors of both participants (e.g., age, country) and intervention (e.g., focus, mode of delivery) are also explored.

Sheldon, K. M., & Lyubomirsky, S. (2019). Revisiting the sustainable happiness model and pie chart: Can happiness be successfully pursued? *Journal of Positive Psychology, 16*(2), 145–154.

An important summary and update of contemporary models of happiness and the potential for its sustainability. This article will introduce the reader to currently accepted models of well-being that attempt to answer the question of how to increase happiness – and keep it there.

REFERENCES

Adams, N., Little, T. D., & Ryan, R. M. (2017). Self-determination theory. *Development of Self-Determination Through the Life-Course, 55*(1), 47–54. https://doi.org/10.1007/978-94-024-1042-6_4

Akhtar, S., & Barlow, J. (2018). Forgiveness therapy for the promotion of mental well-being: A systematic review and meta-analysis. *Trauma, Violence, and Abuse, 19*(1), 107–122. https://doi.org/10.1177/1524838016637079

Banuazizi, A., & Movahedi, S. (1975). Interpersonal dynamics in a simulated prison: A methodological analysis. *American Psychologist, 30*(2), 152–160. https://doi.org/10.1037/h0076835

Boehm, J. K., Lyubomirsky, S., & Sheldon, K. M. (2011). A longitudinal experimental study comparing the effectiveness of happiness-enhancing strategies in Anglo Americans and Asian Americans. *Cognition and Emotion, 25*(7), 1263–1272. https://doi.org/10.1080/02699931.2010.541227

Bolier, L., Haverman, M., Westerhof, G. J., Riper, H., Smit, F., & Bohlmeijer, E. (2013). Positive psychology interventions: A meta-analysis of randomized controlled studies. *BMC Public Health, 13*(1). https://doi.org/10.1186/1471-2458-13-119

Bränström, R., Kvillemo, P., Brandberg, Y., & Moskowitz, J. T. (2010). Self-report mindfulness as a mediator of psychological well-being in a stress reduction intervention for cancer patients: A randomized study. *Annals of Behavioral Medicine, 39*(2), 151–161. https://doi.org/10.1007/s12160-010-9168-6

Bryant, F. B., Smart, C. M., & King, S. P. (2005). Using the past to enhance the present: Boosting happiness through positive reminiscence. *Journal of Happiness Studies, 6*(3), 227–260. https://doi.org/10.1007/s10902-005-3889-4

Burton, C. M., & King, L. A. (2009). The health benefits of writing about positive experiences: The role of broadened cognition. *Psychology & Health, 24*(8), 867–879. https://doi.org/10.1080/08870440801989946

Carr, A., Cullen, K., Keeney, C., Canning, C., Mooney, O., Chinseallaigh, E., & O'Dowd, A. (2020). Effectiveness of positive psychology interventions: A systematic review and meta-analysis. *Journal of Positive Psychology, 16*(6), 749–769. https://doi.org/10.1080/17439760.2020.1818807

Carrillo, A., Etchemendy, E., & Baños, R. M. (2021). My best self in the past, present or future: Results of two randomized controlled trials. *Journal of Happiness Studies, 22*(2), 955–980. https://doi.org/10.1007/s10902-020-00259-z

Chakhssi, F., Kraiss, J. T., Sommers-Spijkerman, M., & Bohlmeijer, E. T. (2018). The effect of positive psychology interventions on well-being and distress in clinical samples with psychiatric or somatic disorders: A systematic review and meta-analysis. *BMC Psychiatry, 18*(1), 1–18. https://doi.org/10.1186/s12888-018-1739-2

Chan, I. S., & Ginsburg, G. S. (2011). Personalized medicine: Progress and promise. *Annual Review of Genomics and Human Genetics, 12*, 217–244. https://doi.org/10.1146/annurev-genom-082410-101446

Cheavens, J. S., Feldman, D. B., Gum, A., Michael, S. T., & Snyder, C. R. (2006). Hope therapy in a community sample: A pilot investigation. *Social Indicators Research, 77*(1), 61–78. https://doi.org/10.1007/s11205-005-5553-0

Dickerhoof, R. M. (2007). Expressing optimism and gratitude: A longitudinal investigation of cognitive strategies to increase well-being. *Dissertation Abstracts International: Section B: The Sciences and Engineering, 68*(6-B), 4174.

Diener, E., Pressman, S. D., Hunter, J., & Delgadillo-Chase, D. (2017). If, why, and when subjective well-being influences health, and future needed research. *Applied Psychology: Health and Well-Being, 9*(2), 133–167. https://doi.org/10.1111/aphw.12090

Donaldson, S. I., Lee, J. Y., & Donaldson, S. I. (2019). Evaluating positive psychology interventions at work: A systematic review and meta-analysis. *International Journal of Applied Positive Psychology, 4*(3), 113–134. https://doi.org/10.1007/s41042-019-00021-8

Emmons, R. A., & McCullough, M. E. (2003). Counting blessings versus burdens: An experimental investigation of gratitude and subjective well-being in daily life. *Journal of Personality and Social Psychology, 84*(2), 377–389. https://doi.org/10.1037/0022-3514.84.2.377

Fordyce, M. W. (1977). Development of a program to increase personal happiness. *Journal of Counseling Psychology, 24*(6), 511–521. https://doi.org/10.1037//0022-0167.24.6.511

Frederick, S., & Loewenstein, G. (1999). Hedonic adaptation. In D. Kahneman, E. Diener, & N. Schwarz (Eds.), *Well-being: The foundations of hedonic psychology* (pp. 302–329). New York: Russell Sage Foundation.

Fredrickson, B. L., Cohn, M. A., Coffey, K. A., Pek, J., & Finkel, S. M. (2008). Open hearts build lives: Positive emotions, induced through loving-kindness meditation, build consequential personal resources. *Journal of Personality and Social Psychology, 95*(5), 1045–1062. https://doi.org/10.1037/a0013262

Fritz, M. M., & Lyubomirsky, S. (2019). Whither happiness? *The Social Psychology of Living Well*, 101–115. https://doi.org/10.4324/9781351189712-7

Gander, F., Proyer, R. T., & Ruch, W. (2018). A placebo-controlled online study on potential mediators of a pleasure-based positive psychology intervention: The role of emotional and cognitive components. *Journal of Happiness Studies, 19*(7), 2035–2048. https://doi.org/10.1007/s10902-017-9909-3

Gander, F., Proyer, R. T., Ruch, W., & Wyss, T. (2013). Strength-based positive interventions: Further evidence for their potential in enhancing well-being and alleviating depression. *Journal of Happiness Studies, 14*(4), 1241–1259. https://doi.org/10.1007/s10902-012-9380-0

Heintzelman, S. J., & Kushlev, K. (2020). Emphasizing scientific rigor in the development, testing, and implementation of positive psychological interventions. *Journal of Positive Psychology, 15*(5), 685–690. https://doi.org/10.1080/17439760.2020.1789701

Heintzelman, S. J., Kushlev, K., Lutes, L. D., Wirtz, D., Kanippayoor, J. M., Leitner, D., Oishi, S., & Diener, E. (2020). ENHANCE: Evidence for the efficacy of a comprehensive intervention program to promote subjective well-being. *Journal of Experimental Psychology: Applied, 26*(2), 360–383. https://doi.org/10.1037/xap0000254

Hendriks, T., Schotanus-Dijkstra, M., Graafsma, T., Bohlmeijer, E., & de Jong, J. (2021). Positive emotions as a potential mediator of a multi-component positive psychology intervention aimed at increasing mental well-being and resilience. *International Journal of Applied Positive Psychology, 6*(1), 1–21. https://doi.org/10.1007/s41042-020-00037-5

Hendriks, T., Schotanus-Dijkstra, M., Hassankhan, A., de Jong, J., & Bohlmeijer, E. (2020). The efficacy of multi-component positive psychology interventions: A systematic review and meta-analysis of randomized controlled trials. *Journal of Happiness Studies, 21*(1). https://doi.org/10.1007/s10902-019-00082-1

Hendriks, T., Schotanus-Dijkstra, M., Hassankhan, A., Graafsma, T., Bohlmeijer, E., & de Jong, J. (2018). The efficacy of positive psychology interventions from non-Western countries: A systematic review and meta-analysis. *International Journal of Wellbeing, 8*(1), 71–98. https://doi.org/10.5502/ijw.v8i1.711

Huynh, K. H., Hall, B., Hurst, M. A., & Bikos, L. H. (2015). Evaluation of the Positive Re-Entry in Corrections Program. *International Journal of Offender Therapy and Comparative Criminology, 59*(9), 1006–1023. https://doi.org/10.1177/0306624X14523385

Iddon, J. E., Dickson, J. M., & Unwin, J. (2016). Positive psychological interventions and chronic non-cancer pain: A systematic review of the literature. *International Journal of Applied Positive Psychology, 1*(1–3), 133–157. https://doi.org/10.1007/s41042-016-0003-6

Jayawickreme, E., Forgeard, M. J. C., & Seligman, M. E. P. (2012). The engine of well-being. *Review of General Psychology, 16*(4), 327–342. https://doi.org/10.1037/a0027990

King, L. A. (2001). The health benefits of writing about life goals. *Personality and Social Psychology Bulletin, 27*(7), 798–807. https://doi.org/10.1177/0146167201277003

Kim, H., Doiron, K., Warren, M. A., & Donaldson, S. I. (2018). The international landscape of positive psychology research: A systematic review. *International Journal of Wellbeing, 8*(1), 50–70. doi:10.5502/ijw.v8i1.651

Koszycki, D., Raab, K., Aldosary, F., & Bradwejn, J. (2010). A multifaith spiritually based intervention for generalized anxiety disorder: A pilot randomized trial. *Journal of Clinical Psychology, 66*(4), 430–441. https://doi.org/10.1002/jclp

Kushlev, K., Heintzelman, S. J., Lutes, L. D., Wirtz, D., Kanippayoor, J. M., Leitner, D., & Diener, E. (2020). Does happiness improve health? Evidence from a randomized controlled trial. *Psychological Science, 31*(7), 807–821. https://doi.org/10.1177/0956797620919673

Lambert, L., Passmore, H. A., & Joshanloo, M. (2019). A positive psychology intervention program in a culturally-diverse university: Boosting happiness and reducing fear. *Journal of Happiness Studies, 20*(4), 1141–1162. https://doi.org/10.1007/s10902-018-9993-z

Layous, K., Lee, H., Choi, I., & Lyubomirsky, S. (2013). Culture matters when designing a successful happiness-increasing activity: A comparison of the United States and South Korea. *Journal of Cross-Cultural Psychology, 44*(8), 1294–1303. https://doi.org/10.1177/0022022113487591

Layous, K., & Lyubomirsky, S. (2014). The how, why, what, when, and who of happiness: Mechanisms underlying the success of positive activity interventions. In J. Gruber & J. T. Moskowitz (Eds.), *Positive emotion: Integrating the light sides and dark sides* (pp. 473–495). Oxford: Oxford University Press. https://doi.org/10.1093/acprof:oso/9780199926725.003.0025

Lopez, S. J., & Snyder, C. R. (Eds.). (2009). *Oxford handbook of positive psychology* (2nd ed.). Oxford: Oxford University Press.

Loveday, P. M., Lovell, G. P., & Jones, C. M. (2018). The best possible selves intervention: A review of the literature to evaluate efficacy and guide future research. *Journal of Happiness Studies, 19*(2), 607–628. https://doi.org/10.1007/s10902-016-9824-z

Lucas, R. E., Clark, A. E., Georgellis, Y., & Diener, E. (2003). Reexamining adaptation and the set point model of happiness: Reactions to changes in marital status. *Journal of Personality and Social Psychology, 84*(3), 527–539. https://doi.org/10.1037/0022-3514.84.3.527

Lyubomirsky, S. (2011). Hedonic adaptation to positive and negative experiences. In S. Folkman (Ed.), *The Oxford handbook of stress, health, and coping* (pp. 200–224). Oxford: Oxford University Press. https://doi.org/10.1093/oxfordhb/9780195375343.013.0011

Lyubomirsky, S., Dickerhoof, R., Boehm, J. K., & Sheldon, K. M. (2011). Becoming happier takes both a will and a proper way: An experimental longitudinal intervention to boost well-being. *Emotion, 11*(2), 391–402. https://doi.org/10.1037/a0022575

Lyubomirsky, S., King, L., & Diener, E. (2005). The benefits of frequent positive affect: Does happiness lead to success? *Psychological Bulletin, 131*(6), 803–855. https://doi.org/10.1037/0033-2909.131.6.803

Lyubomirsky, S., & Layous, K. (2013). How do simple positive activities increase well-being? *Current Directions in Psychological Science, 22*(1), 57–62. https://doi.org/10.1177/0963721412469809

Lyubomirsky, S., Sheldon, K. M., & Schkade, D. (2005). Pursuing happiness: The architecture of sustainable change. *Review of General Psychology, 9*(2), 111–131. https://doi.org/10.1037/1089-2680.9.2.111

Magyar-Moe, J. L., Owens, R. L., & Scheel, M. J. (2015). Applications of positive psychology in counseling psychology: Current status and future directions. *The Counseling Psychologist, 43*(4), 494–507. https://doi.org/10.1177/0011000015581001

Mancini, A. D., Bonanno, G. A., & Clark, A. E. (2011). Stepping off the hedonic treadmill: Individual differences in response to major life events. *Journal of Individual Differences, 32*(3), 144–152. doi: 10.1027/1614-0001/a000047

Martela, F., & Sheldon, K. M. (2019). Clarifying the concept of well-being: Psychological need satisfaction as the common core connecting eudaimonic and subjective well-being. *Review of General Psychology, 23*(4), 458–474. https://doi.org/10.1177/1089268019880886

Meyers, M. C., van Woerkom, M., & Bakker, A. B. (2013). The added value of the positive: A literature review of positive psychology interventions in organizations. *European Journal of Work and Organizational Psychology, 22*(5), 618–632. https://doi.org/10.1080/1359432X.2012.694689

Nyklíček, I., & Kuijpers, K. F. (2008). Effects of mindfulness-based stress reduction intervention on psychological well-being and quality of life: Is increased mindfulness indeed the mechanism? *Annals of Behavioral Medicine, 35*(3), 331–340. https://doi.org/10.1007/s12160-008-9030-2

Otake, K., Shimai, S., Tanaka-Matsumi, J., Otsui, K., & Fredrickson, B. L. (2006). Happy people become happier through kindness: A counting kindnesses intervention. *Journal of Happiness Studies, 7*(3), 361–375. https://doi.org/10.1007/s10902-005-3650-z

Peterson, C. (2006). *A primer in positive psychology*. Oxford and New York: Oxford University Press.

Proyer, R. T., Wellenzohn, S., Gander, F., & Ruch, W. (2015). Toward a better understanding of what makes positive psychology interventions work: Predicting happiness and depression from the person × intervention fit in a follow-up after 3.5 years. *Applied Psychology: Health and Well-Being*, *7*(1), 108–128. https://doi.org/10.1111/aphw.12039

Quoidbach, J., Mikolajczak, M., & Gross, J. J. (2015). Positive interventions: An emotion regulation perspective. *Psychological Bulletin*, *141*(3), 655–693. https://doi.org/10.1037/a0038648

Rashid, T. (2015). Positive psychotherapy: A strength-based approach. *The Journal of Positive Psychology*, *10*(1), 25–40. https://doi.org/10.1080/17439760.2014.920411

Ryan, R. M., & Deci, E. L. (2000). Self-determination theory and the facilitation of intrinsic motivation, social development, and well-being. *American Psychologist*, *55*(1), 68–78. https://doi.org/10.1037/0003-066X.55.1.68

Schork N. J. (2015). Personalized medicine: Time for one-person trials. *Nature*, *520*(7549), 609–611. https://doi.org/10.1038/520609a

Schotanus-Dijkstra, M., Pieterse, M. E., Drossaert, C. H. C., Walburg, J. A., & Bohlmeijer, E. T. (2019). Possible mechanisms in a multicomponent email guided positive psychology intervention to improve mental well-being, anxiety and depression: A multiple mediation model. *Journal of Positive Psychology*, *14*(2), 141–155. https://doi.org/10.1080/17439760.2017.1388430

Schueller, S. M. (2010). Preferences for positive psychology exercises. *Journal of Positive Psychology*, *5*(3), 192–203. https://doi.org/10.1080/17439761003790948

Schueller, S. M., Kashdan, T. B., & Parks, A. C. (2014). Synthesizing positive psychological interventions: Suggestions for conducting and interpreting meta-analyses. *International Journal of Wellbeing*, *4*(1), 91–98. https://doi.org/10.5502/ijw.v4i1.5

Schueller, S. M., & Parks, A. C. (2012). Disseminating self-help: Positive psychology exercises in an online trial. *Journal of Medical Internet Research*, *14*(3), 1–10. https://doi.org/10.2196/jmir.1850

Seligman, M. E. P. (1999). Executive summary: Positive psychology network. University of Pennsylvania. Retrieved from https://ppc.sas.upenn.edu/sites/default/files/PP%20Network%20Concept%20Paper.docx.

Seligman, M. E. P., & Csikszentmihalyi, M. (2000). Positive psychology. An introduction. *The American Psychologist, 55*(1), 5–14. https://doi.org/10.1037/0003-066X.55.1.5

Seligman, M. E. P., Rashid, T., & Parks, A. C. (2006). Positive psychotherapy. *American Psychologist, 61*(8), 774–788. https://doi.org/10.1037/0003-066X.61.8.774

Seligman, M. E. P., Steen, T. A., Park, N., & Peterson, C. (2005). Positive psychology progress: Empirical validation of interventions. *The American Psychologist, 60*(5), 410–421. https://doi.org/10.1037/0003-066X.60.5.410

Senf, K., & Liau, A. K. (2013). The effects of positive interventions on happiness and depressive symptoms, with an examination of personality as a moderator. *Journal of Happiness Studies, 14*(2), 591–612. https://doi.org/10.1007/s10902-012-9344-4

Sheldon, K. M., Abad, N., Ferguson, Y., Gunz, A., Houser-Marko, L., Nichols, C. P., & Lyubomirsky, S. (2010). Persistent pursuit of need-satisfying goals leads to increased happiness: A 6-month experimental longitudinal study. *Motivation and Emotion, 34*(1), 39–48. https://doi.org/10.1007/s11031-009-9153-1

Sheldon, K. M., & Elliot, A. J. (1999). Goal striving, need satisfaction, and longitudinal well-being: The self-concordance model. *Journal of Personality and Social Psychology*, *76*(3), 482–497. https://doi.org/10.1037/0022-3514.76.3.482

Sheldon, K. M., Hauser-Marko, L. (2001). Self-concordance, goal attainment and the pursuit of happiness. *Journal of Personality and Social Psychology*, *80*(1), 152–165. https://doi.org/10.1037/0022-3514.80.1.152

Sheldon, K. M., & Lyubomirsky, S. (2006). How to increase and sustain positive emotion: The effects of expressing gratitude and visualizing best possible selves. *Journal of Positive Psychology*, *1*(2), 73–82. https://doi.org/10.1080/17439760500510676

Sheldon, K. M., & Lyubomirsky, S. (2012). The challenge of staying happier: Testing the hedonic adaptation prevention model. *Personality and Social Psychology Bulletin*, *38*(5), 670–680. https://doi.org/10.1177/0146167212436400

Sheldon, K. M., & Lyubomirsky, S. (2019). Revisiting the sustainable happiness model and pie chart: Can happiness be successfully pursued? *Journal of Positive Psychology*, *16*(2), 145–154. https://doi.org/10.1080/17439760.2019.1689421

Shin, L. J., Margolis, S. M., Walsh, L. C., Kwok, S. Y. C. L., Yue, X., Chan, C.-K., Siu, N. Y.-F., Sheldon, K. M., & Lyubomirsky, S. (2021). Cultural differences in the hedonic rewards of recalling kindness: Priming cultural identity with language. *Affective Science*, *2*(1), 80–90. https://doi.org/10.1007/s42761-020-00029-3

Sin, N. L., & Lyubomirsky, S. (2009). Enhancing well-being and alleviating depressive symptoms with positive psychology interventions: a practice-friendly meta-analysis. *Journal of clinical psychology*, *65*(5), 467–487. https://doi.org/10.1002/jclp.20593

Tejada-Gallardo, C., Blasco-Belled, A., Torrelles-Nadal, C., & Alsinet, C. (2020). Effects of school-based multicomponent positive psychology interventions on well-being and distress in adolescents: A systematic review and meta-analysis. *Journal of Youth and Adolescence*, *49*(10), 1943–1960. https://doi.org/10.1007/s10964-020-01289-9

van Straten, A., Seekles, W., van't Veer-Tazelaar, N. J., Beekman, A. T. F., & Cuijpers, P. (2010). Stepped care for depression in primary care: What should be offered and how? *Medical Journal of Australia*, *192*(Suppl. 11), 7–10. https://doi.org/10.5694/j.1326-5377.2010.tb03691.x

Walsh, L. C., Boehm, J. K., & Lyubomirsky, S. (2018). Does happiness promote career success? Revisiting the evidence. *Journal of Career Assessment*, *26*(2), 199–219. https://doi.org/10.1177/1069072717751441

Weiss, L. A., Westerhof, G. J., & Bohlmeijer, E. T. (2016). Can we increase psychological well-being? The effects of interventions on psychological well-being: A meta-analysis of randomized controlled trials. *PLoS ONE*, *11*(6), 1–16. https://doi.org/10.1371/journal.pone.0158092

Wellenzohn, S., Proyer, R., & Ruch, W. (2016). Humor-based online positive psychology interventions: A randomized placebo-controlled long-term trial. *Journal of Positive Psychology*, *11*(6), 584–594. https://doi.org/10.1080/17439760.2015.1137624

Wong, W. J. (2006). Strength-centered therapy: A social constructionist, virtue-based psychotherapy. *Psychotherapy*, *43*, 133–146. https://doi.org/10.1037/0033-3204.43.2.133

World Health Organization. (2017). Depression and other common mental disorders: global health estimates. World Health Organization. https://apps.who.int/iris/handle/10665/254610

Index